S0-BQC-829

THE BAPTISTS IN AMERICA

LIBRARY
COLLEGE OF THE REDWOODS
EUREKA, CALIFORNIA 95501

THE BAPTISTS IN AMERICA

O. K. Armstrong

and

Marjorie Armstrong

A DOUBLEDAY–GALILEE BOOK

Doubleday & Company, Inc., Garden City, New York, 1979

70087

The Baptists in America was originally published in 1967 by
Doubleday & Company, Inc., under the title *The Indomitable
Baptists*

Library of Congress Catalog Card Number 78-22150
ISBN: 0-385-14655-8
Copyright © 1967, 1979 by O. K. Armstrong and Marjorie Armstrong
All Rights Reserved
Printed in the United States of America

To the memory of
The Reverend John Leland (1754–1841)
In grateful appreciation for his successful efforts
to induce James Madison to write the first amendment
to our Constitution, which forever guarantees
freedom of religion in the United States,
this volume of the Baptists in America
is sincerely dedicated.

O. K. Armstrong
Marjorie Moore Armstrong

CONTENTS

THE BAPTISTS IN AMERICA

Authors' Introduction

As authors of *The Indomitable Baptists: A Narrative of Their Role in Shaping American History* (Doubleday, 1967) and the sequel, *Baptists Who Shaped a Nation* (Broadman, 1976), we are humbled and gratified by the opportunity to produce a "quality paperback" for Doubleday-Galilee.

"Much has happened in eleven years," as the religion editor of Doubleday, Alex Liepa, truly said, adding, "One of you Baptists even got himself elected President." A new chapter of this book tells the story of "Baptists in the White House."

It is a privilege to revise and update the original volume. Corrections of the known errors have been made. Deletions of small portions which from the perspective of the late 1970s seem less significant make room for additions to sections to show what has developed since 1966.

We are especially grateful that we were asked to tell the story, not write a history of the Baptists. Encyclopedias and history books are available for the serious student.

Case histories and thumbnail sketches from the authors' personal acquaintances and knowledge of events are used freely. We make no apology for the inclusion of some examples and the omission of others that are just as worthy.

We write what we know about. We tell the story as we saw it or see it. We are "members in good standing" of a Baptist congregation which is located in the Missouri Ozarks but by charter is affiliated with both the Southern Baptist Convention and American Baptist Churches, U.S.A.

The revised version of the original book is offered with the hope that Baptists and non-Baptists will read and better understand this "peculiar people."

O. K. Armstrong
Marjorie Moore Armstrong

January 1979
The Highlands
Republic, Missouri

RELIGION IN AMERICA

A Statement by the Editor (1966)

If it were possible to sum up in a word the temper and spirit of a religious group as diverse and numerous as the Baptists, the word indomitable would do it: "that cannot be overcome or subdued by labors, difficulties, or opposition; unyielding." In their early days on these shores the Baptists suffered opposition, endured injustice, and underwent widespread persecution. Yet, far from being subdued or overcome, they thrived to become far and away the largest Protestant body. And they have been unyielding in their original and peculiar doctrines. At no time have they sought to curry public favor or to modify their tenets for the sake of general acceptance.

Part of the purpose of the Religion in America Series was to assess religious influence in the development of American culture. The effect of this influence on believers is apparent to any student of religion. The traditions of religious belief convey ideas from the past in terms vivid and moving enough to stir men's emotions. It sets up organizations to carry forward habits of worship and practice that provide a climate of faith. But religious influence can also be brought to bear directly on affairs of state. The effects of belief are not confined to those who recite creeds and hold doctrines; religious beliefs may guide social or political action.

Baptist influence has operated on both the personal and social levels in America. In the matter of shared belief there has been consistency. Insistence upon immersion as the proper form of baptism, opposition to infant baptism, a survival of medieval ritualism, belief in the autonomy of every one of the local churches —these are tenets on which Baptists unite in mind. The presence of identifiable groupings in the United States testifies to the range of variety within the denomination and to the allowance for the intense individuality of opinion within the faith—to the right of Baptists to worship as they please.

The defense and extension of this right has been from the first a characteristic activity of the Baptists. They are allied with the cause of religious liberty and it is in this cause that they have shown demonstrable influence on American political history.

Those who cried out loudest against this taxing practice were the Baptists. When they spoke of religious liberty they were not talking merely about an abstract principle. They were talking about the specific rights of individual believers and of organized church bodies. And when the Baptists agitated successfully to include provision for religious liberty in the Bill of Rights added to the Constitution they were in harmony with their own history as well as their faith.

In this respect the story of the Baptists occupies a prominent place in the panorama of American religion. One cannot read such accounts as those of Roger Williams in seventeenth-century Rhode Island and Isaac Backus in eighteenth-century Massachusetts without getting some insight into the relatedness of religion to the background of American culture.

The extent of the neglect of religion is most noticeably illustrated in the curriculum of our schools. "Today pretty much everything, one way or another, gets into our best schools—sports, music, art, drama, economics, civics, sociology, psychology, psychiatry, and so on—everything except religion. Freud, for example, is proper educational material, but to present Isaiah would be to lug in religion." This summary by Harry Emerson Fosdick states the situation in the schools and at the same time it describes what results come about when the religious activities of the nation are overlooked. A kind of ignorance in perpetuity grows up. Persons versed in our secular history are hard put to answer simple questions about the differences, much less the nuances, among Americans grouped in churches, chapels, cathedrals, tabernacles, temples, and synagogues. And they are even more hard put to understand the connection between religious belief and social action—or the lack of it.

Relief from the general ignorance of American religion will not come from works of ready reference, from hasty accounts written for the unwashed, or from full accounts written by church historians for the faithful. The picture needs to be presented by writers with a sense of popular interest who are alert to high dramatic values and able to see broad lines as well as sharp details.

Fortunately, the materials for the unfolding of the American religious story are readily and abundantly at hand. Records abound. The devout have not been inarticulate; they have held few views back. They have given first-hand accounts. Packed in files and libraries are narratives that attain epic proportions, that are peopled with gifted, eloquent, unquenchable, and, not infrequently, theatrical characters. Reading their lives one feels that American religion may best be seen as people rather than doctrines. It is a story of emotions back of events, of forces operating beneath the surface of the mainstream of America. It is hidden history and, once brought to light, it may well give us a new dimension of perception.

Charles W. Ferguson

THE BAPTISTS IN AMERICA

About the Authors

O. K. Armstrong has a master's degree in journalism from the University of Missouri School of Journalism. In 1925 he founded the Department of Journalism (now the College of Journalism and Communications) in the University of Florida, Gainesville. He did freelance writing for several years and, beginning in 1944, was a member of the editorial staff of *Reader's Digest* until his retirement in 1977. He is the author of seven books, three of them in collaboration with his wife, Marjorie: *Religion Can Conquer Communism* (Thomas Nelson, 1964); *The Indomitable Baptists* (Doubleday, 1967); and *Baptists Who Shaped a Nation* (Broadman, 1975). He is a deacon of University Heights Baptist Church, Springfield, Missouri. Mr. Armstrong served for three terms in the Missouri Legislature and for one term in the U. S. House of Representatives.

Marjorie Moore Armstrong has a master's degree in journalism from Northwestern University, 1950. She is an alumna of the Southern Baptist Theological Seminary with a master's degree in Religious Education. For seven years she was assistant editor of *The Baptist Student,* Nashville, Tennessee, and for seven years managing editor of *The Commission,* Richmond, Virginia. She was the first coeditor of *The Baptist World,* Washington, D.C., 1954–56. Besides collaborating with her husband on three books, she has authored three youth books, *George Green of Africa, Face Today's World,* and *School Someday.* She serves as press relations officer of their church.

I

JOHN LELAND AND THE
BILL OF RIGHTS

An Earnest and Vigorous Preacher

Into the Williams Meeting House in Goochland County, Virginia, on the bright morning of March 7, 1788, strode about a score of the gentlemen of the Virginia Baptist General Committee. The majority were ministers, the others active laymen. They had ridden in from various parts of the state, but most of them lived in Goochland, Orange, and Culpeper counties where Baptist churches were strongest and Baptist influence most powerful.

Leader of these devout men was John Leland, an earnest and vigorous preacher and writer, who lived on a spacious farm near Orange on the Fredericksburg road. Leland was born at Grafton, Massachusetts, in May 1754 and had migrated to Virginia in 1776 for the principal reason that he felt impelled to combat the persecution of Baptists and other nonconformists in the Old Dominion. He was now recognized as the eloquent spokesman for Baptists in the state, pleading the cause of religious liberty and complete separation of church and government.

John Leland counted Thomas Jefferson, Patrick Henry, and James Madison his personal friends. Each of these Virginia politicians had sought and accepted his advice through the years. When John Leland spoke, men of all faiths and of all callings listened attentively.

Leland had issued the call for this meeting of the Baptist General Committee to consider a matter of great importance: Should the

Baptists of Virginia support the ratification by the General Assembly of the new federal constitution?

The question had been raised by the Baptists, but not because they opposed the plan for a federal union. Their leaders and members generally were not antagonistic to a higher sovereignty, which the new constitution proposed. The question had been raised because of concern over an apparent lack of guarantees for complete religious liberty in the new basic law.

In the main, citizens of all faiths in Virginia were satisfied with the proposed constitution. Baptists had shared the pride of Episcopalians, Congregationalists, Quakers, Methodists, and others that the commonwealth's noblest son, George Washington, had presided over the Constitutional Convention in Philadelphia. Truly, this man who had been first in war and who had led the Continental Army to victory was proving himself to be first in peace. That Washington would be named the first President when the Union was formed was taken for granted.

There had been anxiety over the slow progress of the convention during the first weeks of that historic session. As the information from Philadelphia trickled back in summaries of the proceedings in the weekly newspapers, many feared that differences of opinion would prevent any union's being formed. The delegates faced such big questions as what sort of legislature should be established, whether the small states could trust the large ones in a federated republic, and how to divide the powers so that no man or set of men could ever seize control of the government.

There was general satisfaction when it was announced that aging Benjamin Franklin had suggested that since the convention had reached no major agreement in six weeks the members should begin the sessions with prayer "to seek the guidance of Divine Power." There was a saying among Baptists: "Even if Old Ben Franklin is not a Baptist, he is acting like one!"

The facts that the proceedings moved along after that with greater speed and less dissension, that the difficulty of forming a union out of big and little states was settled by a compromise that allowed each state two senators, and that a division of powers was agreed to that seemed to protect the people with suitable checks and balances, were taken as an indication of divine leadership.

"Where Are the Guarantees?"

There was additional satisfaction throughout the Old Dominion that her delegates had supported the wording in Article VI which read: ". . . but no religious test shall ever be required as a qualification to any office of public trust under the United States." The provision effectively outlawed any chance that the federal government could make religious beliefs or nonbeliefs a qualification for office, a principle that Baptists everywhere had traditionally held to.

So the new constitution had evoked favorable reactions all over the commonwealth. Could anyone raise any doubts about a constitution formed under the leadership of such great minds as Virginia's own George Washington and James Madison, as Benjamin Franklin and Samuel Adams?

The Reverend John Leland had such doubts, and he raised them with his well-known vigor. "Where are the guarantees of complete religious liberty?" he asked. "Where is the protection for the individual to believe or not to believe, to worship or not to worship, to be free to support his church or any religious cause, and free also from all compulsion of the government to support some church? Remember—we stand for religious liberty!"

On the great Virginia plantations of the Tidewater, in all the towns from the coast to the mountains, among religious leaders of all denominations and kinds, Leland's statements were repeated and debated.

"The prohibition against any religious qualification for holding office is protection enough!" some argued. "Would any Congress or executive dare to abridge religious liberty with the principle of no religious test for office so clearly stated?"

In his many discussions on the subject during the months that followed the announcement of the new constitution, John Leland persisted in his theory that some future President or Congress just *might* seek to favor some church or some religious belief over another, or might even prohibit by law or regulation the free exercise of conscience and worship. In many communities over the broad expanse of Virginia, with a persistence that marked his whole life, he won religious leaders to his view.

Now in the Williams meeting Leland was determined to put the entire Virginia fellowship on record. The gentlemen who gathered at the Meeting House on that March morning in 1788 needed no further arguments. Their minds were made up. They agreed upon a statement that included these words:

"We the Virginia Baptist General Committee unanimously hold that the new federal constitution, proposed to the States for their ratification, does not make sufficient provision for the secure enjoyment of religious liberty; and therefore it should be amended to make such provision."

Not a man at that gathering could possibly have imagined how far and wide would spread the ripples caused by their tossing this pebble of religious principle into the lake of national politics. For the Baptist spokesmen did more than call for an amendment to the constitution. One of those present, Colonel Charles Barbour, had announced as a candidate for delegate to the state convention called to consider ratification of the new federal constitution. Now he declared that he would withdraw if Leland himself would enter the race to represent Orange County. The influential former officer in the War for Independence told the Baptist leader:

"Announce for delegate! In that way you will be able to block the ratification of the constitution. Without Virginia the constitution will never be accepted. A new convention will be forced to permit a clear statement guaranteeing religious freedom!"

Colonel Barbour's proposal was heartily seconded by several of those present. At first Leland strongly demurred. He reminded his colleagues that James Madison, the very man honored as the father of the Constitution because of his work and influence at Philadelphia in shaping the document, had announced for delegate to the Convention on Ratification. Leland did not want to be pitted against his friend Mr. Madison.

"But without Baptist support Mr. Madison can never be elected from Orange!" Colonel Barbour insisted.

The best the men could get out of John Leland was a promise to consider the matter and do what his conscience might dictate.

Following the dictates of his conscience was a firm and constant practice of the Reverend John Leland. It was his conscience that called him into the ministry and that sent him to champion religious liberty in Virginia. He had not been born of the cloth. His father was a Massachusetts farmer. John was apprenticed to a shoemaker in Hopkinton, and he became an expert cobbler.

A young belle of the community, Sallie Devine, brought in her shoes to be mended and fell in love with the handsome mender. Sallie's parents were devout Baptists and regularly attended the services at the Hopkinton Baptist meeting house. Sallie talked John into hearing Preacher Everett Jones, a man who had been severely whipped as punishment for preaching without the permission of the Massachusetts authorities. In time John professed religion, was baptized, and took up preaching himself.

Soon after he and Sallie Devine were married, they pulled up stakes for the long journey to Virginia. Self-educated by constant reading, a man of tremendous energy, Leland found and established churches in which to preach. He became known and respected as the outstanding minister of his faith in the Old Dominion.

From the Goochland County meeting of the Baptist General Committee John Leland rode back to his home under the great oaks on the Fredericksburg road, a deeply troubled man. Here was the opportunity of a lifetime to strike the greatest possible blow for religious freedom—not for Virginia alone, but for all future citizens of the new Union of states. While he did not want to run against the very popular Mr. Madison, Leland had decided to do everything within reason and honor to defeat the ratification of the new constitution unless it included a guarantee of full religious liberty with separation of church and state.

During the days of soul-searching that followed, Preacher John Leland must have reflected many times on the reasons for his unshakable determination in the matter. He must have reviewed the persecutions of his own Baptist dissenters, and highly resolved to do all in his power to see that such unjust treatment could never again blot the record of human freedom in America. He had come to Virginia for that purpose, and his battle had been won. He knew that now was the time to lay the foundation of full religious freedom in the basic law of the new nation.

From the earliest Jamestown settlements, Virginia had been the cradle of Anglican faith in America. By the mid-eighteenth century a few struggling Baptist churches had been established in the colony. Their numbers soon grew to proportions that alarmed and distressed the clergy and leaders of the Episcopal Church, recognized by law and custom as the establishment for religion. The Baptists made themselves exceedingly unpopular with the authorities, nearly all of whom were of the establishment, by their doctrinal beliefs and practices. They refused to have their babies baptized on the ground that church membership should be entirely a voluntary matter and should follow regeneration by faith. They cried out against what they called wickedness in high places, not sparing members of the establishment if they suspected them of such things as dancing, card playing, or usury. They energetically proselyted for converts whenever they could find them—especially among the poorer classes of people. All in all, the Baptists refused to observe the decorum considered proper for members of a tolerated sect.

The Dissenters of Virginia

By 1760 a bitter battle was underway, launched by Episcopal clergy and representatives of the Crown, to persecute and if possible exterminate these troublesome dissenters. There followed hundreds of arrests and imprisonments of ministers of the Baptists, Quakers, and other nonconformist groups who refused to abide by the regulations for licensing of religious bodies and payment of taxes for support of the established church.

There were laws and ordinances in Virginia, as in all the colonial states, against disturbances of the peace and vagrancy. The latter offense included "strolling," a charge which could be stretched to cover walking along without any set destination or any immediate gainful activity. These offenses were alleged in most of the charges lodged against the Virginia dissenters.

In Spotsylvania County on June 4, 1768, five Baptist ministers were seized by the sheriff and his deputies and brought before the court at Fredericksburg. James Childs, Lewis Craig, William Marsh, James Reed, and John Waller were charged with being disturbers of the peace. They had been preaching without authority of the local magistrates. Besides, said the prosecutor for the court, "They cannot meet a man upon a road, but they must ram a text of Scripture down his throat."

Clearly, ramming Scriptures down throats was *prima facie* evidence of breach of the peace. The magistrates set bail for each of the five at £1,000 sterling, knowing full well that these poor men could not raise that amount of money. The preachers were sentenced to jail. The magistrates reported to the General Court at Williamsburg that these disturbers were "in the habit of running into private homes and making discussions."

From the jail Lewis Craig sent the Court a denial of the charges. He declared that while they were zealous in the spread of the gospel, they did not trespass on the time, property, or beliefs of other persons. Many indignant Baptists came to the jail and to the magistrates to plead for the men. The commonwealth's attorney, John Blair, felt it best to advise the release of the ministers, and after forty-five days in confinement they were freed.

Another Craig named Elijah, a Baptist preacher in Orange County, was imprisoned for illegal preaching. In 1771 Morgan Edwards of Pennsylvania, a founder of Rhode Island College, visited Virginia and wrote of Elijah Craig: "He was in Gaol at Orange for a considerable time in 1768 preaching through the bars to the people who reported to the prison, till he was confined to the inner dungeon where was no opening save a hole in the door through which he received his bread and water."[1]

Among scores of such cases, that of James Ireland of Culpeper is typical as illustrating the bitterness of the campaign against the Baptists. Ireland was an immigrant from Scotland, who felt called to preach to his Virginia neighbors. The year was 1769. The authorities ordered him to desist. Ireland later wrote:

"I sat down and counted the cost, freedom or confinement, liberty or prison? Having ventured all upon Christ, I determined to suffer all for him."

When his congregation next assembled and Ireland stood before them to preach, the constables promptly arrested him. The Culpeper magistrates sentenced him to prison. His treatment there is vividly described by Baptist historian Joseph Martin Dawson:

"The jailer, seeing the fondness of the people for the preacher, collected four shillings and eight pence from those eager to visit him. Despite weakening from cold and improper food, he preached through the bars of the small iron gate. Lurid tales persist as to swords hacking at his outstretched hands when he preached. It is recorded that in order to terrify with warnings of

possible punishments to come, Negroes were cruelly whipped outside the prison where he could see and hear their distress. A plot
to blow up the jail was uncovered. A physician rescued him from
attempted poisoning. His tormentors burned pods of Indian
pepper to smoke him to death. Yet the sturdy Scot maintained
composure, continued his witness, and wrote letters to friends,
headed 'From my palace in Culpeper.'

"At length the resourceful Elijah Craig procured Ireland's
release. He journeyed at once to Williamsburg to appeal to the
governor. Lord Botetourt received him graciously and advised
how he might proceed. He returned to Culpeper for trial. The
magistrates, having got wind of his favorable reception at the capital and awed by the calm of the defendant, betrayed utter confusion. He walked out of the courtroom a free man. At once he tried
to resume preaching, but was too debilitated to recover his old
power."[2]

Another Baptist preacher, Jeremiah Moore of Fairfax, was a
special target of the establishment authorities because he had previously been an active Episcopal layman. Moore was arrested for
unauthorized preaching, and in the charge committing him to the
magistrates were these words: "I send you the body of Jeremiah
Moore, who is a preacher of the Gospel of Jesus Christ and also a
stroller."

Into Alexandria came galloping that well-known lawyer and
fiery orator, Patrick Henry, to defend Preacher Moore. The vigorous advocate of religious freedom stormed into the courthouse at
the beginning of Moore's trial and is quoted as saying:

"Great God, gentlemen, a man in prison for preaching the gospel of the son of God!" Henry's impassioned plea secured Moore's
release.

Far from exterminating the nonconformists, or even reducing
their numbers, such persecutions aroused an intense zeal among
these people to secure guarantees of religious liberty.

James Madison Enters the Battle

While John Leland considered the matter of opposing Mr.
Madison for the position of delegate to the Virginia Convention
on Ratification, he must have recalled his friend's long record in

behalf of freedom of conscience. It was young James Madison, an Episcopal student at the College of New Jersey in Princeton, who had strongly disapproved of the persecutions for religious beliefs and practices that were carried on in his native state. On January 24, 1772, he wrote from Princeton to his college friend William Bradford in Philadelphia:

"Poverty and luxury prevail among all sorts; pride, ignorance, and knavery among the priesthood; and vice and wickedness among the laity. This is bad enough; but it is not the worst I have to tell you. That diabolical, hell-conceived principle of persecution rages among some; and, to their eternal infamy, the clergy can furnish their quota of imps for such purposes. There are at this time, in the adjacent county, not less than five or six well-meaning men in close jail for publishing their religious sentiments, which in the main are very orthodox. I have neither patience to hear, talk, or think anything relative to this matter; for I have squabbled and scolded, abused and ridiculed so long about it to little purpose that I am without common patience. So I must beg you to pity me, and pray for liberty of conscience for all."[3]

After his graduation James Madison did more than write letters expressing his disapproval of religious intolerance. He appeared several times in court as a volunteer pleader in behalf of dissenters arrested for religious activities. He became convinced that Baptists were right in their contention that government should have no control over church affairs. Motivated by his desire to do something about this problem, he entered active political life.

In the spring of 1776 James Madison was elected a member of the Virginia Constitutional Convention. At twenty-five he was its youngest delegate. In that historic convention, youthful James Madison startled the staid gentlemen of the establishment by offering an amendment to the Declaration of Rights, substituting for the word *Toleration* the words *Religious Liberty*. In his first speech on the floor of the convention Madison gave his uncomfortable elders a lecture on the difference between toleration and liberty. Toleration, he pointed out, presumed a favored church or religious organization, established by governmental recognition and deriving some of its support from the public treasury while permitting other sects to exist but in an inferior status. Religious liberty, he explained, meant freedom of conscience and worship without either governmental interference or support. His arguments were unanswerable, and a majority of the convention delegates voted the amendment. His arguments were also squarely in line with the Baptist position on the matter.

The War for Independence had called men to arms. Washington as commander-in-chief of the Continental Army was fighting the British in New England. Thomas Jefferson was a member of the Continental Congress in Philadelphia. On July 2, 1776, the Congress passed a Declaration of Independence, announced two days later, in which Jefferson had enshrined the immortal words:

"We hold these truths to be self-evident: that all men are created equal; that they are endowed by their Creator with certain inalienable rights; that among these are life, liberty and the pursuit of happiness."

After completing his service in the Virginia Constitutional Convention of 1776, James Madison had been elected to the House of Burgesses. There he further endeared himself to the Baptists and other dissenters by successfully sponsoring a Declaration of Rights for Virginia. The statement declared that "all Citizens of the Commonwealth shall be free from coercion by the State in matters of religion." Thus the Declaration went far toward the Baptist ideal of separation of church and state.

During the war years John Leland had extended his preaching, on horseback and on foot, from Orange to Yorktown more than one hundred twenty miles away. He preached as many as a dozen sermons a week during revival services in churches near and far known among Baptists as "protracted meetings." Once on a June day in 1779, when his horse's back was too sore for riding, Parson Leland walked from his home to Culpeper twenty miles away, preached a funeral service and walked back home. And always he got in his vigorous licks for freedom of conscience based on the Baptist ideal that every person is "precious in the sight of the Lord" and has full authority to decide religious matters for himself.

All Leland's biographers refer to his quick wit and his good humor. One tells of an encounter Leland had with an Anglican clergyman, who challenged Leland at a meeting in which the Baptist was denouncing state support of the ministry of any church.

"The minister should get tax support so he will not have such a hard time preparing his sermons," contended the clergyman.

"But I can expound the Scriptures without any special preparation," answered Leland.

"Let's see if you can," challenged the Anglican pastor. "What, for instance, would you do with Numbers 22:21, which reads 'And Balaam . . . saddled his ass?' "

Leland gave the setting of that reference, and added: "First, Balaam, as a false prophet, represents the state-hired clergy. Second, the saddle represents the enormous tax burden of their salaries. Third, the dumb ass represents the people who bear such a tax burden!"[4]

A Victory and a New Threat

It was during that 1784 session of the General Assembly that the keen, logical persuasiveness of Madison won a majority to vote for Jefferson's Statute for Religious Freedom. The act made complete the separation of church and state in the Old Dominion and was accounted by Jefferson as one of the three great accomplishments of his career. It contained these significant words:

"Be it therefore enacted by the General Assembly, that no man shall be compelled to frequent or support any religious worship, place or ministry whatsoever, nor shall be enforced, restrained, molested, or burdened in his body or goods, nor shall otherwise suffer on account of his religious opinions or belief; but that all men shall be free to profess, and by argument to maintain, their opinions in matters of religion and that the same shall in nowise diminish, enlarge, or affect their civil capacities."[5]

Here was a splendid victory for religious freedom, but at the very time that the battle for Jefferson's Statute for Religious Freedom was being won, another threat to spiritual liberty arose in the Old Dominion: A bill was introduced in the General Assembly to levy an assessment of taxes on all property owners for the support of teachers of religion. It provided that each taxpayer could designate the denomination or church to which his assessment would apply.

That was bad enough from the Baptist standpoint. But matters were made much worse by another section of the bill which proposed that the Protestant Episcopal Church be recognized as an incorporation by the state. There was an added stipulation that lay vestries could not remove their clergy, thus proposing to give the favored Anglican ministers a life tenure. The assessment provision applied to all sects and was a sop to gain support of the Presbyterian clergy and lay leaders, and possibly the few Methodists, to overcome the known opposition of Baptists, Catholics, and Quakers.

Sponsors of the bill, members of the old establishment, vowed they could see nothing in the provisions of this bill inconsistent with the Statute for Religious Freedom. Their argument ran thus: "The Statute forbids compulsion to support any religious worship and to believe a certain way; it grants freedom of conscience without penalty. This act is first of all a simple taxation measure for the necessary support of teachers of religion, even allowing each taxpayer his privilege to designate where his payment shall go. Secondly, in bringing order to the administration of the Anglican Church it does not interfere with complete liberty for other sects."

Persuasive arguments those—for some. But not for Baptists, nor for other dissenting sects. Nor for James Madison!

The delegate from Orange County wrote a lengthy "Memorial and Remonstrance against Assessments for Support of Religion," which was printed and widely distributed as a pamphlet. It contained these significant words: "Religion by its very nature is exempt from the authority of society at large; still less can it be subject to that of the legislative body."[6]

Virginia Baptists rallied enthusiastically to Madison's support in his fight against the bill. In a session at Dupuy's Meeting House in Powhatan County on August 13, 1785, their General Committee called for use of what they considered their "natural right of petition to the Government." In their document were these words:

"Resolved, that it be recommended to those counties, which have not yet prepared petitions to the General Assembly, against the engrossed bill for a general assessment for the support of the teachers of the Christian religion, to proceed in matters of religion; that no human laws ought to be established for that purpose; but that every person ought to be left entirely free, in respect to matters of religion: That the Holy Author of our religion needs no such compulsive measures for the promotion of His cause; that the

Gospel wants not the feeble arm of man for its support: That it has made, and will again through Divine power make its way against opposition, and that should the Legislature assume the right of taxing the people for the support of the Gospel, it will be restrictive to religious liberty."[7]

Madison was impressed by the Baptist statement. He wrote to his friend and neighbor James Monroe that although several church groups were *for* the assessment bill, the Baptists were "standing firmly by their avowed principle of complete separation of church and state."

In January 1786, when the taxation bill went down to defeat, Madison wrote to Jefferson, who was then in Paris: "I flatter myself that we have in this country extinguished forever the ambitious hopes of making laws for the human mind."

"No Taxation, No Controls, No Favoritism."

Madison went on to the Constitutional Convention in Philadelphia to assume what proved to be the major responsibility in the writing of that document. By that time Leland and his Baptist co-workers had become convinced that full religious liberty required an absolute prohibition against all legislation affecting worship, its free exercise, and its support. In correspondence with fellow Baptists in other states, especially in his native Massachusetts, Leland confirmed that his convictions on the matter were shared with growing intensity throughout the land.

In Leland's writings of that day we find the details of the Baptist position on religious liberty, and they may be summarized thus:

First, there must be complete freedom of conscience. No one must be subject to penalties by any civil, military, or ecclesiastical authority because of religious belief or nonbelief.

Second, there must be complete freedom to practice religious beliefs and activities, including the propagation of the faith at home and abroad, so long as they conform to respect for the person and the laws of human decency and safety.

Third, there must be effective separation of church and state, specifically: (a) No *taxation* in any amount for any church, religious activity, or establishment. (b) No *control* of any religious organization by an agency of the government. (c) No *favoritism* by the government toward any religious organization, whether by extending diplomatic relations or by concessions to its ministers, leaders, or programs.

In several letters to Madison, the gravely concerned Leland and other crusaders for religious liberty pleaded with their friend and representative to write these cherished principles into the new constitution. Then the blow fell. Madison balked, asking for delay. Finally, in his candid and earnest manner, he declared that since the federal government was to have only delegated powers, there surely could be no opportunity for that government to abridge freedom of religion. Congress, he explained, could pass laws only on such subjects as the constitution granted it the authority to deal with. *It would have no power to legislate for or against religious liberty.*

Thus Madison had sided with Yankee John Adams, considered by Baptists as a champion of established or state-favored religion because he had declared: "Congress will never meddle with religion further than to say their own prayers, and to fast and give thanks once a year."

Leland was disappointed, but his disappointment only stirred him to further action. He wrote a pamphlet entitled "Objections to the Constitution." There were ten objections, and the first one began with these words:

"There is no Bill of Rights. Whenever a number of men enter into a state of society, a number of individual rights must be given up to society, but there should be a memorial of those not surrendered, otherwise every natural and domestic right becomes alienable, which raises Tyranny at once, and this is as necessary in one Form of Government as in another."[8]

After presenting eight other objections, Leland ended his last one by demanding protection for the people against the dangers of unrestrained political power:

"What is clearest of all—Religious Liberty, is not sufficiently secured. No religious test is required as a qualification to fill any office under the United States, but if a majority of the Congress with the President favour one system more than another, they may oblige all others to pay to the support of their system as much as they please; and if oppression does not ensue, it will be owing to the mildness of Administration, and not to any Constitutional defense, and if the manners of people are so far corrupted, that they cannot live by Republican principles, it is very dangerous leaving Religious Liberty at their mercy."

Before James Madison left Philadelphia, he had read Leland's objections and doubtless had studied them carefully. Was Leland right? Was there danger, despite the specific delegation of powers which began with "Congress shall have power," that any human liberties could be infringed? The convention was drawing to a close, so what could be done now? Such questions must have given Madison careful thought.

Just as the convention ended, a letter came to Madison from James Gordon, Jr., of Orange, informing him that several men of the county were contemplating filing their names for delegate of the Convention on Ratification, with the announced purpose of opposing ratification. One of these, the letter said, was Colonel Charles Barbour; in addition, Parsons Bledsoe and Leland, with Colonel Z. Burnley, were all opposed.

Another letter, this one from Captain Joseph Spencer, a Baptist who had served time in prison for his religious faith, discussed the rising tide of opposition to the constitution, and added: "Mr. Leeland and Mr. Bledsoe and Sanders are the most publick men of the society in Orange, therefor as Mr. Leeland lyes in your way home from Fredericksburg to Orange would advise you to call on him and spend a few hours in his company . . ."[9]

Meeting Under Oak Trees

Some of Leland's biographers give considerable credit to Sallie Leland, that devout and spirited woman who had counseled her husband on every move he made after their marriage, for suggesting the solution to the problem of how John might gain his purpose without going to the Convention. Others give the major credit to Colonel Barbour. It seems certain that Sallie did not want to be left alone with their brood of children while John attended a long-winded convention. It is certain that the Colonel, at the Goochland meeting in March 1788, offered to withdraw if Leland would announce for the position.

Perhaps both the wife and the close friend advised John to

strike a bargain with Madison. The new constitution provided for amendments. If Madison would agree to be a member of the First Congress and present amendments that the Baptists wanted, John could announce that he would not run for delegate to the Convention and would support James Madison.

Madison stopped at Mount Vernon overnight to visit the Washingtons, then hurried on to Fredericksburg. There he was warned by several friends and supporters that he would have a hard time being elected a delegate to the Convention unless he gained the support of the influential Baptist leader.

With John Leland's "Objections to the Constitution" in his pocket, Mr. Madison dismounted from his carriage at the front door of the Leland farm home. After the greetings and pleasantries were exchanged, Madison and his host excused themselves from Sallie and the children and strolled out into the side yard. There, under the great oak trees, the two men talked earnestly.

Madison still had to be convinced that additional guarantees of religious liberty and other freedoms mentioned in the Objections were necessary. Leland brought all his persuasive power to bear upon his distinguished friend. Apparently, no record of their conversation was ever made, but soon afterward Candidate James Madison spoke to a picnic crowd in an oak grove near Gum Spring, six miles from Orange. Standing on a hogshead of tobacco so he could be easily seen and heard, he told his listeners that he would indeed run for the First Congress and if elected, would introduce the amendments suggested by the Reverend Mr. Leland and many honest and intelligent citizens.

Once committed to the task of formulating amendments, James Madison became engrossed in the work. As an elected member of the First Congress, he consulted farmers, merchants, lawyers, editors. He reported occasionally to George Washington, who heartily approved the idea of what Madison called a "Bill of Rights." He carefully considered such pleas as these:

"Let no one be imprisoned for saying or printing his opinions!"

"The British put their soldiers in our home without our consent!"

"Mr. Madison, let it be writ that no official can take property without just payment."

"Let no constable search my house without a warrant!"

And of course he consulted Preacher Leland, who had one firm request: "Let freedom of religion lead all the rest in the Bill of Rights."

On January 2, 1789, Madison wrote to the Reverend George Eve, pastor of the Blue Run Baptist Church in Orange County: "Circumstances have now changed. It is my sincere opinion that the Constitution ought to be revised, and that the first Congress . . . ought to prepare and recommend to the States for ratification the most satisfactory provisions for essential rights, particularly the rights of conscience in the fullest latitude, the freedom of the press, trials by jury, security against general warrants, etc."[10]

One afternoon early in that first session of the Congress all eyes in the House of Representatives were turned toward the small man with sparse dark hair and piercing gray eyes, as James Madison stood and announced:

"Mr. Speaker, I have the honor to present for the consideration of this body certain proposed amendments to the constitution of the United States. I shall read them. The first one states:

" 'Congress shall make no law respecting an establishment of religion, or prohibiting the free exercise thereof; or abridging the freedom of speech, or of the press, or of the right of the people peaceably to assemble, and to petition the government for a redress of grievances.' "

The Bill of Rights had started on its way to adoption.

II

THE ZEALOUS ANABAPTISTS

"We Follow the Same Faith"

"We Baptists began at the Jordan River, and have had a continuous existence ever since!" Those words express the firm conviction of those devout people, a small group known as the Landmark Baptists. They earnestly contend that John the Baptizer was indeed a Baptist, that the fellowships of those who believed in the Master during and immediately following his earthly ministry were without doubt Baptist churches; that the first Christian church was the First Baptist Church of Jerusalem, and that there is an unbroken line of Baptist churches down to the present time.

The Landmarkers readily admit that there are some gaps in the record of direct succession from the days of the first Christian believers, but this creates no great problem for them. As one of their spokesmen has described the matter: "If I see a white horse in a pasture, and he disappears for a time in the woods, then I see a white horse coming out from the woods on the other side, I can be fairly sure it is the same white horse, even though I could not see him while he was in the forest!"

However, the vast majority of modern Baptists, whatever their branch, fellowship or convention, say that trying to prove they are successors to the early Christian churches is not important. They agree that it matters not just where and when Baptist churches began. They assert that their supreme task is to follow the teachings of the Master in all things, and declare: "The important thing is not unbroken succession, but unbroken *principles*. We follow the same faith, and largely the same practices, as the early Christians. Our kinship with them is based upon our common source of beliefs and practices—the New Testament."

Baptist church historian Albert Henry Newman has described the kinship thus: "That the apostolic churches were in all essential respects Baptists, or rather the Baptist churches are in all essential respects conformed to the apostolic norm, is generally admitted by impartial students of New Testament church policy who have taken the trouble to compare the two."[1]

Other Baptist historians point out that the Christians of the first and second centuries were scattered abroad, as the writer Luke described it, by civil and religious rulers who tried to exterminate them. They believe that many had gone to faraway Britain, settling in Wales to escape persecution. It is possible, they conclude, that these and other refugees and their descendants continued their practice of baptism by immersion, their belief in the autonomy of each church, and their democratic congregational procedures—in a word, their New Testament practices, down to the modern era. While conceding this, the great majority of Baptists agree that *spiritual succession* is the hallmark of their fellowship, and hold firmly that baptism by immersion, considered a symbol of faith in a risen Christ and a prerequisite to fellowship in a congregation called a church, was practiced by Jesus and his early followers.

As for baptism, by the middle of the third century the Church of Rome had decided that the act of baptism was essential to the salvation of the soul. It logically followed that infants had to be baptized to avoid the dangers of hell in case they died. This dogma centuries later came into direct conflict with the beliefs of the so-called freethinkers, the radical reformers who rejected the infant baptism and recognized baptism only of those who voluntarily expressed faith in Christ.

The Reformation Is Born

The trail leading to the spiritual Reformation began in the year 1170. At that time there arose in France a religious leader, Peter Waldo, to found a sect whose members tried to restore and practice the ways of living of the early Christians. Waldo, a wealthy merchant, inspired by the story of the rich young ruler, decided that true Christianity required a life of poverty. He sold all his goods, distributed the money to the poor, and became a wandering evangelist. Believing that all people should have the Bible in their own languages, he had scholars unlock the Scripture from its Latin prison and translate it into the tongue of the common people.

Peter Waldo gained a wide following—and the determined opposition of the established church. Battered by more than a century of persecution, the Waldensians migrated to the valleys of the Alps. In their Piedmont retreats many of these nonconformists, who became known as the Vaudois, revived and carried on the forms of worship that included believer's baptism by immersion and the democratic organization of their churches—the very heart of later Baptist faith and method.

The Waldensians influenced the formation of many nonconformist groups and congregations, challenging the established Roman Catholic Church and enduring persecutions and death to assert their right to read and interpret the Scriptures and to worship as they pleased.

There was John Wycliffe, born in 1320, the English ecclesiastical reformer who caught a vision of what reading the Scriptures could do for the spiritual life of the common people and had the Bible translated into their vernacular. Wycliffe helped to prepare the ground for the Reformation by preaching that Christ was the true head of the church and that believers needed no mediator to approach him in prayer and faith. His followers, called Lollards, although severely harassed, spread the doctrine of spiritual liberty throughout England and into parts of the continent.

There was John Huss in Bohemia, a priest who dared to assert the supremacy of the Scriptures as the guide for religious faith, and who was burned at the stake. There was Martin Luther, a Catholic monk of the monastery at Wittenberg, Germany, who on October 31, 1517, nailed a protest in the form of "Ninety Five Theses" to the door of his chapel and asserted his belief that "the just shall live by faith."

There was the great reformer, John Calvin, born in 1509 in France and living his adult life in Geneva, Switzerland, who worked out an intricate theological formula at the heart of which was man's right to have direct communication with God.

The Re-Baptizers

The great religious upheaval began at a time when the established Roman Catholic Church and the established governments of Europe were so closely blended as to be inseparable. Emperors, kings, and princes ruled by what was considered divine right, their coronations blessed and certified by the Pope or his appointed deputies. The religion of the ruler was the religion of all his subjects, the dogmas and rulings of the church were the same as temporal law in their impact upon the people, and deviation from authorized thinking was considered a violation of the established order. Disobedience of spiritual edicts was heresy, and the heretic was by the very nature of state-church control guilty of treason and therefore a criminal. Torture was still the accepted method for the trial of the accused, and burning at the stake the favored method of execution. Beheading and drowning were also used, but were less acceptable because they exacted far less suffering. Especially was burning alive the most favored punishment for deviation in religious beliefs, for fire was the great eradicator, and elimination of heresy by eradicating the heretic was the goal of church leaders who felt their positions threatened by unorthodox opinions.

These cruelties fell upon countless thousands of the devout men and women of the Reformation movements. And none suffered more than the spiritual forerunners of the Baptists, those radicals of the Reformation known as the Anabaptists.

Ana in Greek means *again,* and in derision and contempt the Anabaptists were called baptizers again or re-baptizers, because they baptized their members upon individual professions of faith even though each had been baptized as an infant by a priest of the church.

The Anabaptist movement began in Switzerland. For years its ideas and principles had smouldered in the minds and the secret conversations of many religious leaders who felt stifled in the compress of forced religious conformity. With Martin Luther's open break with the church hierarchy, the coals of rebellion against the established church burst into flame. In that same year of Luther's protest, Ulrich Zwingli, a Catholic priest of Einsiedeln, concluded from his study of the New Testament that infant baptism was not necessary for salvation of the soul, and that baptism should follow what he termed a regeneration by faith.

Zwingli came to Zurich and assembled a group of young humanists with whom he studied the Greek New Testament. Among these was Conrad Grebel, son of an influential member of the Zurich Great Council. Early in the year 1525 Grebel and about a dozen of his fellow humanists decided it was time to light the lamps of the Reformation in their own community by being baptized again as evidence of their voluntary conversion and membership in a new church fellowship, a congregation of believers.

Zwingli refused to join them as he hoped to bring about reforms by agreement with the city and church authorities, so the young men broke with their former teacher. One wintry night in early 1525 they gathered secretly at the house of Felix Manz. Conrad Grebel baptized the leader of the group, Jorg Blaurock, by pouring water upon his head, whereupon Blaurock baptized all the others present in the same manner. The young men pledged to hold firm to the New Testament faith and to teach its principles to their fellow men.

The Swiss Brethren

At that secret night meeting in Zurich the Anabaptist movement was born. These reformers and their followers became known as the Swiss Brethren. Through their influence, doubts about the scriptural basis for infant baptism spread over Switzerland and into Germany and Moravia. Their writings were filled with references to the New Testament as the true spiritual authority, especially as relating to baptism as a symbol of entry into church fellowship. As William R. Estep, Jr., modern historian of the Anabaptists, has written of these Reformation zealots:

"Probably the most revolutionary act of the Reformation was the institution of believer's baptism by a handful of Swiss Brethren in Zurich. Of course, believer's baptism had been practiced before, but after the apostolic period only spasmodically by various dissenting groups. Outside of the early period, rarely if ever had believer's baptism been practiced so consistently under such adverse circumstances. Yet its reinauguration was a premeditated act by a little band of dedicated disciples. Their theological convictions demanded action in spite of clear knowledge of its bitter consequences. Immediately baptism became the burning issue of the hour. And the symbol of Anabaptist discipleship became the occasion of severe oppression."[2]

Whereas Martin Luther retained in his reformed principles the practice of infant baptism, his belief in the union of state and church for order in religious affairs, and his doctrine of the Universal Church, Anabaptists repudiated each of these tenets. In addition to believer's baptism, these radicals of the Reformation held unshakably to other doctrines that became the spiritual heritage of modern Baptists. Among these were freedom to worship with no interference or control by the State, conversion through voluntary repentance and faith in Jesus Christ, a determination after baptism "to walk in newness of life," fellowship in a congregation of believers making up what was described as the visible church, and discipleship for mutual comfort and for the spread of the gospel.

We shall note only the most outstanding of the leaders of this revolution in religious beliefs and methods, those whose influence was felt in their spiritual successors for generations that followed.

One of the young men who met to form the new fellowship, Conrad Grebel of Zurich, was born into a family of wealth and educated in the higher schools at Basel, Vienna, and Paris. He brought down upon himself the condemnation of his parents by his marriage to a working-class girl. Grebel's conversion to the beliefs of the Anabaptist reformers made him practically an outcast. Undaunted, he became an evangelist, going with his close friend Felix Manz from house to house, preaching and exhorting in his newfound faith.

Grebel baptized hundreds of converts. Proving his willingness to accept spiritual liberty in the method of baptism, he baptized Wolfgang Ulimann, a former priest, by immersion in the Rhine River on this convert's request. In April 1525 Grebel immersed what a chronicler of that day described as a great company of believers.

Anabaptist Martyrs

Alarmed at such spread of Anabaptist heresy, Zurich authorities rounded up all the leaders of the movement they could find, including Conrad Grebel and Felix Manz, and imprisoned them. For many months the Zurich "Witch's Tower" rang with the hymns and prayers of the devout baptizers. Grebel used the time in jail to write a paper to justify by the New Testament his views on baptism. He declared:

"It is clearly seen what baptism is and to whom baptism should be applied, namely, to one who has been converted by the Word of God, has changed his heart, and henceforth desires to walk in newness of life . . . For this I have already learned and know assuredly, that baptism means nothing else than a dying of the old man, and a putting on of the new, and that Christ commanded to baptize those who had been taught."[3]

The authorities refused to allow the manuscript to be made public. In March 1526 Grebel and all the Anabaptist prisoners in Zurich were sentenced by the magistrates to life imprisonment. At the same time a city ordinance was passed which prescribed punishment by death for anyone performing baptism outside the established church.

Through the help of some secret sympathizers Grebel, Manz, and twelve other prisoners escaped. Weak from his imprisonment, Conrad Grebel became victim of the plague and, cheating the magistrates of their plan to execute him upon his recapture, died during the summer of 1526.

Felix Manz then teamed up with Jorg Blaurock to spread the Anabaptist message, principally among peasants and workers in northern Switzerland. He expressed the spirit of these early members of the reformed fellowship in words such as these:

"Love to God through Christ shall alone avail and subsist; but boasting, reviling, and threatening shall fail. Charity alone is pleasing to God . . . Christ hated no man; his true disciples are likewise devoid of hatred, thus following Christ in the true way, as he went before them. . . ."

Manz was captured with his companion and fellow-worker Jorg Blaurock in a forest and sentenced to death. Explicit details for his execution stipulated that he would be bound and pushed into the water, "thereby he shall have atoned to the law and justice."

Tied to the end of a long pole, he was submerged in the water of Zurichzee for a time, then brought above the surface. When revived, he was asked if he would recant and thus save his life. Each time his answer was "No! I will be true to my belief," and each time he was brought up, his mother, standing on the bank, called out to him "Felix! Do not recant! Do not recant!"[4]

This martyr left behind a number of hymns that breathe the courage and zeal of the early Anabaptists. One song of eighteen stanzas is still sung in German by the closest spiritual descendants of the Swiss Brethren in America, the Amish and Hutterite worshipers. Its English equivalent begins:

> With gladness will I sing now;
> My heart delights in God,
> Who showed me such forbearance,
> That I was saved from death
> Which never has an end,
> I praise thee, Christ in Heaven,
> Who all my sorrow changed!

Jorg Blaurock was a tall, handsome, aggressive man, whom Zwingli called a presumptuous fool. In his misguided zeal young Blaurock did not hesitate to invade a meeting already in progress and take over the services, sermon and all. But over much of Germanic Switzerland he preached, exhorted, and baptized converts, on their profession of faith, either by pouring or by immersion.

Blaurock was arrested, beaten and expelled from one city only to continue his ministry in the next. Hearing that an Anabaptist church in the Adige Valley had lost its pastor, Michael Kurschner, by execution at the stake, Blaurock boldly came in and took up the duties.

In August 1539 Blaurock and a companion evangelist were arrested in the Austrian town of Innsbruck. The authorities cruelly tortured them, hoping to gain information as to other Anabaptist leaders, and some weeks later both were burned at the stake.

Balthasar Hubmaier

Two other shining meteors flashed across the Anabaptist sky in that troubled early sixteenth century. They were Balthasar Hubmaier and Michael Sattler, whose lives, teachings, and martyrdom gave a tremendous impetus to Anabaptist progress and greatly influenced public thinking against persecution for religion.

Hubmaier earned his Doctorate of Theology from the University of Freiburg in 1512. Soon afterward he was ordained to the priesthood and became vice-rector of the University, which he left in 1515 to become priest of the cathedral of Regensburg in Bavaria. In that city Dr. Hubmaier found a campaign raging.

"Expel the Jews! Death to the Jews!" were the cries of militant gentiles. Hubmaier became one of the leaders of the vicious anti-Semitic movement. Writing, speaking, agitating, he had the satisfaction of seeing the City Council confiscate the money and property of the dispossessed Hebrews—including their synagogue, which was turned into a Catholic chapel in honor of the beauteous Mary.

Hubmaier officiated at this chapel and reported numerous miracles of healing, with huge offerings from pilgrims to Mary's shrine. Jealousy on the part of less fortunate priests brought trouble and Hubmaier thought best to leave for a more secluded parish at nearby Waldshut. There the thunderstorm of Luther's reforms broke about the learned, shrewd, successful priest. He recorded that he began to study the New Testament, especially the writings of the Apostle Paul. By 1525, he wrote, he was "a captive to the word of God."

Hubmaier visited Zurich, met Zwingli and also spoke to those who had deserted that reformer for the more radical Anabaptists. In June 1524 he published his *Schlussreden,* a statement of religious principles, which summarized many of the doctrines of the reformers most hated by his own church. In April 1525 Wilhelm Reublin, an Anabaptist refugee, came to Waldshut. Hubmaier, now convinced that the Anabaptists were right, received baptism from him. Then Hubmaier, on Easter Sunday, himself baptized more than three hundred persons with water sprinkled from a milk pail.

From that time forward Hubmaier served the Anabaptists as a humble and penitent, but ardent and energetic, believer. He took Elizabeth Hugline as his wife. He wrote numerous tracts and pamphlets explaining his conversion and his beliefs. He went to Zurich and carried on a disputation with Zwingli. He also wrote a pamphlet which some historians consider one of the best defenses of adult baptism ever written. Said Hubmaier:

"Baptism in the name of the Father and of the Son and of the Holy Ghost is when a man first confesses his sins, and pleads guilty; then believes in the foregiveness of sins through Jesus Christ, and turns to live according to the rule of Christ . . . Then he professes this publicly, in the eyes of men, by the outward baptism of water. He is then truly baptized."[5]

Hubmaier went on to Moravia, and at Nikolsburg made numerous converts. So great was the power of his persuasion that during one year he baptized some 6,000 converts, including the Barons of Lichtenstein, Leonhard, and Johann, thereby arousing the anger of Emperor Ferdinand, the Catholic ruler of Austria.

Arrested and taken to Vienna, the apostate priest was tortured and condemned to death. An eyewitness of the execution, Stephen Sprugel, who was dean of the philosophy faculty at the University of Vienna, related how Hubmaier's faithful wife exhorted him not to recant or to waver. She, too, was executed a few days later by drowning.

From Monk to Anabaptist

Michael Sattler, born near Freiburg, Germany, became a Benedictine monk. Eager for learning, he mastered Greek and Hebrew, which led him to study the New Testament. Convinced that the leaders of the church had moved far away from the simple fellowships of the early Christians, and challenged by the reforms of Martin Luther, Sattler severed all ties of his Catholic ministry.

He, too, had to flee from the emperor's wrath and went to Zurich, where, for a while, he found spiritual peace among the Anabaptists. Then his secret meetings with the baptizers were discovered, and he was expelled from that city, too. He carried on his crusade for reform in southern Germany, in the areas about Horb and Rottenburg, always in secret for fear of instant arrest.

At a meeting of Anabaptists at Schleitheim in February 1527, Michael Sattler preached the principal sermon and offered a thesis on Anabaptist order and discipline that became noted as the Schleitheim Confession. While this meeting was in progress the Rottenburg authorities discovered the Anabaptist activities, and

Sattler was taken into custody, along with his wife and several others of the fellowship. The lengthy accusation included charges that Sattler and his adherents acted contrary to the doctrines of the church with respect to baptism, communion, the Virgin Mary, defense of the country by war, and many other items.

The trial was held before an imposing panel of twenty-four judges, headed by Count Joachim of Zollern. The accused preacher acted as spokesman for all the defendants, taking up the charges in detail, and thus leaving a record of explanations of the Anabaptists' stand that shows clearly how important and enduring were the beliefs of these reformists in shaping modern Baptist principles of spiritual liberty and freedom of conscience.

As to the charge that he and his followers "despised and reviled the Mother of God, and condemned the saints," Sattler declared: "We never reviled the Mother of God, and the saints; but the mother of Christ should be esteemed above all women; for she had the favor of giving birth to the Savior of the world; but that she shall be an intercessor is not known in Scripture . . . As to the saints, we say, that we who live and believe are the saints; those who die in the faith, we consider the blessed."

To the stern judges Sattler expounded a doctrine of nonresistance, on which not all Anabaptists were agreed but which laid the basis for conscientious objection to military service centuries later among several groups of spiritual descendants of these peaceful Brethren. "For it is written," Sattler said, "thou shalt not kill. We ought not to defend ourselves against the Turks, and our persecutors; but earnestly entreat God in our prayers, that he would repel and withstand them. For my saying, if I approved of war, I would rather march forth against the so-named Christians who persecute, imprison, and put to death, the pious Christians. . . ."[6]

Such statements enraged the judges, and the sentence of the court read: "Michael Sattler shall be committed to the executioner. The latter shall take him to the square and there first cut out his tongue, and then forge him fast to a wagon and there with glowing iron tongs twice tear pieces from his body, then on the way to the site of the execution five times more as above and then burn his body to powder as an arch-heretic."

Sattler had promised his followers that if during the public torture he found the pain was endurable, he would raise two fingers.

The sentence was carried out to the letter. When the flames had burned away the ropes that bound his hands he raised two fingers as his last mortal gesture of assurance. His wife, who refused all efforts of a priest to convince her that she should recant, was drowned in the Neckar River.

If the authorities had hoped that Sattler's martyrdom would strike fear into any who might stray into heresy, they were disappointed. It had the opposite effect. William Reublin of Zurich wrote an account of the infamous execution that was circulated secretly all over Switzerland and the German and Austrian realms. Sympathy for the Anabaptists, mixed with curiosity as to their beliefs, rose like a tide.

The Lunatic Fringe

As has been true in the development and progress of all great movements of reform, fanatical leaders, bordered by a lunatic fringe, sprang up among the Anabaptists. The most radical of the fringe were Thomas Munzer, Melchior Hoffman, Jan Matthys, and Jan Beukelssen. These irresponsible zealots, and several minor ones, brought great discredit to the Anabaptist cause.

Munzer, well educated in theology, claimed to be under special guidance of the Holy Spirit. He vigorously denounced Luther's teachings, probably to create attention for his own, which centered upon what he termed the need for a new theocracy in which all persons would share in common without the rule of civil authorities. Because of his disturbing radicalism, Munzer was expelled from Zwickau, and later from Prague. In the spring of 1525 he collected an armed rabble of peasants at Frankenhausen to fight in open battle against the legal authorities, but his misguided army was dispersed; and he was executed.

Melchior Hoffman was an early Dutch follower of Martin Luther, who in 1530 joined the Anabaptist brotherhood in Strasbourg. He predicted that he would return from the dead in 1533, with the Savior from the heavens, and would assist in establishing the seat of Christ's spiritual kingdom of Strasbourg. He was imprisoned.

Two Dutch missionaries, Matthys, a baker in Haarlem, and Beukelssen, a tailor of Leyden, startled the world in the early

1520s when they announced that all civil governments were evil and that there should be a return to the rule of Zion. The city of Munster, across the border in northern Germany, was to be the New Jerusalem. In 1533 Beukelssen announced himself the "King of Zion," and with Matthys led a group of followers, infected beyond reason by fantastic prophecies and promises, to overthrow the city officials of Munster by armed force. They actually controlled the city for two years. Munster was finally liberated from the grip of the self-proclaimed King Beukelssen by military siege and capture, followed by execution of the Anabaptist ringleaders.

• These tragic events cast dark shadows upon the entire Anabaptist movement. The very name became unjustly associated in popular thinking with fanaticism. Certainly the adherents of Martin Luther looked upon them with complete disfavor, considering these radicals as disturbers of the orderly Reformation. The truth about the Anabaptists doubtless lies between the extreme opinions of their bitter critics and their ardent supporters, and modern objective religious historians seem to agree that out of the crucible of their turbulent existence there came the refined metal of spiritual liberty.

Mennonites and Hutterites

No account of the spiritual antecedents of modern Baptists would be complete without recognition of Menno Simons, the Dutch Anabaptist whose name is memorialized by the modern Mennonites, and Jacob Hutter of Moravia, whose faithful adherents took the name of "Hutterite Brethren."

The Anabaptist movement in the Netherlands was well underway when Menno Simons, a parish priest of Witmarsum, found himself caught up in discussions of the Reformation and began to doubt many tenets of the church. After much reflection on the scriptural accounts of the lives of the early Christians, Simons rejected the fanaticism of Hoffman and the extreme radicalism of the Anabaptists of Munster. Then there occurred an event that made him a convert and a leader of one branch of the movement.

In 1530, on orders of Emperor Charles V, a campaign to exterminate the Anabaptists began all over the Netherlands. Many local authorities ordered the families of these re-baptizers to pack up and leave under pain of being jailed and losing all their property by confiscation. About 300 of the wretched wanderers, men, women, and children, assembled at an abandoned monastery called Old Cloister, where they camped while trying to decide where they might find a place to set up a colony. Among these refugees was Menno Simons' brother.

One morning the Anabaptists awoke to find the entire monastery surrounded by troops. The men were herded out, stood against the walls and slaughtered by volleys of the wide-muzzled firearms of the soldiers. Then the women and children, cringing inside one of the shelters, were massacred by the gunfire.

Shocked at this atrocious mass execution, Simons wrote: "My heart trembled within me. I prayed to God with sighs and tears that He would give to me, a sorrowing sinner, the gift of his grace, create within me a clean heart, and graciously bestow upon me the wisdom, spirit, courage, and a manly way that I might preach his exalted and adorable name and holy word in purity."

Menno Simons found that it was impossible for him to continue preaching as a priest of the established church, so in 1531 he cut his former ties to become an evangelist of the Netherland Anabaptists and their acknowledged leader. He steered them away from divisive disputations and taught them a doctrine of fellowship in love and peace.

The Emperor placed a reward of one hundred gold gilders on Menno Simons' head, but the preacher escaped arrest. He continued his labor of exhorting and organizing over Holland and northern Germany. He wrote many tracts, and several books, of great importance to the Anabaptist movement. Many of his writings are still used by his followers, the devout and pacifist Mennonites, as supplemental to Scripture. Simons died peacefully in his home in 1561.

Jacob Hutter was a native of the Puster Valley in the Tyrol. Unlike many Anabaptist leaders who were reformed priests, Hutter was a poorly educated hat maker. He became an Anabaptist convert and preacher in 1529. Harassed by persecution in the Tyrol, he fled to Moravia, a refuge for Anabaptists of that day.

Hutter believed that the example of the early Christians in having "all things in common" was to be followed literally by later Christians, and his leadership among Moravian Anabaptists was distinguished by his establishment of a Christian form of communism. He set up colonies called *Bruderhofe,* or Farms of the Brethren, in which no one owned property but all shared what the land produced. Hutter and his adherents were in all other respects typical of the Anabaptist faith and practice.

Emperor Ferdinand's intolerance of heresy, this time combined with contempt for the communal farming, resulted in the 1533 edict to expel all followers of Jacob Hutter from Moravia. Driven like sheep from one area to another, often walking for days without food or water, the wretched men, women, and children wandered about seeking someone who might befriend them. More than half their faithful in Moravia perished by privation or execution in the decade following Ferdinand's edict.

Hutter himself fled to his native Tyrol, where he was captured and brutally tortured in futile efforts by the authorities to induce him to recant. In February 1536 he was burned at the stake.

Blood of the Martyrs

Many Hutterite Brethren fled to Hungary and Transylvania. There in their Bruderhofe they found peace for a time, only to become victims of new intolerance in 1758 when Empress Maria Theresa sent her agents to all the Hutterite colonies to force the people to become Catholics. Their books were seized, their pastors forbidden to preach, their instructors forbidden to teach. All the principal Hutterite leaders were imprisoned and many were executed, but still the remnants of the colonies worshiped as had their fathers, bravely and zealously for the faith.

So the story of the European spiritual forebears of the modern Baptists was written in the blood of their martyrs, on the parchment of their eagerness to live cheerfully for their faith or their willingness to die for it. The "Martyrs' Mirror," compiled in the eighteenth century, tells of mass executions of the Anabaptists, often as many as a score at one time. In Swabia, the record discloses, four hundred constables were hired to hunt down the Anabaptist heretics and execute them on the spot. The four hundred proved insufficient, so the number was increased to a thousand. The largest mass execution on record was that of three hundred fifty persons at Altzey, ordered by Emperor Ferdinand on recommendation of the Count of Altzey. This spectacle offered a long line of blazing fagots and burning human flesh, but sometime later the Count lamented: "What, pray tell me, am I to do with these heretics? The more I execute, the more they increase!"[7]

Among themselves, the Anabaptists were not always in agreement on details of their new faith as they hammered them out on the anvils of investigation and disputation. Some, like Sattler, were extreme pacifists, while others were not. The majority of Anabaptist leaders baptized by sprinkling or pouring water upon the head, while an increasing number began in the seventeenth century to insist upon a return to what they believed was the example of Christ, immersion of the entire body in water.

Whatever their differences, the Anabaptists believed in the competence of the individual before God, in salvation by grace, and the responsibility of the believer to live a moral life and to propagate the faith. At the same time they vigorously denied that the Pope as the vicar of Christ on earth had both spiritual and secular power, and that the hierarchy of the church had authority to make its interpretation of the Scripture binding upon the faithful.

These certainly were basic ideas for the growing number of Mennonites who migrated to England, there to clash with another established church, the Church of England.

III

ENGLAND'S FIRST BAPTISTS

The Dissenters Suffered

By 1533 King Henry VIII had removed all jurisdiction of the Roman Catholic Church from his kingdom. He had abolished the monasteries, banished the monks, and taken over the enormous wealth of the Church, beheading many Catholic leaders in the process.

Henry's greatest personal triumph in substituting an established religion under his own control for the old papal rule had come in the divorce from his queen, Catherine of Aragon, and his marriage to Anne Boleyn in hope of a male heir. When he and Anne failed to produce the heir, another marriage (after the beheading of Anne) was in order, and the heir, Edward VI, was born.

During the remaining years of his troubled reign, Henry VIII strengthened state control of the religious establishment and increased the power of parliament, generally for his own selfish purposes. He never neglected for a moment keeping his hand in the great game of power politics as played by Europe's foremost rivals, Francis I of France and Charles V of the sprawling realm from Italy to the Netherlands known as the Holy Roman Empire.

Always the scheming, dissolute English monarch found time to collaborate with his bishops in the persecution of the dissenters, especially the heretical Anabaptists. The preserved records show that in May 1525 twenty-five Dutch Anabaptists, who had come to England to encourage and instruct their brethren in the faith, were arrested. Fourteen of these were burned at the stake and the

others imprisoned for life. In 1538 a group of English Anabaptists, led by Jan Matthigiz and Joan Boucher, secretly published a book on the incarnation. Some of its opinions as to the
extent to which God became flesh in his Son ran counter to the
official doctrine on the subject. Both authors were executed by
fire. One historian of the period asserts that the number of Anabaptists executed by Henry VIII exceeded the number of Lollards
executed in England during the whole previous century. It seems
certain that 80 per cent of those put to death for their faith during
the reign of Henry's daughter, "bloody" Queen Mary, were Protestant dissenters.

Through all the intrigues, alliances, betrayals, wars, and tyran-
nical antics of the absolute monarchs of sixteenth-century Europe,
monarchs who justified their actions by the claim of a divine right
to rule, the seeds of Anabaptist beliefs took root and grew.

Near the middle of that century there arose within the Church
of England a group demanding that the established church be
"purified" of all vestiges of Roman Catholicism. These "Puritans," strongly influenced by the teachings of the reformer John
Calvin, called for greater simplicity in worship and strict austerity
in personal life. They insisted upon scriptural authority for doctrines, rites, and ceremonies; but they fell far short of the ideal of
spiritual liberty; they were active and relentless advocates of the
eradication, by imprisonment, banishment, and death, of all nonconformists who did not agree with their doctrines.

In the 1570s a well-educated Anglican minister of London,
Robert Browne, announced his conviction that the Scriptures
alone should be followed in matters of faith and Christian living,
that there should be separation of the church from state control,
and that local congregations should be independent of one another, each a democracy in itself. He held that the established
Church of England had fallen into corrupt ways and that true
believers should separate from its fold. In 1581, under threat of
imprisonment and execution for his beliefs, Browne fled with his
small congregation to Middleburg, Zealand, in the North Sea
province of Holland. Before his death he became mentally
deranged, but the seeds of Separation had been sown and the result was a harvest of dissent from the Church of England, which

furnished recruits to the ranks of believers soon to become known as Baptists.

John Smyth, the Erstwhile Physician

Most important recruit, for the story of Baptist beginnings, was John Smyth. He was a graduate of Cambridge and in 1594 was ordained in the Church of England. He taught at Christ College, Cambridge, and was considered an intelligent and able lecturer. He was identified with the Puritan branch of the established church, and as a good Puritan he endorsed the principle of state-enforced conformity in religious beliefs. "The magistrates," he said, "should cause all men to worship the true God, or else punish them with imprisonment, confiscation of goods, or death as the quality of the cause requireth." In John Smyth's way of thinking, the "quality of the cause" of heresy always required the heaviest penalties possible.

While the details of Smyth's early career are obscure, it is known that from 1598 until 1602 he was city preacher in Lincoln. He was dismissed from his duties as pastor and lecturer because of political differences with city authorities. Moving to Gainsborough, he supported himself for a time by engaging in the primitive practice of medicine of that day.

At Gainsborough, the erstwhile physician found that the local Anglican parish was neglected. The vicar, Jerome Phillips, received the pay of his office but did not bother to hold services or perform other spiritual duties. Smyth impulsively called the parish members together and became their minister. Since he had failed to get his license from the bishop for this bold step, he was severely condemned for his zeal and discharged from the parish.

Smarting under the disgrace, Smyth spent several months in deliberation and renewed study of the teachings and beliefs of the Separatists. Concluding that these reformers were right, he withdrew from the Church of England and gathered a congregation of friends and adherents to organize a congregation at Gainsborough. Among his members were two names that later became noted in religious leadership in America, William Brewster and William Bradford. He had in his congregation, also, a man whose name was to be written high on the roll of those who advanced the cause of spiritual liberty in Europe, Thomas Helwys.

While Smyth was pastor of the Gainsborough Separatist congregation, a branch of this group met at nearby Scrooby with John Robinson, a former Puritan, as pastor and Richard Clifton as lay reader. Fate and Smyth's own convictions and zeal were preparing this former Anglican parson and his protégé Helwys to be remembered among those who laid the cornerstone of a future religious fellowship, the Baptists.

King James VI of Scotland, son of Mary, Queen of Scots, came to the throne of England as King James I in 1603. Selfish and unstable, James cared little for the Scriptures except as they helped to bring the established Anglican Church more firmly under his control. However, early in his reign he sponsored the production of the Bible in English. In 1611 the authorized edition appeared, the famed and revered King James Version of the Scriptures. This Bible, printed in the speech of the educated people yet understood by all in Britain, was hailed with prayers of thanksgiving by members of the Anglican faith and by English dissenters as well. It has remained for more than three centuries the most cherished version of the Word of God for all evangelical sects, and will always be revered for its beauty of expression.

In 1607 King James, backed by his Anglican bishops, intensified his persecutions of Separatists, Anabaptists, and other dissenters. Several of the Gainsborough and Scrooby members were arrested and held in York Castle. Smyth, Robinson, and their followers decided to flee to Holland. Meanwhile, Smyth wrote a book called *Principles and Inferences Concerning the Visible Church,* in which he declared that a church should be "a visible communion of Saints . . . joined together by covenant with God and themselves, freely to use all the holy things of God, according to the word, for their mutual edification and God's glory."[1]

Early in 1608 the congregations made their flight to Holland, settling in Amsterdam where they found a measure of religious freedom. There Smyth came in close touch with the Anabaptist Mennonites. Again he carried on a serious study, attempting to reconcile his position as a Separatist with the Mennonite doctrine of believer's baptism. And again he adopted a new faith. He convinced himself, and then his congregation, that baptism should be a voluntary matter on the part of a person who had reached the "years of accountability" and made profession of faith in Christ as Savior. He and his followers took the drastic step of dissolving their congregation and creating a new one, based not on what was known as a "covenant," but upon believer's baptism. In 1617 Pastor Robinson related in a brief account what had happened:

"Mr. Smyth, Mr. Helwys and the rest having utterly dissolved, and disclaimed their former church, state, and ministry, came together to erect a new church, by baptism. Unto which they also ascribed so great virtue, as they would not so much as pray together, before they had it. And after some straining of courtesy as to who should begin . . . Mr. Smyth baptized first himself, and next Mr. Helwys, and so the rest, making their particular confessions."[2]

The new congregation became known as the "Church of Baptists." Pastor Smyth explained his action in a lengthy *Epistle to the Reader,* which began (in modern English):

"To everyone that loveth the Truth, Salutations: It may be thought most strange that a man should oft times change his religion, and it cannot be accounted a commendable quality in any man to make many alterations and changes in such weighty matters as are the cases of conscience, but if constancy is commendable in anything it is religion." In his discourse Pastor Smyth considered it necessary to explain to the Separatists the doctrine relating to believer's baptism, which brought about his own separation from them. His position was identical with that of his Anabaptist-Mennonite teachers:

"This, therefore, is the question: whether the baptism of infants be lawful, yea or nay; and whether persons being baptized, being infants, must not renounce that false baptism and assume the true baptism of Christ, which is to be administered upon persons confessing their faith and their sins, this being the controversy betwixt us and the Separation commonly called Brownists. Considering what baptism is, an infant is no more capable of baptism than is any unreasonable or insensible creature. For baptism is not washing with water; but it is the baptism of the spirit, the confession with the mouth, and (then) the washing with water."

Smyth accurately foreshadowed in his Epistle, and in later writ-

ings, principles that became the structure of modern Baptist beliefs. He contended that a "true church" must be founded not
merely upon separation from the established Church of England
but upon the principle of baptism after repentance and confession
of sins. He made a vigorous answer to those who were accusing
him and his congregation of ignoring the Old Testament, the common argument made in behalf of the duty of the civil power to enforce obedience to the first four of the Ten Commandments. He
declared that "we deny not the Scriptures of the Old Testament,
but with the apostles acknowledge them to be inspired of God,
and that we have a sure word of the prophets whereunto we ought
to attend as unto a light shining in a dark place, and that whatsoever is written aforetime is written for our instruction that we
through patience and comfort of the Scriptures might have hope,
and that we ought, as Christ counselleth, to search the Scriptures
of the Old Testament as the men of Berea did, because that in
them we may find everlasting life, and that they do testify of
Christ. This we believe according to the Scriptures."

Pastor Smyth followed all his statements with citations from the
Bible, at times many heaped together to pile proof on proof. He
set out other fundamental Baptist tenets in his treatise, dealing
with why the first day of the week was observed for rest and worship, the power of the civil authorities, and the nature of Christ—
all with the appropriate scriptural citations:

"We acknowledge that according to the precedent of Christ's
Disciples and the primitive churches, the saints ought upon the
first day of the week, which is called the Lord's Day, Rev. 1:10,
to assemble together to pray, prophesy, praise God, break bread
and perform other parts of spiritual communion for the worship of
God, their own mutual edification, and the preservation of true
religion and piety in the church. . . .

"Concerning magistrates, we acknowledge them to be the ordinances of the Lord that every soul ought to be subject unto them;
that they are ministers of God for our wealth; that we ought to be
subject to them for conscience's sake; that they are the ministers
of God to take vengeance on them that do evil; that we ought to
pray for them that are in dignity, nor to despise the government,
but to pay tribute, toll, custom, etc. and that according to the
Scriptures. . . .

"Concerning the flesh of Christ, we do believe that Christ is the seed of Abraham, Isaac and Jacob, and of David, according to the prophecies of the Scriptures, and that He is the Son of Mary, His Mother, made of her substance, the Holy Ghost overshadowing her. So have other children the bodily substance of their parents. Also we believe that Christ is one person in two distinct natures, the Godhead and the manhood. . . ."

Smyth gave his own tart definition of a heretic by questions and answers: "Do not the Papists call the Protestants (Lutherans, Calvinists, Zwinglians, Church of England) heretics and call for fire and fagot? Do not the Protestants call the Separation schismatics and heretics and judge them worthy of the gibbet? Not the affirmation of men without proof, but the evidence of wilful obstinancy in error makes men heretics."[3]

First Baptist Church on English Soil

In northern Holland lived and worshiped the branch of the Mennonites known as "Waterlanders." Up to this time the influence of John Calvin had led many groups of the Anabaptists to embrace his principle of predestination, but the Waterlanders held to the doctrine expounded by Jacobus Arminius, the noted Dutch theologian, that of general atonement and salvation for any and all persons willing to confess and embrace the Christian faith. Won to the Waterlander point of view, Smyth began to doubt the efficacy of his own baptism. He and a majority of his congregation applied for membership with the Waterlanders.

Smyth's foremost co-laborer, Thomas Helwys, and about ten others of the congregation refused to go along with Smyth and the majority in asking for Mennonite baptism. Helwys assumed leadership of the small new congregation.

Although it was entirely a coincidence, the year 1611 saw both the publication of the King James Bible, authorized by the Crown and produced by leaders of the established church, and still greater persecutions of dissenters, likewise authorized by the Crown and supervised by bishops of the established church. News of the harassments and executions of nonconformists in England greatly influenced Thomas Helwys and his congregation in Amsterdam in their decision to return to their native land. There,

Helwys told his members, they might share in what he called their "Baptist witness," and if need be share also in imprisonment and martyrdom.

Late in 1611 this pastor and his faithful followers came back to England, and established themselves near the edge of London as a congregation of baptized believers.

It was the first Baptist church on English soil. It was the visible, vital, connecting link between the postmedieval builders and preservers of Baptist principles, and the spiritual forefathers of modern Baptists who were soon to carry those principles to America where spiritual liberty would find ground for unlimited growth.

To remove any stigma which the name "Anabaptist" implied in England of that day, Helwys disassociated himself from the Mennonites but remained Arminian in his doctrinal outlook. He plunged into evangelizing his community and adding to his church the growing number of converts. He found time to write a small volume entitled *Booke of Ye Mystery of Iniquity,* in which his religious beliefs were forthrightly expressed.

His Majesty Got a Booke

It must have come as a surprise to King James one day to receive a copy of this *Booke,* sent by special messenger from Helwys himself. The monarch's surprise must have grown into a major shock, followed by anger, when he discovered what was in the work written by this former country squire of Broxtome Hall, who was now preaching for the obscure dissenter sect. His Majesty read a vigorous plea for freedom of conscience and a refutation of the established principle that the king was the authority in his realm on matters of religion as well as civil rule.

"Heare, o king, and despise not ye counsell of ye poore, and let their complaints come before thee," the book began. Continuing, in Mr. Helwys' original spelling and expressions, were these startling introductory words from this unknown parson to his king:

"The king is a mortall man, and not God therefore hath no power over ye immortall soules of his subjects, to make lawes and ordinances for them, and to set spiritual Lords over them . . . O king, be knot seduced by deceivers to sin so against God whome thou oughtest to obey, nor against thy poore subjects . . ."[4]

Whether Preacher Helwys presumed his arguments for freedom of conscience and for separation of the power of the government from control of religion were powerful enough to convert His Majesty, King James, or that he was willing to be made an example of persecution for the cause of religious liberty can only be conjectured. It is certain that the King considered Helwys' writing rank heresy, and all copies of his *Booke* that could be found were burned. The author was imprisoned. He was given opportunity to explain his doctrines, and to recant what the authorities considered treasonable. He explained his principles thoroughly, but refused to recant and was held in prison in London for the rest of his life, which probably ended in 1616.

The rash act of this English dissenter revealed the depth of feeling on the part of the spiritual descendants of the Anabaptist believers. Back of Helwys was the spirit and fervor of the Reformation throughout Europe. All about him in England was the urge of the common people to study the Scriptures, spurred by the popularity of the King James Bible. There can be no doubt that this edition of Holy Writ, intended originally for use only by clergy and laity of the established church but read eagerly by persons of all classes and stations, stimulated the growth of the early Baptist congregations in Great Britain. A copy of this English translation of the Scriptures was passed from one family to another in Helwys' congregation. Sermons were joyously preached from its texts; young people were instructed in both Old and New Testaments, which were "the Law and the Gospel." The stories of the early Christians were studied and pondered carefully as guides for doctrine and worship.

Several publications by these first struggling Baptist leaders strengthened the faith of their members. One appeared in 1612 from the pen of Pastor Smyth in Holland. It was entitled *Confession of Faith of John Smyth and His People in 102 Articles*. The *Confession* dealt forthrightly with the civil power:

"We believe that the Magistrate is not by virtue of his office to meddle with religion, or matters of conscience, to force and compel men to this or that form of religion or doctrine, but to leave Christian religion free to every man's conscience, and to handle only civil transgressions (Romans XIII 3, 4), injuries and wrongs of man against man, in murder, adultery, theft, etc., for Christ only is the King and Lawgiver of the Church and conscience (James IV, 12)."

A Young Man Rebels at Intolerance

The more King James and his bishops tried to fasten down the lid of repression of dissenters in his realm during the early seventeenth century, the greater grew the pressure generated by the nonconformists' eagerness for religious freedom.

The Reverend John Murton, one of Helwys' followers, took over the leadership of the Baptist congregation during the founder's long imprisonment and continued to lead after Helwys' death. In 1615 Murton wrote a discussion entitled *Persecution for Religion Judged and Condemned.* Following Helwys' courageous example Murton presented a copy to the king, in which His Majesty could read:

"No man ought to be persecuted for his religion, be it true or false, (just) so they testify their faithful allegiance to the king . . . What authority can any mortal man require more, than of body, goods, life, and all that appertaineth to the outward man? The heart God requireth."

Inspiring as were such courageous statements of faith by the Baptists of the early seventeenth century, they possessed a significance for the future of the Baptist fellowship that no one at that time could have foreseen. They were read and pondered, earnestly and thoughtfully by a young man of London, a student at the Charter House who worked as a reporter in the Court of the Star Chamber. His name was Roger Williams, and he carried the principles of religious freedom to America.

IV

ROGER WILLIAMS

Punishments for Religious Beliefs

The man destined to found the first Baptist church on American soil, Roger Williams, was born probably in late 1603. It was the year in which Elizabeth, known as Good Queen Bess, having reigned for two generations, passed from mortal life, and James I was proclaimed King.

Roger Williams' birthplace is in dispute. It is known that his parents lived for a time in Wales, and some church historians believe that Roger was born in that British principality. The weight of evidence favors the conclusion that the Williamses were living in London from about 1600 and that Roger was born there. It is certain from his own writings that he worked at his father's tailor-merchant shop as a boy.

The Williams home was near the square in front of Newgate Prison, the favorite site of the authorities for the execution of condemned heretics. As a lad Roger witnessed many such executions. The people in the crowds who came to take in the ghastly spectacles generally considered them a time for laughing, mocking, and jeering at the condemned wretches. Roger, however, developed a sense of pity which grew to shame and abhorrence at such inhumanity toward persons whose only crime in many instances was nonconformity in matters of conscience.

It was through his mother's side of the family, rather than his father's, that young Roger Williams came in close contact with persons of political influence in England. His mother was of the prominent Pembertons, close friends of Sir Edward Coke, a liberal-minded lawyer and jurist. Noting Roger's exceptional talents, Sir Edward placed him under a master who taught the lad to take shorthand notes. When Roger was eighteen years old, Coke secured a scholarship for him at the Charter House. Appointed to the King's Bench as chief justice, Sir Edward employed young Williams to record the proceedings in the Court of the Star Chamber.

Day after day there came before the Star Chamber court for trial the men, women, and, frequently, young children accused of crimes. Roger Williams heard and transcribed all the arguments in use against those considered heretical criminals. The injustice of punishment for refusal to believe religious principles prescribed by the state, for denying what conscience in persons of honest religious convictions would not let them accept, developed in the young man an intense hatred of bigotry and intolerance. He resolved that someday he would strike a blow for protection of each individual's right to follow his own conscience in spiritual matters.

Sir Edward continued to sponsor Roger Williams through Pembroke College, Cambridge, from which the young man was graduated in 1627. While a student, Williams followed with keen interest the debates and discussions between his sponsor, Sir Edward, and William Laud, Bishop of London and later Archbishop of Canterbury, who was an implacable enemy of the Puritans, Calvinists, and all other nonconformists. Bishop Laud, a high churchman, restored many of the rites and ceremonies of Roman Catholicism; Coke firmly opposed such moves. Roger Williams sided with the point of view of his patron, writing and speaking for the Puritan cause.

Williams took two years of postgraduate work at Cambridge, studying for the ministry, mastering Latin, Greek, and Hebrew, and becoming proficient also in Dutch and French. By the time he left the university he was recognized as an eloquent young preacher, a forceful debater, an ardent rebel against conformity in religion. He served as a chaplain in the home of Sir William Masham for a time, and this position brought him in touch with such men as Oliver Cromwell and John Hampden.

Chaplain Williams proposed to a young lady of noble birth, but when the family refused to allow the union, Williams married a maid in the Masham household, Mary Barnard. His friends severely criticized him for marrying beneath his station, but Mary proved a staunch and loyal companion during the turbulent years they lived and labored together.

With dismay, Roger Williams saw his sponsor, Sir Edward Coke, degraded and sent to prison in the Tower of London by King James. And worse days lay ahead after King Charles I succeeded King James in 1625. Autocratic and contemptuous of Parliament and democratic procedures, Charles gave full rein to Archbishop Laud to persecute the Puritans and other dissenters. By 1630 the campaign to exterminate nonconformists reached a high pitch. Numerous dissenters were imprisoned and punished by fines and mutilation, sometimes by execution. With burning indignation Williams witnessed the cruel treatment assessed against Dr. Alexander Leighton, a minister who had become an influential Puritan and had written a protest entitled *Zion's Plea Against the Prelacy,* which was critical of the intolerance of established church leaders. For this offense he was arrested on Archbishop Laud's orders, and the bishop stipulated in detail the following punishment:

"Committed to the Prison of the Fleet for Life, and pay a fine of ten thousand pounds; that the High Commission should degrade him from his ministry; and that he should be brought to the pillory at Westminster while the Court is sitting and be publicly whipped; after whipping be set upon a pillory a convenient time and have one of his ears cut off, one side of his nose split, and be branded in the face with a double SS for a sower of sedition; then that he should be carried back to prison, and after a few days be pilloried a second time in Cheapside, and have the other side of his nose split and his other ear cut off, and then be shut up in close prison for the rest of his life."[1]

Roger Williams decided that the time had come to fight such shocking punishments for differences in religious opinions, regardless of the consequences to himself. He identified himself with the Separatists-Baptists and penned a moving protest called *Dissent.* Addressed to Archbishop Laud, it voiced in forceful words his undying opposition to all religious intolerance.

Williams' thinking on the vital issue of religious liberty was strongly influenced by a most tragic, senseless, destructive conflict that began in 1618 and was to rage over many areas of Germany and Bohemia until 1648, the Thirty Years' War. The causes lay deep in the rivalries of European rulers and their determination to maintain the religion that they favored. It was indeed a conflict to the death between Catholics and Protestants, a struggle for supremacy of princes loyal to Rome against princes supporting Luther and the Reformation. Along with all intelligent and thoughtful English Separatists, Roger Williams became increasingly confirmed in the belief that the combination of church and state resulted in coercion, persecution, and conflict of the type then raging in middle Europe; and that only separation of church and state could prevent such evils in the future.

Exile in America

Williams' *Dissent* produced the inevitable result. Laud ordered that the defiant author be seized and brought to trial forthwith. However, Roger Williams had come to a calm decision. He would not become a victim to the spleen of this church leader and the pliant monarch. He would preserve his life and continue his fight for religious freedom.

Many Separatists, particularly Baptists and Quakers, had fled to Holland. Williams decided that he, too, would become an exile from his native land. But he would not go to Holland. He had received an urgent invitation from the church of the Puritans in Boston to migrate to that city and preach to their congregation. Considering this a providential opportunity, Williams embarked secretly on a ship sailing for America on December 8, 1630. It was the *Lyon,* putting out from Bristol and bound for Boston. By Roger's side was his wife Mary, as eager as he to begin a new life in a new world.

In the diary of Governor John Winthrop of Massachusetts under the date February 5, 1631, there is an entry that tells of his welcoming the good ship *Lyon,* arrived at Boston Harbor with its twenty passengers. His Excellency the Governor mentioned four of these passengers by name, and two of these were "Mr. Williams (a godly minister) with his wife."

It had been a long, stormy voyage, and Roger and Mary Williams were heartily glad to set foot on land. Along with Governor Winthrop, several other important church leaders in the Massachusetts Bay Colony were waiting to welcome the still-young man. They had heard of his eloquent preaching in England and of his becoming an exile to escape the rigid conformity that King Charles insisted upon. There was an acute shortage of trained preachers among the Boston Puritans. Surely this tall, intelligent, handsome, twenty-eight-year-old minister was the answer to their prayers.

Hardly had Roger Williams found lodgings for himself and his wife when he began to inquire thoughtfully into the exact doctrines and practices of the Massachusetts Bay Puritans. He had supposed that the separation of three thousand miles of ocean, if no other factor, had given them freedom to separate from the rigid beliefs of their Puritanical leaders in the homeland. He discovered that like their cousins in England, these Puritans clung to the principle that the government must insure the financial support of an established church and, more important, must protect that church from error. Williams was staunchly opposed to this view.

Doubtless, Williams understood the fundamental reasons for Puritan intolerance. He must have learned that the Puritan mind held tenaciously to a train of reasoning which seemed to that mind to be the soul of logic, the essence of unquestionable truth, namely: The Scriptures are the source of all authority for creed and practice. The Scriptures are clear and plain, the answer to every problem and situation, spiritual or civil. It is the responsibility of the minister, as Christ's spokesman, to interpret the Holy Writ. If any person does not agree with the interpretation, he is obviously in error; it is then the duty of the minister to dispute with him and correct the error. If the person still does not agree, it is because he stubbornly holds to his error and, like an erring child, must be punished until he forsakes his error. So that the church might not suffer from persistent error, the state must help the church force the truth upon the person by proper punishment.

The Massachusetts colony was in fact a mixture of democracy and theocracy, in which civil and religious laws were so intermingled as to be inseparable. These Puritans called their state the Holy Commonwealth. Roger Williams had pulled far away from belief in such a church-state relationship before leaving England. He had every intention of carrying a torch for freedom of conscience in the new land, a land that he had supposed would be receptive to the encouragement of spiritual liberty.

Assuming that Roger Williams would be honored to serve them as pastor-teacher, the Boston Puritan leaders formally offered him the position. They had not counted on Williams' hardening conviction against any and all control of religious affairs by what he called the civil power. He shocked them by refusing the offer and by his explanation: "I durst not officiate to an unseparated people."

The Boston Puritans considered themselves separated enough and looked upon Williams' announcement as insulting. They marked him as a man to be dealt with firmly in due course of time.

Thundering from Salem

Roger and Mary visited among churchgoers of other communities of the Massachusetts Bay settlers. At Salem they found a neighborhood of independent thinkers who had emigrated from England in 1628 and had separated from the Boston Puritans for precisely the same reasons Williams refused to become the Boston teacher: They refused to accept the idea of public control over conscience and worship. They were, in his opinion, a true congregational type of church. The vigorous young minister preached for them, and the members liked him. They called him to be their teacher, and he accepted. He found keen satisfaction in preaching and lecturing to a people who supported his doctrine that the authority of the state, whether in Boston or in London, lay only in civil affairs.

"According to Divine Law," Williams proclaimed in his sermons, "officers of the Crown cannot rightfully interfere with the right of a person to worship as he pleases!" He even carried his argument to the conclusion that magistrates were without the right to punish Sabbath-breaking, swearing, and other violations of the first four of the Ten Commandments, since those matters were in the realm of the spiritual. As though to answer this brash young preacher, the General Court of the Massachusetts Bay Colony, the legislative group for the settlers, on May 18, 1631, passed an ordinance that stated:

"Noe man shall be admitted to the freedom of this body polliticke, but such as are members of some of the churches within the limits of the same." Williams roared back that there could be no true freedom without freedom of conscience to join a church or not to join a church as one might please. Such teachings shocked and angered the Boston Puritans. Here was heresy of the rankest kind.

Perhaps an even greater offense on the part of Parson Williams alarmed the smug and straitlaced fathers of the colony. Williams went out among the Narragansett Indians, from whom the land of the colony had been purchased, and told them of the Great Spirit. He told the Indians that this Great Spirit was the creator and father of all mankind, and that like a father he cared for his children. Furthermore, the earnest evangelist declared, the Great Spirit wanted men to treat one another as brothers.

This was bad enough, so far as the Calvinistic Puritans were concerned, for surely none of these aborigines could be counted as among God's elect and so to preach to them was foolish and futile. But even more disconcerting was Williams' discovery that the Narragansett tribe had been paid only a pittance for the land of the colonists. In this nosey preacher's view, the Indians had been swindled by people supposed to be pure of heart.

After six months at Salem, harassed and threatened with arrest and punishment, Roger Williams and his wife found refuge at Plymouth among the Pilgrim separatists, who were much more humane in religious views than were the Puritans. There the Williamses remained for nearly two years, while Roger served the congregation as assistant pastor. Governor William Bradford was a regular worshiper in the Plymouth congregation and highly esteemed this fiery young minister and his independent views.

Williams again went out to the Indians, the Massasoits, to make friends and to teach the Christian gospel. Again he was received gladly. The chiefs and their braves were delighted to find a paleface who met them as a brother and spoke of all being children of the Great Spirit. Williams actually drafted a treaty of friendship with the Massasoit tribe, which was to serve as an important item in his establishment of his own colony.

Despite their stand that a government should not force religion upon anyone, the Pilgrims believed in the support of the church by the government. Unable to change their views, Williams became restless at Plymouth. In the summer of 1633 he received an official call from the congregation at Salem to return as the pastor. He gladly accepted, and back to Salem came Roger and Mary Williams. Soon afterward their first child, a son, was born.

Now the battle between the Boston Puritans and this contentious young minister began in earnest, as Williams grew more outspoken against religious intolerance and the authorities grew more determined to silence him.

"I affirm that there was never civil state in the world that ever did or ever shall make good work of it, with a civil sword in spiritual matters," he declared in a vigorous sermon that he defiantly published. He chided the religious leaders for using the civil authorities to carry out their persecutions, charging that "under a pretense of holy orders in themselves, they put over a drudgery of execution to their enslaved seculars."[2]

"The state should give an absolute permission of conscience to all men in what is spiritual!" was the theme of many a Williams discourse.

It seems certain that Roger Williams' rebellious attitude was a principal reason for the passage by the General Court, on May 14, 1634, of a Freeman's Oath. It specifically provided for "the right of Magistrates to punish for breaches of the First Table (of the Ten Commandments) and to rule in religion." The clear purpose of this act was to eradicate all opposition to the Holy Commonwealth in both civil and religious matters. It required all men to take an oath of loyalty to the General Court. Failure or refusal to do so was punishable by banishment.

Parson Williams Goes to Trial

Williams promptly accepted this new challenge. He vehemently attacked the act as both illegal and unjust, and was served with a summons for trial on the charge of "entertaining dangerous opinions." Even Governor John Endicott, who had befriended Williams in the past, agreed that the trial should be held.

The court assembled in Boston on October 8, 1635. It was composed of all the magistrates of the colony, who were at the same time the complaining witnesses, the prosecutors, the jury, and the judges. Sitting among them as advisers to the court were Puritan ministers, the principal witnesses against the culprit. Williams had no legal defender, as no one learned in the law dared volunteer as his counsel for fear of reprisals.

The complaints were heard, one after another, with quotations from Williams' speeches and sermons to prove the charge of "dangerous opinions," which in themselves constituted sedition against the Holy Commonwealth. When Williams rose to his own defense, he startled the court with his calm but forceful words. All that he had learned in his reporting days in the Court of the Star Chamber in London came back to help him now. He remained respectful and courteous throughout the long day and into the night of the trial, quoting Scripture to combat the accusations of sedition. He declared his support of the Ten Commandments, but remained firm in his opinion that the First Table was not to be enforced by the civil power. He actually won several of the magistrates to his viewpoint, and they refused to vote for his conviction.

But the Puritan advisers were constantly at the elbows of the magistrates, urging them to do their duty for the peace and quiet of the community, and the result was a foregone conclusion: a sentence of banishment from the Massachusetts Bay Colony. However, Williams was given an opportunity to recant and to announce his decision on the next day. When the court reassembled to hear if he would recant, Williams declared:

"I shall be ready . . . not only to be bound and banished, but to die also in New England for my convictions and for the truth as I see it!"

Refuge Among the Indians

Roger Williams returned to his home and his wife and child. The court had allowed him six weeks to prepare to leave the colony. He stayed close to Salem, plotting how he might outwit the Puritan ministers and their helpers, the magistrates. Many friends came to visit him, usually at night, to offer sympathy and wish the family well.

Among the visitors was Henry Vane, Jr., son of Sir Henry Vane of London, one of England's outstanding statesmen of that day. The young man was impressed with Williams' sincerity and deplored his banishment. Vane's visit began a friendship that stood the dissenting parson in good stead in later years.

One day a close friend brought Williams a secret message from Governor Winthrop. The Boston authorities were planning to seize Williams and put him aboard a ship bound for England, the message said. Again Williams decided he would not be a martyr if he could escape and continue his fight for liberty of conscience. That night he bundled himself in his greatcoat, stuffed some food into his pockets, kissed his wife and baby good-by, and stole out into the darkness.

A storm was blowing up and by midnight it had turned into a blizzard. Williams headed southwestward toward Narragansett Bay, shuffling in the drifting snow over fields and through forests. It grew bitter cold and the wind howled and shrieked about him. During the next day, utterly exhausted and nearly frozen, he reached a camp of the Narragansett Indians. Greeting him as a brother, these friends took him in, fed him, thawed him out, and insisted that he remain in hiding with them.

Through all the rest of that winter the exiled minister stayed with his Indian benefactors, sharing their food and their shelter, telling them more about the Great Spirit. A quarrel developed between two rival chieftains, and war was about to begin when Williams traveled from one chief to the other, urging to keep the peace. He brought the tribal leaders together and the quarrel was settled. In gratitude, Chief Massasoit gave Williams a tract of land on the east bank of the Seekonk River.

During the winter the exiled parson had made a momentous decision. He would establish his own colony, and it would be open to all who wanted to live in the enjoyment of religious freedom. The gift of land from Chief Massasoit seemed just the place for such a settlement and Williams began to build a house and plant a field there. Governor Winthrop of Plymouth advised him that he was on land of the Massachusetts Bay Colony, and it would be safer if he moved, as Williams later wrote, "to the other side of the water, and then, he said, I had the country free as themselves and we should be loving neighbors together."[3]

A Village Called Providence

By this time several of Williams' Salem friends had joined him, and the small group moved across to the west side of the Mooshassuc River. There Williams bought land from the Indians and began laying out a village which he called Providence. His family joined him in their new home, and there the second child was born, a daughter whom Mary named Freeborn.

Roger Williams invited settlers to come to his "Providence Plantations," making it clear that he had set up "a shelter for persons distressed for conscience." The colony, he announced, would have a civil government with no authority over religious matters. All who came could worship in their own way, if they cared to, or be free not to worship.

The settlers came, singly and in families. There were dissenters from Boston and other areas of the Massachusetts colony; Quakers from communities where they had been persecuted by Puritans and Congregationalists; a few families of Jews from New Amsterdam, fleeing the discriminations and harassments of the Dutch.

With high satisfaction Roger Williams watched this experiment for three years, then decided to organize his own church. It would be a congregation based upon the Anabaptist principles of the churches of John Smyth and Thomas Helwys in Holland and England. It would be a church of baptized believers, with immersion the symbol of death to sin and resurrection to a new life.

One day in March about a dozen men and women assembled at the Williams home. In the chilly waters of a nearby stream Roger Williams had himself immersed by Ezekiel Holliman, who had been a member of the Salem church; then Williams baptized Holliman and the others. Thus was organized the Providence Baptist Church, the first Baptist church on American soil, and still in honored existence.

Just as he had opened the door of his colony for all to enjoy religious liberty, so Roger Williams opened his church for any to come and worship who wished to do so. The congregation held services in the Williams home until a meeting house was built. The founder and pastor made it a point to inform his neighbors that they were welcome not only to worship with his congregation but also to join the fellowship if, as he put it, they were "like-minded" in the Baptist faith.

The Rhode Island Compact

Roger Williams became assailed with doubts as to the validity of his own baptism. While he left no specific record of those doubts, his ruggedly honest nature prompted him to resign from the pastorate and the membership of his church in July 1640. All the remainder of his life Williams termed himself a "seeker."

But Roger Williams never repudiated or denied any Baptist principles which he had embraced when he assembled his congregation. Rather, he emphasized his belief in them, in Rhode Island, and later in England during his stay in his native land as he worked to obtain a charter for his colony. In fact, Williams went the whole distance for complete religious liberty. To qualify as a citizen of Rhode Island one signed a compact of tremendous historic significance in the development of the separation of church and state in America. In the simple language of the common man it read:

"We whose names are hereunder written, being desirous to inhabit the town of Providence, do promise to submit ourselves in active or passive obedience to all such orders or agreements as shall be made for the public good of the body, in an orderly way, by the major consent of the present inhabitants, masters of families incorporated together in a township, and such others when they shall admit into the same, only in civil things."

Surely none who signed the compact, including the founder himself, could have foreseen that in less than one and one-half centuries the principle embodied in those four words, *only in civil things,* would be accepted as part of the fundamental law of the new union of states and written into the constitutions of its various commonwealths.

Roger Williams was not content merely to see that spiritual liberty was guaranteed in the citizens' compact and in Rhode Island's laws. He stood by vigilantly to insure that his principles were followed and enforced. On several occasions the matter of the interpretation of religious liberty came to the test.

"Should not our council pass a Sunday-observance law, as enacted by the Puritans, since it is man's duty to rest on the Sabbath?" was asked and discussed among the settlers. Williams' answer was a definite "No!" This was a matter of conscience, he said, so long as the citizen obeyed the civil laws on Sunday as on all other days. No compulsory Sunday-observance act was ever enacted in Rhode Island while Williams lived, nor any other law relating to duties that a man might owe to God.

"What about such heretics as Seventh Day Baptists, who defy the accepted Christian concept of worshiping on Sunday and insist upon observing Saturday as the day of rest and worship?" was asked. Here again Williams asserted that this was a matter of conscience, and even though the practice of worshiping on the seventh day ran counter to the majority in the community, the religious minority, however small, should not be troubled for their beliefs. He welcomed these seventh-day worshipers, who were persecuted and discriminated against in almost every other American colony, and they came in such numbers that in 1671 they organized a conference. Later, one of their faith served as governor of the state.

Records of the colony show that one of the settlers, Joshua Verin, "restrained his wife from going to meeting as often as she desired." Whether Mrs. Verin's plaint was based upon sound reasons or whether it might indicate unmentioned domestic difficulties is not known. However, Joshua Verin was "withheld from liberty of voting in the Council until he shall declare to the contrary," which meant until he agreed to let his good wife go to meeting without interference even from her husband. Thus Williams and his band of believers in freedom of conscience and worship struggled to establish their community.

Williams versus Cotton

It is difficult for modern minds, accustomed to freedom of conscience and worship, to grasp how generally accepted was the belief that the union of church and state was necessary in order to insure conformity in religious affairs in the period of American colonial history. The feeling was tersely expressed by a Boston attorney, Nathaniel Ward, who styled himself "Lawyer Divine," presumably because he was the legal representative of the established church. Ward had drawn up the church and civil rules that were the first legal code for the community. In discussing Williams' argument that no one should be forced to believe or practice religion in a prescribed manner, Ward exclaimed: "It is an astonishment to think that the brains of men should be parboiled in such impious ignorance!"

Such criticism failed to shake Roger Williams' firm belief in the principle of complete spiritual liberty. When he was accused by Boston's outstanding Puritan minister, John Cotton, of encouraging anarchy and discouraging the progress of Christianity by his stand against control of religion by the state, Williams answered with this illustration:

"There goes many a ship to sea, with many hundred souls on one ship, whose weal and woe is common, and is a true picture of a commonwealth, or a human combination or society. It hath fallen out sometimes that both Baptists and Protestants, Jews and Turks, may be embarked into one ship; upon which supposal I do affirm that all the liberty of conscience that ever I pleaded for turns upon these two things; that none of the Baptists, Protestants, Jews or Turks be forced to come to the ship's prayers or worship; nor secondly, be compelled from their own particular prayers or worship."

In 1643 Williams sailed for London to obtain an official charter for his colony, so that it could be secure from enemies within and without. Sir Henry Vane was now a member of Parliament and volunteered to help smooth the way for consideration of Williams' request. Even so, the ponderous bureaucracy of the Crown's government consumed several months as Williams was sent from one influential official to another, finding them in greater haste to go fox hunting than to concern themselves with a small colony in far-off America led by a dissenting parson.

While waiting for action on his request, Williams' restless spirit prompted him to write a lengthy discussion entitled *The Bloudy (Bloody) Tenet of Persecution for Cause of Conscience.* In this work he summarized all his arguments showing the danger to human liberties flowing from state control of religion. In the quaint, stilted English of his day, flavored with his wordy but expressive language, the champion of freedom denounced compulsion of mind and conscience in spiritual matters.

"It is the will of God," he wrote, "that since the coming of his Sonne the Lord Jesus, a permission of the most Paganish, Jewish, Turkish, or Antichristian consciences and worships, bee granted to all men in all Nations and Countries: and they are onley to bee fought against with that Sword which is onely (in Soule matters) able to conquer, to wit, the Sword of God's spirit, the Worde of God. True civility and Christianity may both flourish in a state or Kingdome, notwithstanding the permission of divers and contrary consciences, either of Jew or Gentile."

John Cotton took on the task of debating with Williams in what turned out to be a long exchange of letters and statements. The Bay Colony's most ardent exponent of the control of religion by the state brought out the usual arguments favoring the enforcement of the authority of an established church upon all the population under its jurisdiction, while Williams parried every thrust of the learned theologian with the sharp blade of his own arguments in behalf of complete liberty. Their historic discussions may be summarized:

Cotton: "It is a carnal and worldly, and indeed an ungodly imagination, to confine the magistrate's charge to the bodies and goods of the subject, and to exclude them from the care of their souls."

Williams: "If it be the magistrate's duty or office, then is he both a temporal and ecclesiastical officer: the contrary to which most men will affirm. That doctrine and distinction, that a magistrate may punish a heretic civilly, will not here avail."

The Charter Is Secured

Williams felt that he had the plain lessons of history to support his contention that the union of church and state, with enforcement of established religion and beliefs, resulted in countless injustices and widespread tyranny. He condensed much English history with the remark that the realm had been filled with blood and confusion for a hundred years and this explanation:

"Henry the Seventh leaves England under the slavish bondage of the Pope's yoke. Henry the Eighth reforms all England to a new fashion, half Papist, half Protestant. King Edward the Sixth turns about the wheels of state, and works the whole land to absolute Protestantism. Queen Mary, succeeding to the helm, steers a direct contrary course, breaks in pieces all that Edward wrought, and brings forth an old edition of England's reformation, all Popish. Mary not living out half her days, Elizabeth, like Joseph, is advanced from the prison to the palace, and from the irons to the crown; she plucks up all her sister Mary's plants, and sounds a trumpet, all Protestant. What sober man is not amazed at these revolutions!"[4]

Roger Williams' patience, with the help of Sir Henry Vane's influence with members of Parliament, finally won out. On March 14, 1644, the charter for The Rhode Island and Providence Plantations was granted by the Parliamentary Board for Commissioners for Plantations. In triumph the founder brought back to Providence his cherished patent, and in triumph he was welcomed home by his fellow colonists. The charter defined the boundaries of the small colony and gave the settlers the power to form their own government, elect all their officers, and make all their laws. Williams was promptly given the title of president of the colony.

Firmly embodied in the Rhode Island charter was the principle of government of, by, and for the people. All persons in the colony (male, and over twenty-one years of age, of course) were given an equal voice in the government if they were law-abiding and peaceful men. Williams expressed his principle of rule by the people in these words:

"The Civill Power is originally and fundamentally in the People . . . a People may erect and establish what forme of Government seemes to them most meete for their civill condition: It is evident that such Governments as are by them erected and established, have no more power, nor for a longer time, than the civill power of people consenting and agreeing shall betrust them with. This is cleere not only in Reason, but in the experience of all commonweales, where the people are not deprived of their naturall freedome by the power of Tyrants."

The Rhode Island settlers' nonconformity brought down upon them the contempt of officials and members of other American colonies. This situation was well illustrated when a ship bearing Quakers fleeing the persecutions of England and the Netherlands docked at New Amsterdam. The master of this Dutch port refused to allow these strange persons, who would not bear arms and tended to shut themselves up within the enclosure of their own people, to embark. He recorded:

"We suppose they went to Rhode Island, for that is the receptacle of all sorts of riffraff people, and is nothing else than the sewer of New England. All the cranks of New England retire thither. We suppose they will settle there, as they are not tolerated by the Independents in any other place."

The Quakers on that ship did settle there, and so did other shiploads of Quakers. They were generally as contentious in religious doctrines as was Williams himself, and were a source of irritation to the founder. But Williams showed his opposition to their debates with their leaders and let the people judge as to which side had the truth.

Williams maintained his close friendship with the Indians, even learning their tribal languages. He wrote a brief Narragansett dictionary and also a Key to other Indian dialects. "It was not price nor money that could have purchased Rhode Island; Rhode Island was purchased by love," he said.

Once a townsman missed six of his cows and demanded that the Providence officials declare war on the thieving Indians. Williams investigated and found that some Indian children playing near the pasture had frightened the herd. The parson went to the chief of the tribe and stated the trouble. Together the two men searched the woods until the lost cattle were rounded up and returned.

When agents of the Massachusetts Bay Colony needed an interpreter for some important treaty negotiations with the Narragansett chiefs, they chose Roger Williams, the man they had banished, to entrust with this responsibility.

In the years that followed the life and work of the founder of the first Baptist church in America, some Baptists have severely criticized Roger Williams for his leaving the Baptist fellowship and becoming a seeker. Other Baptists are more charitable, pointing out that he never swerved from his belief in spiritual liberty and all other historic Baptist principles. They point out, also, that Williams' becoming a seeker only exemplified his rugged spiritual honesty when assailed by doubts about the wisdom of continuing his own spiritual leadership as pastor.

V

JOHN CLARKE OF RHODE ISLAND

Haven of Religious Freedom

In establishing Rhode Island as a haven of religious freedom among the American colonies, the name of John Clarke must be written beside that of Roger Williams. This well-educated, free-thinking young English immigrant was born in London in 1609. Apprenticed to a doctor, John became a skillful physician. He was also an earnest student of law and theology.

Clarke became a dissenter from the Anglican Church, and to avoid persecution he lived for a time in Leyden, Holland, where he came in contact with the Baptists, although he did not join their fellowship in that city.

Hoping to find freedom of conscience and a profitable new life in America, Clarke sailed for Boston in November 1637. He reached the Massachusetts Bay capital in time for a rude shock. The town was all stirred up over the teachings of a cultured, independent-thinking woman, Anne Hutchinson. The mother of fourteen children, she was attracting wide attention by holding religious discussion meetings in her home every Thursday evening. At these gatherings she would encourage anyone to express his or her opinion on spiritual matters, and would lead discussions on subjects supposed not to be open to diversity of opinions, such as the meaning of the Scriptures, the way of salvation, and the duties of the Christian life.

Not all Anne Hutchinson's ideas and beliefs conformed to the Puritan way of thought and practice, so the Boston authorities became alarmed at her influence and the possibility that she might lead some of the parishioners astray. The Puritan elders drew up a long list of what they called erroneous opinions this woman was accused of holding and called her to appear for an accounting. She came and stood fearlessly before her inquisitors, answering their questions and refuting their accusations, often by quoting Scripture. Some days later she was denounced openly, at a worship service in the Puritan Meeting House, by the leading elder of the city, John Wilson. From the pulpit of his church Wilson thundered:

"I denounce you, Anne Hutchinson, in the house of God, as a woman of dangerous and heretical errors. I denounce you as a servant of Satan. I cast you out as a leper that you no more blaspheme, seduce, and lie. I do order the congregation to treat you as a heathen and publican!"[1]

Anne Hutchinson turned and walked slowly out of the meeting house. Before she reached the door a small lass, Mary Dyer, sprang up, ran to her side, and walked out with her, an act of childlike kindness that enraged the righteous Puritan elders. It was a crime for any person to help or give comfort to a branded heretic.

"The girl must pay for this!" the elders vowed. Mary Dyer did pay for her deed, and for many other actions which showed her devotion to humanity. She became a follower of the contentious Quakers and publicly defended their beliefs. On a spring afternoon, twenty-four years after the Anne Hutchinson incident, Mary Dyer was led to the Boston Common with hands chained and legs shackled as a criminal, charged with being a "vile Quakeress," and from a rude scaffold she was hanged by the neck until dead.

Anne Hutchinson left Boston and the Massachusetts Bay Colony in late 1638 and with several of her younger children fled to the shelter of Roger Williams' Providence community.

The Founders of Newport

The persecution of Anne Hutchinson sickened John Clarke. He wrote in his diary: "A year in this hotbed of religious tyranny is enough for me. I cannot bear to see men in these uttermost parts of the earth not able to bear with others in matters of conscience and live peaceable together. With so much land before us, I for one will turn aside, shake the dust of Boston off my feet, and betake me to a new place. There I shall make a haven for all those who, like myself, are disgusted and sickened by the Puritan dictatorship. I shall make it a place where there will be full freedom of thought and religious conscience."

The only place affording freedom of thought and religious conscience was Providence town and plantations. To that haven John Clarke and several of his associates went, and there they were greeted and welcomed by Roger Williams, who helped Clarke and his small band of freedom seekers to purchase from the Indians a pleasant coastal island called Aquidneck in Narragansett Bay. There Clarke started his settlement and town, which he named Newport.

In 1640 Clarke and several of his colonists announced themselves as professed dissenters, and during that year they organized the First Baptist Church of Newport, the second Baptist church on American soil. John Clarke became the minister and continued as pastor and leader until his death in 1676.

It is not certain from the records whether John Clarke adopted immersion for the baptism of believers who formed his congregation or who joined it soon after its founding. In 1644 Mark Lukar, an English Separatist who had been immersed two years previously and immigrated to America soon afterward, joined Clarke's colony and church. Lukar's influence seems to have been the deciding factor in the acceptance by Clarke and his congregation of immersion as the official mode of baptism, as it was for the First Baptist Church of Providence.

John Clarke was inspired with missionary zeal, and occasionally left Rhode Island to preach for Separatist and other dissenting congregations in Massachusetts. In 1649 he attempted with the help of one of his most active churchmen, Obadiah Holmes, to organize a Baptist church at Seekonk, Massachusetts, but he and his helpers were thwarted by the authorities.

Obadiah Holmes had immigrated from England, settling in Salem, where he set up the first glassworks on American soil. He joined the Congregational church at Salem, but after some years he moved to Rehoboth in the Plymouth colony. Deciding against the presbyterial type of Puritan control he became a Separatist, and gathered a small band of like-minded people for worship. For this step he was called before the court at Plymouth in June 1650, where Governor Bradford dismissed him with a warning that he and his Separatist believers would have to desist from their meetings. To find religious freedom, Holmes moved to Newport, where he continued his highly skilled trade of glassmaking and became a most active and influential member of Elder Clarke's Baptist church.

Clarke joined Williams in the long and bitter verbal battle with John Cotton of Boston, Calvinist Puritan leader of Massachusetts. Through speeches, sermons, and printed pamphlets the controversy raged. Williams and Clarke insisted upon the principle that civil magistrates had no authority over the souls of men; Cotton maintained that the authority of the civil officer included control over religious beliefs and practices. He was determined to have a theocratic state.

A Well-Publicized Whipping

Cotton was in a position to enforce his doctrine in the Massachusetts colony, as Clarke learned when he went up to Lynn, near Boston, to visit an aged and blind Baptist friend, William Witter. He was accompanied by Obadiah Holmes, and an active layman of his congregation, John Crandall. The men walked the eighty miles' distance in two days and arrived at Witter's home on Saturday night.

Boston authorities were informed that the three dissenters had entered the Massachusetts jurisdiction, and they sent marshals to watch their movements. The Baptist visitors decided to stay with their blind friend overnight and comfort him with a private religious service in his home on Sunday morning.

Suspecting that this was what the three were up to, a marshal and his deputies burst into the blind man's home next morning and caught them in the act of worship. Here was a serious offense, for it was strictly a violation of the law for anyone to hold divine services except under the auspices or with the consent of the established Congregational Church of the Massachusetts Bay Colony. The three culprits were hustled off to a tavern. Then, informed that they would have to cleanse their souls for their disobedience in the matter of worship, they were taken to the afternoon worship in the established church.

Lodged in the Boston jail, the men faced an official charge containing the accusation that they were "certain erroneous persons, being strangers," though actually their offense was understood to be holding a religious meeting without license from the authorities.

Determined to make an example of these somewhat prominent invaders from Rhode Island, the officials staged a well-publicized trial. John Cotton was invited to state the case against these Rhode Island heretics, and he swept grandly into the courtroom to carry out his mission. Sitting in the prisoners' box, Clarke, Holmes, and Crandall heard Cotton shout that the culprits denied the saving power of infant baptism, and thus they were soul-murderers. This offense, declared Cotton with all his fervor, deserved capital punishment just as did any other type of murder.

For their defense, all three affirmed the fact that they were holding a religious service, with reading from the Scripture to their blind friend, and prayers. However, Clarke further pled, it was not a public service; a home should not be invaded by civil authorities, under the ancient English maxim that a man's house, however humble, is his castle.

"Not when a crime is being committed!" John Cotton countered.

The trial judge agreed with the eloquent and learned defender of the established faith. These men, he said, deserved to be put to death. However, he would let them off with a fine. And if they did not pay the fine and leave at once the territory of the colony, they should be "well whipped." So back they went to the jail.

Friends in Newport promptly raised the money for the fines of all three men. Crandall was released from the fine. John Clarke and Obadiah Holmes refused permission for their fines to be paid. As Clarke was being led to the whipping post, a friend pressed the money into the hands of the Puritan official accompanying the party, and Clarke was released. But Holmes remained adamant.

"Agreeing to the payment of my fine would constitute admission of wrong-doing," he stubbornly maintained.

The streets of Boston from the jail to the public whipping post were lined with spectators. Some raised their voices above the jeering to bid this dissenting preacher to be of good courage. As he was being stripped to the waist, Holmes preached a brief sermon to the dense crowd of men, women, and children that formed a circle about the whipping post, exhorting them to remain faithful to their beliefs.

The whipper took seriously the sentence the judge had pronounced, that his victim be well whipped. According to Holmes's own account, the flogger used a whip with three hard-leather lashes, stopping three times to spit on his hands and laying on with all his might. Each of the thirty strokes cut three gashes through the skin. Holmes recorded that a holy strength and serenity possessed and sustained him through the ordeal. Several voices were heard encouraging and praising him despite the stern looks and hostile gestures of the civil officers present. In Holmes's account is this passage:

"And as the man began to lay the strokes upon my back, I said to the people, though my flesh should fail and my spirit should fail, yet God will not fail: so it pleased the Lord to come in, and to fill my heart and tongue as a vessel full, and with an audible voice I break forth, praying the Lord not to lay this sin to their charge, and telling the people I found he did not fail me, and therefore now I should trust him forever who failed me not; for in truth, as the strokes fell upon me, I had such a spiritual manifestation of God's presence, as I never had before, and the outward pain was so removed from me, that I could well bear it, yea, and in a manner felt it not, although it was grievous."[2]

As soon as Holmes, dripping with blood, was untied, two men rushed up to shake his hand. They were promptly arrested and taken from the crowd to the jail, although, Holmes recorded, all they said was "God bless you!"

John Clarke welcomed back to the peace and freedom of Newport his scarred associate from the Boston jail and whipping post. For twenty days and nights Obadiah Holmes could sleep only by lying on his stomach, or propped upon his knees and elbows. In the meantime news of the trial and the whipping spread far and wide over Massachusetts and Rhode Island communities. The account also reached London, and there Sir Richard Saltonstall asked for full details. He had lived in Boston and had served as magistrate in that city years before. Appalled at the news, he addressed a letter to the ministers of Boston, in which he declared:

"It doth not a little grieve my spirit to hear what sad things are reported daily of your tyranny and persecution in New England; that you fine, whip, and imprison men for their consciences. First, you compel such to come into your assemblies as you know will not join with you in worship, and when they show their dislike thereof, or witness against it, then you stir up your magistrates to punish them for such (as you conceive) their public affronts. Truly, friends, this practice of compelling any in matters of worship to do that whereof they are not fully persuaded, is to make them sin, for so the apostle tells us, Romans 14:23. And many are made hypocrites thereby, conforming in their outward man for fear of punishment. We pray for you, and wish your prosperity every way; hoped the Lord would have given you so much love and light there, that you might have been eyes to God's people here, and not to practice those courses in a wilderness, which you went so far to prevent. These rigid ways have laid you very low in the hearts of the saints. I do assure you that I have heard them pray in public assemblies, that the Lord would give you meek and humble spirits, not to strive so much for uniformity as to keep the unity of the spirit in the bond of peace."[3]

That civil authorities could enter a home without a warrant just on the suspicion that a so-called crime by way of religious worship was being committed was a topic of frequent conversation, not only among dissenters, but among other thoughtful citizens as well. The event proved to be an important factor in creating among those rugged pioneers the sentiment to assert the right of all men to be secure in their persons, papers, effects, and homes against unwarranted searches and seizures.

Cromwell Wasn't Interested

By 1651 Elder John Clarke was determined to secure a permanent charter for all the Rhode Island communities, of which Providence, Newport, Warwick, and Portsmouth were now the principal towns. That meant a long, arduous sojourn in London. He left on this mission late in the year only to find that a rugged military genius, Oliver Cromwell, had conquered the forces of King

Charles I, had been installed as captain-general of the army and was fast becoming the dictator of the British realm.

The Baptist minister, now returned to his native city of London, supposed the Protestant man at the head of the military and civil regime, with the title of Protector of the Commonwealth, would be sympathetic to the cause of religious liberty and would speedily grant the request for a Rhode Island charter. After all, were not the Baptists of Great Britain solidly behind Cromwell, hoping for a greater measure of religious freedom from his own hand?

But disappointment dogged Clarke's steps as he made the rounds from bureau to bureau in the Protectorate government trying to interest someone in seeing Cromwell in behalf of the dissenters in that faraway American colony. It is not known if Oliver Cromwell ever heard of Clarke's petition, or if he did, ever seriously considered granting the charter. Old Ironsides, as the Protector was called, was quite taken up with plans to advance the Protestant cause in Europe, but with little thought for the affairs of the colonies. His overriding ambition was to push the power and prestige of Britain to the highest possible level. Furthermore, all through the years of his rule, Cromwell's orientation was toward centralized control, with individual freedoms, including religious freedom, subordinate.

Baptists of England, however, flocked to Cromwell's banner, filled the ranks of his army, supported his leadership, and profited from his favors. The temper of the times gave to the English people such Baptist molders of opinion as John Bunyan, son of a tinker, who in Bedford jail wrote *Pilgrim's Progress;* and the other noted writers, who are identified by many historians as Baptists—John Milton, who in his blindness produced *Paradise Lost;* and after the Restoration, Daniel Defoe, whose pen gave to English literature *Robinson Crusoe.*

Clarke's stay in London stretched out to twelve long years. To support himself he returned to the practice of medicine among old and new friends in London. At last patience and persistence won the battle for this Baptist minister and doctor of medicine. On a September day in 1658 Oliver Cromwell passed from the scene of power. During the next two years a restoration of the monarchy was brought about and Charles II was crowned king. Clarke found it possible to interest a minister of the Crown, and then Charles himself, in the matter of a charter for Rhode Island.

In 1663 the coveted document was secured and John Clarke returned in triumph to his adopted colony, as had Roger Williams before him. In ringing words the charter declared:

"Our royal will and pleasure is, that no person within said Colony, at any time hereafter, shall be in any wise molested, punished, disquieted, or called in question for any differences of opinion in matters of religion, and do not actually disturb the civil peace of said Colony; but that all and any persons may, from time to time, and at all times hereafter, freely and fully have and enjoy his and their own judgments and consciences in matters of religious concernments throughout the tract of land hereafter mentioned, they behaving themselves peacefully and quietly, not using this liberty to licentiousness and profaneness, not to civil injury or outward disturbance of others, any law, statute or clause therein contained, usage or custom of this realm to the contrary thereof in any wise notwithstanding."[4]

To this forthright statement were added these words of the monarch, later engraved upon the state house in Providence for all future generations of Rhode Island people to ponder: "It is much on their hearts (if they may be permitted) to hold a lively experiment that a most flourishing civil state may stand and best be maintained, and that among our English subjects, with full liberty in religious concernments."

It is most likely that King Charles had the help of the learned and determined John Clarke in wording the principal clauses of the charter. It is almost certain that the sovereign, thinking upon the unusual request he had just granted, added the postscript, never realizing fully to how great an extent the "lively experiment" in religious liberty in Rhode Island would shape the pattern of the American way of life and government when the people of the colonies brought forth a new nation, as Abraham Lincoln later said, "conceived in liberty and dedicated to the proposition that all men are created equal."

Legalized Intolerance

If all the American colonies had caught the ideal of granting freedom of conscience and worship that was Rhode Island's, the dark pages of persecutions for spiritual beliefs in the new world would not have been written. But twelve decades were to pass before the principle of separation of church and state, cherished and nurtured by the Baptists, became the official policy of the American people. More than a century was required for the people of the new nation to gain complete religious liberty, to embody its guarantee in their Constitution, and build it into the fundamental laws of the states as well.

Much of the intolerance of the colonial period was directed squarely at the stubborn, freethinking Anabaptists, as they were still called in derision. Their practice of baptizing only those who were mature enough to accept religious beliefs was the principal factor that brought down public condemnation on their heads. In 1644 the General Court of the Massachusetts Bay Colony spelled out the offense of refusing to have babies baptized and prescribed punishments for parents and others who sanctioned such refusal. This step was necessary, it was explained by the civil and religious authorities, for two reasons: To save the souls of the infants from hell-fire in case they should die, and to bring uniformity to the administration of religious affairs.

The law struck full force at all dissenters against the established Puritan Church. The General Assembly of Virginia in 1659 enacted a similar law and made its punishments even more severe by amendments in 1662.

In 1636, when the Massachusetts Bay Colony was only six years old, an institution for higher education was founded at the community of New Towne, near Boston. Two years later a young immigrant minister, John Harvard, passed away, leaving half his fortune and all his library to the school. In honor of this benefactor the institution was named Harvard College. Since Cambridge in England was the seat of a noted university the General Court changed the name of New Towne to Cambridge.

Dr. Henry Dunster, a foremost scholar and teacher in the colony, was elected Harvard's president in 1640. He launched the college on its illustrious career by selecting the best available professors of Latin, Greek, mathematics, and what was known as moral science. He encouraged freedom of study and beliefs—the beginning of academic freedom in the new world.

Doing some freethinking of his own, Dunster became convinced that these peculiar people, the Baptists, were right on two counts: first, in holding to believer's baptism, rather than to the baptism of infants; second, in pleading for freedom of conscience and for spiritual liberty generally. In 1655 he let it be known publicly that he had embraced the Baptist faith.

The blow fell quickly. The overseers of Harvard College summarily dismissed Henry Dunster from his position as president and professor. He moved to Plymouth colony to live in inactivity and disgrace until his death in 1659.

To understand the attitude of intolerance in religious beliefs and practices prevalent in the seventeenth and eighteenth centuries in the American colonies one must place himself in the setting of that day. The spiritual leaders of the established churches were not more cruel, more sadistic, more prompted by evil motives, than those of other areas of Christendom. They merely lived at a time when state-supported religion was the traditional and accepted thing, backed by the power of the civil authorities.

In New England, the Puritans, and then the Congregationalists, made up the Establishment, tolerating the Episcopalians but not the Anabaptists or any other "separated" faiths. As the other colonies developed, most of them officially recognized and favored some establishment of religion. In Virginia the transplanted Church of England was by law the only recognized church and continued so through the Revolution and the adoption of the United States Constitution, as we have seen in the account of John Leland and his influence upon James Madison in the drafting of the Bill of Rights.

A few colonial areas offered toleration for Baptists and other dissenters. The General Assembly of Maryland, for example, in 1649 passed a much-heralded Act of Toleration. It was hailed as granting religious liberty. Actually, by its own words, the act allowed religious freedom only to those "professing to believe in Jesus Christ . . . and to those who believe God's holy and true Christian religion." The Maryland act further provided:

"That whatsoever person or persons within this Province and the Islands thereunto belonging shall from hence forth blaspheame God, that is, curse him or deny our Saviour Jesus Christ to bee the sonne of God, or shall deny the holy Trinity the father sonne and holy Ghost, or the Godhead of any of the said three persons of the Trinity or the Unity of the Godhead, or shall use or utter any reproachfull speeches words or language concerning the said Holy

Trinity, or any of the said three persons thereof shal be punished with death and confiscacon or forfeiture of all his or her lands and goods to the Lord Proprietary and his heires."[5]

One can well understand that this legislation by Maryland failed to satisfy the demands for religious liberty on the part of such sects as the Baptists and the Quakers, to say nothing of that small and despised group, the Jews.

Law Based on the Commandments

It must be remembered that under a legally favored religion, supported by taxation, the civil authorities had a job to do. They were entrusted with making and keeping the people good by law.

Much of the civil law of that day was based upon the Ten Commandments. If the Decalogue required keeping the Sabbath day holy, then it was the duty of the civil officers to see to it that violations of keeping the Sabbath holy were punished—according to their own interpretation of what constituted the Sabbath day, and also of what was holy. John Cotton spelled out the principle:

"And therefore it cannot be truly said the Lord Jesus never appointed the civil sword for a remedy in such case; for he did expressly appoint it in the New Testament; nor did he ever abrogate it in the New; the reason of the law, which is the life of the law, is an eternal force and equity in all ages. 'Thou shalt surely kill him, because he hath sought to thrust thee away from the Lord thy God.' Deut. 13:9–10. This reason is of moral; that is, of universal and perpetual equity, to put to death any apostate seducing idolater or heretick, who seeketh to thrust away the souls of God's people from the Lord their God."[6]

Ministers and parishioners of the established churches in the American colonies, as in their mother countries, permitted no freedom to question the authorized interpretation of the Bible. The medieval concepts of heaven and hell had not been softened and blurred. At every point of time in his life, from birth to death, a person was destined for one place or another—for heaven or for hell.

To understand further the actions of the leaders of the established churches and their champions, the civil authorities, it is essential to keep in mind that to them truth was doctrine as they saw it, and error was a belief that differed from theirs. If baptism was essential to save the soul of an infant from damnation, then infant baptism it must be, and cursed be anyone who stood in the way, whether parent or pastor. The attitude was tersely expressed by the noted Boston preacher, Increase Mather, in a sermon of May 23, 1677, in which he declared:

"I believe that anti-Christ hath not at this day a more probable way to advance his kingdom of darkness, than by a toleration of all religions and persuasions."[7]

It was against this very premise of the established churches that Baptist faith and practice held firm. The Baptists could find no Scripture to support the doctrine of infant damnation or of infant baptism for the salvation of the infant's soul. Not even the strongest Calvinist Baptist could believe that an ordinance administered without the knowledge and free acceptance of the individual could bring about a regeneration of the soul. So the persecutions continued, and suffering for the cause of religious freedom became the badge of honor for Baptist ministers and congregations.

VI

HOW BAPTISTS GREW

The Seeds of Baptist Faith

Two significant results flowed from the restrictions and persecutions of early American Baptists:

First, they scattered the seeds of Baptist faith and practice widely over the developing colonies. Second, they crystallized in the minds and hearts of Baptists, as well as others who were of like opinions, the determination to work for guarantees of complete religious liberty—the guarantees that became the foundations of all freedoms in the American nation.

By the year 1677 the Baptists in Boston had grown to a sizable congregation, meeting quietly in the homes of the faithful. They organized themselves into a church, and in January 1678 they began building a meeting house without informing the authorities that it was to be used for worship. On February 15, 1679, the congregation met for the first time in the new building. John Russell, a well-educated man, was ordained the first pastor.

By this time, of course, the fact that a Baptist church had been established in Massachusetts' capital city had become well known. At the meeting of the General Court in May an act was passed authorizing the officials of the city to confiscate the Baptist property. The spirited pastor and his congregation moved into the hearing room of the Court, where Elder Russell contended that the act was unjust, since it was passed after the church was built. The law made a crime of something that was not declared a crime before the deed was done. It was, the pastor contended, *ex post facto,* and therefore not justified.

After heated discussion the court voted that the congregation could still own the property, but "it is our judgment that you who are Baptists shall not meet in it again."

Word of this matter reached His Majesty, King Charles II, who did a most unusual thing. He dictated a personal letter, written in his secretary's hand, to the governor and authorities of the Massachusetts Bay Colony. It contained these severe words:

"We shall henceforth expect that there shall be suitable obedience in respect of freedom and liberty of conscience, so as those that desire to serve God in the way of the ch. of Eng, be not thereby made obnoxious or discountenanced from sharing in the government, much less that of any other of our good subjects (not being Papists), who do not agree in the Congregational way, be by law subjected to fines or forfeitures, or other incapacities, for the same; which is a severity to be the more wondered at, whereas liberty of conscience was made a principal motive for your first transportation into those parts."[1]

The Boston authorities decided not to permit the Baptists to know about this royal letter, but the news of it could not be long suppressed. Defiantly, the congregation opened the doors of their meeting house again and resumed services. In March 1680 the General Court ordered the constables to nail shut the doors once more, and a new act with the threat of severe punishments forbade the Baptists to worship there again.

Once more Pastor Russell and Baptist leaders pled that the *ex post facto* action was contrary to simple justice. But to no avail. The doors of the First Baptist Church of Boston were not reopened until 1689, when the Act of Toleration was signed by King William III in behalf of himself and his royal companion, Queen Mary. This act gave the greatest measure of religious liberty to dissenters of Great Britain that they had enjoyed to that day, and its influence for religious freedom was felt throughout the American colonies.

William Screven Goes South

An early example of the expansion of Baptist churches and their influence is found in the story of Elder William Screven and his congregation. To find religious liberty they journeyed all the way from the northernmost colony, Maine, to the settlement farthest south at that time—South Carolina.

Screven was born in Somerton, England, in 1629, and emigrated to Boston about the year 1668. He became a successful merchant of the city. Deeply religious, he planned to organize a dissenters' church in Boston. Informed that he would be violating the laws of the Massachusetts Bay Colony, he moved to Kittery in the province of Maine. When Massachusetts acquired the area of Maine, Screven joined with several others in petitioning the king to establish direct rule over the province. While this step was never taken, the petition placed William Screven's name on the list of those who might entertain dangerous heresies.

Authorities watched him closely, and on July 6, 1675, they lodged a charge against him, misspelling his name, which read: "We'll present William Scrivine for not frequenting the public meeting according to Law on the Lord's Day." Before the case came to trial the court issued a clearance, stating: "This person presented is remitted because per evidence it appears that he usually attends Mr. Mowdy's meeting on the Lord's day." (The "Mowdy" referred to was Elder Joshua Moody, a Congregational minister in Postsmouth.)

Screven married Bridget Cutts, daughter of a sea captain who had immigrated from Barbados. To become full-fledged Baptists, in July 1681 Screven and his wife, with Humphrey Churchwood, a young man of Kittery who later married Bridget's sister Mary, went to Boston and were baptized into the membership of the First Baptist Church. Several of their neighbors who were dissenters also wanted baptism so that they might have their own Baptist congregation. Accordingly, Screven went again to the Boston church and asked that he be licensed to preach and to baptize. A certificate from the church, dated January 11, 1682, and signed by the pastor, Isaac Hull, and Deacon John Farnum, reads:

"These are to certify, that our beloved brother, William Screven, is a member in communion with us, and having had trial of his gifts among us, and finding him to be a man whom God hath qualified and furnished with the gifts of his Holy Spirit, and grace, enabling him to open and apply the word of God, which through the blessing of the Lord Jesus may be useful in his hand, for the begetting and building up of souls in the knowledge of God, do therefore appoint, approve and encourage him, to exercise his gift in the place where he lives, or elsewhere, as the providence of God may cast him: and so the Lord help him to eye his glory in all things, and to walk humbly in the fear of his name."

Now the battle against this dissenter by Kittery religious and civil authorities began in earnest. Before Screven and his friends could form their congregation they were called before a magistrate, who threatened them with fines and imprisonment if they proceeded with heretical worship or even attended Baptist meetings. On June 28, 1682, Screven was brought by a marshal before the entire General Assembly of the Province of Maine convening at York, and charged with blasphemy in that he "spoke against the holy ordinance of Baptism." He promised (at least the record so states) either to stop holding public services, or to leave the colony.

But in a spirit of defiance, or prompted by a stubborn belief that his cause was just, William Screven made no immediate move to leave Kittery. In September he wrote to the Boston Baptist church and asked for an elder to come to help organize the Baptists into a congregation. Later that month the church was organized, with a covenant signed by William Screven as elder. By his name was that of his wife, Bridget. Signing also were Humphrey Churchwood with his wife, Mary, and eight other men, most of them adding the names of their wives.

When officials of Kittery made known their intention to deal harshly with Screven and his congregation if they tried to hold church services, the preacher finally decided he had had enough of persecutions for conscience's sake. Several of the relatives of the Cutts family had chosen to settle in the Carolinas rather than in the far-northern province of Maine. Bridget and Mary declared that reports from their kin in the southern colony proved there was religious toleration there. Packing as much of their belongings as they could carry, most of the Kittery Baptist families took ship for the Carolinas. The year was 1696.

As far back as 1521 the Spaniards had explored the inlets and bays of the pleasant Carolina region, laying claim to the land in the name of the sovereign of imperial Spain. They had also established several forts, together with their Catholic mission stations to convert the heathen Indians, along the Atlantic coast from Florida to the southern border of Virginia.

Ignoring the claim of the Spaniards, King Charles II in 1663 by a royal grant chartered the Carolina colony to eight noblemen whom he designated as the Lords Proprietors. The grant covered a vast territory in that southernmost British claim in the North American continent, embracing what became the states of North and South Carolina, Tennessee, Georgia, parts of Alabama and Mississippi, and northern Florida. Among the proprietors were Sir Anthony Ashley Cooper and Sir John Colleton. The name Carolina honored both kings, the beheaded Charles I and the sovereign of the restored monarchy, the grantor himself, Charles II.

The First Southern Baptist Church

French Protestant believers, the Huguenots, led by Captain Jean Ribault, had made an attempt in 1562 at colonizing the region that became South Carolina, but they had been chased away by Spanish soldiers and freebooters. The first permanent settlement came in 1670 when a band of hardy English, commissioned by the Lords Proprietors, landed at Albermarle Point and there began to build Charles Town. Soon a group of dissenters arrived, under leadership of Joseph Blake, from Screven's native community, Somersetshire in England. More immigrants, including several of the Cutts family relatives, came from Barbados. Settlers in greater numbers came from England, and in every group there were dissenters who joined the Baptist ranks.

In 1672 a new town site was laid out by the men of Charles Town at Oyster Point, a wedge of land between the Cooper and Ashley rivers, where, as loyal Charlestonians declare, these two rivers join to form the Atlantic Ocean. New business houses and residences were built, and almost the whole community moved into them.

Meanwhile, the colony in South Carolina was constantly harassed by the Spanish, who claimed all the coastal area from Florida northward to the Virginia grant. By land and sea the Spaniards would come, destroying, burning, capturing as many hostages as they could for slave labor at their St. Augustine fort and other Florida strongholds. Hostile Indians and pirates also scourged the Carolinas. But the land was fertile, the climate pleasant; oysters, fish and game were plentiful; and other resources for survival and growth abundant.

About 1696 Elder Screven moved with the congregation from their rural homes into Charles Town, where they took the name "First Baptist Church." The records show that in 1698 Elder Screven purchased land to add to his 1,500 acres, and that another grant, in 1700, brought the holdings of this energetic parson to 2,600 acres.

For a time the members of this First Baptist Church in the southern colonies held services in the home of William Chapman. On July 18, 1699, William Elliot, one of the congregation, gave to his fellow Baptists "Lot No. 62 on Church Street," with a statement which declared:

"As well for and in consideration of the brotherly love which he hath for, and doth bear unto the people of the Church of Christ, baptized on profession of faith, distinguished from all others by the name of Anti-paedobaptists, of which Church he professeth himself a member, as to promote and encourage so good and pious a work as the building a place for the said people to meet and worship. . . ."

A meeting house, forty-seven by thirty-seven feet, was completed in late 1700. Screven continued to serve as pastor until about 1708, when the minutes of the church show that the membership had grown to ninety. In a letter to the members, Elder Screven wrote:

"My dear brethren and sisters (for whom God hath made me, poor unworthy me, an instrument of gathering and settling in the faith and order of the gospel), my request is that you as speedily as possible supply yourselves with an able and faithful minister. Be sure you take care the person be orthodox in the faith, and of blameless life, and does own the Confession put forth by our brethren in London."

Screven's labors ended on October 10, 1713. A tribute to his effective leadership was unwittingly given by a representative of the Anglican Bishop of London who was in Charles Town at the time, when he characterized Screven as "extremely ignorant," but added: "Next to the Presbyterians, the Anabaptists are most numerous."

In all the American colonies, as the new century began, the seeds of Baptist faith and practice had been planted which were to make these peculiar and indomitable people the most numerous of the United States Protestants.

The Welsh and the Tunkers

As the year 1700 dawned, there were only fourteen Baptist churches in the American colonies from Maine to South Carolina. But the new century brought a stirring of interest in religion for the pioneers, and no group benefited more than did the Baptists.

In William Penn's Sylvan Land dissenters found a climate of toleration, and Baptist congregations took root. In 1688 several Welsh immigrants joined settlers from Rhode Island to organize a church in their community. It was the first Baptist church in Pennsylvania, and still exists as Lower Dublin Baptist Church. Members of this congregation proudly announced there would be "preaching or exhorting" every Sunday, and two meetings a year especially to transact the business of the church. Their greatest missionary contribution was to help the Philadelphia Baptists to organize their own first church in 1698.

By 1707 there were five Baptist churches in the Philadelphia area. Inspired by the desire to aid one another in every way possible, the pastors and members of these five churches organized the Philadelphia Baptist Association. Each church sent messengers, with strict instructions that they could not bind their churches to any agreement, since the autonomy of a Baptist church had to be preserved. The messengers could confer, consult, and discuss matters pertaining to doctrine, ordinances, discipline of members, and polity, then report back to their parent churches "for consideration and edification."

Here was the beginning of a significant influence in Baptist life, the *association of churches,* first on the local level, expanding later into *conventions* of messengers representing the churches of entire states and the nation. Here was the tool that shaped the structure of common activities among Baptists and that still surmounts differences in doctrinal matters and creates unity in methods and programs.

In 1719 there came the first shiploads of so-called "Tunkers" from Germany. Also known as Dunkards, they were direct descendants of the Anabaptists in their country. Among them was Elder Paul Palmer, a General Baptist, who moved from Maryland to North Carolina in 1727 and established the first Baptist church in that state near the settlement of Cisco. An enthusiastic, vigorous evangelist, Palmer held numerous revival meetings and organized several churches in various communities of the North Carolina colony. On October 12, 1729, Royal Governor Richard Everard protested to his London bishop: "This Baptist preacher is stirring up a tide of fervor with his wild preaching and exhorting."

The records do not disclose what, if any, action was taken by either His Grace the London Bishop, or His Excellency the Royal Governor.

Morgan Edwards, a noted Baptist historian of the pre-Revolutionary period who lived in Philadelphia, in 1772 issued in his own handwriting a book called *Materials Towards a History of the Baptists in the Provinces of Maryland, Virginia, North Carolina, South Carolina, and Georgia*. A careful writer of names, places, dates, and other details of Baptist life in the southern states, Edwards tells of the founding of churches, persecutions of ministers and their congregations, the disputes between Particular and General Baptists. He begins his account of the spread of Baptist faith to Virginia by remarking:

"Next to Maryland, towards the south, is Virginia; a province famous for tobacco, and antiquity; being the first of all the British provinces in America, and affording much gratification to snuffers, smokers, and chewers in all the rest and in other parts of the world. This weed makes the planters and manufacturers rich and swells the public revenue but must fail, as the raising of it hath already made a barren waste of a great part of the country."[2]

Following this blast at Virginia's principal crop in that pre-Revolutionary day, the learned Baptist writer confirmed that progress for the Baptists was painful and slow for many years due to the fact that the charter granted to the Virginia founders in 1607 officially established the Anglican Church, supported from public funds to the extent necessary to maintain the meeting places and pay the salaries of the rectors. However, Dr. Morgan Edwards added, the Baptists had a way of "persevering to the end," even though it was not until 1714 that the first Anabaptist church was organized in Virginia, in the wilderness of Prince George's County.

The Great Awakening

By the 1720s the established churches in both the American colonies and in the British Isles had for the most part become so established as to be rigid. Their worship services were formal, with little warmth and feeling. Few churches in America offered their worshipers the experience that those peculiar people, the Baptists, called heartfelt religion. The result was a steady decline in church attendance and interest in spiritual matters. The times demanded a revival of religious feeling.

The revival came, on both sides of the Atlantic, in what became known as the Great Awakening. Its first trumpet notes to arouse the people from their spiritual lethargy were blown by Theodore Frelinghuysen of New Jersey; by Oliver Hart of Pennsylvania, an earnest Baptist who came as missionary to the Carolinas; and by a father-and-son team of Presbyterian ministers, William and Gilbert Tennent.

William Tennent lived in a community north of Philadelphia, where he had set up an academy called the Log College, a precise description of the rude building that housed it. Gilbert Tennent studied for the ministry in his father's Log College and became pastor of the New Brunswick, New Jersey, Presbyterian Church in 1726. Two years later he began a revival service in his church with remarkable success. Young Tennent preached a fiery, heart-stirring sermon, and people crowded in to hear him. Assisted by his father, Gilbert carried his evangelistic crusade to many communities of New Jersey and Pennsylvania.

Like the Tennents, other outstanding leaders of the Great Awakening in America were not Baptists. Yet the Baptists became the principal beneficiaries of this spiritual movement, since it spread far, wide, and deeply an acceptance of the Baptist ideal of heartfelt religion.

In New England there was Jonathan Edwards, Connecticut-born minister of a Congregational church in Massachusetts. As a child Jonathan was precocious, writing learned essays on religion and philosophy in his early teens and graduating from Yale College with high honors at the age of seventeen. At twenty-four he was called to be pastor at Northampton, a church which his maternal grandfather, the Reverend Solomon Stoddard, had served.

A magnetic speaker, Jonathan Edwards delivered his sermons with an almost fanatical conviction that every word he said was gospel truth and would be disbelieved at the peril of his hearers. Hundreds were added to the membership of Edwards' church, and his influence spread to many other communities.

At the same time a stirring of religious emotion began in England and Wales. Foremost leader of the movement in England was George Whitefield, a preacher of tremendous power and a New Light Congregationalist who believed that the souls of men could best be quickened by an emotional experience resulting in a changed life.

At the urging of John Wesley, Whitefield arrived in Savannah in May 1738 and preached for three months in all the communities along the coast and in the neighboring islands. Returning to England, he found that the clergy of his homeland had turned against him because of his unorthodox evangelizing, so he took to preaching in the open air to such crowds as never before in England had come to hear a minister. He came back to America in 1740 and in the following decade made five additional journeys to preach to throngs of American people who assembled to hear him from Maine to Georgia. From every congregation, whether in churches or in the open air, men and women moved forward at his invitation to touch him or to press his hand and to ask for his prayers for their salvation.

Numerous converts of this revival period trooped into Baptist congregations, seeking freedom from the established churches. Many became Baptist preachers and founded their own free congregations. Typical of these was John Clayton, an immigrant to the Georgia colony. A forthright exhorter given to speaking his mind, Parson Clayton declared in a sermon: "No man can be a Christian who keeps a concubine, be the keeper a king and the concubine a countess!"[3]

Although Clayton had called no names, his remark was taken as a reflection, as indeed the preacher intended it to be, upon the honor of the late King George I, who had as one of his mistresses a lady of royal blood. For this offense, the indiscreet preacher was arrested and brought before the magistrate at Savannah. In answer to the accusation Clayton made this plea: "I expressed only my private opinion, and I should have the right to do so because I spoke what I considered to be the truth!"

This did not help him much. The magistrate levied a fine upon the parson. Yet without realizing the importance of his protests, Elder Clayton of colonial Georgia was expressing an ideal strenuously defended by Baptists in later years. They called it *Freedom of Speech*.

VII

ISAAC BACKUS—BAPTIST CHAMPION

Mary Lane Had a Will

James Lane, who had owned a farm near the town of Richmond, Virginia, from the early years of the eighteenth century, had a son Dutton who disobeyed his explicit orders not to go hear that fiery evangelist, George Whitefield, preach. Not only did Dutton Lane go to hear Whitefield, but under the spell of the great preacher's magnetic voice, personality, and ardor, the youth made a profession of faith. While Dutton Lane knew that Whitefield was an English Separatist and not a Baptist, he liked what Whitefield preached about religious freedom. So Lane joined a small Baptist church there in the heart of Virginia, was ordained to preach, and began his own remarkable career as an evangelist.

This disobedience and drift into heresy so enraged James Lane that he disowned his son and warned his wife never to go hear Dutton preach. However, she was a strong-willed woman. At the time when the promise to obey in the marriage ceremony was taken literally by wives and strictly enforced by husbands, Mary Lane did what she thought was right, with or without her husband's consent. So, on a Sunday morning when Dutton came to hold what was known as a protracted meeting in the Baptist church nearest the Lane plantation, Mary slipped out of the house, put the sidesaddle on her mare, and went to hear him.

Mary Lane readily admitted to her husband that she had gone to the Baptist meeting house to hear their son preach. Seizing his horsewhip, James Lane stood his wife against the wall and beat her unmercifully. Then he took his musket, loaded it with powder and ball, vowed to heaven he would find his heretic son and kill him, and rode away.

For some reason, probably the sight of Lane's musket and his obvious anger, no one around the vicinity of the Baptist meeting house seemed to know where the young preacher had gone. The father returned home, somewhat cooled off by his ride. There the spirited Mary, still nursing the wounds from her husband's whip, quietly challenged his sporting blood: "You give a bird a chance to wing afore you shoot it," she said, "Why not give Dutton a chance? Go hear him just once."

After some hesitation, James Lane agreed. He would go hear his son—just this once. When the service was over, Lane shook his son's hand and walked out without a word. But he came back—time and again, and sat as under a spell while his son called people to repentance and salvation through faith in Jesus Christ. In relating what happened, many times in his career as a pastor and evangelist, Elder Dutton Lane would say:

"At last he decided I was preaching the truth. He came forward under conviction of sin. I baptized him, and he became a pillar of that church!"[1]

Lane's power as an eloquent preacher and powerful evangelist became known all over Virginia. Morgan Edwards, eighteenth-century Baptist historian, had this to say about one of Lane's converts: "William Cocker had conceived such a malignity against the Baptists that he was wont to say He had rather go to hell than to heaven if going to the latter required his being a Baptist; but coming accidentally to hear Dutton Lane this same malignant fell to the ground, roaring, 'Lord, have mercy on me! I am a gone man. What shall I do to be saved?' In this manner he went on for about an hour; and now is a humble and pious Baptist."

Salvation for the Common People

Parson Dutton Lane was one of hundreds of Baptists of the mid-1700s who professed religion and answered the call to preach in the period of the Great Awakening. More definitely than they could ever have known, the leaders of the revival movement, whether Baptists or not, paved the way for Baptist growth in

America. They followed the example of Whitefield in proclaiming: "Salvation is yours for the taking! Think for yourselves. The common people heard Jesus gladly. You are the common people—you can hear and heed him, too!"

Since Baptists generally were indeed of the common people, they gained a major share of the converts who listened to the trumpet call to salvation and church membership.

There was the Reverend Robert Feke of Oyster Bay, New York, for example, who in 1741 organized a Baptist church there, the first congregation of Baptists in that state. Elder Feke wrote to his friends in Newport who had encouraged his efforts: "God has begun a glorious work among us, and I hope he will carry it on to his own glory, and the salvation of many souls. There have been seventeen added to our little band in about three months."[2]

The Baptist pastor's hope was amply justified as many New England settlers came westward and founded Baptist churches along the Mohawk, Susquehanna, and Genesee rivers, and by Otsego Lake. In 1762 the first Baptist church in New York City was formed with the Reverend John Gano as pastor. After a distinguished career in the city, Elder Gano journeyed to the wilds of Kentucky to take the Baptist message to the West.

Another lasting influence of the revival period in the American colonies was increased resistance of Baptists, aided by other dissenters, to laws they considered unjust and intolerable, laws sponsored by established churches to govern religious affairs. In 1718 the General Court of Massachusetts had put on the books an act that assessed all the families of the towns in the colony for the payment of salaries of the Congregational ministers, regardless of whether the families were Presbyterians, Quakers, Baptists, or of any other faith, or no faith at all. The tax was levied upon everyone, "assessed in the king's name," as the General Court declared.

At Swansea, settled by Baptists as a small colony, there were two Baptist churches and none other. Here the pastors and congregations refused to pay the tax to support a Congregational minister living in another town serving not one single family in Swansea. "Taxation without representation, and without benefit of any public service!" the Baptist faithful cried.

After appeals and threats failed to convince these stubborn people that they had to pay the assessment, the authorities put the property of the Baptist congregations up for sheriff's sale. The buildings and their furnishings, together with several fields and even a cemetery, were sold for a fraction of their money value. The Congregational minister himself was a successful bidder for one parcel.

"Taxation without representation!" the Massachusetts Baptists cried, anticipating the slogan that was to be raised three decades later against the tax collectors of Great Britain.

In Virginia, the Act of Toleration, passed in 1689, proved an empty gesture for religious dissenters. It still required a license from the authorities at Williamsburg to hold services, but in Camden County in 1743 a convert of George Whitefield's preaching, Samuel Morris, defied the authorities and invited his neighbors to come to his home for Baptist worship. By some fortune Morris secured a book of sermons preached by Whitefield and taken down after a fashion of shorthand. To an ever-growing group of his neighbors, hungry for any evangelistic sermon and especially one "writ down" from the great English preacher, Morris read and re-read the burning words of the evangelist.

Before long the zealous, literate convert was traveling all over Hanover County to read to groups of listeners at night. The next move was to start building a meeting house. Now the authorities stepped in. A warrant was issued, calling Samuel Morris before the magistrate, where he was charged with "nonattendance at church."

Morris pled that the Act of Toleration applied to Virginia, as to all other of His Majesty's colonies in America, and that thus it applied to him and to his fellow Baptists. The magistrate did not agree, but let Elder Morris off with a stiff warning. After a period of quietude the Baptist missionary-evangelist again took up his preaching and completed the building of a meeting house for his congregation.

Isaac Backus Made Two Decisions

For Baptists of colonial America the most important product of the aroused spiritual movement was Isaac Backus. As a youth just come of age, he went forward to shake Whitefield's hand one night in the spring of 1743 in the Congregational church house at Norwich, Connecticut.

Isaac's late father, Samuel Backus, had passed away six years before, leaving a comfortable fortune made from his iron works and a large estate of land. Samuel Backus was a descendant of one of the first families of Connecticut. Isaac's mother, Elizabeth Tracy Backus, was from the Winslow family of the Mayflower pilgrims.

The Backus family had always been prosperous, but unlike most prosperous people of that day they were independent in religious thinking. Both Isaac's grandfather and great-grandfather had withdrawn from the state-supported Congregational Church in protest against lack of religious freedom in the combination of civil and spiritual rule exercised by the established church. Isaac's mother, however, had remained in the Congregational Church, and at eighteen Isaac himself had joined this favored fellowship in Norwich. It had seemed the proper thing to do.

By a covenant officially approved by the General Court of the Massachusetts Bay Colony in 1657, the Congregational establishment admitted to membership persons who professed to be only moral but not converted, and who agreed to come under the discipline of the church. Both Widow Backus and her son were unhappy in a fellowship that did not require what the Congregational dissenters, known as New Lights, called a true inward change. In 1745 Elizabeth Backus and Isaac cut their ties with the regular Congregational Church and joined the New Light worshipers in Norwich.

Within a few months Isaac Backus made another great decision: He would be a preacher. He applied to his church for ordination, was accepted, and in a solemn ceremony was examined and commissioned by the New Light fellowship to preach. Two years later he began his remarkable career as a minister and spiritual leader. He assembled a congregation at Titicut, Massachusetts, drew up its articles of faith, and became the congregation's first pastor.

Young Preacher Backus looked upon John Locke as his hero and often quoted him in his early writings. He was especially impressed with Locke's treatise *On Toleration,* with its significant words: "Civil laws are not to provide for the truth of opinion but for the safety and security of the commonwealth, and of every particular man's goods and person. And so it ought to be, for truth certainly will do well enough if she were once left to shift for herself."[3]

From the start of his ministry Backus refused to pay the church tax. On February 6, 1749, he was clapped in jail for this refusal, and only the intervention of some influential members of his congregation got him out. Still refusing to pay the tax, he was released with a warning that the levy must be paid or he would be confined for a long term.

Unterrified, Backus stepped up his efforts to repeal the church tax, and in late May 1749 wrote in his diary:

"On May 24, 1749, many of the saints met together in Attelborough; to seek the Lord's direction and to confer about petitioning the court for to set us free from the oppression of being forced to pay for the support of a worship that we can't in conscience join with—and we had considerable clearness in sending and we drew up a petition and sent copys around to the saints in various parts of the governments; and it fell to my lot to carry a copy down to the cape."[4]

The New Light saints at the Cape warmly endorsed the protest, but the members of the General Court were not impressed. They ignored all such petitions, whether from New Lights, Baptists, Presbyterians, or other troublesome minorities. However, Isaac Backus had exercised a right that he vigorously defended all the rest of his life, that of petition for redress of grievances.

Back in Norwich, Widow Backus fared even worse than her son for her stubborn refusal to pay the tax for support of the established church. One chill autumn night the constables came to her home and escorted her to jail. She had only the clothes she had on her back. For thirteen days and nights she was kept in a cheerless, cold cell of the prison until finally a friend paid the tax for her, and she was released. The spirited woman wrote to her son Isaac: "Though the punishment was grievous, I did not fear; for the Lord was with me."

Drawing ever closer to Baptist beliefs and practices, in August 1751 Isaac Backus had himself immersed in the open waters of a lake near Titicut. Several of his congregation followed his example. He continued in his position as pastor of his church until June 1756. Then came his open espousal of the Baptist faith.

It is likely that his members were not too surprised. For years Backus had been preaching and defending the ideals for which Baptists were most noted: spiritual liberty, believer's baptism for membership in the church, the autonomy of each church congregation, and complete freedom from governmental control.

The congregation of the First Baptist Church of Middleborough, Massachusetts, called Elder Isaac Backus to be the pastor, and he accepted. There he began the pastorate that extended until his death in 1806.

Backus continued the campaigns he had begun as a New Light Congregationalist against taxation of religious bodies, even though the laws of both Massachusetts and Connecticut had been modified to permit Baptists to avoid paying taxes to support the state-approved church and its ministers, provided they signed certificates of exemption announcing that they were bona fide Baptists. Civil and religious authorities of these colonies considered this a very tolerant arrangement, and most Baptist congregations were signing the certificates, glad to be rid of the unjust tax.

But the Reverend Isaac Backus denounced this scheme, holding that to force Baptists to sign the certificates before they could secure tax exemption was as much an invasion of personal rights as the tax itself. He continued to declare that to comply with this law implied that the civil rulers had the right to favor one religious group over another, and that by levying this tax the authorities were appropriating a power that belonged only to God as the spiritual head of all believers. Finally, he condemned the practice because, he said: "In all civil governments some are appointed for others, and have power to compel others to submit to their judgment; but our Lord has most plainly forbidden us, either to assume or submit to any such thing in religion."[5]

Backus realized that the Baptists, drawing their members in largest part from farmers and laboring people with little education, were generally led by ministers of meager schooling. It was a rare thing to find an academy graduate among them. For the future good of the growing sect, Backus decided, this must be remedied. He joined with other well-known Baptist leaders, particularly those in Philadelphia, to establish a college especially for candidates for the Baptist ministry, and in 1766 they founded Rhode Island College at Providence, later to become Brown University. The scholarly James Manning, a Princeton graduate, became its first president. Backus served as a trustee of the school for thirty years, helping to bring high recognition to the institution among early colleges in America. For many years it was the chief training ground and seminary for young Baptist ministers. Proud of its reputation as a Baptist institution, the college refused to consider any plan for state support or control.

By 1762 the Philadelphia Baptist Association had grown to twenty-nine churches with more than 4,000 members, chiefly in Pennsylvania, New Jersey, and New York. Following the pattern set by this first co-operating group of Baptist churches, other groups formed themselves into associations for united efforts and mutual benefit. The second such association was made by congregations of the Charleston, South Carolina, area, grouping about the Old First Baptist Church. Next came the Sandy Creek Baptists in North Carolina in 1758 and Ketockton Baptist Association in Virginia in 1766.

The Sandy Creek churches were known as Separate Baptists, and in 1770 they had grown strong enough to divide into three associations, one each in Virginia, North Carolina, and South Carolina. Leader of the Separates in the latter state was Elder Daniel Marshall, a fervent evangelist and organizer of churches. He was arrested by South Carolina authorities at the insistence of Anglican Church leaders for his preaching and pleading the cause of religious liberty. Discussing the influence of those who went out from old Sandy Creek, the contemporary historian, Morgan Edwards, with some pardonable exaggeration declared:

"All the Separate Baptists sprang hence: not only eastward towards the sea, but westward towards the great river Mississippi, but northward to Virginia and southward to South Carolina and Georgia. The word went forth from this sion, and great was the company of them who published it, in so much that her converts were as the drops of morning dew."

The Grievance Committee

Urging that New England Baptists fall in line, in 1767 Elder Backus and Dr. Manning took the lead in establishing the Warren Baptist Association, made up of churches scattered over the wide region of Massachusetts, Connecticut, and Rhode Island, with Warren, Massachusetts, as its center.

The Warren Baptist Association took the unusual step of setting up a grievance committee composed of eight members so that differences of all kinds among the ministers, congregations, and individual members could be explored and settled. Even more important, the organization appointed an agent to be spokesman for the member churches in all matters of public concern and especially in clashes with the authorities over church taxation. The Reverend John Davis, youthful pastor of the Second Baptist Church, Boston, was named agent. He lived only three years after assuming this work, and when Backus was chosen to succeed he wasted no time announcing that he would "give advice and aid to persons who might be oppressed and harassed for refusing to pay taxes to support the ministers and work of the Congregationalists." Within a few months he brought out in printed form an *Appeal to the Publick for Religious Liberty,* which asserted:

"And it appears to us that the true difference and exact limits between ecclesiastical and civil government is this, That the church is armed with *light and truth,* to pull down the strongholds of iniquity, and to gain souls to Christ, and into his Church . . . While the state is armed with the *sword* to guard the peace, and the civil rights of all persons and societies, and to punish those who violate the same . . . I before declared that the Scripture is abundantly clear for a free support of ministers, but not a forced one; and observed, that there is as much difference between them, as there is between the power of truth in the mind, and the power of the sword in the body."

On May 5, 1773, Elder Backus led the Grievance Committee of the Warren Baptist Association to send a letter, signed by himself as their agent, to all the affiliated churches asking them to petition the state and local governments against requiring the signing of certificates for tax exemption. "We desire you to consider whether it is not our duty to refuse any conformity to their laws about such affairs, even so much as giving any certificates to their assessors," the letter urged.

There is no record that the General Court of Massachusetts, or any local authorities, paid any attention to the petitions, but Backus was exemplifying the use of a right he lived to see guaranteed in the federal Constitution.

The clouds of rebellion against the mother country were gathering over the colonies, and under those clouds the First Continental Congress met in 1774. Delegates from all the thirteen colonies except Georgia convened in Philadelphia intent upon discussing the common problems of the uncertain future.

Backus, agent of the Warren Baptist Association, presented the honorable gentlemen another and unwanted problem: what to do about religious liberty. He won support among fellow ministers for a plan to petition the Continental Congress for an end to the use of public funds for any church or religious group. While few of the agent's associates and friends held much hope for the success of the audacious idea, several willingly accompanied him to Philadelphia to see what his arguments and eloquence might accomplish.

John Adams Was Irritated

Massachusetts had originated the call from the Continental Congress, and one of the state's outstanding leaders, John Adams, had helped to draft its wording. Backus knew that Adams' support for his petition would go far to influence the other fifty-four members from the twelve states gathered in that historic session.

The Baptist delegates from Massachusetts arranged for a conference with the representatives from their state to be held the evening of October 14, 1774, in Carpenters Hall. Because of the high interest in the matter of religious freedom in Massachusetts, several members of the Congress from other states were also present when James Manning read the petition, and Backus rose to explain it.

The Massachusetts delegates, led by John Adams, were visibly embarrassed and irritated. They heartily resented any group implying that their great state did not grant all the religious freedom allowed in all others. Mr. Adams spoke, followed by Samuel Adams, both of them admitting that there was what they called an ecclesiastical establishment but protesting that it was "very slender" and that it permitted full religious freedom. If there were any restrictions on religious liberty in Massachusetts, John Adams declared, it was the fault of local officials who might not understand the law, rather than the General Court.

Backus reminded the group that the General Court had seized the Baptist property at Ashfield in payment of taxes levied for a Congregational minister who did not even live in that parish, and asserted that it was not so much a matter of the money involved, as one of principle in which freedom of conscience, with freedom also from state control, was at stake.

John Adams closed the four-hour discussion with a promise that the Massachusetts delegates would do what they could for the relief of the Baptists, then, according to Backus, added these words: "Gentlemen, if you mean to try to affect a change in Massachusetts laws respecting religion, you may as well attempt to change the course of the sun in the heavens!"

John Hancock Ordered a Reading

Determined to change the course of the sun in the heavens if necessary, Backus and his committee armed themselves with another and more strongly worded petition, and presented their plea directly to John Hancock, presiding over the Continental Congress. Mr. Hancock ordered the petition read and considered. After some discussion the members took action. It was expressed in this resolution:

"In Provincial Congress, Cambridge, December 9, 1774: On reading the memorial of the Reverend Isaac Backus, agent to the Baptist churches in this government: Resolved, that the establishment of civil and religious liberty, to each denomination in the province, is the sincere wish of this Congress; but being by no means vested with powers of civil government, whereby they can redress the grievances of any person whatever, they therefore recommend to the Baptist churches, that when a general assembly shall be convened in this colony, they lay the real grievances of said churches before the same, when and where their petition will most certainly meet with all that attention due to the memorial of a denomination of Christians, so well disposed to the public weal of their country. By order of the Congress, John Hancock, President."[6]

That suggestion was all that the persistent Backus and his resolute Baptist associates needed. When the General Court met at Watertown in July 1775, early in the session the members heard and pondered this vigorous memorial from Baptists of their state:

"Our real grievances are, that we, as well as our fathers, have from time to time been taxed on religious accounts where we were not represented: and when we have sued for our rights, our causes have been tried by interested judges . . . and for a civil legislature to impose religious taxes, is, we conceive, a power which their constituents never had to give, and is, therefore, going entirely out of their jurisdiction . . . We beseech this honorable Assembly to take these matters into their wise and serious consideration before Him, who has said, *with what measure ye mete, it shall be measured to you again.* Is not all America now appealing to Heaven, against the injustice of being taxed where we are not represented; and against being judged by men, who are interested in getting away our money? Yet as we are persuaded that an entire freedom from being taxed by civil rulers to religious worship, is not a mere favour, from any man or men in the world, but a right and property granted us by God."

The memorial was read twice, discussed, referred to a committee, and reported favorably. A bill was drafted which stated that "no person shall be hurt or restrained, in person, liberty or estate, for worshiping God in the manner most agreeable to the dictates of his conscience." A time was set for its second reading, and Backus and his fellow Baptists were ready to celebrate what they thought would be a significant triumph. But a vote on the bill was postponed from day to day and finally the bill itself was tabled, according to agent-lobbyist Backus, because John Adams had been quietly at work behind the scenes.

Backus was often referred to by his opponents as the most contentious person they ever encountered. Even by his friends he was recognized as one who liked to debate for debate's sake, often with harsh words better left unsaid. To gain a point Backus was known to lead the discussion into several side fields, only to drag his unwary participants in the dialogue into concessions they did not intend to make. Too often for Backus the end justified the verbal means.

At the same time, Backus also learned what it meant to be villified and condemned by those opposing his principles. Every week the newspapers of Massachusetts printed tirades against him, some of the writers calling him a fanatic, others a "treasonable scoundrel." He was accused of going to Philadelphia "to attempt to break up the Union of our Colonies," and one editor asserted: "For this man, the halter and gallows would be fitting reward."

Some of the denunciations Backus answered in his usual stilted prose with its long, involved sentences. Some attacks he ignored as not worthy of answer. Disappointed but still undaunted, he would wait his time to return to the battle.

"We Hold These Truths to Be Self-Evident . . ."

In the meantime, clouds of a greater conflict over human liberties continued ominously to gather. The dispute between the government of His Majesty George III and his American colonies was reaching the point of no return. Open rebellion on the part of American leaders was now the steam which the kettle of political control could no longer restrain.

Patrick Henry, the eloquent Virginia lawyer who had upheld the right of Baptists and other dissenters to worship freely, had asserted the right of the colonial states to legislate independent of the British Parliament, especially with respect to taxation. On April 19, 1775, the first shots of the War for Independence sounded on the village green of Lexington, Massachusetts. The Continental Congress assigned the command of the Continental Army to General George Washington.

On July 2, 1776, the Congress adopted a forthright Declaration of Independence, written by a delegate from Virginia, Thomas Jefferson. Announced to the public two days later, it contained these historic words: "We hold these truths to be self-evident, that all men are created equal, that they are endowed by their Creator with certain unalienable rights, among these Life, Liberty, and the Pursuit of Happiness."

From that time forward, Thomas Jefferson, although not a

Baptist, became in the mind of Isaac Backus and of countless other Baptist leaders the ideal statesman.

Buttressed by the Declaration, even before independence was won, all the states except Rhode Island and Connecticut adopted new constitutions. The General Court of Massachusetts called a convention for that purpose in 1779. Noah Alden, a Baptist of Boston, urged Backus to offer the draft of a bill of rights for the new constitution. Noah Alden's letter, preserved among Backus' papers, has a notation on the back which reads: "Wrote a Bill of Rights, and sent in a letter to him. August 11, 1779."

Backus must have had before him a copy of the bill of rights already adopted by Virginia, and possibly also by Pennsylvania, for the wording of his proposal contained phrases almost identical to those in the constitutions of those states. Some words were similar also to those Backus used in his Memorial of 1774. The first article declared: "All men are born free and equal, and have certain natural, essential, and unalienable rights."

A second article asserted that "no subject shall be hurt, molested, or restrained, in his person, liberty, or estate, for worshiping God in the manner and season most agreeable to the dictates of his own conscience."

In Backus' draft was an article that actually prohibited the levying of taxes to support *any* church. Again to his disappointment, this wording was deleted from the final draft of the Massachusetts constitution. Backus vigorously protested this omission in a paper entitled *An Appeal to the People of Massachusetts Against Arbitrary Power,* published in the December 2, 1779, issue of the *Boston Chronicle.* The paper could not affect the wording already adopted. Still, Isaac Backus' ideal of religious liberty was taking root.

VIII

THE FREEDOM TRAIL

For the Cause of Religious Liberty

No church fellowship in America was more hearty in its support of the War for Independence than the Baptists. According to Isaac Backus only two Baptist ministers, whose names he did not mention, refused to support the struggle. The great majority of Baptist ministers, in their sermons and their evangelistic tours, actively announced that they stood with General Washington, the Continental Congress, and the armed forces fighting for freedom from Great Britain.

As the acknowledged leader of colonial Baptists and their chief spokesman for the cause of religious liberty, Backus himself lost no chance to endorse the Revolution. He repeatedly declared that it was the right of the people to establish their own government, especially if it meant greater personal freedoms. Said Backus:

"The great end of government being for the good of the governed and not the honor or profit of any particular person or families therein: the community hath an inalienable right to reform, alter, or newly form their constitution of government, as that community shall judge to be most conducive to the public weal."[1]

It was well known and appreciated by all Baptist leaders in the colonial states that the Virginia country squire and statesman, Thomas Jefferson, had supported them and the leaders of other faiths who were struggling to secure religious liberty. They rejoiced when he wrote into the Declaration of Independence the stirring words: "That to secure these rights, governments are instituted among men, deriving their just powers from the consent of the governed."

"This is what we have believed and taught all along!" was the exultant cry of Baptists from New England to Georgia.

Many Baptists went back to the statements of Roger Williams and found striking similarities in the words of the Rhode Island founder and those of the Virginia delegate to the Congress. They wondered if Thomas Jefferson might have been reading Roger Williams' writings on human liberty. As freedom had been the watchword of Baptists in matters of conscience and worship, so freedom and self-government in political affairs became their goal once war with the mother country was joined.

While Baptist leaders generally supported the obligation of every able-bodied male citizen to take part in the war by bearing arms, they also defended the right of any man who in conscience could not bear arms, "who conscientiously scruples the lawfulness of it, if he will pay such equivalent," as a resolution of the Warren Baptist Association stated it. This stand brought Baptists to the defense of Quakers and Mennonites who traditionally were staunch pacifists. Dr. Backus proudly recorded:

"The Baptists were so generally united with their country in defence of their privileges, that when the General Court at Boston passed an act, in October 1778, to debar all men from returning to their government, whom they judged to be their enemies, and named 311 men, such there was not one Baptist among them. Yet there was scarce a Baptist member in the Legislature who passed this act."[2]

Baptist preachers joined those of other denominations—principally Episcopalians, Methodists, and Presbyterians—as voluntary chaplains to the Revolutionary soldiers in all the thirteen states. Where commanders of the troops permitted, these ministers set up rude altars in the camps on Sunday mornings and among the campfires at night. They preached to men dirty with the dust of the march and the bivouac and often wearing bandages red from the wounds of battle, but eager to hear what they used to hear in the churches back home.

In Georgia there was Daniel Marshall, serving as a chaplain to the Southern troops under General Nathanael Greene. Tory sympathizers took him prisoner, but he is reported to have "preached" them into releasing him, whereupon he rejoined the Revolutionary army and marched northward with it against Cornwallis' Redcoats.

Against English Rule and Satan

Elder Oliver Hart, pastor of the First Baptist Church at Charleston, South Carolina, during the first years of the war preached independence for South Carolina and the other American states as vigorously as he did the gospel. It was said of him that Parson Hart never made any distinction between freedom from English rule and freedom from the rule of Satan. This preacher helped to organize all the coastal areas of South Carolina to supply equipment, clothing, and food for the American troops. He frequently visited the camps of the buckskin-clad Carolina marksmen fighting under the commands of General Francis (Swamp Fox) Marion and General Nathanael Greene, and other units of the American line, with boxes and bales of supplies as they drove the British steadily back toward Virginia. Such activities marked Parson Hart as a traitor in the eyes of the British, and when the Redcoats captured Charleston in 1780 the patriotic preacher fled to Hopewell, New Jersey. There he served as pastor of the Baptist congregation until his death in 1795.

When on October 19, 1781, General Charles Cornwallis, British commander, surrendered his troops to the victorious alliance of American and French forces under General Washington and General Rochambeau at Yorktown, Virginia, members of the Philadelphia Baptist Association were meeting. The historic news was carried northward by riders on fast horses and reached Philadelphia near midnight of the next day. In the still of that night the people of the city, most of whom had retired at their customary hour of nine o'clock, were awakened by the cries of the watchmen. Some in German, others in English, were shouting, their voices echoing among the buildings of the town: "Past twelve o'clock, and all is well—and Cornwallis has surrendered to General Washington!"

The rejoicing members of that Baptist convention passed this resolution:

"And now, dear Brethren, we feel ourselves constrained to acknowledge the great goodness of God toward us, and to call on you to join with us in thankfulness and praise, as well for the unanimity and brotherly love which prevailed throughout our meeting, as for the recent signal success granted to the American arms in the surrender of the whole British army under the command of Lord Cornwallis."[3]

Soon after victory was won, General Washington, Episcopal vestryman, wrote to the Baptist churches of Virginia through the officers of their state association: "I recollect with satisfaction that the religious society of which you are members have been throughout America, uniformly and almost unanimously, the firm friends to civil liberty and the persevering promoters of our glorious Revolution."[4]

At the beginning of the Revolutionary War, nine of the thirteen American colonies officially recognized and gave support to so-called "established" churches. Among the four New England states, only Rhode Island permitted complete freedom of worship —the legacy of Roger Williams and his Baptist followers. Congregationalism was the state religion of Connecticut, Massachusetts, and New Hampshire. The Episcopal Church was favored, in more or less degree, as established by law, in New York, Maryland, Virginia, North Carolina, South Carolina, and Georgia. New Jersey, Pennsylvania, and Delaware had no established religion.

Disestablishment came fairly early in the war for the southernmost states and for New York. In those states the influence of the Baptists, aided by Presbyterians and Methodists, the latter still part of the Episcopal Church although pulling steadily away, was the deciding factor for religious freedom. For the Baptists, the struggle was for complete separation of church and state, while Presbyterians and Methodists demanded only the safeguarding of their rights under acts of toleration.

In South Carolina the name of Richard Furman emerged as the man who led the forces against the established religion. In 1776 he sponsored a meeting at High Hills to discuss religious liberty and to lay plans to secure it in the Palmetto State. Two years later Furman visited the convention in Charleston that had met to draft a new state constitution, and his eloquent arguments resulted in the adoption of a provision that put an end to the special status of the Anglican Church in South Carolina and placed all churches on an equal footing of freedom.

The Episcopal Church in Virginia held out staunchly to preserve its established position. In the face of a flood of petitions from Baptists all over the Old Dominion, in December 1779 the Assembly repealed parts of the act that had provided for the support of the clergy and for the collection and paying of parish levies. Another act of that Assembly provided that salaries for ministers would no longer be paid by the state.

These steps, restricting financial support for the Establishment, Baptists conceded, were in the right direction. But they were not enough to satisfy Baptist demands. The struggle in Virginia continued until after the war, when Thomas Jefferson's "Bill for the Establishment of Religious Freedom" brought victory for complete religious liberty in 1785. Not until 1817 did New Hampshire end its Congregational establishment. In 1818 Connecticut followed its neighbor's example.

A Wall of Separation

In Massachusetts, meanwhile, Dr. Backus continued his unrelenting war against levying taxes for the established church. The high point of his battle was reached in October 1780, when he and his Baptist associates presented to the General Court of Massachusetts a vigorous protest against a provision in the proposed new state constitution which placed public education virtually under control of church leaders. The protest set forth specific reasons why Baptists opposed the plan, including these:

"Because it asserts a right in the people to give away a power they never had themselves; for no man has a right to judge for others in religious matters; yet this Article would give the majority of each town and parish the exclusive right of covenanting for the rest with religious teachers, and so of excluding the minority from the liberty of choosing for themselves in that respect.

"Because this power is given entirely into the hands of men who vote only by virtue of *money* qualifications, without any regard to the church of Christ.

"Because said Article contradicts itself; for it promises *equal* protection of all sects, with an exemption from any subordination of one religious denomination to another; when it is impossible for the majority of any community to govern in any affair, unless the minority are in subordination to them in that affair.

"Because by this Article the civil power is called to judge whether persons can conveniently and conscientiously attend upon any teacher within their reach, and oblige each one to support such teachers as may be contrary to his conscience; which is subversive of the unalienable rights of conscience."[5]

Elder Backus was elected a delegate to the Massachusetts convention called to ratify the proposed federal Constitution in 1787. The veteran crusader for religious freedom was gratified to know that the document, brought forth after long travail in Philadelphia, contained the words: "No religious test shall ever be required as a qualification to any office or public trust under the United States."

Still, Backus and his associates felt that this negative provision should be strengthened by a positive restraint upon the new government to prevent either public support, or interference in any manner, with religious affairs. They applauded James Madison's successful moves for the amendments, especially for the First Amendment, which erected what Thomas Jefferson later succinctly called the "wall of separation between church and state."

To the Baptists of the new American Republic the guarantees of the Bill of Rights were simply those for which they had fought and for which their forebears had suffered martyrdom in many areas of the world for centuries. They saw nothing remarkable about the provision that "Congress shall make no law respecting an establishment of religion, or prohibiting the free exercise thereof."

" 'Tis only the right of every person to believe or not to believe, and to be free of the meddling of the state in matters of conscience!" was the idea earnestly expressed by Baptist leaders and believers of that day.

Long after the adoption of the federal Constitution, Massachusetts retained its provision for recognition and support of the Congregational Church. "This is not just!" thundered Isaac Backus from his pulpit, as he spoke in the meetings of the Warren Baptist Association, and as he wrote letters of advice and encouragement to Baptists all over the state. In 1791 he issued a pamphlet calling attention to the conflict between the provision for religious liberty in the United States Constitution and that of the laws of his state, which clearly provided for an establishment of religion. He was answered by being reminded that the federal Constitution had no power to modify state constitutions and laws. Backus countered with the argument that the federal Constitution was by its own definition "the supreme law of the land," and that no state had the right to make and enforce laws that violated its provisions. In this fight Backus had the active support of such diverse fellowships as the Unitarians and the Quakers.

It was in 1833 that Massachusetts finally abandoned its provision for an established religion by a Bill of Rights in its constitution. Dr. Backus had planted among Baptists and others the seed of a political principle, deeply embedded in the rich soil of his religious faith, that in a Union of States the rights of all citizens must be equally guaranteed. From that seed flowered the words of the Fourteenth Amendment to the United States Constitution:

"No state shall make or enforce any law which shall abridge the privileges and immunities of citizens of the United States, nor shall any state deprive any person of life, liberty, or property without due process of law, nor deny to any person within its jurisdiction the equal protection of the laws."

The Westward Tide of Settlers

Despite the hardships and hindrances of the War for Independence, Baptists continued their co-operation among neighboring congregations, and even across far distances, where communications and mutual assistance were still possible. In 1775 South Carolina Baptists raised funds to aid their brethren in New England who were being persecuted as nonconformists and nonsupporters of the established church.

Spurred by the realization that religious liberty had been secured through independence and the First Amendment in the Constitution, Baptists throughout the new Union moved forward in the establishment of congregations, forming associations, planning and carrying on missionary work among the Indians, and helping the struggling churches of the raw frontiers.

New Hampshire Baptists set up an association of churches in

1776, and helped to sponsor a similar group among Baptist churches of Maine. In 1781 the Shaftsbury Association brought together a number of Baptist churches in southern Vermont, western Massachusetts and the eastern areas of New York state. In 1785 the Groton Conference was organized to serve many of the Baptist churches of Connecticut.

By 1795 there were enough Baptist churches in the vicinity of Otsego Lake, New York, to form an association. This organization proved to be a pioneer in what later became known as the Baptist Home Mission Society, for its member churches cooperated in raising funds to send the first missionary to preach to the Six Nations Indians of northern New York.

Ever westward flowed the tide of settlers. With them went Baptist families in increasing numbers. Into the great northwestern states and territories they went, these immigrants principally from New England, New York, and Pennsylvania. They settled in the foothills of the Alleghenies, in the fertile farmlands and along the streams of the Ohio and the Mississippi valleys.

Especially attractive to Baptist immigrants was the Northwest Territory, lying north of the Ohio River, west of Pennsylvania and extending to the Mississippi River. An act of Congress known as the "Ordinance of 1787" guaranteed complete religious liberty and gave promise of free public schools in all that vast region. Article III of the Ordinance began with these words:

"Religion, morality, and knowledge being necessary to good government and the happiness of mankind, schools and the means of education shall forever be encouraged."

In the area that became Ohio a band of twenty-five pioneers staked out their homesteads near the village of Columbia, now within the limits of Cincinnati. It was November 1788. Among them were two Baptists, Benjamin Stites, a Revolutionary major and recognized leader of the group, and John S. Gano, son of Dr. John Gano, the first Baptist pastor in New York City. In early 1790 came the Reverend Stephen Gano, another son of Pastor Gano. He helped the handful of Baptists who had settled at Columbia to organize their church, with the Reverend John Smith as the first pastor.

Smith was a popular leader in public affairs in the pioneer community, an eloquent orator who became United States senator.

Unfortunately, while in Washington he became associated with Aaron Burr and was involved in some of the schemes of this adventurer who barely missed defeating Thomas Jefferson for the presidency of the United States.

Cincinnati, with its land and water commerce, became the metropolis of the Northwest and also the center of Baptist activities and expansion. The Miami Association of Baptist Churches was organized in Cincinnati in June 1798. The first Baptist church in Illinois was organized in 1796 at a village with the picturesque name of New Design. One family among the founders of this church produced six Baptist preachers—James Lemen and his five sons.

Baptists were the first Protestant denomination to carry the gospel and organize churches west of the Mississippi River. The first such congregation was formed in 1795 at a settlement in Missouri on the trail between the villages of St. Louis and St. Charles. It was called Fee Fee Baptist Church, and has had a continuous existence from its beginning.

By 1800 there were several Baptist congregations worshiping in homes or in small meeting houses in settlements along the Mississippi and the Missouri rivers. In 1805 a group of about twelve Baptists organized a church at the community of Tywappity, eleven miles south of the French town of Cape Girardeau, Missouri. These earliest churches in the Louisiana Territory drew worshipers by wagons or horseback for miles around on meeting days —usually "oncet a month."

Plentiful as Blackberries

A study completed in 1900 by Baptist historian J. M. Carroll of Texas pictures the growth of the Baptists in the southern states during the last decade of the eighteenth century and the first ten or twelve years of the nineteenth. In Virginia, where Dr. Carroll declared "Baptists were as plentiful as blackberries," there were about 200 Baptist churches with 20,000 members in 1790. One decade later the numbers had grown to about 400 churches with 35,000 members.

Typical of the rugged pioneers who assembled the dissenters known as Baptists in humble homes or in groves of trees and organized them into congregations was Elder Joshua Morris. He preached in the numerous communities of the state, and one June evening in 1780 he conducted a prayer meeting in the home of John Franklin on Union Hill in Richmond. Thirteen other persons of Baptist leanings were present.

The house where the worshipers met for that service was like most of the homes of the common people of that day who became Baptists. It has been described as "a small wooden building containing a single room of scarcely more than sixteen or eighteen feet in dimensions, with a smaller shed-room attached on the eastern side, and a chimney in the middle."

In that small shelter, despite the threat of invasion by the British forces moving northward from the Carolinas, the fourteen worshipers organized themselves into the First Baptist Church of Richmond. When some members of the small congregation urged caution in view of the possibility the town might be captured, Parson Morris is reported to have said: "Brethren! Let us take care of our souls, and the Lord—with the help of General Washington—will take care of the British!"

Brother Morris' faith proved well founded. The British never took Richmond, and the First Baptist Church of Richmond grew to be honored as a leading congregation of Virginia and the nation.

Baptists experienced similar leadership and expansion in the Carolinas. Their leader in that area in the post-Revolutionary period was Richard Furman, whose name is honored in a university founded by Baptists in Greenville, South Carolina. Furman grew up on a large cotton and tobacco plantation, son of wealthy parents who became ardent Whigs and supporters of the Revolution. Richard was ordained to preach and held revival services in numerous communities of his state.

When the War for Independence broke upon the Carolinas, Furman volunteered to join the troops. Governor John Rutledge persuaded him to remain a civilian and propagandize the American cause among the Tory-minded planters of western South Carolina. The eloquent young Furman spoke one evening at the settlement of Waxhaw, and in his audience were Widow Jackson and her two sons, John and Andrew Jackson. The British overran Waxhaw and a Redcoat officer ordered Andrew to shine his boots. The spirited lad refused, and the officer gave him a slash with his sword that left a scar Andrew Jackson carried into the President's mansion and to his grave. Furman performed his task so well that the British general Lord Cornwallis posted a reward for his capture. In later years Furman became an outstanding leader in establishing a true denomination from the scattered and independent Baptist churches of America.

In Georgia the two great Baptist organizers of the pioneer era were the Reverend Henry Holcombe, who in 1800 organized the First Baptist Church of Savannah, and Dr. Jesse Mercer, a preacher and educator who founded a college at Penfield, that bears his name and was later moved to Macon. Principally from Georgia and Tennessee, the settlers pushed westward and southward into Alabama and Mississippi, where they set up their cotton plantations with slave labor.

South of the Ohio River, into the territories that became the states of Kentucky and Tennessee, the first settlers came mostly from the mountainous areas of Virginia and North Carolina. Then came the planters with their slaves, their predominant ethnic background Scotch-Irish and their religion strongly Calvinist. While Presbyterians were most numerous among pioneers before the Revolution, Baptists outstripped them in the first decade of the nineteenth century.

Occasionally in the migrations to Kentucky and Tennessee an entire congregation would decide to move at the same time, including the preacher, deacons, and the members old and young. They kept their worship going as they plodded westward, holding their prayer meetings, singing their hymns, and listening to the parson preach by the flickering light of their camp fires.

Sunday schools had their small beginnings near the turn of the century and grew to exert a powerful influence in the nationwide and worldwide Baptist fellowship. An example set in 1780 by a wealthy printer of Gloucester, England, was followed widely by Protestant churches in America. The printer was Robert Raikes, who, in a spirit of compassion for the dirty, ragged boys of the slums of his city, gathered several of them in his home on Sundays and gave them instruction in the Bible and the "three R's." A Baptist deacon, William Fox of England, expanded the movement in 1785 with an organization called "The Society for the Support and Encouragement of Sunday Schools." The first Sunday school in America was launched by three women of the First Baptist Church of Philadelphia in 1815, despite the protest of some leaders of their church who felt that the children would merely clutter up the house of worship.

Gradually, many Baptist ministers saw merit in the plan to teach religion to children meeting on Sunday in the churches and set up Bible classes. Often these preachers met the determined resistance of leaders of their congregations, who could find no scriptural basis for such goings on within the church walls. On the other hand, often the more liberal religious leaders decided that a Bible school for the young people was needed to instruct them in doctrine and morality. Thus many Bible classes were established despite the opposition of the pastors.

One factor stimulating the founding of Sunday schools in Baptist churches, as in the churches of other Protestant denominations, was the eagerness of children and youth, and for that matter of many adults, to hear something more than a steady diet of the dreary, long discourses delivered by most pastors to those early nineteenth-century congregations. The Sunday school brought Bible study down to the level of the immature and the uneducated, even when the minister himself was the only teacher.

The Frontier Communities

The fervor and intensity of the Great Awakening was never lost to the pioneer Baptist preachers and evangelists. "Seeking the lost" was their favorite theme. They preached it in their sermons and exhortations, in their Sunday services and in their "protracted meetings." They believed in a literal heaven and a literal hell, and they called men and women to repentance and faith in Jesus Christ with the principal aim to help the sinner to enjoy heaven and to avoid hell. As Dr. Nathan E. Wood expressed it in his discussion of the growth of Baptist theological thought:

"Preaching was azoic in its simplicity, literalness, and directness. Current philosophies appear to have had little influence on our preachers. French infidelity, whose brilliant reign in the United States during the last quarter of the Eighteenth and the first quarter of the Nineteenth centuries seems to have been a congenial sequel to the social and moral chaos incident to the Revolutionary War, was met by us not with intellectual subtleties or argument, but by a rigid application of biblical truth to the consciences of men . . . Sneers at morality, jests at religion, and the whirl of worldly pleasure were met by a 'thus saith the Lord,' or the thunders of a prophesied judgment."[6]

Such was the dedication of the pioneer Baptist preachers and missionaries who went west with the settlers that they endured the hardships and risked all the dangers about them. Many brought with them their brides of a few days or their wives of many years, who shared with their husbands the rugged life and work in the wilderness communities of the immigrants. They had faith in God and they were convinced that out on the frontier were people who needed the old-time religion. They had a message and they aimed to tell it. Their aim struck the hearts of the pioneer people, a people hungry for something that would bring hope and faith into their drab lives, something to lighten their loads of toil and to brighten the dismal boredom of the perpetual fight for existence against nature and the elements.

At the beginning of the nineteenth century most Baptist meeting houses in the cities and towns of the eastern states had progressed to neat structures of brick or white-painted wood. They usually had a bay window extension which partially surrounded the pulpit where the minister delivered his sermons. Many were heated by Franklin stoves, considered adequate since cold-natured members could move nearer for greater comfort.

The typical church building of the pioneer Baptist congregation, however, was a rude log structure about twenty by thirty feet, often with split-log benches with or without backs. A stick-and-mud fireplace when packed with seasoned logs provided heat during the cold season, and open windows permitted cooling breezes when the sun bore down. The meeting houses were usually built by volunteer labor of the men and boys of the congregations with only a boss carpenter to supervise the work. Women and girls of the families supplied and served the noon meal.

A center aisle in the meeting house divided the congregation so that the male worshipers sat on one side and the females on the other. Singers might be seated on benches to the right or left of the raised pulpit platform, but never with men and women on the same benches. In front and at the sides of the meeting house were hitching posts for the horses that brought in the worshipers, sometimes from as far as twenty miles away.

The Preacher Got a Dollar a Day

The preacher was "called" by the congregation, whose members decided his tenure and pay. He rode his own horse and brought his own Bible in his saddlebags—along with his nightshirt and little else. It was his due to be entertained by the members of the church, although it usually meant that he slept with one or more of the boys of the host family. Once-a-month preaching services allowed him to hold as many as four pastorates at one time although many were content with two. His pay was generally one dollar per meeting day—considered a fair wage and in keeping with the scale for a skilled worker. Many pioneer preachers, the most educated men of their communities, set up subscription schools to teach the children of their members to read and write, and to add to their meager incomes.

The frontier Baptist churches had no budgets, no finance committees, no literature to buy, practically no expenses and therefore no worry about them. If the church building needed repairs or paint, the men of the congregation supplied the need. Fuel could be had for gathering it in the clearing. Families took turns sweeping out the meeting house and keeping its grounds neat.

A cemetery was as much a part of the pioneer place of worship as the building itself. The burial place filled slowly with the mortal remains of the families within the fellowship—the aged, the infants and children who could not survive the rigors of frontier life, those in their prime who died from mysterious diseases supposed to be incurable—all those snatched away by the Grim Reaper. The cemetery became a tie that bound the worshipers all the closer in memories of the joys and sorrows of the departed ones.

Discipline was severely enforced in the pioneer Baptist churches. Hardly a scheduled business meeting convened but what some hapless member was mentioned by the elders as needing spiritual chastisement. It might be a deacon seen taking a hospitable dram, or a young man who, rumor had it, went to a square dance at an unbeliever's home and thus got into bad company.

From the minutes of the Forks of the Elkhorn Baptist Church in Kentucky, compiled from 1800 to 1820, Dr. Archie Robertson has gleaned these items in his work *That Old-Time Religion:*

"Bro. Blanton complains against Bro. Major for playing carnal plays. Bro. Edward Roberts is excluded from this church for playing fives and for offering to bet One Hundred Dollars. Mr. Asa Bolls Caty is Excluded for the sin of a Dultery. Sister Esther Boulware's Winney (a slave) was given a hearing on charges that since the Lord converted her, 'She had never believed that any Christians kept Negroes a slave, and that she believed There was thousands of White people wallowing in Hell for their treatment of Negroes and she did not care if there was as many more.' Winnie was excluded from that church."[7]

Never did the Baptist pioneer preachers and church leaders lose sight of the principle of freedom in church control, with each congregation, however few in numbers or humble in the social standing of its members, autonomous and free to select its pastor, ordain its deacons, admit new members, administer its discipline, care for its religious teaching and training, and co-operate with other congregations as its members might decide.

And never did they forget that freedom of conscience and worship was their cherished right, to be fought for without retreat or compromise.

IX

ADONIRAM JUDSON AND THE HEATHEN

Ten Small Churches

The people called Baptists emerged from the eighteenth century in America with some pronounced traits. They had a congenital fear of churches recognized by law as "established." In addition, they had a sense of independence that caused each congregation to assume total responsibility for itself and abhor any threat of hierarchy. Having severed all ties with mother countries where religious liberty was denied, the Baptists enjoyed a security in the new world that became self-centeredness. The prevailing Calvinist sentiment encouraged it.

Only ten small churches could be found in all of North America in 1700 that claimed to be Baptist. Their total membership was scarcely 300. By 1740, the number had grown to 60. By 1776, when the nation was born, the total number of Baptist churches had grown to 472.

In 1795, the census of the sixteen states and territories of the United States showed 1,152 Baptist churches, widely scattered and related only by name, except in a few cities where several churches formed a Baptist association or mission society.

A half century later, Baptists could boast 9,385 congregations with 720,046 members, led by 6,364 ordained ministers. During a period when the population increased 140 per cent, Baptists increased 360 per cent. What was even more remarkable, the churches were related to one another through a national body, with a foreign mission agency, a home mission agency, a monthly magazine, several weeklies, a publishing house—and a world outreach.

What happened during the early nineteenth century to induce a fanatically independent people to rationalize their fears of centralized church control and pool their spiritual and material resources?

The historian is forced to look for an event or episode which Baptists could clearly recognize as supernatural, for they called themselves the "people of the Book" with deep respect for the work of the Holy Spirit. It would have had to be revealed to them as their specific responsibility, for they would accept orders from no bishop or pope, synod or presbytery. Such an episode would have had to be dramatic enough to arrest attention and stimulate their faith. To do that, it would have had to be newsworthy, for the channels of communication in the early 1800s were few and small.

Meeting all these criteria was an event that took place in Calcutta, India, on September 6, 1812. It was the baptism by immersion of a young Congregational missionary, Adoniram Judson, Jr., and his wife, Ann, into the Baptist faith, the climax of a series of incidents involving several young Americans dedicated to the service of God among the heathen.

Two important influences induced Adoniram Judson to become a missionary. First, as a student at Andover Seminary he had a profound religious experience. It came from reading, and pondering long and thoughtfully, a sermon entitled *Star of the East* by Dr. Claudius Buchanan. The sermon was a call for volunteers to carry the Christian religion to the heathen peoples of Asia, and Judson became convinced that God was calling him.

Does the Lord Want to Convert the Heathen?

A second influence that impelled Judson to become a missionary was the news of an English Baptist, William Carey, a cobbler turned preacher, who was already in India and is known as the father of modern missions. Reports were trickling back to England, and then to America, that Carey and several other English missionaries were blazing a new and glorious pathway for the Christian message in the land being exploited by British traders. Where

Carey had gone, Judson could go, the earnest Andover Seminary student reasoned.

Adoniram Judson, Sr., was a Congregational minister, so Congregationalism was born and bred in Adoniram, Jr. Still he honored the courage of this British Baptist who was the first to volunteer as a Baptist foreign missionary. Church people of all denominations in America had heard the expression for which William Carey had become noted: "Expect great things from God; attempt great things for God."

As far back as 1784 the Nottinghamshire Baptist Association in England adopted a resolution setting apart an hour on the first Monday of each month "for extraordinary prayer for the revival of religion and for the extending of Christ's Kingdom in the world." During the following year a British ship's doctor, John Thomas, who had been on duty with his vessel as it plied between England and India, became impressed by the need for the spread of Christianity to Asia. Most of the people in the small colony of British subjects in Calcutta were professing Christians who persuaded Dr. Thomas to remain there and preach to them. William Carey heard of Thomas' efforts in behalf of this faraway group, and getting to India to spread the gospel became the fixed goal of his life.

Carey came to the meeting of the Nottinghamshire Baptist Association in the spring of 1791 with a manuscript which he called *An Inquiry into the Obligations of Christians to Use Means for the Conversion of the Heathen.* After a series of doctrinal sermons from the elders of the group, Carey took the floor to present his writing and to plead that at their convenience the delegates read it. Then he introduced a resolution that urged upon the preachers and congregations of the Association the responsibility to send the gospel to foreign lands, "that the heathen may know the saving grace of the risen Lord."

Carey's resolution blew up a heated debate. Some supported the young man in his plea for foreign missions; others vigorously opposed him. The voices of the opponents expressed clearly the doctrine of the Calvinists among these Baptists who took literally every scriptural reference to such words as "the elect" and "whom he did predestinate." They argued that it was little short of blasphemy to imply that the omniscient Creator did not already know those whom he would save, and therefore it was futile to try to influence that which had been decided from the beginning. The feeling of these Calvinists was well expressed by one of the elders who pointed a long, bony finger at Carey and shouted: "Sit down, young man! If the Lord wants to convert the heathen he'll do it without your help—or mine!"

On the other hand, there were ministers in that meeting who argued that Christ's admonition to "go into all the world and preach the gospel to every creature" meant he needed just such human instrumentalities as this William Carey to help accomplish his purpose.

So the debate went on with no decision on Carey's resolution. The best the young preacher could get was advice from his elders that he publish his *Inquiry* and thus make it available for general study. The group further agreed that William Carey should preach the annual sermon at the next meeting, set for May 1792.

Here was a fortunate break for the youthful shoemaker who wanted to devote his life to foreign missions. At the May meeting, with practically all the ministers of the Association present, Carey took for his text Isaiah 54:2–3: "Enlarge the place of thy tent, and let them stretch forth the curtains of thine habitations: spare not, lengthen thy cords, and strengthen thy stakes; for thou shalt break forth on the right hand and on the left; and thy seed shall inherit the Gentiles, and make the desolate cities to be inhabited." Carey poured out his heart in his plea for missions, stressing the theme that taking the gospel to heathen lands was both scriptural and a duty, and repeating several times the words "Expect great things from God; attempt great things for God."[1]

Carey sensed that his sermon was making a most favorable impression upon many in his audience, but in an agony of disappointment, he saw the meeting adjourn without any action taken on his plea. However, the seed he had planted took root, and on October 2, 1792, Carey's supporters met in the parlor of Mrs. Beeby Wallis and organized the "British Society for the Evangelization of the Heathen." A committee of five was named to get the work of the Society underway.

Looking for some handy receptacle in which to take up a collection to start their work, one of the group picked up their hostess' snuffbox. When he opened the box the men were astonished to find on the inner side of the lid a small scene of the conversion of Saul of Tarsus on the road to Damascus—as the Apostle Paul became the first foreign missionary.

"A good omen!" all agreed, and the sum of £13/25, chiefly pledges, was raised then and there.

The Baptist visitor to London who is quite persistent may see that priceless memento at 93 Gloucester Place, where the Baptist Missionary Society has its headquarters—a block from where Elizabeth Barrett Browning once lived. The snuffbox is stored in a safe, and only the executive has the key!

William Carey pledged to be the Society's first missionary. He had in mind asking to be sent to Tahiti. He had read tales of a pirate captain's visiting that tropical, romantic, isolated region, and assumed it would be a good place to spend his life as a Christian missionary. But Dr. Thomas, returned from India, wrote Carey that Tahiti was comparatively sparsely populated, and that India, with its teeming millions of pagan peoples, was the needier field. Carey agreed, and at a meeting of the society on January 9, 1793, both he and Dr. Thomas were appointed Baptist missionaries to India.

Carey's wife Dorothy flatly refused at first to leave England. Patiently her missionary husband convinced her that he was going to India for life, and he needed his family there. The powerful East India Company wanted no praying, psalm-singing parsons interfering with their business of exploiting the resources of the subcontinent, so officials of the government in London refused passports to missionaries. However, a Danish trading vessel gave them passage and in June 1793 Dr. Thomas, Mr. and Mrs. Carey and their five children, and Mrs. Carey's sister, sailed for Calcutta, arriving almost five months later.

During their first three years of service in India only £200 were sent from England for their support. Their financial hardships were sharpened by active opposition of the British traders and government officials. Carey could not make a living at his old trade where people wore only sandals. In 1800 he and his associates moved their tiny mission station to Serampore, a town thirteen miles up the river from Calcutta, under the protection of the government and flag of Denmark.

At Serampore, after seven years of missionary service in India, they won their first convert from Hinduism to Christianity. He was Krishna Pal, who had fallen on the river bank and dislocated his shoulder. He was brought to the mission station for treatment, remaining several weeks and professing what devout Hindus scornfully called the white visitors' religion, three days before Christmas, 1800. A mob formed, seized Pal and had him imprisoned. Carey secured his release and baptized him in the Hooghly River.

Slowly, patiently, Carey and his fellow missionaries won a band of converts and established a Christian church. Carey mastered numerous Indian languages, set up a printing plant, and translated the Bible into forty-two different languages of the people of that Asian land. When the new government college for training colonial administrative officers was opened, Carey was invited to join the faculty. The position gave him not only financial security but the chance to teach England's future officials his philosophy of humanity. Carey personally translated the governmental directive that put an end to *suttee,* the centuries' old custom of burning widows alive on their husband's funeral pyre.

In 1806, son Felix went to Burma, a land even more shrouded in heathen darkness than India, and set up a mission station at Rangoon. In the years following William Carey's slow and discouraging beginnings in India, several British Baptist volunteers for that mission field visited America en route to India. They were given a most cordial welcome by Baptist churches, families, and individuals, and they awakened an interest in foreign missions among their New World hosts. Also, they formed a link in the chain of correspondence between William Carey and the Baptists in America. Some of their letters and writings found their way into the *Massachusetts Baptist Missionary Magazine,* established in 1803, thus stimulating youthful readers to turn their eyes toward foreign lands. Most important of all for the cause of Christian missions under Baptist auspices, they sealed the dedication of Adoniram Judson's life to the cause of missions. He became convinced that American Christians should assume their share of the task of going into all the world with the gospel.

The Haystack Prayer Meeting

Two of Adoniram's fellow students at Williams College, Samuel Mills and James Richards, had dedicated their lives to foreign missions. With three other young men of the college these two had assembled in a maple grove one August afternoon to talk and pray about missions. A heavy rain came up and the five students took shelter under a haystack. While the rain came down, these earnest young men discussed and prayed about the need for missionaries to carry the gospel to heathen Asia. The "haystack prayer meeting" was remembered as an important day in their lives. At Andover, Mills and Richards led several other students in organizing a group they called The Brethren. Each member pledged to "hold himself in readiness to go on a mission when and where duty may call."

Adoniram Judson joined The Brethren at Andover. Encouraged by local pastors and seminary professors, he and three others of the group drew up a petition and presented it to the annual assembly of the Congregationalists of Massachusetts, meeting at Bradford. They offered themselves for service overseas, even though they heard some of their elders describe this as a wild, romantic undertaking.

At the Bradford Congregationalist convention the delegates and visitors were entertained in the spacious home of Deacon John Hasseltine. And it was there that Adoniram Judson met a vivacious, bright-eyed girl of sixteen, Ann Hasseltine, nicknamed Nancy by her family and friends. The youngest of five children in a well-to-do family, she was a student at Bradford Academy.

It was love at first sight for Adoniram, and with the determination that marked all his decisions, he resolved to marry Nancy Hasseltine.

No church in the United States had ever sponsored or supported a missionary on a foreign field. So Judson, still as determined as ever, appealed for help to the London Missionary Society. First he wrote a letter of inquiry in April 1810. Members of the Society were mildly interested, so Judson made the voyage to London to appeal in person for sponsorship for his plan to go to

India. The London Society gave him no assurance that the money could be provided.

Back in America, Judson renewed his plea before the Massachusetts Congregationalists. After much deliberation, debate, figuring the probable costs, and delay, the leaders of that church decided to take the historic step. They voted to set up an agency "for the support of missionaries to foreign parts," and named it the American Board of Commissioners for Foreign Missions. They appointed Adoniram Judson "to open a mission in some Asiatic field," along with three other men—Samuel Nott, Samuel Newell, and Gordon Hall. They fixed the salary of foreign missionaries at $666.66 per year for a married man, and $444.45 for a single man.

A fifth student suddenly applied for ordination with the others. He was Luther Rice, who lacked a year of finishing his schooling at the Seminary. Also, he planned to be married, but found to his sorrow that his sweetheart felt no call to go to India or any other foreign land. So Rice made quick arrangements for his academic credits, and offered himself, as a bachelor, for appointment. He was accepted by the Board, with the stipulation that he raise his own travel funds. Only six days before sailing time, in the depths of winter, Rice set out on horseback to visit churches and church friends. He came back with enough money for his one-way passage to India.

In the meantime Judson, though luckier with his choice of a bride, wrote a letter to her father:

"I have now to ask whether you can consent to part with your daughter early next spring, to see her no more in this world; whether you can consent to her departure for a heathen land, and her subjection to hardships and sufferings of a missionary life; whether you can consent to her exposure to the dangers of the ocean; to the fatal influence of the Southern climate of India; to every kind of want and distress; to degradation, insult, persecution, and perhaps a violent death."[2]

Go, Ye Heralds of Salvation

This youthful indulgence in melodrama proved to be an accurate prediction, but the suitor's honesty recommended him to Deacon

Hasseltine. On February 5, 1812, in the Hasseltine home, in the very room where Adoniram had first met Nancy, they were married by Dr. Jonathan Allen, pastor of the Bradford Congregational Church, and a man who had known Nancy and her sisters and brother all their lives.

Samuel Newell had in the meantime won the hand of another young woman, Harriet Atwood of Haverhill, a close friend of Nancy since their childhood. On the afternoon of the day Nancy was married, Parson Allen performed the wedding ceremony also for Newell and his bride Harriet. The two newlywed girls began eager preparations for their departure with their missionary husbands for faraway pagan lands.

Samuel Worcester, clerk of the committee sponsoring the appointees, was a good publicist. He spread the word in all the Massachusetts Congregational Churches and in newspapers, announcing the forthcoming ordination of the young volunteers. Typical was this notice in the *Salem Gazette* and the *Essex Register:*

"Next Thursday, February 6, by appointment of the Prudential Committee of the American Board of Commissioners for Foreign Missions, Messrs. Adoniram Judson, Samuel Newell, Samuel Nott, and Gordon Hall are to be set apart by a solemn ordination as Christian Missionaries to carry the Gospel of Salvation to the Heathen. The public exercises are to be holden at the Tabernacle in this town, and to commence at 11 o'clock A.M. A collection will be made on the occasion in aid of the Missionaries, which, to embrace a very unexpected opportunity for conveyance to India, is now fitting out with all possible dispatch."

As the news spread, public interest in the ordination service ran high. Numerous volunteers collected money to give to the missionaries, and by the day of the ordination the total had reached more than $2,000—swelling to a thousand more by sailing time. Salem Tabernacle Meeting House, a huge, barnlike structure seating about 2,000 people, was packed for the solemn ceremony of the church in the dedication of the young men. The congregation listened attentively to the words of Parson Allen's sermon:

"My dear children, you are now engaged in the best of causes. It is that cause for which Jesus the Son of God came into the world and suffered and died. You literally forsake father and mother, brothers and sisters, for the sake of Christ and the promotion of His Kingdom."[3]

When the five young men came forward and knelt in front of the altar of the Tabernacle for the laying on of hands, a dainty young woman fell to her knees beside Adoniram Judson. And thus Adoniram's bride of one day was consecrated along with him.

Many in the audience wept as they sang the final hymn, composed especially for the occasion by Parson Allen. Its first stanza ran:

> Go, Ye Heralds of Salvation,
>   Go and Preach in heathen lands.
> Publish loud to every nation,
>   What the Lord of Life commands.
> Go, Ye sisters, their Companions,
>   Soothe their cares, and wipe their tears,
> Angels shall in bright battalions
>   Guard your steps and calm your fears.

Faraway India, populous and "benighted," according to the faithful in America, seemed the logical Asiatic field for these eager young missionary volunteers. British traders had established foothold colonies in several areas of that land, and in true British tradition the armed forces of the developing Brittanic Empire had arrived to protect them. First commissioned in 1600 as The Governor and Company of Merchants of London Trading into the East Indies, it had come to be known as the East India Tea Company. It had spread its trade during the seventeenth century to include tea, spices, indigo, and many other products of this remote but financially profitable area. Overcoming the rivalry of the Portuguese and Dutch shippers, the British merchants, under guns of British ships of war, had gained supremacy in buying and selling the products of India. Surely, Judson and his eager associates in the missionary venture reasoned, they would be given good British protection.

On February 19, 1812, the newlyweds, Adoniram and Ann Judson, and Samuel and Harriet Newell, boarded the *Caravan* at Salem, Massachusetts, for the 114-day voyage that would take them across the Atlantic, around the tip of Africa, and northeastward to India. Two weeks later, Luther Rice and the two other ordained missionaries with their wives sailed on the *Harmony* from Philadelphia.

A Missionary Was Converted

On small sailing vessels, whose decks were crowded with chicken coops and pig pens to provide fresh meat for the voyage, the passengers had little space for exercise, though they had plenty of time for reading. Judson, an avid language student, resumed a translation of the Greek New Testament which he had begun at Andover. He began an intensive study of the Greek word for *baptize*.

The Board had given explicit instructions to baptize "credible believers and their households," and this worried the young minister. He knew that the basis of the Christianity he was to represent in Asia was the New Testament, but he decided that according to the gospels membership in a church was restricted to individuals who showed evidence of being followers of Christ. Baptism, he discovered, was always mentioned in connection with belief.

As the slow-sailing ship plowed its long journey across the Atlantic, around the Cape and into the Indian Ocean, Judson continued his thoughtful study of the New Testament. He could find no reference to the baptizing of infants, so his doubts increased as to the Congregational Church practice of sprinkling babies, and finally he confided to his wife: "Nancy, I am afraid the Baptists may be right!"

Ann reacted in fear at first. She realized that if they turned away from their Congregational sponsorship they might become just two Americans stranded in a foreign land, cut off from their families and their sources of income—and with a war about to begin between the United States and England. She could see all sorts of trouble for Adoniram and herself if he became a Baptist.

But Ann Judson was no coward. She joined her husband in the study of the New Testament and came to the same conclusions on baptism by immersion of believers as had he. Later she wrote in retrospect of her reluctance to change affiliation: "Baptists in America were yet a feeble folk. So peculiar were they regarded to be as a people that the hand of every other denomination was against them. Thus they were an object of contempt."

In the meantime the persistent William Carey had been allowed to set up a mission in Calcutta. Now, he and his English associates in that city had been notified that the Americans were coming. They agreed among themselves to raise no questions with these Congregationalists about denominational differences. Recruits for the mission field were too rare for the veterans to challenge the credentials of newcomers so long as they were Christians duly appointed by a mission society.

Thus there were cordial welcoming ceremonies. The new missionaries were given quarters in homes of the Baptist members of Carey's mission, and the Judsons made friends quickly and easily. In a few weeks Adoniram sought out Carey for a long talk. Soon afterward members of the mission were astonished when Adoniram and Ann Judson made formal request for baptism by immersion. On September 6, 1812, they were immersed in the baptistry of Carey's Calcutta Lal Bazar Chapel with the Reverend William Ward performing the ordinance. Thus the two recruits from America were voted into the fellowship of the Calcutta Baptist Church.

The second contingent of American missionaries landed safely and were given the same hearty reception. After the excitement of reunion Luther Rice, not knowing of his colleague's experience, asked Judson for some advice. He had done some intensive study of the New Testament during the voyage, he said, and was deeply concerned about the prevailing custom of baptizing infants.

"Just study your Greek New Testament," Judson advised. Eventually Rice declared that in all honesty he would have to adopt the Baptist position in regard to believer's baptism. Then Judson presented to him a copy of the sermon on baptism he himself had preached in Calcutta. Luther Rice requested immersion and followed the Judsons into the baptismal pool. In his diary he made this entry for November 1, 1812: "Was this day baptized in the name of the Holy Trinity. The Lord grant that I may ever find His name to be a strong tower to which I may continually resort and find safety."

Alone in India

The three Americans soon faced the consequences of their actions. Now they could not pretend to represent the Congregationalists. Judson wrote to Dr. Worcester a frank and full discussion of why he and Ann had become Baptists. He pled for an understanding of their plight. It was a difficult letter to write, and it was received by Worcester and his American Board for Foreign Missions with surprise and distress. Another letter, this one from Luther Rice, informed the Board that he too had become a Baptist.

The Judsons and Rice realized that Baptists in America had no foreign mission agency or money. The war with Great Britain had begun. It was disrupting shipping, and the mails were uncertain. The presence of the missionaries in India was challenged daily by the East India Company, acting as agents of the British Crown. Its officers harassed William Carey and his associates at every opportunity. Finally the Americans were ordered to return home by the first ship to sail, or to face deportation to England.

Watched daily by the police, the missionary group decided to go to Madras, a seaport city far to the south of Calcutta, and there to make plans to reach a new mission field. Samuel and Harriet Newell went on ahead by a sailing vessel whose master could take only the two passengers. En route, tossed by storms and drenched by cold rains, Harriet became very ill. On October 8, two days before her nineteenth birthday, she gave birth to a baby girl as she lay on the cabin floor with no one to attend her, except, as she wrote in her diary, "my dear Mr. Newell." The baby died on its fifth day of life. The Newells landed at Port Louis where after lingering for some days Harriet quietly passed away. Her grieving husband buried her near an evergreen tree in the local cemetery.

It was a disconsolate, discouraged quartet of would-be missionaries, the Judsons, Newell, and Rice, who were reunited at Port Louis on the Isle of France. A full year had gone by since they had left their homeland. They had been prevented from beginning the work for which they had pledged their lives. To complicate matters further, Rice's old stomach trouble, a bad liver ailment, which must have been an ulcer, was flaring up under the constant strain. Samuel Newell found passage to Bombay and served in a Congregational mission there until his death in 1821.

There seemed to be only one practical course of action left to the new Baptists. Rice would go back to America, regain his health, solicit funds to support a new Baptist mission somewhere in India, and then return. Rice agreed to the plan and did his best to revive the spirits of his discouraged companions. He promised to do all he could do to win support for their mission, wherever it might be.

The war had cut off all shipping to the United States, but Rice was lucky enough to find a ship, the *Donna Maria,* bound for San Salvador, Bahama Islands. From there he made his way to Boston as a chaplain on a small Portuguese freighter.

On to Burma

The turn of fate for the Judsons came when, at the Madras wharf one day, Adoniram discovered a Portuguese ship, the *Georgiana,* making ready to set out for Rangoon, Burma. He decided to consider that mission field. But all their newly made British friends in Madras warned them: "Stay away from Burma! It is a land of heat, poverty, disease, and the most unspeakable cruelties in the world!"

In addition, the Judsons were told, Burma was a land of impenetrable heathen darkness. It was ruled, they were informed, by an absolute despot, whose officials, in league with Buddhist leaders, were corrupt beyond imagination. And Buddhism had such hold on the minds of the people that its followers were not open to Christian truth in any form. However, Judson knew that the lone English Baptist, Felix Carey, was still laboring in Rangoon, and he wrote in his diary: "Dissuaded by all our friends at Madras, we commended ourselves to God, and embarked the 22nd of June."

The *Georgiana* was an old, creaking, smelly vessel. Ann Judson was more than eight months pregnant. During the torturous voyage she gave birth to her firstborn, a son. Like Harriet Newell, she was unattended except for her husband. The child never lived, and the tears of Ann and Adoniram Judson followed the tiny form beneath the waters of the Indian Ocean.

The *Georgiana* sailed up the Rangoon River and the Judsons saw for the first time the golden-domed Shwe Dagon pagoda, most venerated Buddhist shrine in Burma. They went ashore, surrounded by every possible proof in sights, sounds, and smells that here indeed was a land of poverty and strange, heathen beliefs—a land, they decided, where their Christian message was most needed.

The Judsons made their home with the Felix Careys for a time while both began the study of the difficult Burmese language. Hardly had they unpacked before an English businessman of Rangoon, a friend of the Carey family, told Judson earnestly:

"My dear young sir, let an older man advise you—and a man who knows his Burma. I know what I am talking about when I say to you, *go back to America!* Go back tonight. There's nothing here but heartache. These people have a fine, strong religion of their own. They'll resent you. And while they're the kindest, pleasantest people in the world they're also the most passionate and cruel. Go back while you're still a youth full of the fire of your faith!"

Adoniram Judson firmly replied: "Sir, my wife and I have come to stay!"[4]

Rangoon was a motley collection of mud huts, built mostly in a swamp except for the palaces occupied by the Viceroy, his numerous wives, and his favored officials. A few substantial buildings also housed the representatives of European governments and business concerns. For months, sheltered in the Felix Carey home, the Judsons studied the Burmese language and used every chance to learn the habits, customs, and religious beliefs of the Burmese people.

Felix' wife was the daughter of a Burmese mother and an English trader. The mother also lived with the Careys, and she and Mrs. Carey proved most helpful to the Judsons in their efforts to master the Asian language. Adoniram found a renegade Buddhist priest willing, for a price, to teach him the basic Burmese words. He was Maung Noo, and he helped Judson with his first efforts to construct a Burmese dictionary and grammar. Maung Noo was astonished when first asked to teach Ann also, for he clung to the accepted oriental idea that females were not capable of learning to read and write.

The Carey house, actually a small three-room bungalow, was outside the city walls of Rangoon on explicit orders of the Viceroy. Here was evidence of the low esteem in which officials in Burma held the white man from across the seas who came with a new religion. The Careys had accepted this condition as one of the sacrifices of being missionaries. The house was at the edge of the dump for the city's refuse, and the stench was heavy and constant.

Far more distressful for the Judsons was the fact that the house was also close to an open field used as the site for executing criminals. That could mean any person who had unwittingly offended the Viceroy or one of his numerous officials. The cries of victims, ignored by the passersby, became almost unendurable to the sensitive Americans: the screams of men and women being beaten to death with clubs, the muffled pleas of those being buried alive, the shrieks of those disemboweled and left in the blazing sun to be attacked by vultures while still alive.

The Judsons concluded that indeed Burma, a pagan land of unspeakable cruelties, badly needed the mercy, faith, hope, and love of the Christian religion.

Ann Judson took the courageous step of appealing directly to the Viceroy for permission to find a house inside the city walls. The Viceroy met her, wearing a long sword dangling from his girdle. Amused at this white woman's audacity, the all-powerful factotum granted Ann's request. In time the new Judson mission quarters were ready.

Good News from America

Meanwhile, Luther Rice had appeared before the American Board of Commissioners for Foreign Missions that had sponsored him and the Judsons, and in sorrow heard the expected words: "Brother Rice, you are no longer one of us!"

The Massachusetts Baptists received him cordially. News of the ready-made Baptist mission enterprise in Asia had reached America before Rice's return. Thomas Baldwin, a leading Baptist minister of Boston, had already organized a small group with the resounding name The Baptist Society for Propagating the Gospel in India and Foreign Parts. Money was coming in from congregations all over Massachusetts. The Society's members heartily endorsed Luther Rice's plan to travel about gathering donations for the cause.

So the volunteer missionary who had so easily raised his own passage money two years before now hit the trail on behalf of the Judsons in one of the most remarkable campaigns of money raising in religious history. At a meeting of Baptist leaders in Philadelphia in May 1814, Rice took part in the formation of the "General Missionary Convention of the Baptist Denomination in the United States of America, for Foreign Missions," which became known as the Triennial Convention. They voted to appoint Adoniram Judson as their Baptist missionary, adding that he should be informed of the appointment without delay.

Because the War of 1812 between the United States and Great Britain had stopped all mail to the Orient, it was sixteen months later, on September 5, 1815, the third anniversary of their joining the Baptist fellowship at Calcutta, that the Judsons received news of their new sponsorship and promise of support. On that day Judson entered in his journal:

"These accounts from my dear native land were so interesting as to banish from my mind all thought of study. This general movement among the Baptist churches in America is particularly encouraging as it affords an additional indication of God's merciful designs in favor of the poor heathen. It unites with all the Bible and Missionary societies in Europe and America serving the last twenty years, in furnishing abundant reason to hope that the dreadful darkness which has so long enveloped the earth, is about to flee away before the rising sun."

Heartened by the news that they were now bona fide Baptist missionaries, and that their loyal, energetic friend, Luther Rice, was traveling over the United States on their behalf, Adoniram and Ann Judson moved forward in their work of bringing the gospel to the people of Burma. Actually, Ann had not been officially made a missionary, for being a woman she could not be given that status of equality with her husband. It was sufficient for the members of the American board to know that she was there with her husband and would doubtless perform such tasks as he directed her to do.

Just five days after the good news from America arrived, Ann gave birth to a son whom they named for that Baptist champion of religious liberty, Roger Williams. Tropical fever claimed this infant's life when he was eight months old. The loss was almost too much for Ann and for weeks she went about as in a daze. Adoniram, driving himself unmercifully to complete his Burmese dictionary and grammar, suffered acute headaches. The Burmese diet of rice and curried chicken, or chicken in stewed cucumbers, three times a day, proved inadequate for the Americans, accustomed to milk, butter, meat, and green vegetables.

Good news came with the arrival of two more Baptist missionaries sent by the board created by the Triennial Convention, Mr. G. H. Hough and his wife, from Boston. Mr. Hough was selected in answer to Judson's plea that they find a printer. Dr. Carey sent a small printing press, with Burmese type, from Serampore. Now Judson's translations could be published. Mrs. Hough gave Ann Judson the sorely needed companionship of a woman of her own race and language.

"Every time I mention religion to anyone," Judson told his new associate, "he immediately asks for our 'holy books.' Now we can produce our own."

First to come from the press were two small books—the first ever printed in Burma: one about the meaning of Christianity, and a little question-and-answer pamphlet Ann had written for women. Then followed the translation of the Gospel of Matthew, and after that, Judson's pride and joy, the completed Burmese grammar.

After Six Years—the First Convert

The Judsons realized that their first converts would have to come from the common people who had learned to trust them and who believed that this strange white couple had come to Burma only to be helpful. Noting that the Buddhist priest had *Zayats,* or rest houses, on the roadways leading to their pagodas so that pilgrims could stop and discuss religion, Judson built such a house with a veranda near his home and often stood in the door inviting wayfarers to stop in. Very few did. Buddhism was the state religion. Heretics were cruelly punished. But Judson made careful note of those brave enough to visit the mission. This excerpt is typical:

"Moung Thahlah appears to be really earnest, in his desires to become a disciple of Christ. His sister Ma Baik, who was lately drawn into a high quarrel with a neighbour, expresses much sorrow, and says that the circumstance had convinced her more than ever, of the evil of her heart, and the necessity of getting a new nature."

It was not until Sunday, July 4, 1819, six whole years after their arrival in Burma, that the Judsons gained their first convert. He was faithful Maung Noo, their language teacher.

The third missionary sent from America was a physician, Dr. Jonathan Price. He urged the Judsons to take a furlough and visit the United States. Adoniram refused to consider the idea for himself, but agreed that Ann should make the trip. She told her husband and the mission good-by, and sailed for America via England, where she was overwhelmed with honors, meetings, and invitations to speak. That, however, was but a prologue to her reception in the United States. Her family and her old friends treated her almost with reverence. Churches were thronged with people who came to see and hear the first woman missionary among "the heathen." She made public appearances all over New England and as far south as Washington City.

One of Ann Judson's greatest joys on her visit home was to hear Luther Rice explain how the new Baptist denomination was being built around the missionary enterprise. To assure their friends that the mission was going well, she wrote a very readable booklet entitled *Account of the American Baptist Mission to the Burman Empire.*

When Ann Judson rejoined her husband in Rangoon, there were eighteen converts worshiping at the mission. Adoniram had translated the entire New Testament into *Pali,* the classical language of Burma. In Ann's absence he and Dr. Price had gone to Ava, capital of the empire, to confer with King Bagyidaw and to beg him to grant a greater degree of religious liberty to his subjects and to the American missionaries. The king had reacted favorably and had even invited Judson to move his mission to Ava. Soon after Ann's return they made the move, settling in a comfortable home.

Every moment that Adoniram could spare went into his careful translation of the Scripture into Burmese. Finally one part of the task was done—the entire New Testament in Burmese, written on foolscap paper and neatly stacked in a pile.

War in Burma

In May 1824 a blow of fate struck the missionaries in Burma. Tension had mounted steadily between the British and the Burmese rulers, and now it broke into war. Word reached Ava that British troops had captured Rangoon. That was the signal for the arrest and imprisonment of all the Englishmen at Burma's capital. In vain Judson pleaded that he and Dr. Price were not English, but American. For six months they and the other Caucasian men languished in prisons, most of the time in heavy irons, in filthy and vermin-infested cells, with barely enough food to keep them alive. Often their feet were drawn up so that only their shoulders touched the slimy floor.

Through those torturous months of the war Ann Judson brought food to her husband and his comrades in misery. With winsome tact the courageous woman made friends with the jailers when possible and even bribed them to make her husband's lot more endurable.

Fearing the loss of the manuscript of Adoniram's translation of the New Testament, Ann first wrapped it carefully and buried it in the mission yard. But she and her husband knew that the hot, moist soil would soon destroy it, so she dug up the bundle and after wrapping it in heavy paper and linen she placed it inside a pillow tick. On a visit to her prisoner husband she had Maung Noo bring the pillow with its precious contents and leave it in Adoniram's care. For weeks Judson slept with the manuscript under his head.

For about three weeks Ann's visits to the prison ceased. Then one day she came back bearing in her arms their baby girl, whom she had named Maria.

As superior British arms began to win the war, the Caucasian prisoners were hurried from one prison to another with no time to gather up their personal effects. In anguish of mind and spirit Judson realized that he had lost the pillow with his manuscript of the Burmese New Testament.

Again fate called the turn of events. Discussions leading to ending the war began at Ava, and someone thought of that American missionary who understood the Burmese language. Adoniram was brought out of prison, weak and emaciated, and, still under guard, he served as interpreter for the British and the Burmese officials.

This new status gave him liberty to see again his wife and some of their friends. One day the guards informed the American preacher that his wife had arrived—carrying a bundle. Ann thrust into his hands the pillow with the manuscript intact. Maung Noo had picked it up just after Judson had been hurried out of that first prison and had kept it close to him, thinking that his friend might want to keep the hard pillow. By this slim chance Judson's labor of years was saved.

Saw Judson Aung of Rangoon, graduate of Berea College, Kentucky, stated in a personal letter from Burma in 1979: "Judson's translation of the Burmese Bible is firmly in use today for the richness of the old King's Burmese and not necessarily because it is the most authentic. I like to compare it to the King James Version. After reading the several modern translations in English, I cannot point up any glaring errors in Judson's translation. A year ago we got 10,000 copies [of Judson's Bible] printed at the Government Press and many members of the state Legislature bought copies."

Back in Rangoon, the Judsons found their mission in ruins. Their faithful language teacher and several other converts had died of cholera. The missionaries built a new station some miles away, at a town the British had named Amherst, near the coast of the Bay of Bengal. Adoniram Judson, now known as Dr. Judson from his honorary degrees given *in absentia,* was called to Ava again as interpreter for the peace negotiators. While he was away Ann supervised the construction of their bamboo house and two schoolhouses.

Adoniram returned to find that cholera had struck down his wife. Ann's mortal remains had been laid away under the shade of a hopia tree. A few months later little Maria also fell victim to the fatal disease, and Judson watched sorrowfully as his associates, white and Burmese, dug another, and smaller, grave under the hopia tree.

X

LUTHER RICE AND COLUMBUS

Winning Support for the Judsons

Tall, dark-haired and dignified, every inch a debonair bachelor, exuding confidence and friendliness, Luther Rice set out to win support of Baptists for the Judson mission, which he presumed was still in India. He began his campaign, naturally enough, in his native Massachusetts, starting with the city that already considered itself the Hub of the Universe—Boston. He visited most of the Baptist congregations of the Bay State during the remainder of that autumn of 1813 and was successful from the first. Who could refuse a man with such graphic reports of what God had done for the Judsons and their prospects for a Baptist mission to the heathen?

"Go to the middle Atlantic and the Southern states," New England Baptist leaders urged. "Those churches will help the Judsons in their divine dilemma."

On horseback and by stagecoach, sometimes on foot, through rain and sunshine, snow and sleet, whatever the condition of the weather and the roads and trails, Rice visited Baptist churches and homes. Often he traveled all night to reach his destination and plunged at early morning into his rounds of visiting and speaking. He played a flute to keep himself company as he rode or walked along, and to amuse the children in the homes that had him as a guest. Wherever he went, individuals and audiences responded to the appeal for money to support the recently baptized missionaries in India. When Rice learned that the Judsons had gone to Burma he called their place of service the mission at Rangoon.

Women south and north, members of Female Mite Societies, were delighted to give this man of God a good supper and a night's rest, to sew on a button or launder a white shirt in exchange for the latest news of the Judsons. Children listened in rapture to the true story of Americans on the other side of the globe, a never-ending serial of which nobody knew the ending. Farmers and merchants, doctors and lawyers, Baptist ministers and laymen weighed the evidence of this series of events and yielded to Luther Rice's appeal to support what he called this God-given mission undertaking.

With his ready smile and lighthearted manner, Luther Rice made himself at home with Baptist families from Boston to Savannah. His hosts offered to this traveling missionary a stall for his horse, hot food, and a comfortable bed for himself, and the warmth of family fellowship. In exchange, Luther Rice told them of India and the Judsons, and of his own travels in America. Always before he went to bed he would join the family in worship.

A Baptist farmer of that day recalled an overnight visit of Luther Rice: "He prayed with all my family, and that prayer I shall never forget. Everyone in the house was named, and all the churches of the state, all ministries, schools, colleges, all mission stations and the missionaries—the city of Washington, all our cities, our nation, and the world."

No hardship could stop the travels of Luther Rice. A letter to his brother told of a typical experience:

"Being obliged to ride in the night, I got lost. The roads in this part of our country are none of them fenced, and are most through wood; I had to go that night in byroads but little traveled —missed the way, got out of roads, at length, into mere paths, and ultimately lost the path—found myself alone in a dreary wilderness, unable to discover the point of the compass . . . I stopped and besought the Lord to lead me out—rose from my supplications and attempted to advance. In less, perhaps, than two minutes, certainly in less than five, fell into the road which conducted me to the place that I calculated to reach that night, at which I arrived about one o'clock. Have now just come from attending Sandy Creek Association and am now on the way to Charleston."[1]

As Rice made his way to homes in the plantations of the South and the farmlands of the North; to the churches and associational meetings in hamlets and towns up and down the eastern states, he began to ponder this problem: No single congregation, and no single Baptist Association, could hope to support a missionary couple in Burma—or on any other foreign field; but the conscientious efforts and sacrifices of *all* the Baptists of America could sustain not only the Judsons but a worthy corps of missionaries in many stations, even to the uttermost parts of the earth.

The Baptists Unite

One day as Rice rode the stagecoach from Petersburg to Richmond, Virginia, on a road too broken and rutted to allow him to write in his diary or make notes for his next sermon, he sat wrapped in thought. As though, he declared later, it came from divine revelation, an idea struck him: Why not call a convention of Baptists to consider the formation of a nationwide organization? If the Congregationalists could do it, why not the Baptists? If representatives of Baptist churches strung out along the seaboard and along the western frontier once met together, they would feel a unity they had not dared depend on.

Luther Rice talked to the Baptists about this wherever they gathered to hear him. He wrote persuasive letters at the end of each day's journey. By the slow mail of that day and by personal visits Rice enlisted the help of men he knew would stand firm for such an organization. They included such Baptist luminaries as Dr. Richard Furman of Charleston, South Carolina; the Reverend Lucius Bolles of Salem, Massachusetts; and Dr. William B. Johnson of Savannah, Georgia. There was Dr. William Staughton of Philadelphia, who had come to America from England, one of the men who had attended the meeting in Widow Wallis' home in England when William Carey was appointed missionary to India and who had passed a snuffbox for the collection.

Furman and Johnson were especially helpful to Rice in calling the proposed conference. They spread the word among Baptist pastors and associational leaders from Richmond to Savannah, pleading for support for the project. Many others promised Rice that they would write letters urging Baptist leaders in all areas to be represented at the meeting and otherwise to use their influence to enlist a good group of those favorable to the idea of Baptist missions.

At Furman's suggestion the Philadelphia Baptist Association, oldest such organization in the country and most centrally located, issued the call for the conference. Dr. Henry Holcombe, pastor of the Philadelphia First Baptist Church, offered his meeting house as the place for the gathering. The date was set for May 18, 1814.

The call went out to Baptist missionary societies and associations all over the country. Each society, association, or other religious body pledging to contribute at least $100 a year to the work of the new convention was eligible to send two delegates. Distance and the expense of travel by stagecoach or horseback limited the number who assembled to thirty-three—seventeen of them from outside Philadelphia. All together they represented eleven states and the District of Columbia.

On that May morning in the Philadelphia church, the distinct pronunciations of the Yankees from Massachusetts, the so-called middle-staters, and those from the far South mingled in praise and prayer. Of course, Luther Rice was on hand, eager to see whether his idea would be adopted. Actually, he was determined to see that it was.

That Revolutionary War chaplain, noted theologian and scholar, Dr. Furman, was unanimously elected to preside over the conference. For regional balance Dr. Thomas Baldwin, pastor of the Second Baptist Church of Boston, who had given Rice such encouragement from the start, was named secretary. The group voted to organize The General Missionary Convention of the Baptist Denomination in the United States for Foreign Missions. The members decided to meet every three years.

"Then why not call it the Triennial Convention—for short?" Dr. Johnson suggested, and that proposal was adopted.

In the next step taken by the group, Luther Rice saw the complete success of his idea—the creation of a foreign missionary organization to represent all the Baptists of America willing to co-operate in the support of the Judsons and other foreign missionaries and to co-ordinate all such efforts in the future. The body was named The Baptist Board of Foreign Missions for the United States.

On May 24 the new Board held its first meeting, with Dr. Baldwin as chairman. For its recording secretary the Board elected Dr. William Staughton. With these details out of the way, Dr. Baldwin declared that resolutions were in order. The first motion warmly commended Luther Rice "for the success with which his labours have been crowned." The second resolution appointed Rice as a missionary under the new Board, with this significant wording: "Brother Luther Rice, with a view to excite the public mind more generally, to engage in missionary exertions, and to assist in organizing societies or institutions, for carrying the missionary design into execution."

"Brother President, I move the following resolution," announced Dr. Johnson. His resolution was entered in the minutes with this spelling and punctuation:

"On motion Resolved, That the Rev.d Adoniram Judson, now in India, be considered as a Missionary, under the care and direction of this Board; of which he shall be informed without delay: That provision be made for the support of him and his family accordingly: and that One thousand Dollars be transmitted to him by the first opportunity: That the Secretary of the Particular Baptist Society for Missions in England, be informed of this transaction: and that this Board has assumed the Pledge given by the Boston Mission Society, and to pay any Bills which may be drawn on them, in consequence of advances they may have made in favor of Mr. and Mrs. Judson."[2]

"Excite the Public More Generally!"

With keen disappointment Luther Rice heard read the resolution about himself. He saw at once its significance. The Baptist fathers starting the new missionary venture did not intend to lose the services of their best-known and most energetic spokesman. He would not be encouraged to go back to the Orient. He was needed right at home, to continue his travels and his money raising for missions. In fact, the group solemnly gave him the title General Agent of the Board, with a salary of eight dollars a week—two dollars more than skilled laborers could make at one dollar per day.

Dr. Holcombe, host pastor, rose to say they must be practical in money matters, and since Brother Rice had collected some funds for the mission enterprise it would be well to have a report from him. Brother Rice was ready. He had kept a strict account of every penny he had received for the Judson mission. He reported that he had $1,274.62½ on hand, and broke down the total into the amounts by states: South Carolina donors topped them all with $702.40½: Georgia $181.37½, Virginia $119.89¾, and so on. Rice even reported that a lady in South Carolina and another in Maryland each gave him a pair of gloves, and that a gentleman in Washington City donated a pair of badly needed shoes.

Rice then told of how two Negro slaves in Georgia gave him twenty-five cents for the cause. They had rowed him down the river, for hire, on one of his trips in that southernmost state. When Rice told them of the need for missions among the men of Asia they not only refused to take any pay, but they gave their passenger every cent they carried in their trousers.

When the meeting ended, members of the new board impressed upon Luther Rice that in order to "excite the public more generally" he would have to continue what he had been doing so effectively—visit Baptist leaders, families, church congregations, and associations, to tell the story of what he saw and heard in distant Asia and the big task ahead for the Judson mission.

Thus it was Luther Rice who was chiefly responsible for creating a denomination out of hundreds of autonomous Baptist churches scattered principally over the states of the Atlantic seaboard. Through his efforts, inspired by his imagination, persistence, and determination, Baptists of America were drawn together in a truly national organization. They kept their ideal of the independence of each congregation, but they added the aims and ideals, the plans and programs, the zest and enthusiasm, of nationwide co-operation.

The Judsons in the exotic country on the other side of the world furnished the impetus for the campaign. Rice furnished its power.

After the organization of the Triennial Convention, the Baptist crusader for missions discarded the stagecoach for a small one-horse wagon. Now he could come and go as he pleased, penetrating isolated rural areas to towns and communities that had never seen nor heard a preacher from outside their little world. He named his sturdy, faithful horse Columbus, after the man who set out for India and discovered America. In time he gave up the four-wheeled wagon for a two-wheeled cart, lighter and easier on Columbus as they jogged along over rocky, stumpy, or muddy roads.

Rice always carried a packet of Bibles and Testaments to dispose of at cost, or to give away to families who had never felt able to buy the Holy Book. He carried also copies of the *American Baptist Missionary Magazine,* and other publications such as back issues of the *Columbian Star*. Thus he became the first itinerant Baptist bookseller, or colporteur. Rice took along some packages of food, and he gathered nuts and berries in season as he found them along the roadside. He planned his journeying carefully, so that he could wind up a day's travel at a Baptist home. The host family had no warning that Brother Rice was coming until they heard the shrill sound of his flute.

The Most Preached-to Horse

One of Luther Rice's sympathetic biographers, Saxon Rowe Carver, presents this sidelight on his activities:

"Between stops, there were long, lonely miles to travel. Luther always had a sermon to get ready for the next place, for the people loved to hear him preach. He liked to study his Bible and knew much of it by heart. As he was often invited to the same place twice during a short while, he decided to preach his way through the New Testament. That way, he would almost never repeat a sermon. Driving along as fast as Columbus could make it, he planned exactly what he would say at the next church. Often he talked out loud. Columbus was likely the most preached-to horse in the United States."[3]

Luther Rice kept strict account of all money received for the mission cause, and made periodic reports to the General Convention. His entry for March 25, 1815, is typical:

"By my journal, it appears that I have travelled, since entering upon my thirty-third year, which closes this day, 7,800 miles, and, since leaving Philadelphia the 25th of last July, have received from various sources, and on various accounts, $3,629.44¼. As this amount has been mostly contributed for missionary purposes, the fact, and the amount, furnish gratifying proof of the progressive state of missionary views, impressions, and zeal among the

Baptists in the United States. May this cause advance with increasing vigor and success, till the world shall be full of the knowledge of the Lord."

At the second meeting of the Triennial Convention in May 1817, Luther Rice gave a glowing report of his work. As a result, the activities of the General Convention were expanded to include home missions, with Rice as the first agent. His salary was set at $400 a year. At the third meeting in 1820 the arrangement was changed with the General Convention continuing its control of foreign missions and the home mission work assumed by the Massachusetts Domestic Missionary Society under the direction of Rice's staunch friend and supporter, Dr. Jonathan Going. In 1832 the domestic mission work of the Baptist churches in America gave birth to an organization named the American Baptist Home Mission Society.

Rice left everywhere in the wake of his visits a spirit of unity and purpose for missions. Numerous Baptist missionary societies were organized by congregations that heard his message and felt the warmth of his enthusiasm. Ministers who had never before given the matter serious thought were prompted to preach sermons on the need to convert the heathen. Inspired by Rice's glowing accounts of Ann Judson's heroic service with her husband, the birth and death of each of her children, and how she looked to her sisters in every Baptist church in America to sustain her in prayer, women quickly organized "mite societies" and "female missionary societies"—this at a time when most Baptist pastors considered that women should be seen in a church, if they remained inconspicuous and decorous, but never heard.

Luther Rice clearly understood that for Baptists the local church was the strategic element for evangelizing a community, and consequently for making up an active unit of the denomination. When a pastor, the deacons, and the members generally accepted his vigorous plea for contributions and for future interest in missions at home and abroad, Rice counted that visit a success. And he seldom failed.

Perhaps Rice's greatest contribution to the new Baptist unity of effort was his turning the tide of sentiment away from Calvinist predestination and toward the ideal of offering the truth and the abundant life to every man, woman, and child in every community of the United States—and of the world. He combatted the anti-missionary forces with all his energy and eloquence. He convinced whole congregations, beset by teachings of Primitive Baptist ministers, that they should pray and give money to Christianize the people in foreign lands. Grey said of him at the celebration in 1964 of 150 years of the denomination's growth in America:

"It was what Luther Rice achieved as a promoter of high public sentiment which was translated into action among Baptists that gives him eminent place. He came upon the scene at a time when the denomination stood at the parting of the ways. He, more than any other single force, turned the masses of Baptists to the highways of progress."[4]

Colleges, Periodicals, and African Missionary Societies

The indefatigable ambassador to the Baptist churches took a personal interest in every project that he considered vital to the building and strengthening of the Baptist denomination. At a time when most rural Baptist ministers had little education beyond reading, writing, and ciphering, Rice led in establishing Columbian College in Washington City, later to become George Washington University, especially for training young Baptist men who felt called to preach. His influence was a major factor in founding at least ten other colleges, including four that remain to this day Baptist-oriented institutions of higher learning: These are Furman University, Greenville, South Carolina (1826); Georgetown College, Georgetown, Kentucky (1829); Richmond College, now the University of Richmond, Virginia (1832); Mercer University, Macon, Georgia (1833).

Rice realized the importance of creating a religious press to inform the members of the churches about denominational needs and progress. In 1816 he inaugurated a quarterly which he called *The Latter Day Luminary*. In 1822 he launched the *Columbian Star,* the first weekly news magazine to be published by Baptists in America. The *Star* eventually became the Georgia Baptist state paper, *The Christian Index. The Religious Herald* of Richmond, Virginia, was launched under Rice's sponsorship in 1826, and a complete file of this publication was once sent to Burma for the Judsons' enjoyment. *The Western Recorder* of Kentucky and *The*

Christian Watchman of Boston were also founded in the period of Rice's influence.

Luther Rice gave a definite impetus to the education of Negro leaders in the South. He stimulated the organization of "African Missionary Societies." From his efforts, there emerged into recognition one of the great Negro leaders of that period, Lott Cary of Richmond, Virginia. Raised as a slave, Cary bought his freedom. Eloquent and dedicated, he had become known and respected as pastor of a Negro church in his city. On Rice's recommendation this former slave was sent by the General Convention as a missionary to Monrovia, capital of Liberia, where he founded a colony of Christians.

The Letters from Rangoon

Caught up in the need to keep working in the United States, Luther Rice was forced to postpone his return to the foreign field. But the correspondence between the Judsons and their closest American friend reveals their partnership to the end. From Rangoon on February 6, 1833, Judson wrote:

"I have received your two short, and almost illegible letters of last March, and it is hardly necessary for me to say how fully I enter into all your views and wishes in regard to the new college, and whatever tends to raise the character of the Baptist denomination, and promote the cause of Christ at large, in the United States. Your labours will be ultimately appreciated, and the page of history will do you ample justice, notwithstanding the dissentient voice of the narrow-minded of the present day . . . I wished that we might live and labor together; but I hope that, though separated, we are both doing important service for the same Master, and perhaps, in ways best adapted to our respective capacities."[5]

Several horses served in succession to the original Columbus, but Rice kept the two-wheel gig. His horse and cart became his trademark as he pulled into a community, doffing his stovepipe hat, bowing pleasantly to one and all, and seeking out the Baptist leaders.

Rice's only vacations were the short days he might spend at his home town of Northborough, Massachusetts, among his relatives and boyhood friends. True to the love he always felt for the young woman who refused to marry him and go with him to foreign lands, Luther remained a bachelor. He resisted all temptations to ask for the hand of any of the countless eligible females whom he met almost daily on his travels and who would gladly have shared his work and hardships. He gave back to the causes he sponsored almost all the small salary paid him. To meet the needs of the struggling Columbian College in 1826, he paid over all his small savings, along with some $3,000 he inherited as a patrimony. He then had to acknowledge that he was "without a cent in the world."

Luther Rice was a chief source of information about the Judsons for all the Baptists, and others interested in foreign missions, in America. In sorrow he received from Adoniram the accounts of the passing of Nancy and little Maria. He passed on to the missionary and mite societies the story of how the Judsons' close friends, George and Sarah Boardman, missionaries from Massachusetts like the Judsons, had befriended Adoniram after his loss of wife and child. After George Boardman died there was Rice's story of the romance between Adoniram and widow Sarah Boardman, and their marriage.

Judson Remarried

Baptists learned that Sarah, like Ann Judson before her, was well educated, articulate, and poetic. After she became Mrs. Judson, Sarah contributed her part to the saga of missions in the Far East with poems, widely used in publications for churches and religious groups in America. Two children were born to Adoniram and Sarah before her death in 1840.

Luther Rice did not live to greet his hero Adoniram Judson when the missionary from Burma made his only trip home to the United States in 1845, but Rice had prepared the way for the unprecedented reception given any visiting missionary by the American people to that day. Judson later wrote that his chief worry as the ship sailed into Boston's harbor was how to look for a place to sleep after thirty-two years' absence. He was totally unprepared for the tumultuous welcome at the dock. A hundred homes were opened to him. He was entertained at Brown University and heard President Francis Wayland's eulogy:

"You went forth amid the sneers of the thoughtless . . . You return to your native land, and you find that the missionary enterprise has kindled a flame that can never be quenched in the heart of the universal church. Every Christian and every philanthropist comes forward to tender you the homage due to a man through whose sufferings, labors, and examples these changes have, to so great a degree, been effected."[6]

In Philadelphia at the home of a friend Dr. Judson met an attractive young woman, Emily Chubbuck, who was writing a frivolous sort of column for a local newspaper under the pen name of Fanny Forrester. Rather abruptly Adoniram asked her to be his wife. Many of Emily's friends tried to dissuade her from accepting the noted missionary's proposal because of the difference in their ages and, perhaps of a more serious nature, the apparent fact that Judson had spells of moody melancholy and was often irritable. Some of Emily's friends declared that she was allowing herself to be swept off her feet by a glamorous hero. But Emily had a mind of her own.

Whether Fanny Forrester's devotees considered she was throwing herself away or entering into an exalted career, they faithfully followed her to Rangoon and back in her sprightly reports. With skill born of practice, Emily C. Judson described the events at the mission in Burma with a flavor that made her writings excellent reading, and Americans who had no church connection and only contempt for foreign missions became interested. Emily convinced them that her husband's work was supremely important. One commentator said of her: "The Christian world gained much, the literary world lost nothing, when Fanny Forrester became a missionary."

It was Emily Chubbuck Judson who sent back the account of Adoniram's death and burial. She told of taking him on board a French ship for a voyage, hoping to improve his health, and how his life ebbed away near the Andaman Islands. Judson's burial was related by his best biographer, Courtney Anderson, in these words:

"At fifteen minutes after four on Friday afternoon, April 12, 1850, Adoniram Judson reached his Golden Shore . . . That evening at eight the *Aristide Marie* hove to. The crew assembled silently. The larboard port was opened. There were no prayers, except those silent ones in the hearts of the living. The captain gave an order. The coffin slipped through the port into the night."[7]

Luther Rice had gone on before Judson. Traveling through South Carolina on a fund-raising tour for the college in September 1836, Rice fell gravely ill. Informed that his condition was critical, he requested that his horse, the cart, and his baggage—his entire worldly estate—be given to Columbian College. His remains were laid to rest at Pine Pleasant Baptist Church near Saluda.

It is likely that Luther Rice never realized the importance of the creation of a denomination from its scattered and previously isolated congregations. But already Baptists in all communities of America were saying that without the Judsons the work of Luther Rice would not have found its inspiration, and without Rice the Judsons could not have accomplished their work in Burma nor blazed the trail for Baptist foreign missions around the world. And it was President Francis Wayland of Brown University who later said of both Judson and Rice:[8]

"We knew nothing of our numbers, and were scarcely aware in all points of the doctrinal sentiments embraced by the churches in different parts of our country. Ignorant of our strength, and unaware of the reliance which we could place on each other, we were unprepared to attempt any important enterprise, for we knew not who could be relied on to carry it forward. The change of sentiment in Messrs. Judson and Rice was just the event which was required to awaken the dormant energies of the Baptists in America."

What of Burma Today?

According to *The American Baptist,* in its May and June issues, 1978, the Burma Baptist Convention reported 340,176 baptized believers in 2,735 congregations. At the 107th general meeting of the Convention, 1977, the peak attendance was 15,000 registered delegates, in spite of the fact the place of meeting was in the remote Chin state and difficult to reach.

Most dramatic event of the year was the centennial celebration of Baptist missions among the Kachin hills people—"the equal of any Billy Graham crusade in size, organization, and spiritual experience," according to one eyewitness.

This secluded area, forty miles from the China border, not less than six hundred miles from Rangoon, was penetrated first by an American Baptist missionary, Josiah N. Cushing, and a Baptist teacher from the Karen tribe. Its people got the brunt of World War II battles and now suffer economic and political limitations.

To celebrate a hundred years of the Christian faith in that territory, the leaders of the Kachin Baptists planned for a full year to welcome fellow Baptists to Nawng Nang, ten miles from Myitkyina, December 21 to 25, 1977. Fifty thousand were expected, but 73,421 actually registered attendance and at least 25,000 more were present. The campus of the Baptist Seminary was the convention site.

Opening with the traditional Kachin processional dance in which several thousand, dressed in silver-decorated costumes, took part, the procession was headed by a ninety-four-year-old pastor who had assisted the pioneer American in his Bible translation half a century earlier.

On Christmas Eve a baptismal service was held. One hundred Kachin pastors moved into the Irrawaddy River, while the 6,215 candidates for baptism formed a hundred lines leading to the riverbank, and tens of thousands of delegates looked on. Prayerfully, each convert was immersed.

On Christmas Day a memorable communion service was held from 11 A.M. to 3 P.M. Individual communion cups made of green bamboo became souvenirs of the event.

The logistics of this convention, in a country where nobody can purchase a cake of soap or a tube of toothpaste, aspirin or film, was impressive. The Kachins as host accepted their full responsibility in providing food and shelter. The simple tabernacle constructed for 15,000 proved too small. One hundred long sleeping shelters were not enough. Yet the crowds were made comfortable. Food was ample: The various associations provided buffalo, cattle, hogs, and chickens, a total of 5,000 baskets of rice, and bags of salt, various spices and seasonings, plus abundant supplies of firewood for the cook fires.

Music by the official choir of 3,000 voices was matched by the singing of 2,000 Lisu tribespeople, and several other choirs participated. A challenge to young people to be missionaries, issued the year before the celebration, resulted in the "Gideon's Band" of

600 volunteers—twice the goal—who would give themselves to evangelism in strange areas for three years without pay.

Only one disappointment marred the well-planned celebration. The Socialist Republic of the Union of Burma denied repeated formal requests for permission to receive foreign visitors and fellow Baptists from abroad to attend the celebration. The Judsons and the Cushings were there, without a doubt, in spirit!

XI

PECK AND THE WESTWARD EXPANSION

The Hungry Visiting Preacher

In a June day in 1815 Luther Rice was preaching under a grove of trees in a community of the Catskill Mountains in New York State. The occasion was a meeting of the Warwick Baptist Association. Rice made his usual fervent appeal to support the work of the Board for Foreign Missions. At the close of the service a robust young man came up to shake his hand, and to say:

"Brother Rice, I am John Mason Peck. I am pastor of a Baptist church at Amenia, not far from here. My wife Sally and I would like so much to put you up for the night. I want to talk with you."

Rice accepted the invitation and followed Peck to his home. Sally Peck served the hungry visiting preacher a big meal. After some talk about missions in general, Peck declared he wanted to be a missionary, but he thought he should work in the homeland. Rice responded that the Triennial Convention had only foreign missions in mind, but there would be another meeting of the Convention two years later so Peck might put his plan to volunteer for mission work before that body. Meantime, said Rice, his young host could improve his schooling by studying English, geography, and history, taking up Greek and Latin later on.

The visit of Luther Rice to this rural Baptist minister's place began the home missionary travels of a man who rivaled Rice in his determination and zeal to spread the gospel, a man who literally explored the West of his day for the Christian cause.

John Mason Peck was born October 31, 1789, on a farm near

Litchfield, Connecticut, in the same county that produced the noted preacher Lyman Beecher, his son Henry Ward Beecher, and daughter Harriet Beecher Stowe, whose pen would write the anti-slavery novel *Uncle Tom's Cabin*. John Peck's father was a veteran of the War for Independence with little schooling and little interest in affairs of the Congregational church of which he nominally was a member. But in December 1807 his son John attended a revival meeting at Litchfield and was converted. He joined the Litchfield Congregational Church, and in that congregation he met Sarah Paine, known all her life as Sally. On May 8, 1809, John Mason Peck and Sally were married and moved to a farm near Windham, New York.

In the fall of 1810 they decided that the Baptists were right about believer's baptism, and they were immersed into the fellowship of a little Baptist congregation at New Durham, five miles from their home. Young Peck indicated to this congregation that he would like to preach, and the members were quite agreeable. They voted that he should "improve his gift," a way of saying that the church would be glad to ordain him if he proved he really had a talent for preaching. Peck preached his first sermon from the text "Go ye into all the world and preach the gospel to every creature," and gained experience by "filling the pulpit" of the Catskill Baptist Church. On June 9, 1813, he was ordained by that church. During four years of preaching for the Catskill congregation Peck delivered 174 sermons and was paid $43.03 in donations. He and Sally with their infant son moved to Catskill, where he eked out a living by teaching a subscription school in his home, instructing in the three R's a few children of the town whose parents could afford to pay the small fee.

Late in 1813 Peck was called to be pastor of the Baptist church of Amenia, in Dutchess County, New York, with enough pay that he could give his whole time to the pastorate and to his own education. He became a private student of the principal of the Dutchess Academy of Poughkeepsie. And Luther Rice found him at that meeting of the Warwick Baptist Association near Amenia.

The Western Mission

Peck took Rice's advice about improving his education by studying for several months in Philadelphia at the seminary conducted by William Staughton. In the summer of 1816 he traveled for the Massachusetts Missionary Society among the Baptist churches of western New York. In January 1817 he helped to organize the "American Baptist Society for the Propagation of the Gospel," at Great Valley, Pennsylvania. At the second meeting of the Triennial Convention in Philadelphia in May 1817 Peck volunteered for full-time missionary work wherever he might be needed. Another volunteer, James E. Welch, stood with him. The two preachers were formally set apart to begin the work of what was named the Western Mission.

In their instructions the two men were told that the Board wanted them to start their work at St. Louis or its vicinity and to establish "a school or schools" in that region. At that time there were only about eight Baptist churches in all the Missouri and the Arkansas territories, with a membership estimated at approximately 200. The Board's instructions to the new missionaries further read:

"They wish you also to collect such scattered brethren through districts of the country, as you may be able, and to encourage and assist their formation into regular churches of Christ. It is not improbable that from such brethren and churches, men of God may be found who will rejoice to become your associates in the work before you. The Board is particularly desirous that the Fox, the Osage, the Kansas and other tribes of Indians should engage your particular zeal. In proportion as the Lord shall confirm the capacity of the Board, and as brethren shall be found willing to become adjutors, they will be happy in enlarging the number of Western laborers. . . ."

The Board urged the missionaries to exercise a strict frugality—hardly a necessary warning in view of the pittance they were to be paid. The missionaries were "to collect what you can from the friends of Zion, for the support of Missions and let an account of your receipts and expenditures be prepared in time for insertion in our annual Report."

"We pray that you may abound in personal and domestic religion," the Board admonished. "Your example will speak with a voice as distinct and instructive as your public ministrations."[1]

Peck loaded his wife and their three children, along with some basic household goods, in a one-horse wagon, and on July 25,

1817, set out for the Great West. They made it to Philadelphia in ten days. Then slowly, over trails of rocks, mud, and far stretches of wilderness, they plodded on. In late October they crossed the Ohio River into Kentucky then to Lexington where Welch and his family were waiting for them. On Friday, November 7, they crossed the Ohio again into Shawneetown, Illinois, and on the next day Peck entered in his journal: "I never saw a place more destitute of religious instruction."

When the Peck and Welch missionary caravan was ferried over the Mississippi River and came to a halt in St. Louis on December first, Peck saw a place even more destitute. St. Louis was a rough, tough river town, a cluster of brick business houses facing the muddy river and extending up the slope from the wharves. There were crude houses of brick or wood for the shopkeepers and traders. Missouri had not yet become a state, its territory carved from the Great Louisiana Purchase made by President Jefferson only fourteen years before.

Roaring St. Louis

The background of St. Louis was French, with the Choteau family predominant in the leading industry, fur trading. The streets were seas of sticky mud. The settlers of the town were for the most part hard-drinking, hard-fighting, uncouth, and uneducated frontiersmen. Saloons abounded, and drunken knifings and killings were commonplace. The French Catholics had brought in what little religion there was, except for a small handful of settlers, mostly the farmers, still willing to admit a Protestant background, for the most part Congregational or Presbyterian. The Reverend James Smith had been the first Baptist minister to set foot on Illinois soil, and in the spring of 1796 had organized the first Protestant congregation in that state at New Design, some hundred miles from St. Louis. So Peck and Welch found few "friends of Zion" to help start their work in the St. Louis region.

Before the December of their arrival had passed, the two home missionaries opened a school, spreading the news by word of mouth that either children or adults could come and learn to read, write, and cipher. On Wednesday evenings and on Sundays, religious meetings were held in the schoolroom. By the following

February, nine Baptists among the pupils had been attracted to the school, old and young; and with their own families to augment the number, Peck and Welch organized the First Baptist Church of St. Louis.

John Mason Peck had a penchant for organization. On March first, when the congregation was barely three weeks old, he organized the members hopefully into the Western Baptist Mission Society, instructing them that they were to help him raise money to spread the gospel. Under the spell of Peck's crusading enthusiasm, the small group raised $3,000—much of it from fur traders and saloon keepers who felt that a Protestant church in the heart of their roistering business district might be a good thing. With $600 of the money the congregation bought a lot forty by sixty feet, on the corner of Third and Market streets, and the rest was almost enough to build a small place of worship, complete with diminutive steeple and bell. The roots of Baptist home mission work in the West were taking hold.

Peck's next organizing venture was a school for Negroes, held in the church house in the evenings—certainly the first night school for colored people, slave or free, west of the Alleghenies. About a hundred came to the night classes, men and boys, eager to learn to read and write. For this action Peck and Welch were harassed by the town authorities, who threatened them with imprisonment for interfering with the property of their neighbors, since some of the Negroes were slaves.

On the first Sunday of April came a triumphant event in the story of Western Home Missions—the first baptizing. Peck led two white men, his first converts, into the muddy waters of the Mississippi. The banks of the river were thronged with spectators. One small group comprised the congregation of the church, while massed behind were hundreds of the curious, some scoffing, others reverent. Peck recorded that among the crowd were two Presbyterian ministers, and many Catholics—including two priests.

In a letter to the Board dated St. Louis June 15, 1818, and published in the *American Baptist Magazine,* Peck told of enlarging the school, with its new name, Western Mission Academy. He related:

"This institution at present consists of three departments, which we intend to increase and to extend into the country and to more distant villages. The first department embraces those scholars who pay for their tuition, and contains at present about forty, of which five are the children of Catholics. The second department is a free school limited at present to ten scholars, all except one the children of French Catholics, and who without this means would grow up in vice and without useful knowledge. The third department is our African Sunday school. Were I to speak only of the advantages of learning to read, and the temporal good of this unhappy race, with the progress that some have made, much might be said. From the first beginning we let it be known that religious instruction would be our primary object. . . ."[2]

The authorities were not at all happy about this Sunday school, and sharply reminded Peck and his associates that they had better study "the 7th Section of an Act for the Regulation of Slaves, and leave it to yourselves to decide, whether or not you have incurred heavy penalties by your Negro school." The missionaries were further asked to reflect on "whether it is prudent and humane to give instruction to those who must be made by it either more miserable or rebellious." The two transplanted Yankees could see nothing in a little literacy to make even a Negro slave more miserable or rebellious, so they sent a polite answer to the St. Louis town officials and kept on with their Negro Sunday school.

The immediate years ahead were filled with the expanding activities of John Mason Peck. Leaving Welch in charge of the St. Louis school, he visited communities far and wide, in both Missouri and Illinois, to hunt up Baptist families among the settlers and incoming immigrants, and to organize them into small, struggling congregations. He went as far south as Cape Girardeau where Bethel Baptist Association had been formed of five Baptist churches. He went up and down the Illinois side of the big Mississippi, meeting with Baptist families to preach in their homes and to organize congregations.

Peck had a long visit with the intrepid frontiersman Daniel Boone, who had come in from Kentucky and who urged this Baptist preacher to use his talent for writing to bring in more and more settlers to the Mississippi Valley country. Peck raised money to set up the St. Charles Academy, across the Missouri River north of St. Louis. In April 1819 he moved his family to St. Charles, living in a small wooden home near the new school building and campus. From there he extended his work to the Indian tribes along the Missouri River and reported to the Board:

"Every season, a number of the citizens of this village proceed up the Missouri from 800 to 2000 miles, and spend seven or eight months with the Indians, learn their language, etc., and all for a few paltry Beaver skins or Buffalo hides. And shall a Christian missionary refuse to submit to like inconvenience, for the sake of immortal souls and the glory of God?"[3]

Objections from the "Hardshells"

In July 1820 came the blow that might have utterly discouraged anyone of weaker fiber and faith than John Mason Peck. Members of the Board decided they could no longer raise the money to support the Western Mission—despite the fact that Peck and Welch were raising most of the funds for its activities. One reason given was the hope that increasing immigration would supply all the Baptist preachers needed on that frontier. Back of this and other excuses was a reason of greater significance—and of potential danger for the frontier work. It was the growing opposition of the "hardshells"—the leaders of anti-mission sentiment among the very Baptist immigrants the Board hoped might carry on the extension activities. Peck's inclination to branch out into too many projects—schools, Indians, and new societies—may have influenced the Board to withdraw support. Officially it suggested that some sponsorship would be continued if Welch would remain at St. Louis and Peck would go to Fort Wayne, Indiana, and work among the Indians.

Welch stayed, but Peck refused to go to Fort Wayne. He turned his eyes toward the state of Illinois, which became his field for the rest of his long life. He convinced the Massachusetts Baptist Missionary Society that they needed him in Illinois. In March 1822 this organization appointed him "agent and missionary," at a salary of five dollars a week. Peck moved to Rock Springs in St. Clair County and soon had a thriving congregation organized. He made fast friends with the Baptist leaders at New Design, where the first Baptist church of the state was founded, especially with the five sons of the Reverend James Lemen, one of whom, James Lemen, Jr., also was an ordained Baptist minister. In the spring of

1823 Peck made a twenty-day tour to meet Baptist pastors and leaders in various communities of Illinois and Indiana. His boundless enthusiasm for the Baptist cause and his constant travels spread his fame as a preacher and revivalist.

John Mason Peck found time in his busy life of organizing Baptist churches, speaking at Baptist conventions, raising money for his schools, and otherwise serving as the leading home missionary of his denomination in the West, to hoist the banner against legalizing any further introduction of slavery into Illinois.

When Illinois became a state in 1818 its constitution prohibited importation of slaves. However, a majority of the members of the State Legislature in sessions of 1819 and 1821 were pro-slavery in sentiment. In the latter session they passed an act calling for the citizens to vote whether a convention should be held to change the constitutional provision prohibiting the bringing in of slaves. The date for voting on the matter was set for August 2, 1824.

Here was a battle to Peck's liking. He plunged into the contest with his voice, his pen, and his organizing ability. He assembled meetings of citizens at Belleville, his home county seat, and at neighboring towns, and organized the Society for the Prevention of Slavery in the State of Illinois. All over the Prairie State Elder Peck distributed a call for the organization of similar groups to oppose the convention. He issued a stream of pamphlets pleading for citizens to vote against the proposal. He traveled from town to town speaking on the evils that would follow if Illinois became a slave state.

Newspapers of that day were largely political organs, and they divided sharply on the issue—and on the Baptist crusader. The pro-slavery papers castigated him as a meddler in a political matter with which the church should not be concerned. Peck answered that slavery involved a moral principle, and—far ahead of his time —that his church and denomination had an obligation to speak up.

A total of 11,612 votes were cast in the special election, with 4,972 votes for changing the constitution and 6,640 against. Matthew Lawrence, in his biography of Elder Peck, asserts:

"The victory was great indeed. What the result would have been had the other side won and Illinois become a slave state can only be conjectured. Probably the entire Northwest would have followed her example and the whole history of the nation would have been changed. Surely the men who won this victory, and Peck as one of the chief among them, deserve first rank among the heroes of Illinois history."[4]

A School for Preachers

John Mason Peck caught a vision of what education would do for Baptist ministers, and for their churches, and set his boundless energy to the task of establishing a school especially to train young men who felt called to preach. It would be a true institution of higher learning. He planned to invite ministerial students to his school from three states—Missouri, Illinois, and Indiana. He would give them two years of intensive instruction in English, Latin, Greek, theology, and elocution—the latter a stilted form of public speaking that involved what was considered to be the right posture, use of the voice, and appropriate gestures. He would send the graduates back to their home communities equipped to be real circuit riders for the growing numbers of Baptist congregations.

Peck knew he would require more money for the project than he could raise locally, so on February 22, 1826, he set out for the East—his first trip back after leaving eight years before. In Washington he dropped by the big President's House to see his old Massachusetts friend, John Quincy Adams, for whom the Pecks had named their oldest son, and gave that distinguished Yankee a bright report on the great opportunities for settlers in Illinois. He clasped hands again with the man who had started him on his missionary career, Luther Rice, and told him of the hopes and aims he held for the proposed school. He attended the Triennial Baptist Convention in New York and appeared at meetings of various organizations of Baptists and benevolent societies. Then he visited his aging mother and others of his and Sally's relatives in the Litchfield community.

On to Boston went Peck, where he attended a meeting with members of the Massachusetts Baptist Missionary Society and proposed his plan for the seminary. The Society endorsed the scheme and although the members refused to be responsible for raising the funds needed, they made Peck their agent and missionary with permission to solicit the money. Eagerly accepting the challenge, Peck set out over New England and New York to plead for donations. He also visited several schools of higher education in the East, getting pointers he might use for the proposed Illinois seminary.

According to the *American Baptist Magazine,* the enthusiastic missionary promoter had collected $973.04 for the project by the end of the summer and considered his trip a great success. He had enough to start building his school. He would prove what education could do—even for frontier Baptist preachers.

On New Year's Day 1827, John Mason Peck brought together at his home in Illinois a group of men to organize the Rock Springs Theological and High School. In order to spread out the almost one thousand dollars he had collected from friends and well-wishers, Peck recruited volunteer workers to fit the wood and lay the bricks. He himself donned work clothes and gave many days of labor to the task. By the autumn of 1827 he and his "faculty" of one other teacher enrolled the first students.

While Peck was helping construct the building one day, a young Presbyterian minister, John M. Ellis, rode by. A graduate of Andover Theological Seminary, Ellis was making a name in Illinois as a promising leader of his church.

"What are you building, Brother Peck?" Ellis asked.

"I am building a theological seminary," Peck answered. And he added: "You Presbyterians should be doing the same thing!"

Ellis was impressed with his Baptist neighbor's suggestion, and started a movement among Presbyterians that resulted in the founding of Illinois College at Jacksonville. Soon the Methodists followed suit by establishing McKendree College in St. Clair County. Peck noted with considerable satisfaction that in *some* things the Baptists were taking the lead.

Realizing the lack of a publication for members of Baptist churches, in April 1829 Peck began *The Pioneer of the Valley of the Mississippi,* a four-page paper issued once a month. He hoped there would be some profit from this venture that would add to the income he sorely needed for his family, but he and his printer carried the paper for several years at a loss. He made up some of the loss with his book *Guide to Emigrants,* written, Peck acknowledged, to attract "a good class of people" to his adopted state. In September 1820 Peck found a new printer and started another paper, *The Western Baptist.*

In June 1831 he welcomed Dr. Jonathan Going, president of the Massachusetts Home Missionary Society and technically his employer, and for three months these two Baptist missionaries traveled widely over Illinois, Missouri, Indiana, and Kentucky. They surveyed the towns and settlements to determine the need for congregations to be organized, preachers to be called, Bibles to be distributed, and all other items to make possible the expansion of the Baptist cause. Peck and Going ended their journeying at Shelbyville, Kentucky, where Peck entered in his journal: "Here we agreed on the plan of the American Baptist Home Missionary Society."

Two methods were discussed by those who met in New York City for the Triennial Convention. Should home missions be promoted and sustained by an independent agency or "society" with its own officers and headquarters in New York? Or should the General Convention take on home missions in addition to foreign missions, with a secretary and treasurer for each of the two causes?

The Triennial Convention refused the second plan. Peck and Going urged the first plan. The American Baptist Home Mission Society was organized then and there, April 1832, based in New York City. "North America for Christ" was the ambitious goal.

In 1831 John Peck moved his seminary from Rock Springs to Alton, a growing town on the Illinois side of the Mississippi not far from St. Louis. In time the school became Shurtleff College. In 1834 he led the Baptists of Illinois in organizing a state convention.

Peck wrote incessantly, often from notes he had jotted down as he rode horseback from place to place. He was the author of eight books, including *Gazetteer of Illinois, Guide for Emigrants, Life of Jeremiah Vardeman* (noted Baptist pioneer preacher), and a small biography of Daniel Boone. He turned out newspaper and magazine articles, pamphlets and letters, in a steady stream. He had a standing engagement to preach a sermon to the members of the State Legislature at Vandalia, the capital, at the close of each session, and he frequently mentioned this honor in his letters to fellow Baptist leaders to convince them that Baptists actually had standing among their fellow citizens. Something of Peck's varied activities may be seen in the account by Dr. Coe Hayne in his *Vanguard of the Caravans:*

"During a period of forty-five days he rode on horseback 830 miles, preached twenty-seven times 'regular discourses,' formed five Bible societies, attended four Baptist Associations, two Methodist camp meetings, besides making a number of addresses to prepare the way for other Bible societies. On the trip in question he entered Clay County, on the extreme western side of Missouri, to the very edge of the limitless prairie, then an undisputed domain of Indians and buffalo. He learned of one hundred families in the vicinity of Liberty that did not have Bibles in their homes."[5]

To the Canaan of America

More than any other person of his day, Elder John Mason Peck informed prospective immigrants about the fertile prairies and rolling uplands of Illinois and enticed them to move into the state. His *Gazetteer of Illinois* was produced in 1837 after prodigious research into every geographic and climatic fact about the region that he could lay his hands on. It described every river, the type of soil, the farm products, the rainfall, day-by-day temperatures, and numerous other facts concerning each of the seventy counties of the state. Such facts, Peck disclosed, he obtained partly from his extensive travels into most of the counties as he organized Baptist churches and distributed Bibles and tracts, and partly by appealing to his friends, the members of the Legislature, who represented all areas of the state, for additional items of interest. He wrote:

"The course of the author was, to spend two or three hours each evening with gentlemen from a county, who were well acquainted with every part, and write a brief sketch of the same . . . By this method, no creek, prairie, or settlement, known by name amongst the people, would escape notice . . . No small pains have been taken to obtain the latest information, especially from the recently organized counties in the north, where new settlements are made every month, and villages spring up as the growth of a summer. . . ."

One of those villages that had sprung up was called Chicago, which Elder Peck considered had little prospect for growth. In his opinion, colored doubtless by wishful thinking, Alton was to be the metropolis of the West.

Peck mentioned in his *Gazetteer* every type of animal life, every species of tree found in the state, what fruit trees were best suited to the climate, what vegetables and what types of grapes could best be grown, and so on into thousands of facts, presented in language to attract families to that land of potential plenty: "The wild plum is found in every part of the state. Crab apples are equally prolific, and make fine preserves with about double their bulk of sugar. Wild cherries are equally productive . . . The black mulberry grows in most parts. The gooseberry, strawberry, and blackberry grow wild and in great profusion. . . ."[6]

Peck could not resist quoting the editor of the *Illinois Magazine* as saying: "We know one gentleman who made twenty-seven barrels of wine in a single season, from the grapes gathered with but little labor, in his immediate neighborhood." Not wishing to advance the cause of strong spirits, Elder Peck added: "There has been a considerable falling off in the manufacture of whiskey within a few years, and it is sincerely hoped by thousands of citizens that this branch of business, so decidedly injurious to the morals and happiness of the community and of individuals, will entirely decline."

The reverend gazetteer-compiler set out exact routes to be taken by the Illinois-bound immigrants, with schedules of canal boats from Albany and Buffalo, the dates of the sailing of steamboats on the Ohio River, and what stagecoach service could be found by way of Columbus, Indianapolis, Vincennes, and on to St. Louis. He even gave a table of passenger rates.

"We would say," Peck's *Gazetteer* declared, "for the benefit of those who have determined on coming to the West, that the *State of Illinois* offers every inducement to emigrants . . . Indeed, Illinois may with propriety be called the 'Canaan' of America!"

Thousands of prospective emigrants read Peck's enthusiastic words and many came to his Canaan. Among them were a fair share of Baptists, and the scores of churches he had organized were ready to receive them with hymns of thanksgiving.

In early 1852 at sixty-three years of age Peck found himself so poor that he had to beg publishers to pay him some small fees so that he and his faithful wife, Sally, could subsist. But in November of that year, when a fire destroyed the building of his Rock Springs Seminary, along with his library of thousands of volumes, from all over Illinois and from many parts of the country, came shipments of books to help replace his loss.

John Mason Peck did not live to hear his two political and personal friends, Abe Lincoln and "Little Giant" Douglas, in their historic debates on the slavery issue—one of which took place in Alton. On March 14, 1858, the clockworks of his person ran down and stopped.

XII

BAPTIST GROWING PAINS

The Baptist Master Builders

"America provided fertile soil for Baptist growth," wrote Dr. Lynn E. May, Jr., religious historian. "The simplicity of its doctrine, the democracy of its organization, its ability to propagate itself without overhead machinery, and its appeal to the common man because of its democratic polity, contributed to the rapid growth of the denomination."[1]

This fact was amply demonstrated during the quarter century from 1820 to 1845, when the structure of Baptist growth in churches, associations, education, and missionary activities continued to rise. At the base of this structure was the solid foundation laid by such leaders as Luther Rice, John Mason Peck, and countless other Baptist ministers and laymen.

The master builders were the men of vision and ability who realized that their churches were now a part of a national denomination, and needed to co-operate with one another without sacrificing the historic Baptist principle of the autonomy of each congregation.

Still, there was the constant struggle between the stand-pat Baptists and the progressives. More than 90 per cent of the people of the growing nation lived on farms and plantations or in rural settlements clustered about a church and store with possibly a post office and schoolhouse. A comparatively few rural Baptist pastors found their way to the new seminaries and academies. The vast majority had little education beyond the reading, writing, and arithmetic gained from a few months in a subscription school or the rude, log-cabin schoolhouse of the frontier settlement. Still the Protestant minister in the predominantly Protestant areas of the nation was known as the man of God, the recognized spiritual leader of his congregation whatever his denomination. He was looked upon as an important person in the community he served. He was given due respect whatever his educational advantages or his lack of them.

In fact, most Baptist congregations from the Alleghenies westward were content to have pastors who were not educated. They wished their sermons to be delivered, with full power and unction, straight from the preacher's heart and not as some said from his head. They resented sophistication and snobbery, and the type of preaching they heard was inflicted upon the Christians of the effete East. They were suspicious of book learning that might turn the preacher away from the simple Bible truths.

It became the task of educated Baptist ministers to change this attitude, and they made a start in the period following the organization of the denomination. Some of the names of pastors and evangelists are inseparably linked with the progress of Baptists in America, and therefore with the developing institutions of the entire nation—religious, educational, and cultural.

In the northern states there were such widely known men as Dr. William Staughton, who after helping start the Judsons on their way to Asia and Rice on his way all over the country continued his ministry as pastor in Philadelphia. There was Spencer H. Cone, a converted actor, who began his preaching in 1823 in Washington, D.C., where his eloquence drew thousands to hear him and where he was made chaplain of the House of Representatives, and who for eighteen years was a noted pastor in New York City.

There were such leaders of the denomination in the North as Dr. Francis Wayland, for twenty-eight years president of Brown University of Providence, Rhode Island, who found time to preach in churches all over New England and to plead for an educated Baptist ministry. There were that powerful preacher Elder Jacob Knapp, who held pastorates in New York State and became a fiery evangelist and champion of Baptist doctrines; Bartholomew Welch, pastor of the Emmanuel Baptist Church in Albany, New

York, who numbered Martin Van Buren and other eminent statesmen in his congregation; Nathaniel Colver, pastor at Tremont Temple in Boston from 1839 to 1852, a man of imposing presence and
powerful influence in his city; and Baron Stow, another Boston
Baptist preacher who was so learned and eloquent that crowds of
students from Harvard College in Cambridge and from the Theological Seminary at Newton regularly walked to his church to hear
him.

In the South there were such men as Richard Furman of
Charleston, organizer and president of the first Triennial Convention and easily the best-known Baptist of the country during his
day. There were Andrew Broaddus, Virginia-born pastor at Richmond, a pulpiteer who became famous in the denomination as an
expositor of the Bible; Robert Baylor Semple, pastor of the old
Bruington Church in King and Queen County, best remembered
as the early historian of Virginia Baptists.

Among the distinguished Baptist leaders in the South during
this period also were Samuel Wait, pastor at New Bern, North
Carolina, who became the first president of Wake Forest College;
Thomas Meredith, founder and editor of the *Biblical Recorder,*
which still stands as a monument to his vision of the need for
religious journalism.

Jeremiah Vardeman

Typical pioneer Baptist preacher, whose biography was written by
John Mason Peck, was Jeremiah Vardeman, who as a boy came
with his family from Virginia to the wilds of central Kentucky in
1792.[2] With his father and brothers, Jeremiah often engaged in
running fights with marauding Indians. He loved the outdoors and
took part in all the rough sports of the frontier youths. At seventeen he made a profession of religion in a revival conducted by an
itinerant preacher and was admitted to membership in the local
Baptist church.

Peck related that young Vardeman fell into such worldly ways
as fiddling, dancing, and card playing. These pleasures brought
young men and young women together in a manner frowned upon
by the Puritan-minded Baptist elders and parents of that day.

After being admonished several times for his frivolity, Jeremiah was excluded from the church.

Several years later another itinerant preacher reached the neighborhood and became the Baptist pastor, the Reverend Thomas Hansford, a man totally blind. He took a liking to the hearty, friendly voice of Jeremiah Vardeman, and told the young man he could not "see" any of his faults. However, the preacher added, he saw promise in such an able young man and he wanted Jeremiah to reform and come back into the church. Vardeman did so, making a dramatic confession of his sins of dancing, card playing, and drinking, and promising to give them all up. After Jeremiah's statement his parents joined the deacons and members in praying, shouting, slapping him on the back, and singing "Oh the glory door is always open wide, to welcome the sinner home!"

Thus received, Jeremiah Vardeman became a fervent exhorter and preacher. Some settlers from back East who had heard the great Jonathan Edwards vowed that Vardeman was every bit as good an evangelist. His favorite sermon was "How can ye dwell in devouring flames?" and sinners came trooping to the mourner's bench at his call. He held revivals in Louisville, Nashville, and Cincinnati, which laid the foundations for Baptist growth in each of these towns. He preached over much of Kentucky and Tennessee, then in 1830 emigrated to eastern Missouri. There he continued his evangelizing and served as moderator of the first Baptist Association in that state.

Of such character and ability were the Baptist leaders of the early denomination. Standing with them were hundreds of dedicated preachers, laymen, and women, the latter having no public voice in their congregations but exerting immeasurable influence upon the churches.

Learning to Educate

The efforts of such leaders added to the organized Baptist conventions, or associations, which drew the churches of each state closer together, co-operating in common activities. In the decade from 1820 to 1830, state associations were established in all the New England and the Middle Atlantic states not previously organized. The New York Baptist Association was founded in 1821, uniting with the Hamilton Missionary Society four years later. The Connecticut Convention was organized in 1823, the outgrowth of a Baptist society formed in 1811; the Massachusetts convention in 1824, succeeding the Baptist Missionary Society.

Michigan's first Baptist church was organized at Pontiac in 1822, as was the First Baptist Church of Indianapolis. By 1826 there were five Baptist churches in Michigan, and they formed a state association. Soon after the village of Chicago began to spread beyond Fort Dearborn in 1833, its first Baptist church was founded.

Encouraged by John Mason Peck, Baptist missionaries from Illinois pushed across the Mississippi into Iowa and organized Long Creek Church at Danville. By 1839 there were enough Baptist congregations in the state for an association, and in 1842 the state convention first met.

In the South and West, comparable progress in state conventions was made, with organizations set up in South Carolina in 1821, in Georgia in 1822, in Virginia and Alabama in 1823. By 1844 state Baptist conventions were functioning in every state east of the Mississippi, and in Iowa and Wisconsin.

Typical of the Baptist spirit of autonomy that prevailed among the congregations forming the state bodies is this provision in the Vermont Baptist Association's constitution: "It shall not by any of its acts or agencies infringe on the rights or independence of the churches."

Behind the expansion of Baptist activities in the United States from 1832 forward was the American Baptist Home Mission Society. During the first year of its existence the Society raised money to help support Baptist missionaries in twelve states and Canada. Thirty-seven of these missionaries were sent out to frontier states. By 1838, shortly after the inauguration of Martin Van Buren as the eighth President, the number of home missionaries had grown to 103. Special attention was paid in their assignments to such thriving towns as Cleveland, Indianapolis, Louisville, St. Louis, Detroit, Kalamazoo, and Chicago. Among them was the Reverend Amory Gale, who, though he suffered from asthma, went to the wilds of Minnesota in 1834 to carry the Baptist message. During sixteen years of pioneer work, Gale traveled more than 100,000 miles, much of it on Indian ponies with his packsaddles, sometimes driving a wagon and sleeping under it at night, often fighting wolves and scaring away hostile Indians.

The gospel lamps carried by Baptist ministers and home missionaries lighted the way for the founding of many Baptist seminaries and colleges during the early decades of the nineteenth century. In 1813 the Maine Literary and Theological Institution obtained a charter and opened its doors at Waterville. Its announced purpose was to provide better educated ministers for that region, whether they were Baptist or not. The school became Waterville College in 1821, which was later renamed Colby College.

In 1817 thirteen men formed the Baptist Educational Society of the State of New York and began raising money to build a school, "to educate pious young men for the ministry," as the founders announced. The school they built was Madison College, at Hamilton, from which grew Colgate University.

This pattern of organization and purpose was typical of the efforts of progressive Baptist leaders to develop a trained ministry in America. They fought valiantly to overcome the idea that higher education was the enemy of what the unlearned preacher called "heartfelt religion." They stood against a custom prevailing in many Baptist churches of the rural areas. The practice was for the elders and deacons to assemble in the meeting house and call in the young minister about to go away to study book learning. They would question him at ponderous length as to his beliefs to be sure he was strong in the faith—and the Baptist faith particularly. They would solemnly warn him that whatever he learned at college, he must never allow his learning to dilute his zeal for exhorting and proclaiming the old-fashioned gospel.

Notable among the accomplishments of the progressive Baptist leaders of the period was the founding of Newton Theological Institution, which opened in 1825. Luther Rice's dream of a school for training ministers was fulfilled by the chartering of Columbian College in Washington. The Connecticut Literary Institution, founded by Baptists, was opened in 1823 at Suffield.

Leader of the early Baptist educators in the northern states was the Reverend Williams Rogers, the first student to enroll at Rhode Island College, later Brown University, and who became professor of oratory and *belles-lettres* at the University of Pennsylvania. His son wished to seek his fortune in the South, and since Rogers and

Richard Furman, South Carolina preacher and educator, were close friends, Rogers wrote a letter of introduction to Furman for his son:

"Being a young adventurer in the bustling world, he will stand in need of our Parental-Friendly-and Ministerial advice. Do, my dear Sir, have respect to his deportment and warn him against all evil company and extravagance of every kind. . . Oh that under you he may profess Faith in Jesus! What joy of soul would such tidings impart! You will find him affable and obliging—and for a young man without religion, a strict Baptist."[3]

Baptists in the southern states, meanwhile, were also busy with higher education. Besides the colleges previously mentioned as founded through the influence of Luther Rice (Furman, Georgetown, Mercer, and Richmond), by 1841 their leaders had established Bethel College in Kentucky and Howard College in Alabama. In addition, Judson Female Institute, the first Baptist academy for women, opened its doors in January 1839 at Marion, Alabama. Named in honor of Ann Hasseltine Judson, this venture in educating selected young females was made possible through the vision of Edwin D. King, member of the board of trustees of the University of Alabama, and the generosity of a widow of Marion, Julia Barron.

It was not until 1861 that a wealthy brewer in Poughkeepsie, New York, Matthew Vassar, gave a large sum of money to found a liberal arts school for women, the first women's college to provide faculty and facilities equal to those enjoyed by institutions of higher learning for men of that day.

In the West, following the example of Peck in Illinois, Baptists established Granville Literary and Theological Institute in Ohio, the Michigan and Huron Institute at Kalamazoo, and the Franklin Manual Labor Institution at Indianapolis. The yeast of ministerial education began to leaven the whole lump of Baptist literacy.

Through the quarter century of years before 1845, Sunday schools were organized with increasing frequency in Baptist churches in every area of the country, despite vigorous opposition on the part of the predestinarians. "Lesson helps" were needed to guide the teachers in their Bible instruction, and small publishing ventures began to supply them. In 1817 the Philadelphia Adult and Sunday School Union was established, soon succeeded by the

American Baptist Sunday School Union. In 1824 this organization had 723 Sunday schools in its affiliation, with total membership of about 50,000. In 1840 the Baptist Tract Society merged with the American Baptist Publication and Sunday School Society, and with assets of $4,121.70 began issuing Sunday school lesson aids, as well as books on religious subjects, which were sold at cost.

Arminian versus Calvinist

Meanwhile, for all its forward movements, the stumbling, heavily loaded wagons of Baptist progress encountered many rocky and rutted roads during the years from the first Triennial Convention to the forks of the way which came in 1845. There were sharp differences of opinion over both doctrinal and organizational matters. Most ominous of all, there were the gathering clouds of sectional conflict over the issue of slavery, which brought a complete cleavage between North and South.

In matters of doctrine, the issue of Arminianism versus Calvinism caused the bitterest debates and differences among Baptist leaders. The Arminian belief, distinctive of the Free-Will Baptists, that *all* may be saved through faith in Jesus Christ, increasingly challenged the principle of Calvinism that salvation was for the *elect* only. These divergent beliefs were hotly discussed in many church gatherings, local and statewide, especially in the mountainous area of the Appalachians and on frontiers where settlers from that rugged area had put down their roots. Often the preachers hotly debated, Bibles in hand, quoting Scripture to support their arguments pro and con. Editors of Baptist publications were sharply divided, taking up the battle on one side or the other, sometimes filling half their pages with the discussion. Occasionally laymen joined the fight, but for the most part, members of the congregations seem to have left it to the heated clerical disputants to settle the matter—if they could.

The Calvinists were strongly antimissionary. Something of their unyielding attitude is illustrated by Dr. Coe Hayne, one of Peck's biographers:

"To train ministers, to establish Sunday schools, or to send men and women with the gospel message to destitute fields—all such means were simply the devices of men and not of God's choosing.

Daniel Parker, the leader of the antimissionary Baptists, was untiring in his opposition to Peck, ranging up and down the Ohio and the Mississippi and on both sides of the Wabash, preaching with fiery eloquence a gospel of intolerance and lining up the associations against 'Yankee contraptions.' Many of the churches Peck helped to create denied him their fellowship."[4]

Two-Seed and Primitive Baptists

Leading the Calvinist squadrons among Baptist forces were the Primitive Baptists and the Two-Seed-in-the-Spirit Predestinarian Baptists, both lineal descendants of the early colonial Calvinist Baptists. The two-seed designation came from the doctrine that Mother Eve had within her a good seed and a bad seed, and all those whom God foreordained to be saved to enjoy heaven were descended from the good seed. The Two-Seed Baptists held that since those who are to be saved were elected from the beginning of time, any effort to evangelize the world, or its communities, or to change human nature in any way is an impertinent interference with God's plan.

The stock argument of the Two-Seed Baptists began with the question: "Does not God know all things, from beginning to end?" The answer would have to be "Yes, God knows all things; he is omniscient." "Well, then," was the rejoinder, "if God knows all things from beginning to end, does he not know which of his creatures are to be saved, and which are to be lost?" If the unwary free-will Baptist admitted that question he found himself confronted with the Calvinist conclusion: "Well, that's predestination."

Even more rugged than the opposition given Baptist progress by the Two-Seed Predestinarians were the roadblocks against Sunday schools and missionary societies, erected by the Primitive Baptists, commonly called Hardshells because of their adamant resistance to co-operation with other Christians. They challenged fellow Baptists to cite where in the King James version of the Bible any such thing as a church board or a Sunday school was mentioned, and concluded that if they were not mentioned they were the work of men and not of God.

Furthermore, the Primitives were fervently predestinarian. If only the elect could be saved, they counseled, why send missionaries to point out the need for salvation? If among the children of a family some were marked for heaven and others for hell, why set up Sunday schools to inform them of the Scriptures?

The Hardshell Baptists found an articulate expression in a report from a meeting of the Kehukee Baptist Association in North Carolina in 1827, which read: "It was agreed that we discard all Missionary Societies, Bible Societies, and Theological Seminaries, and the practices heretofore resorted to for their support, in begging money from the public."

The movement spread to other Baptist churches and associations, particularly among the illiterate settlers of the western areas, to the South into Georgia and Alabama, and with the wagon trains across the Mississippi into the hill countries of Arkansas and Missouri. While they could not halt the trends for home and foreign missions among the great body of Baptists, they did become a stultifying influence in all the communities where their small chapels were built.

The Primitive Baptists frowned upon all worldliness in dress and manners. They permitted no such vanities as neckties for the men and ribbons for their women. In their places of worship the Hardshells provided a plain wooden pulpit stand, hard benches, a crude table with a bucket of drinking water and dipper, and no varnish or paint was allowed to indicate the pride and sinfulness of humankind. They separated the men from the females in their churches so that no attraction of the opposite sex—either way—might distract the soul from spiritual contemplation. They often bored large holes in the floors of their rude meeting places as primitive spittoons for the men who chewed tobacco, declaring with fierce independence of spirit that what a man "chawed" was in no wise offensive to fellowmen or to God Almighty.

An example of how far some Hardshell Baptist churches went in their opposition to Sunday schools and in upholding their Calvinist doctrines generally may be found in the minutes of the earliest Baptist church at Carrollton, Illinois, for April 1827, at a time when John Mason Peck's leadership was being felt all over the state: "Resolved, That Mrs. Justus Rider and Miss Phoebe Harris be expelled from the Baptist church, because they favor

Sunday schools which are not mentioned in the Bible, and have harbored a missionary."[5]

Mrs. Rider and Miss Harris, her sister, pleaded guilty to the charge of favoring the organization of a Sunday school, and of harboring a missionary—Elder Peck—so the motion to expel them was passed. Four other members, who expressed sympathy with the two erring sisters, were also excluded.

However, that did not end the matter. Mrs. Rider's husband, Justus, a prominent merchant of the town who had never joined the church because of its Hardshell leanings, backed his wife in calling to their home the five other expelled members. There on April 28, 1827, the seven persons exercised their Baptist freedom to organize a new church, in which, a descendant of the Rider family wrote, "men like Father Peck could find a place, and the reprehensible missionary was 'harbored' whenever he could be persuaded to accept hospitality; the little Riders all went dutifully to Sunday school, and William (one of the boys) was given an incentive to his study in the promise that when he was old enough he should go to Father Peck's new college."

Thus steadily, if slowly, the free-will theme of the missionary-minded Baptists won out over the Calvinists as Sunday schools were organized, as Baptist publications told of Judson and other missionaries working in distant pagan frontiers, and as evangelists pleaded fervently with sinners to come, one and all, to the mourner's bench and accept salvation.

Brother Miller Awaits the Advent

One remarkable upheaval gave Baptists considerable anxiety during its comparatively brief existence. It began in New York State in the early 1830s with the preaching of Parson William Miller, a Baptist pastor born in Pittsfield, Massachusetts, and living in Rochester. His theme: "Christ is returning to the earth—soon!"

Before long Brother Miller convinced himself, with the aid of carefully selected scriptural passages from the books of Daniel and the Revelation, that the exact year of Christ's bodily return could be calculated. It would be during 1843. To set the date, Miller used *literal* interpretations of the Scripture. That his interpretations lifted the Bible passages completely out of context and destroyed the beautiful symbolism of the ancient writings bothered Brother Miller and his followers not at all.

Miller gathered a big following of believers in his Second Advent. While his theme of the very year for the Lord's return became a divisive factor in churches far from his center of activities, he assumed more and more the role of a great prophet, the only spiritual leader on earth with the whole truth. He convinced thousands of followers that he alone had the divine revelation of the second advent, and he brooked no questioning of his authority.

When 1843 came and went without the prophesied advent, Miller refused to be discouraged. He simply revised his calculations and came up with another date for the second coming: It would be on March 21, 1844, in the early morning. Christ's appearance, of course, would be somewhere in the vicinity of where Miller and his faithful would be standing.

As the month and the day for the advent drew near, many of Miller's believers sold their possessions, convinced that they would never be needed again on earth. Shrewd buyers contracted to purchase farms and homes of the Millerites as of the day before the Advent. Miller went to Washington to advise all the politicians who would listen to him that since the world was coming to an end on March 21, 1844, they need make no plans for the elections scheduled for that year.

The faithful assembled before daybreak in the chill air on a hill near town, clad in their white robes, standing barefoot and bareheaded, looking exultantly toward the East. They clustered about their prophet, who led them in songs and prayers. The sun rose and continued to move in its circuit. When noon came, some began to doubt. By late day, disappointment, augmented by hunger and physical needs, began to thin the ranks of the faithful.

"I was right all the time!" Brother Miller assured his flock. "The Lord has simply changed his mind!"

Some of the Millerites left the fellowship, chagrined. But as has been true in similar circumstances, many of the faithful clung to their leader and his teachings. They were truly convinced that since Miller could do no wrong, the Lord had indeed changed his mind, and they had better be ready for the new date. As expressed by Baptist historian Henry C. Vedder at the close of the nineteenth century:

"Eventually thousands of Baptists, and some entire churches, were drawn into this current, which bore them farther and farther away from their faith, and resulted in the establishment of the Second Advent body. Even when there was no formal separation from our fellowship, many churches and individuals received irreparable harm from Miller's vagaries, and growth was greatly retarded in the regions where his influence was most extensive."[6]

William Miller later wrote an *Apology and Defense* in which he acknowledged that it was a mistake to set an exact date for the Advent. However, he held firm to his belief that Jesus is coming soon—and this very motto can be seen on signs posted in many areas of the country today.

Despite some permanently divisive effects of the Millerite movement, the affair contributed one great asset to Baptist progress. It had a lasting influence upon Baptist doctrinal beliefs. A few pastors and itinerant evangelists, principally in the isolated mountain areas of Kentucky and Tennessee, announced the time and place of the Lord's Second Coming in the decade following Miller, but for the most part his failure had a sobering effect upon such self-appointed prophets. It strengthened the preachers in proclaiming the traditional Baptist theme: "Be ready! Ye know not the day nor the hour of the Lord's return!"

Alexander Campbell

One schism among Baptists of this period helped to found a major denomination in America. Towering above most Baptist preachers in the early 1820s was a young minister, Alexander Campbell, an Irish immigrant who came to the United States with his parents in 1809. Alexander's father, Thomas Campbell, was a Presbyterian clergyman who settled in Washington, Pennsylvania. He became convinced that immersion was the proper method of baptism and joined the Baptists, along with his wife and children. He began to preach that a return to primitive Christianity, eliminating societies and groups within the congregations, would ultimately unite all Christendom.

Alexander Campbell embraced his father's ideas, began to preach, and in 1812 organized groups which he called the Disciples of Christ. Well-educated, highly articulate and persuasive, zealous and dedicated, Campbell quickly won a large following. He traveled widely over his home area of western Pennsylvania, then into Ohio, Tennessee, and Kentucky, preaching and exhorting his converts to join the Disciples of Christ.

Alexander Campbell's supreme confidence in his mission proved a tremendous asset as he won converts to his cause by the thousands. He emphasized that each man is free to read and interpret the Bible for himself and explained that immersion is essential to salvation. This was a telling point with many who were troubled at the doctrine of so-called instantaneous conversion involving no action except a mental acceptance of Christ. He simplified other doctrinal beliefs, such as that of the Trinity, for the congregations that followed him out of the Baptist ranks in 1828 and into the growing fellowship of people who preferred to call themselves simply Christians but who were also known as the Campbellites. In time, Campbell's Disciples of Christ movement became a forceful factor in American spiritual life. Today its two main branches are known as the Disciples of Christ and the Church of Christ.

XIII

THE RANKS SPLIT

The Winds of Disunity

Hardly had the Triennial Convention started the work of foreign and home missions before the winds of disunity between Baptist churches of the northern states and those of the South began to blow. It became evident that irritating divisions of opinion were increasing among Baptist leaders.

One major difference revolved about denominational control. Briefly stated, and somewhat simplified, Northern Baptist leaders generally were content to follow the policy of a decentralized denomination, with independent organizations functioning without convention control. They generally felt it was right that the Foreign Mission Society, the Home Mission Society, the Publication Society, all mapped their programs of activity and support separately.

There was no general Baptist organization to which all of these societies were responsible. Each, independent of the others, had its own annual session. Before long they agreed on a general time for their annual meetings, with one following the other in the same city, so that a member of any society could, if he wished, attend all of them. Some belonged to two or more of the societies because they gave money for their support.

In the southern states, Baptist leaders generally inclined toward much greater centralized control of the co-operative activities of their churches. Their chief spokesmen were the president of the Triennial Convention, the widely respected Dr. Richard Furman of Charleston, South Carolina, and Furman's protégé, a vigorous, eloquent young minister, William Bullein Johnson, pastor of the First Baptist Church of Savannah, Georgia. Furman had found in Johnson his worthy successor for Baptist leadership in the General Convention, and after Furman's death in 1825 Johnson used his wide influence to keep all Baptists working together in the Convention, at the same time preparing them for greater central control. He served as the last southern president of the Triennial Convention, from 1842 to 1844.

Johnson well understood another source of irritation among southern pastors. Many felt that their churches were not fairly represented in the two mission societies, and that they had little voice in shaping policies. The Home Mission Society concentrated its efforts principally on the western frontier and among immigrants in the large eastern cities, neglecting such needy fields in the South as Indian communities and the French in Louisiana, and the poorer churches in the towns, plantations, and hill-farms below the Ohio River.

The Issue Was Slavery

These differences might have been resolved. But ever darker and more ominous grew the storm clouds raised by the issue of slavery. Reflecting the rapidly growing abolitionist sentiment of the people of the North, delegates to the Triennial Convention from north of the Mason-Dixon line became outspoken against employing or supporting missionaries, at home or abroad, who owned slaves.

From the late 1830s most Baptist ministers in the northern states, especially in New England, were thundering against human bondage, and their churches passed resolutions against the institution. Antislavery societies sprang up in communities all over the North, and Baptist ministers and leaders leaped to the front of the movement, carrying the banners of abolition.

The Baptist position on slavery was complicated by the fact that the majority of the people of this denomination in the South were not the great slave-owning planters as a class. Most Baptists were the humble people of their communities. Many Baptists owned slaves, some one or more Negro families as household or farm servants, a few as many as a score. But the majority of the big plantation families of Virginia, the Carolinas, and Georgia, and to a less extent of Alabama and Mississippi, were descendants of the colonial aristocrats, and they were of the Anglican or Presbyterian faiths. However, as the abolitionist movement grew in intensity, casting its threatening shadow over this established institution of the South, Baptists generally lined up with their slave-owning neighbors, whether big planters or little farmers and businessmen.

Birth of the Southern Baptist Convention

In 1840 the Reverend R. E. Pattison of Boston, editor of the *Christian Reflector* and secretary of the Foreign Mission Society, wrote that he would not vote to appoint a slaveholder as missionary, and called on all his colleagues to join him in his stand. Hearing of this, the First Baptist Church of Tuscaloosa, Alabama, queried the officers of its state convention: "Is it proper for us at the South to send any more money to our Brethren in the North for missionary and other benevolent purposes before the subject of slavery be rightly understood by both parties?"

In 1844 a committee of that state convention passed a resolution for the consideration of the Triennial Convention's Board of Foreign Missions. It stated:

"Our duty at this crisis requires us to demand from the proper authorities in all those bodies, to whose funds we have contributed or with whom we have in any way been connected, the distinct, explicit avowal that slaveholders are eligible and entitled equally with non-slaveholders to all the privileges and immunities of their several unions, and especially to receive any agency or mission, or other appointment which may run within the scope of their operation or duties."[1]

The Society members answered, frankly and explicitly, that they could not appoint as missionary any person who owned slaves, nor would they be a party to any agreement that seemed to express approval of the institution of slavery.

In April 1845 the American Baptist Home Mission Society, meeting in Providence, Rhode Island, adopted a resolution that declared: "It is expedient that the members now forming the Society should hereafter act in separate organizations at the South and at the North in promoting the objects which were originally contemplated by the Society," and appointed a committee to report a plan to accomplish this separation.

Baptist churches of the slaveholding states faced no other course than to organize their own convention, and this they proceeded to do, with no delay. The word went out that the congregations in the slaveholding states were ready to go it alone. Their decision had the blessing of President Francis Wayland of Brown University, who wrote to the Reverend Jeremiah Bell Jeter, pastor of the First Baptist Church of Richmond, Virginia: "You will separate, of course. I could not ask otherwise. Your rights have been infringed. I will take the liberty of offering you one or two suggestions. We have shown how Christians *ought not* to act; it remains for you to show us how they *ought* to act. Put away all violence, act with dignity and firmness, and the world will approve your course."

The Virginia Baptist Foreign Mission Society took the lead in calling for a meeting to create the new organization of Baptists in the South, and a conference began on May 8, 1845, in the First Baptist Church of Augusta, Georgia. The delegates assembled from Maryland, Virginia, North Carolina, South Carolina, Georgia, Louisiana, Alabama, Kentucky, and the District of Columbia, 293 in number, some representing more than one Baptist organization. They passed a resolution that the Baptist congregations in the South "have been circumscribed in their efforts to work for the world's evangelization by the agency with which they had been cooperating," and appointed a committee to draft a constitution for a new Baptist convention. Its preamble contained these significant words:

"We, the delegates from Missionary Societies, Churches, and other religious bodies of the Baptist Denomination, in various parts of the United States, met in Augusta, Georgia, for the purpose of carrying into effect the benevolent intentions of our constituents, by organizing a plan for eliciting, combining, and directing the energies of the whole denomination . . . for the propagation of the Gospel."[2]

Next it declared: "The Constitution we adopt is precisely that of the original union; that in connection with which, throughout his missionary life, Adoniram Judson has lived, and under which Ann Judson and Boardman have died. We recede from it no single step . . . We use the very terms, as we uphold the true spirit and great object of the late General Convention of the Baptist Denomination of the United States."

The conference at Augusta voted to continue the two major fields of activity for which the Triennial Convention was founded: the spread of the gospel to foreign lands, and the extension of Baptist faith and churches in the homeland.

On May 12 when the final resolution had been passed by the gathering a new Baptist body had been born—the Southern Baptist Convention, destined to be a major factor in shaping the policies of the states that tried to dissolve the Union of States during the following fifteen years.

But the conflicts among Baptists about the slavery issue had by no means come to an end. Arguments of the Northern Baptists were met with vigorous counter-arguments from Southern Baptist preachers and laymen, who sought to consolidate their position that the institution of slavery was of divine origin and support. They cited numerous passages of Scripture such as "the servant is not above his master," and Paul's letter to Philemon concerning the runaway slave, Onesimus, to uphold the position stated by their late leader, Richard Furman, that "the right of holding slaves is clearly established in the Holy Scripture, both by precept and example." The Christian ministers of Richmond, Virginia, including the pastors of all white Baptist churches of that city, passed resolutions denouncing the interference of the people of any state in the domestic relations of masters and slaves.

Officeholders and political leaders generally in the southern states took courage from the stand of Baptist farmers and businessmen using slave labor. Those in the northern states were encouraged to stand fast against any toleration of the institution, by Baptist leaders otherwise holding to the same principles of faith and practice as their brethren in the South.

There were, of course, exceptions to the rule. A few southern ministers, teachers, and journalists raised their voices to point out that slavery was a dying institution because of the industrial revolution, and that free labor, paid more than the meager sustenance usually given the slaves, would result in greater production and higher standards of living for all. In the North, some cautioned against the extremism of the radical abolitionists, pointing out that slavery existed in many northern states until it became unprofitable and that it would die out in the South as conditions changed in that area. But calm considerations were smothered by the clamor of division on both sides; reason was supplanted by prejudice; and negotiation was rejected for conflict. The situation has been succinctly explained by Baptist historian, Robert G. Torbet:

"The sectional impasse came because free labor in the North opposed slave labor in the South. These antagonistic social concepts were disruptive to the national unity. The South was slipping into political and economic inferiority, its dependence upon a staple crop placing it at the mercy of northern industrialists. Southerners fought back with the tariff. Meanwhile, the North objected to revived expansionism in the 1850s on the part of the Southerners in their effort to secure more territory for slavery."[3]

Growth Before the Storm

Meanwhile, the Baptist organizations of both the South and the North made valiant efforts to carry on their normal activities. By 1850 the Baptists, not only of the South but of the entire country, had grown to second place among Protestants in membership, with only the Methodists outnumbering them. Baptists were increasing rapidly in the states and territories of the western frontier, under the exhortations of pioneer evangelists and pastors.

The American Baptist Home Mission Society, organized in 1832 under the motto "North America for Christ," in its first decade of work had sent its missionaries into every area of the country, and especially into the lonely settlements of the West. The intrepid carriers of the Good News and of Baptist doctrine, with these two subjects always joined in their messages, were following the roads that wound among farms and plantations, accepting the hospitality of any who would take them in, preaching, organizing churches from groups of the faithful and their new converts. In 1842 the Society reported that the decade had produced about 400 churches and more than 11,000 baptisms.

When General John C. Frémont's explorations beyond the Great Rocky Mountains called attention to the Far West in 1843,

Baptist pioneers helped make up the wagon trains for the long trek to the Pacific Coast. The first Baptist church on that coast was founded at Oregon City in 1847. The huge Republic of Texas was added as a star in the Union flag in 1845, and in 1848 the War with Mexico brought annexation of vast territories of the Southwest. Then came the Gold Rush to California in 1849 and the years following. The Baptist Home Mission Society sent missionaries into each of these areas, while continuing to augment with youthful recruits those working in the states of the Northwest from Indiana to Iowa and Minnesota. In 1854 the Baptist workers invaded Kansas and two years later they were in Nebraska.

The American Baptist Foreign Mission Society maintained its work in Burma and opened a mission in South India. It began its work in China by sending out Virginia-born John Lewis Shuck to Macao in 1835. Two years later he baptized the first Chinese Baptist convert. His wife, Henrietta Hall, had been baptized by Pastor Jeter of Richmond and became interested in missions by reading the story of Ann Hasseltine Judson. In Macao with her husband she conducted a missionary school for Chinese children. The Shucks moved their mission to Hong Kong, and there they organized the first Baptist church in China.

In 1844 the Society's leaders joined other Protestant groups to urge a treaty between the United States and China, which permitted religious chapels and hospitals in five Chinese ports. Under this arrangement Baptists sent missionaries to Ningpo and Swatow.

The new Southern Baptist Convention was also moving forward in both its home and foreign mission work. Its Board of Domestic Missions, located at Marion, Alabama, combined and co-ordinated the energies and resources of Baptists and their churches in home mission work throughout all the southern states. During the fifteen years before the outbreak of the Civil War, the board sent missionaries to the large cities of the South, to the Indian tribes, to pioneer areas of Texas, Kansas, California, and the Southwest. Its workers helped to secure church sites, and to build houses of worship—many of them from logs hewed from the forests or from bricks made of clay nearby. The Board furnished Sunday school literature and tracts to white pastors and church leaders to be used among the Negro slaves, most of whom worshiped in the galleries of their masters' meeting houses.

Promptly after the formation of their Convention, Southern Baptists, too, began their foreign mission activities.

"The empire of China presents the widest and most important field for Christian missions in the world," declared Pastor Jeter, president of the Foreign Mission Board in a report to its first meeting. "For centuries it has been carefully closed against the ministers of Christ. Recently God has opened the way for the introduction of the Gospel into that dark land . . . Therefore, *Resolved,* That with as little delay as possible, we will proceed to establish missions in the free ports of China, or such of them as may be selected for the purpose."

In 1844, after the death of his wife, Henrietta, at Hong Kong, John Lewis Shuck returned to the United States. Since he was a Southerner, the newly formed Foreign Mission Board offered to send him back to China as its missionary, and he accepted. The Reverend I. J. Roberts, a Kentuckian who had served in China under the Triennial Convention, asked Southern Baptists to appoint him. Shuck and Roberts were sent to Shanghai, and they organized the first Baptist church in that city in 1847. Soon other missionaries were sent to China. A mission was also established in Nigeria, West Africa.

Through the troubled years preceding the War Between the States, the personality of Dr. Richard Fuller stands out among Southern Baptists. A South Carolina-born Harvard graduate, he urged the education of Negroes as well as whites, although he upheld what he considered the biblical sanction for slavery. He became pastor of the Seventh Street Baptist Church of Baltimore in 1847, stating as one of his reasons for locating there that he might be useful in that border city and state to reconcile the advocates of abolition and those supporting the right to own slaves.

From the presidency of the Maryland Baptist Union Fuller moved up to be Moderator of the Southern Baptist Convention in 1857, serving until 1863. A preacher of great power, he was a vigorous leader though not an experienced presiding officer. His methods of dealing with complicated parliamentary situations became the source of numerous legends. One story has it that a messenger rose in a meeting of the Convention and made an involved motion. Fuller was hopelessly confused. After a moment of thoughtful silence he solemnly asked: "My dear Brother, will you not, in the interest of the kingdom we love, withdraw that motion?"

In another meeting a member presented a resolution asking that all should pray for the denominational editors. Fuller was not sure how to handle such a proposal. He stood in full grandeur for a time, then finally ruled: "Well, my dear Brother, we should all think about that motion!"

The German Baptists

While the major division of Baptists in the United States was taking place, Baptist ranks were being augmented with immigrants from northern Europe. Some were members of Baptist churches in their homelands, while others had leanings toward Baptist principles. Leaving countries where Baptists were always in the minority and often a despised sect, the immigrants were delighted to find that in a land of complete religious liberty the Baptists were a major religious influence.

Most important among the immigrant Baptists in the period before the War Between the States were those from Germany and from Sweden. From these groups emerged two new branches of the denomination.

On November 6, 1851, in the German Baptist Church of Philadelphia, a group of eight men, surrounded by members of their host congregation, met and after an opening prayer lustily sang a hymn. Its words and tune were dear to the hearts of Baptists of German descent in that day: *"Ach, Bleib' mit deiner Gnade bei uns, Herr Jesu Christ."* (O Stay with Us, Lord Jesus Christ, with Thy Blessing.)

Elder Johann Eschmann read the stately priestly prayer from the 17th chapter of the Gospel of John and preached a sermon. The group then organized for business. Six of the eight were ministers, two were laymen, all prominent leaders of German-speaking Baptist churches located in New York City, Rochester, and Buffalo, New York; Newark, New Jersey; St. Louis, Missouri; Chicago, Illinois; and Bridgeport, Ontario.

Other German-American Baptist churches, not represented at the conference, had been established in Cincinnati and Pittsburgh, and in various communities of Wisconsin and Indiana. Elder

Eschmann served as moderator of the meeting and Elder Anton Konrad Fleischmann as clerk. In daily sessions that filled six days, the men organized the North American Baptist General Conference, destined to draw together as a separate fellowship the churches whose members were of predominantly German descent in communities from the Atlantic to the Pacific.

Among those eight founders were names highly revered by members of this fellowship through the years. Young Konrad Fleischmann had been a member of a Separatist church in Switzerland. In 1839 he was visiting in England when a Baptist minister planted in his mind the idea of crossing the Atlantic to preach to German immigrants in America in their native language. Fleischmann reached the immigration center on Ellis Island and found himself in New York City. He learned of a German Baptist church in Newark that needed a pastor, but after one difficult year there he moved on to the hill country of Lycoming County, Pennsylvania, into a community with a large German population. The Baptist State Convention helped support him with $20 per month. An eloquent, persuasive evangelist, Fleischmann held revival meetings all over the area, with hundreds of conversions and additions to the churches.

From baptized converts of his revival meetings in Philadelphia, Elder Fleischmann organized a church on July 9, 1843. So that the congregation could be well identified, the charter members called themselves "The German Church of the Lord That Meets on Poplar Street."[4]

Another of the founders of this conference of Baptists was Alexander von Puttkammer, an officer in the Prussian Army and a relative of Prince Otto von Bismarck. This scion of nobility became so dissatisfied with the militarism of the ruling princes of the German states that in 1845 he deserted and escaped to America. Jobless, penniless, and all but hopeless, the young man wandered into the Baptist church at Lawrenceville, New York, where he was converted. Puttkammer worked for a time, and for a pittance, for the American Tract Society, then became a colporteur, a traveling salesman of Bibles and literature, of the American Baptist Publication Society. He founded churches and preached to congregations in various cities of New York.

Another member of the founding group was also a Prussian

who escaped the military despotism of his native land, Wilhelm Grimm. He began preaching to a small group of Baptists at Memel, East Prussia, and ten times he was dragged before the magistrates, charged with preaching an unauthorized faith. In 1847 Grimm and fourteen of his congregation emigrated to Milwaukee, Wisconsin. There they found a small city rapidly growing with German immigrants.

Another name, destined to become best known of all the early German-American Baptists, was August Rauschenbusch, pastor at Bridgeport, Ontario, who reached Philadelphia for the founders' meeting a day late because his stagecoach was delayed by muddy roads. August's family was of the Lenne Valley in Westphalia. His father served as pastor of a Lutheran congregation at Altoona, fifth of a line of ministers that went back for more than a century. Young Rauschenbusch attended the University of Berlin and was strongly influenced by the atmosphere of agnosticism that permeated higher education in that Prussian capital.

Still troubled at the thought of deserting the faith of his devout preacher ancestors, he went on a long walking tour in the Alps, and came upon an inscription cut into a rock, which freely translated read: "Eternal God, the rocks declare Thee, the waters declare thy name. When shall my soul behold thy face?"

Rauschenbusch started studying his Bible again. In 1846 he came to America and went out to St. Louis, then known as the German city of the West, where he found friends among German-speaking Baptists. On a spring day in 1850 he rowed across the Mississippi to the Illinois side with a minister, Christopher Shoemacher, and a small group of friends, and was immersed in the muddy waters. He refused to be baptized on the St. Louis side because Missouri permitted slavery.

These German immigrants forming the North American Baptist General Conference were in accord with the historic principles of the fellowship with respect to believer's baptism by immersion, the autonomy of each congregation, the importance of evangelizing and missionary work, and keeping the state away from control of the church.

One principle the new organization adopted firmly and fervently: The German Baptists were staunchly opposed to slavery. Located almost entirely in areas settled or being settled by German immigrants in the northern states, their sympathies flowed naturally into the river of the abolitionist cause.

Members of the German Baptist convention, as the Conference was popularly called, were also strongly opposed to secret societies of all sorts, including lodges with secret rituals. Much of this feeling was due to concern that activity in a lodge might detract from interest in the church.

And the Swedes

"Our People Were Swedish" was the proud boast of increasing numbers of immigrants following 1840. The Baptist General Conference of America, for many years popularly called the Swedish Baptist convention, began when three immigrants from Sweden who had settled in Rock Island, Illinois, were baptized in the Mississippi River and promptly organized a Baptist church. The date was August 8, 1852. The minister who did the baptizing was also a Swedish immigrant, Gustav Palmquist, of Galesburg, Illinois, a schoolteacher who had been ordained to preach earlier that year.

The northern area of Illinois had many Swedish-born settlers and the hopes of the founders of the Rock Island church for more members were quickly realized. Following the example of these Illinois Baptists of Swedish descent, others from the Scandinavian countries who were Baptists or who held Baptist beliefs established churches and organized associations where songs could be sung, prayers said, and sermons heard in the language of their forebears.

There was practically no doctrinal difference between Baptists of the Swedish immigrants and other Baptists in the United States and Canada who believed in missions, domestic and foreign, except in the emphasis that the Swedish leaders and members placed upon certain fundamental principles. Swedish Baptists strongly supported belief in the verbal inspiration of the Scriptures, the virgin birth of Christ, the atonement, and the premillennial return of Christ to the earth. They clung to baptism by immersion and the observance of the Lord's supper as an ordinance of the church.

From the beginning, the Conference was strongly missionary in spirit, both in work overseas and among the churches of the United States and Canada. Candidates for appointment as foreign missionaries of the Baptist General Conference had to meet strict standards. Their leaders insisted that there must be "personal experience of salvation through Jesus Christ, and a divine call to foreign service; zeal for soul-winning, college training or its equivalent, an acceptable record of Christian service."[5]

Swedish Baptists, located almost entirely in northern states, were as actively opposed to slavery as were their Baptist neighbors of German descent. In 1851 *Uncle Tom's Cabin* came out, the book that crystallized sentiment for the abolition of slavery as did no other single influence. It is safe to say that the overwhelming majority of the immigrant Baptists, with those of other faiths from northern Europe, bought or borrowed the book and made its dramatic message a part of their crusade against slavery. But the crusade was moving rapidly into one of the most tragic conflicts of modern history.

XIV

WAR AND PEACE

The Guns of Charleston

If Baptists of good will in the South, and countless others like them, could have decided the matter, doubtless the tragic War Between the States would have been averted. But the peaceful seas they hoped for became stormier. Upon receiving the news that Abraham Lincoln had been elected President, the South Carolina legislature called for an election of delegates to a popular convention to be held in December. The convention, composed of the most prominent leaders of the state, first met in the First Baptist Church of Columbia, where plans were drawn up for South Carolina to secede from the Union. Because of a smallpox epidemic in Columbia, the convention finished its work in Charleston.

One by one the southern states followed South Carolina out of the Union. On an April day in 1861 the guns on the shore of Charleston began booming. The echoes of the bombardment on Fort Sumter rumbled and reverberated across the nation, calling men of the North and of the South to arms—and more than two hundred thousand of them to their deaths. The echoes sounded the death knell also of the old patrician South, the pleasant land of great homes set among magnolias with slave quarters in the rear, and with black people, the property of the planters, singing rhythmic work songs as they labored.

While the war severely retarded the missionary work of the Baptists in the North, it brought such activities of Southern Baptists almost to a halt. Young men of the Dixie states rushed to sign up under the Stars and Bars of the new Confederacy. Many who had received military training recruited whole companies and battalions from among their neighbors, became officers, and marched away with drums beating and crowds cheering. In its issue of July 1, 1861, a Baptist weekly, published at Louisville, Kentucky, gave this account:

"Colleges have suspended, some of them indefinitely. Doctor Talbird, President of Howard College, has raised a company and gone to the wars, and the students of most of our colleges have enlisted in the Confederate Army. Our female schools, in several localities, show signs of distress. Some six or seven Baptist papers have gone down in the past six months, while the Mississippi and Texas Baptists issue half sheets, and the *Tennessee Baptist* is cut down in size to one-third less than the *Western Recorder*. Added to this gloomy picture, our Foreign Missions are paralyzed, our Home Missions almost suspended, and our State organizations unable to carry on their work. Ministers have been forced through stern necessity to leave their fields of usefulness in order to provide bread for their families."[1]

Baptists in the Forefront

President Jefferson Davis and his associates in the Confederate government looked to the religious leaders of the South to arouse moral and material support for the cause, and certainly the Baptists did not disappoint them. Many Baptist meeting houses were used as recruiting stations, and Baptist young men carried the fervor of the camp meetings into the cause they considered just and righteous. The *South Western Baptist* for February 5, 1863 related:

"A few days since a distinguished Presbyterian Doctor of Divinity inquired of the Reverend James B. Taylor, D.D.: 'Can you explain to me how it is that there are so many Baptists in the army? I have been chaplain from the beginning of the war, and it seems to me that a large portion of all the religious men with whom I have met were Baptists. Is it that your people are so numerous, or that they are patriotic?' Bro. Taylor replied that 'they were both numerous and patriotic.' In one regiment there were, some time since, six hundred Baptists. In a regiment from Alabama there were thirteen Baptist ministers."

The gloomy picture for Baptist work became even darker as the fratricidal struggle dragged on. At the meeting of the Southern Baptist Convention in May 1863 the Board of Domestic Missions reported that its work had turned to the "moral and spiritual well-being of the army." The Board had decided to give its attention to Military Missions, with the principal concern the selection of chaplains to accompany and preach to the troops, and colporteurs to distribute tracts containing passages of Scripture, with exhortations to live a righteous life and avoid temptations. The Colportage Board of Virginia Baptists took the lead in publishing the tracts, with more than five million given out to men who wore the gray of the southern troops.

The same Convention of 1863 expressed its sentiments in a resolution that read:

"The events of the past two years have only confirmed the conviction expressed by this Convention at its last session, that the war which has been forced upon us is, on our part, just and necessary, and have only strengthened our opposition to a reunion with the United States on any terms whatever; and while deploring the dreadful evils of the war, and earnestly desiring peace, we have no thought of ever yielding, but will render a hearty support to the Confederate Government in all constitutional measures to secure our independence . . . While we justify ourselves in this conflict with our enemies, we acknowledge that our sins have deserved the terrible calamities that God has sent upon us, and view them as a solemn and imperative call to penitence, humiliation and a hearty turning to God."[2]

After General Stonewall Jackson was killed at the battle of Chancellorsville, the next session of the Southern Baptist Convention resolved: "That we have just heard with unutterable grief of the death of that noble Christian warrior, Lieut. Gen. T. J. Jackson; that we thank God for the good he has achieved, and the glorious example he has left us, and pray that we may all learn to trust, as he trusted, in the Lord alone."[3]

Less than two months after those words were written, the Union forces of General U. S. Grant took Vicksburg, Mississippi, and cut the Confederacy in two. At the same time on the rolling landscape surrounding Gettysburg, Pennsylvania, the Army of Virginia under General Robert E. Lee was beaten in a battle later described as the last battle fought between gentlemen. These decisive engagements marked the doom of the Confederacy, although it required nearly two years more to exhaust the resources and manpower of the South.

The strict blockade imposed by the United States Navy on the Southern states prevented correspondence with and support for foreign missionaries. Some funds were gathered in Virginia by Richard Fuller and taken to Baltimore under a flag of truce personally approved by President Lincoln, thence distributed to Baptist mission points in China and Africa.

Because of the blockade of southern ports, cotton on the English market rose to fabulous prices. Blockade running in cotton became big business. The risks of capture were great but the profits were attractive. The Baptist Foreign Mission Board solemnly decided to take the venture of blockade running to help its stranded missionaries. Members invested $1,500 in several bales of long-staple cotton. The shipment reached Nassau safely, to the intense relief of the speculating Baptist leaders, and was sold in Liverpool for about $5,000. According to the report made to the Southern Baptist Convention in 1863, the proceeds were acknowledged by grateful missionaries in Asia and Africa. Except for these windfalls, Southern Baptist workers in foreign lands had to fend for themselves during the conflict.

In the North the activities of the Home and Foreign Mission Societies, and of the American Baptist Publication Society, were less seriously affected by the war. Work among the Indians and pioneer churches moved forward. Baptists were among those who gained the consent of President Lincoln to recognize officially the Corps of Chaplains, and Baptist ministers from Maine to Nebraska entered the Union ranks wearing the Christian cross. Work among Negroes by the Home Mission Society took a turn southward as Union armies occupied areas of the southern states conquered by Grant, Sherman, Sheridan, and their fellow commanders in Blue.

The Healing Mission

On March 4, 1865, President Lincoln was inaugurated to begin his second term. A defeated South heard his words with intense interest and awakening hope. "Let us bind up the nation's wounds . . . with malice toward none, with charity for all . . ."

On February 16, 1865, General William T. Sherman and his Union troops, fresh from marching triumphantly through Georgia, arrived at Columbia, South Carolina, and began looting and burning the city. The destruction became so widespread that on the night of February 17, many women, children, and loyal slaves of the town congregated on the grounds of the State Insane Asylum. Legend has it that General Sherman dispatched a lieutenant with a squad of soldiers to the heart of the city with one order: "Destroy that Baptist church where the first secession convention was held!"

Arriving at the stately, columned building, which had no identification at that time, the soldiers accosted an aged white-haired Negro—whom they did not recognize as the sexton—loitering about the place. "Is this the First Baptist Church?" the officer demanded to know. The loyal caretaker, quickly sensing the mission of this detachment, decided that for once he could tell an untruth.

"No, sir! No, sir! That's hit up yonder!" and he pointed to the only other church edifice in sight, a good two blocks up the street. That neighbor church was blown to bits, but the First Baptist Church, scene of the historic assembly, stands to this day.

Surely with Lincoln at the head of a union of states reunited after the scourge of war there would be no vengeful beating of a prostrate South, no mass punishments for the sins of those who had planned and led the rebellion. Lincoln, the man condemned in 1861 as the enemy of the southern people, was now looked to as the one who could "with charity for all," as the President had said, bring about peaceful reconciliation.

On April 9 General Lee surrendered his army to General Grant at Appomattox Court House, Virginia. The war was over and the country, North and South, rejoiced. Five days later the nation was plunged into consternation and grief by the assassination of the President. It is safe to say that, except for the veterans of the defeated Confederate army, as great a proportion of southern people sincerely mourned the passing of Lincoln as among those of the North.

A policy far from the ideal of malice toward none was enforced upon the secessionist state governments and their citizens. Mass guilt by association, a principle repugnant to all enlightened and humane people, became the pattern for the reconstruction of the South. The states were occupied by Union troops and the whole area from Virginia to Texas divided into military districts under the rule of Union generals.

Churches of all faiths in the South felt the lash of the occupation whip, and since Baptists were most numerous in the South, they felt the thongs most keenly. Many churches had been temporarily abandoned during the war since pastors had gone with the troops or back to the soil to make a living. Federal rulers moved quickly to confiscate these buildings for meeting houses for the freedmen—the former slaves.

Some of the difficulty experienced by churches trying to regain their properties is seen in the case of the Coliseum Place Baptist Church of New Orleans. In December 1865 the Board of Domestic Missions dispatched Elder Russell Holman to help this congregation secure permission to use its edifice again. Holman was informed by the military office that the following would have to be furnished: proof that the Southern Baptist Convention was an incorporated body; signatures of all those incorporating this organization; proof of the loyalty to the Union of the incorporators, by way of a certified copy of their amnesty oath or a pardon in case the amnesty oath did not apply to them. In addition, the title to the property would have to be proved, along with certificates that there had been no sale of the property, and that the freedmen had no claim upon it.

All these conditions were finally complied with, and the officer commanding the New Orleans region turned over the keys to what was left of the congregation. Many church groups could not cut through this maze of red tape and simply worshiped in other buildings or built new ones.

It was to a large extent the influence of religious leaders, both North and South, that in time bound up the wounds of war. Baptists on both sides of the old line of division were in the forefront of that healing mission. On September 27, 1865, the American Baptist Home Mission Society first extended the hand of conciliation, with a resolution that the Board would "fraternally welcome" the restoration of co-operation with the brethren in the South, "in the glorious work of publishing the gospel in all its fullness of doctrine, precept and practice, throughout the land."

Dr. Pharcellus Church, pastor of a church in Boston, wrote to Elder Jeter in Richmond: "My idea is this, that the *cause* of alienation between us has disappeared . . . We are citizens of one earthly, and I hope, heavenly polity, and it were an act of madness, as well as of wrong, to perpetuate division and alienation."[4]

In December 1865 the editor of the *Examiner and Chronicle,* organ of the New York Baptists, made this cordial gesture:

"Undoubtedly there are in our Southern churches multitudes of good Christian men and women, as good as are to be found; undoubtedly they have multitudes of good and faithful pastors, sharing with them a common lot of poverty. Let us establish, they with us and we with them, better relations. If our lot is a more favorable one, let them share our blessings in our aid to build up with them the common cause of our country's evangelization; it is not as conquerors or oppressors that Northern Baptists would come to such co-operation, but as brethren, seeking to restore wastes and turn them to joy and gladness . . . The South is to rise, and for the resurrection Baptists should be preparing . . . We never hear of their churches languishing, their colleges dying, their missionary life paralyzed, without an irrepressible desire for the speedy coming of the day which shall make all these interests a common cause of the whole Baptist family."

Southern Baptist Convention Becomes Permanent

The admission by a prominent Northern Baptist that undoubtedly there were good Christian men and women in the southern churches was a long step toward reconciliation, and Southern Baptist leaders welcomed such evidences of a desire to restore friendly relations. However, the humiliation of the South was too deep. The big question for them was: "Shall we continue our Southern Baptist Convention?" Rather quickly they found the answer. It rose like a chant from churches, associations, and state conventions: "We will continue our Convention!"

The matter was confirmed at the 1868 meeting by a resolution that declared that the Southern Baptist Convention "is a permanent institution," and that the need for sustaining it "is more imperative now than at any former time."

Having made the major decision, Southern Baptist leaders were in better position to accept the proffered restoration of friendship with their Baptist friends in the North on the basis of co-operation without any thought of returning to organic union.

Baptists in the three principal border states, Maryland, Kentucky, and Missouri, moved promptly to help the disorganized and demoralized mission boards of the Southern Baptist Convention. Minutes of the first convention held after the war, at Russellville, Kentucky, disclose that representatives of the Board of Domestic Missions had responded to the invitation of the Baptist General Association of Kentucky to come and discuss plans to aid the Board and that the Elk Horn Baptist Association had greeted them "with a genuine old Kentucky welcome." In six weeks' time, $10,000 was raised in the Baptist churches and associations of the state. The report added hopefully that by this generosity the Board was upon its feet again. Similar visits were made to associations in Missouri and to churches in Baltimore. By 1870 Baptists in several of the southern states had resumed their support of both the foreign and home mission work.

At the 1875 meeting of the Convention a delegation from the American Baptist Home Mission Society appeared with fraternal greetings. For the first time since the surrender at Appomattox some of the Baptist veterans of Lee's army clasped hands with Yankees from the North, bent on friendship rather than conquest. The Convention confirmed its decision that the Northern and Southern organizations should not be merged, but added that "we are all the more solicitous that we should preserve the most fraternal relations, while each strives to do the work of the common Master in its own appropriate sphere."[5]

The irritating, burdensome presence of federal troops and carpetbagger politicians in southern communities lasted through the administrations of President Grant. During his second term, which began March 4, 1873, numerous church groups of all faiths petitioned the government to restore full citizenship rights to people of the southland, and to end the tragic era of the so-called Reconstruction. Baptist churches, associations, and conventions did their share of the petitioning, and brought heavy pressure upon Baptist members of Congress to plead for a final binding up of the nation's wounds.

Backing Rutherford B. Hayes

Baptists of the North added the weight of their influence to the cause of amity. Among the most prominent of these was a Baptist editor of the Cincinnati *Journal and Messenger*. He helped to rally Ohio Republicans to back their governor, Rutherford B. Hayes, for nomination as President of the United States, with the understanding that if Hayes was elected he would end military control of the South.

The election of November 1876 was so close that the ballots of Florida, slow to report, would decide the winner. And the voting in Florida was so evenly divided that the votes of the last precinct to be counted would decide the state's three presidential electors. The precinct was Alachua, and its returns were withheld for two days for a supervised recount, which resulted in three electors for Hayes and a majority of one for him in the electoral college. Inaugurated as President, Hayes kept the agreement a Baptist editor had worked out for him and promptly ended military rule in the South.

One Northern Baptist, identified in the record simply as from Philadelphia, attended the 1879 Southern Baptist Convention sessions in Atlanta, and in a friendly speech declared: "If Northern and Southern brethren would meet and mingle more, not in any official or representative character, but simply as Christian brethren, they would discover that apprehensions on one side and suspicions on the other form the principal grounds for all such discussions . . . The country is too great for one convention or even two."

The convention responded with a resolution calling for the appointment of five men "to bear to our Baptist brethren of the Northern States, at their approaching anniversaries, expressions of our fraternal regard, and assurances that, while firmly holding to the wisdom and policy of preserving our separate organizations, we are ready, as in the past, to co-operate cordially with them in promoting the cause of Christ in our own and foreign lands."

Still there were organizational differences between Baptists of the North and those affiliating with the Southern Baptist Convention. The northern Home Mission Society moved promptly to line up churches, leaders, and contributors in the southern states, while the bankrupt southern Board of Domestic Missions, its name changed in 1874 to the Home Mission Board, could do little but hope for better times.

When the Southern Baptist Convention met in 1882, only seven of the twenty-one state conventions and general associations of the southern states were co-operating with the Southern Board, and in the meantime the American Baptist Publication Society of the North was selling literature to Sunday schools and churches nearly everywhere throughout the South. Dr. E. T. Winkler, pastor of the First Baptist Church of Charleston, South Carolina, cried out at the session of the Convention:

"The facts prove beyond the possibility of question that the Southern Baptist Convention is being supplanted in its own domain. Every one of the border states of the South is occupied by the Home Mission Society; and most of our older states are in co-operative alliance with the American Baptist Publication Society in colportage and Sunday school work . . . What the result will be, unless a great change takes place, no prophet is needed to foretell."[6]

A Baptist layman and educator, Dr. Isaac Taylor Tichenor, president of the Alabama Polytechnic Institute at Auburn, took the lead in reviving the Southern Baptist Convention on its home front. He left the presidency of his school, became the executive of the Home Mission Board, moved the organization from Marion, Alabama, to Atlanta, and started projects to reclaim the lost territory. One of Dr. Tichenor's supporters, the Reverend J. B. Gambrell, a veteran of General Pickett's charge across the blood-soaked terrain at the battle of Gettysburg, told another session of the Convention: "Multitudes of people speaking strange tongues will flow into this Southland. At first the Northern man with American ideas will come, but he will be followed by men from every nation under heaven . . . Along the mountain fastnesses and in the great coming cities of the South the battles are to be fought within a generation that will decide the spiritual destiny of this country for a thousand years."[7]

Baptist Journalism

During the post-Civil War period Baptist publications rode the crest of high popularity. Magazines for general circulation were few, and by the standards of that day expensive, so the national and state Baptist papers supplied many families with all the periodical literature that came into their homes.

The publications told the news of missionaries on foreign fields, work among the American Indians, progress of churches erecting new houses of worship, the results of revival meetings, the doings of the associations and conventions. Always there was the weekly or monthly sermon, put together in the formal, stilted language of the times, usually divided into three points, and filled with admonitions for Baptists to do justly and live righteously.

It was the world mission enterprise that gave birth to Baptist journalism; for if the "preach-ed" word was essential to evangelism, the published word was indispensable to missions. It was interest in missions that started what Baptists claim to be the oldest church periodical in the world. It appeared in 1803 under the title *The Massachusetts Baptist Missionary Magazine,* a quarterly in pamphlet format with thirty-two pages. It was the voice of the state missionary society, edited by the pastor of the Second Baptist Church of Boston, Thomas Baldwin.

Letters from William Carey and his associates in India and editorials on missionary effort and support were published to stimulate prayer and giving. When the Judsons and Luther Rice became Baptists, this periodical devoted itself almost exclusively to the publication of communications from them and between them.

At the suggestions of Luther Rice, in 1816 *The Latter Day Luminary* was launched as a quarterly, published in Philadelphia by a committee of the Baptist Board of Foreign Missions for the United States. It apparently failed to win support and lasted only until 1826. In 1819 the *Christian Watchman* was launched in Boston, the first Baptist newspaper, which after several consolidations survived as the *Watchman-Examiner.*

In 1822 Luther Rice again entered the field of Baptist journalism when he launched the *Columbian Star* to promote Columbian College in Washington, D.C. It demanded more time and money than he could give, so in 1828 its offices were transferred to Philadelphia and in 1833 to Georgia. A direct descendant of this paper is the *Christian Index,* state Baptist paper published in Atlanta.

According to the late Frank Luther Mott, author of a three-volume study of American magazines, between 1820 and 1845 Baptist periodicals were produced in bewildering abundance.[8] Controversies over doctrine and slavery, as well as continuing interest in missions, spawned and maintained many of them. Preacher-editors used the printing presses as their public forums as well as to forge a common bond of thought and action for the churches.

When the southern states withdrew from the Triennial Convention and established two mission boards, the Foreign Board immediately established a house organ that was named *The Journal,* and offered the Board of Domestic Missions eight pages of each issue. A monthly news sheet captioned *The Commission* was started by the Foreign Board to supplement the more formal publication.

The Triennial Convention, recognizing the necessity for circulating news of its new missionaries and its efforts to unite Baptists of America for their support, made the Massachusetts periodical its official organ in 1817, and changed its name to *The American Baptist Magazine,* issuing it every other month. By 1825 the resources, both editorial and financial, justified monthly publication. In 1836 it was renamed *The Baptist Missionary Magazine,* and in 1910, combining with a monthly devoted to home missions, it chose the title *Missions.* The subtitle "An International Baptist Magazine" was added later.

Its first editor, Dr. Baldwin, undoubtedly had access to one or more copies of the first Baptist periodical on record. Dr. John Rippon of London, pastor of the Baptist Church in Carter Lane, edited a yearbook from 1790 to 1802 entitled *The Baptist Annual Register, including Sketches of the State of Religion Among Different Denominations at Home and Abroad.* It was officially dedicated to "all the baptized ministers and people in America,

England, Ireland, Scotland, Wales, the United Netherlands, France, Switzerland, Poland, Prussia, Russia, and Elsewhere."

And for readers who had not guessed from the eighteen-word title and twenty-two word dedication that this was a missionary document, the editor spelled out the content as "foreign news and missionaries' letters."

Dr. Rippon drew heavily upon the even more remarkable document that William Carey had prepared to convince his colleagues that the cause of foreign missions was not only appropriate for Christians in the late eighteenth century but entirely feasible. Carey's pamphlet, for all its colloquial English, remains a highly readable document, even with its lengthy title: "An ENQUIRY into the OBLIGATIONS OF CHRISTIANS, to use means for the CONVERSION of the HEATHENS, in which the Religious State of the different nations of the world, the success of former undertakings, and the practicability of further undertakings, are considered."

Baptist women were ardent readers of the missionary magazines. To bind the various women's state groups and the numerous local missionary societies together, several Southern Baptist women in the late 1870s launched a paper they called *The Heathen Helper,* published at Louisville. The secretary of the Foreign Mission Board, doubtless prompted more by the urge to encourage what he termed "the dear Sisters" than to appraise objectively their entry into journalism, described the paper as "a bright, eight-page sheet, handsomely illustrated, and filled with reports, letters, and pithy editorials."

The Baptist Sunday School Board

It was during the post-bellum period that the Baptist genius for organizing became clearly apparent throughout America. Striking examples of this trait were the establishment of the Sunday School Board by the Southern Baptist Convention, and the Baptist Young People's Union, first in churches of the North, then among those all over the nation.

For many years after the Civil War, during the Reconstruction period with its painful, slow recovery of industry and transportation and the adjustment of the southern people to free labor, all Baptists depended upon the American Baptist Publication Society for church literature. Its monthly, *The Young Reaper,* first Sunday school "story literature paper" for young people in the United States, was widely read. Attempts of the Southern Baptist Convention to establish a publication society failed, although the first periodical for use in Sunday schools, entitled *Kind Words,* survived these years of poverty and uncertainty by transferral to the Home Mission Board.

The Publication Society founded in 1824 in Philadelphia had a thriving business in 1860. It enjoyed the monopoly in Baptist periodical literature and naturally hoped to keep it by providing Sunday school lesson materials acceptable to Baptists everywhere. It engaged young preachers as colporteurs to visit from church to church in the more remote states, and to introduce the Baptist publications and sell the Bibles printed by the Baptists.

It required no professionally trained eye to detect that the literature from that source was biased. Local preachers and professors engaged to write the materials were educated in the well-established seminaries and preacher-training schools—all of them north of the Mason-Dixon line. For the most part they were city-bred writers, whose urban tastes and sophisticated interests were as obvious in their written prose as their northern accent was in their oral expressions. The content of this literature inevitably reflected the cause the writers knew best—Northern Baptist churches, frontier missions, and foreign missions. With no ulterior motive, the authors of American Baptist Publication Society products devised materials most congenial to the more numerous Baptist Sunday schools in the northeast and the middle Atlantic states. Southern Baptist leaders, churches, missionaries, and fields were rarely mentioned.

The man who recognized and evaluated this influence, the Reverend James Marion Frost, pastor in Richmond, Virginia, set about to convince Southern Baptists that they could never build a strong denominational spirit without their own literature.

Frost was born in 1849 at Georgetown, Kentucky, the son of a Baptist minister who had graduated from John Mason Peck's school, Shurtleff College at Alton, Illinois. The elder Frost was both a preacher and a teacher, for he was a member of the faculty at Georgetown, the Baptist school in central Kentucky, at the time of James's birth. The younger Frost grew up in Kentucky, then wooed and won Nanney Riley, described by Baptist writers of her day as "a daughter of the Georgetown Female Academy, a beautiful bluegrass belle." James took his belle to various pastorates in their native state and to Alabama, and in his late thirties they went to Leigh Street Baptist Church, Richmond.

One evening in 1889 young Frost worked late on a resolution he proposed to offer at the next annual session of the Southern Baptist Convention. He proposed the formation of a Southern Baptist board of publication. He delivered his statement to the office of the editor of the state paper, and in the *Religious Herald* for February 27, 1890, his resolution was set forth. Along with the text was a discussion of the proposal by Frost.

He rejected the suggestion that his plan was malicious in nature. He declared he was not provincial in his sympathies or unappreciative of the service that the American Baptist Society had rendered to Baptist churches nationwide. He clearly indicated his willingness for churches to exercise their historic right to use whatever literature they preferred, and order it from whatever source they wished, but he pointed out the significance of having literature sympathetic toward the interests and projects of the Southern Baptist Convention if there was to be adequate support for these.

An editorial in that issue of the *Religious Herald* protested. "We cannot agree to the wisdom of the proposed organization," the editor said. "The precedents are all against it. Previous experiments along this line have, all of them, been embarrassing and troublesome while they lasted, and have closed their fitful and unsatisfactory lives in disastrous failure."[9]

Undaunted by a flood of similar criticisms, Frost offered his resolution to the Convention at Fort Worth in May. It was the session that broke Convention precedent by electing a layman as president, Judge Jonathan Haralson of Alabama, a man of great dignity and a strict parliamentarian.

An address on temperance by a well-known pastor, J. B. Cranfill, was stopped short by the judge's gavel when the speaker used the word "devil."

"Dr. Cranfill!" the judge interrupted. "Don't you think that is a rather strong word to use in this presence?"

"Brother Moderator, it is a strong word," the preacher admitted without irritation. "I apologize. With your consent and with the consent of the Convention, I withdraw the word and substitute 'Satan' instead."

Tension was broken, and some of the fight on Frost's resolution was postponed by referring the matter to a committee. For a whole year the subject was debated by pastors and laymen, some pleading for the new agency to give Southern Baptists their own literature, others insisting that what they ordered from Philadelphia was good enough for any Baptist church. Who could say how many periodicals southern churches would order? Who could predict success for such a venture when paper was scarce, printing expensive, and so few Southern Baptists had experience in writing about the Bible for children?

Primed for a good debate to air Baptist differences of opinion, messengers thronged into Birmingham, Alabama, for the next session of the Convention. Many preachers came with pockets of their Prince Albert coats bulging with speech manuscripts which they hoped might turn the tide one way or the other, and even make names for themselves among their brethren.

Frost introduced his resolution, changing the name of the proposed agency from "board of publication" to "Sunday School Board." He was ready to speak for it when Dr. John A. Broadus, president of the Southern Baptist Theological Seminary, former teacher of many of the ministers present, stepped to the podium and without waiting for recognition from the presiding officer pleaded with the churchmen to adopt the proposal. The vote was taken before anyone else could speak, and only thirteen among the hundreds of messengers were recorded against it. James Marion Frost was named the first executive secretary of the new board, and Nashville was designated as its base.

Thus in 1891 came into being the Sunday School Board of the Southern Baptist Convention. The perspiring Baptist leaders in the opera house in Birmingham that warm May day—some of them bitterly disappointed that they had lost their chance for a great speech—could not have known it at the time, but they had established an organization that became the major factor in the growth of their Convention from that year forward. A conscious rival of the Publication Society, the board succeeded from the

start, both financially and as the center of numerous Southern
Baptist educational activities.

Not only did the new board quickly win the literature orders of
most Southern Baptist churches, it led in organizing a church
school for every congregation that lacked one. It developed
graded literature, teacher training courses, standards for adult
classes as well as children's Sunday-school work, and promotional
efforts.

Enter the Young People

The founding of the Baptist Young People's Union of America
marked a long step forward in Baptist growth. The dates of the organizing convention were July 7, 8, and 9, 1891. The place was
the Second Baptist Church, Chicago. The man chiefly responsible
for launching the movement was the Reverend O. W. Van Osdel,
pastor of the First Baptist Church of Ottawa, Kansas. He had observed two such youth organizations and was convinced that they
were valuable adjuncts of the churches sponsoring them: the Epworth League in Methodist churches and the Christian Endeavor
in congregations of the Christian, Presbyterian, and some other
fellowships. In 1887 Van Osdel published a plan for organizing
the young people in Baptist churches, needed, he maintained, "as
a department for work and special training." The exponent of this
idea emphasized that such an organization could train youths in
Bible study, Baptist doctrine, missionary enterprises, and systematic giving to religious causes.

Van Osdel carried on a voluminous correspondence with other
Baptist pastors and denominational leaders all over America, including many in the Southern Baptist Convention, urging the formation of a "Union of Young Baptists." The churches of Kansas
called a convention of young people in Clay Center in October
1889. During that month a similar convention met in Grand Island, Nebraska, and formed the "Nebraska Convention of Baptist
Young People." The movement spread to Wisconsin, then to several other states in the North. Planning to call the new youth
training groups the "Loyalists," Van Osdel began a monthly publication with that name.

That was the signal for a storm of opposition to break upon the movement. "Nothing but a courting society in the church!" several Baptist papers screamed. Pastors by the score denounced the proposal as a scheme that would create a "tail to wag the dog." The idea that young people of both sexes could work together in church activities, with all the risks of scandal, proved alarming to countless Baptist leaders.

Undaunted, Van Osdel moved ahead, with a vanguard of enthusiastic supporters among the progressive leadership in Northern Baptist ranks. Dr. Benjamin Griffith of the First Baptist Church of Philadelphia called a preliminary conference at his church on April 22, 1891. Following this meeting the actual invitations went out for an organizing convention in Chicago in July.

At ten o'clock on the morning of July 7 the sessions began, with more than 1,600 representatives from thirty-three states and territories, the District of Columbia, and the provinces of Ontario and Nova Scotia. There were many young men and a few young women present, but the guiding hands were those of veteran Baptist leaders.

The movement was a success from the start, with Baptist churches all over the northern states organizing B.Y.P.U.'s despite the vigorous and vocal opposition of some pastors who, like those who stood against the Sunday schools, feared the new organization would steal the limelight from them. Dr. John H. Chapman became president of the B.Y.P.U.A., with Dr. E. E. Chivers corresponding secretary. The latter took over the publication of the magazine, now called *The Young People at Work*. In 1893 a junior department was organized, and by 1900 thousands of young Baptists were completing study courses in the Bible and Baptist doctrine.

Churches of the Southern Baptist Convention seized upon the B.Y.P.U. idea enthusiastically and made it their own. At the annual session of the Southern Baptist Convention in May 1896 the young people's work was officially recognized as an auxiliary activity. By 1900 thousands of unions were training young people in church membership and enlisting them as candidates for the ministry and for mission work at home and abroad. Baptists had developed a sure method for recruiting young, dedicated workers.

The fact that young people of both sexes freely mingled in discussions, study courses, and social events under church auspices proved a blessing. Many a pastor learned that romances begun in the B.Y.P.U. led to lasting happiness, and these marriages produced new and welcome crops of Baptists.

RAUSCHENBUSCH AND THE SOCIAL
GOSPEL

Pastor from the West Side

In the autumn of 1886, a tall, neatly dressed man, wearing a Van Dyke-style beard, the very picture of clerical dignity, appeared before the councilmen of New York City to plead for places for the children of his neighborhood to play, and—of all things—for sandpiles for them to play in. The man had a slight German accent, for he was of German descent. He commanded respect, for it was obvious that he was highly educated. And he was articulate, positive, and convincing.

He was Walter Rauschenbusch, a Baptist pastor from the section of New York's West Side known as "Hell's Kitchen," a man soon to be praised by some and denounced more heartily by many as a religious fanatic.

"Our children *must* have places to play," he argued before the city authorities. He also discussed the matter with fellow ministers of New York and with anyone who would listen. Tuberculosis was prevalent among children of the poorer families, denied sunshine and fresh air. Surely anyone could see the need for outdoor playgrounds for the health of such children, said Rauschenbusch. Surely they needed to be taken off the streets and away from temptations to steal, to fight, and to become generally delinquent.

Rauschenbusch argued about other social conditions, too. He brought up matters never discussed in polite home or church society, such as how church people should be helping "fallen" girls who become unwed mothers. He talked about such unpopular subjects as how employers should pay living wages, and how, if Jesus were on earth at the time, he would do as he had before—concern himself with the right use of money, care for the aged and the sick, the unemployed and the handicapped, and other social problems that needed to be solved in order to help people know abundant living.

Here was a man bravely charting a new course for Baptists, and for church people of all faiths in the America of the last two decades of the nineteenth century. When Rauschenbusch was called by his fellow Baptists a "social gospeler," it was an accusation not lightly given or accepted. It implied that the crusader was unorthodox, if not downright heretical. Up to that day preaching concerned itself overwhelmingly with getting souls saved and safely on the road to heaven. With that accomplished, the church provided for them a comfortable pew where they could hear sermons that carried no wearisome alarms about the need to improve the lot of unfortunate people. What Jesus had to say about justice and social uplift was considered irrevelant or secondary. Speaking as a Baptist, but more definitely as a Christian minister, Rauschenbusch said of his church:

"Our business is to make over an antiquated and immoral economic system; to get rid of laws, customs, maxims, and philosophies inherited from an evil and despotic past; to create just and brotherly relations between great groups and classes of society; and thus to lay a social foundation on which modern men individually can live and work in a fashion that will not outrage all the elements in them."[1]

Walter Rauschenbusch was born in Rochester, New York, on October 4, 1861, six months after the Civil War began and fifteen years after his parents emigrated from Germany to America. His father, Elder August Rauschenbusch, as we have noted, was immersed on the Illinois side of the Mississippi River, became pastor of a Baptist church in Bridgeport, Ontario, and was in Philadelphia as one of the organizers of the German-American Baptists. He helped create the North American Baptist General Conference. He organized the German Department in the Rochester Theological Seminary and served as its teacher of theology.

Walter grew up in the devout home of his parents, one of five children. It was a typical Baptist preacher's home of the period, with daily family worship, Bible reading and prayer, Sunday school and church services on Sunday. Walter was a precocious youth, easily mastering Latin, Greek, Hebrew, and French, in addition to English and the German speech used in the home. A story has it that when a visitor asked Walter what he wanted to be when he grew up, he answered: "I want to be a John the Baptist!"

Elder August Rauschenbusch sent the family to the old country for a year, and then joined them for his summer vacation. On the banks of the Rhine River he pointed out a spot where one of Walter's cousins had drowned. Promptly peeling off his clothes Walter plunged in, swam across the river, and without touching the bank swam back again to prove to his father his lack of fear!

The same lack of fear characterized all his life and work. When he was seventeen, Walter had a personal experience which he described in these words: "I felt I was in a far country and I wanted to come back to my own country. I did not want to tend hogs any longer. This experience influenced my soul down to its depths."

This vital, vivid, personal touch with God left young Rauschenbusch with a permanent conviction that spiritual rebirth is essential to salvation. It became his answer to those who feared that his social gospel would become a substitute for repentance and belief. The experience prompted him to decide to become a minister, as had his father and five grandfathers before him.

Further schooling for Walter in Germany was followed by studies in the seminary at Rochester, where his father became his principal teacher, and where he began to express his unorthodox ideas about the Christian's social responsibility.

By the time Walter Rauschenbusch was graduated from the seminary he was a handsome, virile, six-footer, with red hair, hazel eyes, a sporty pair of "burnsides" and a mustache. He answered a call from German Baptists in Louisville, Kentucky, to spend the summer of 1885 helping to rehabilitate a run-down church in that city. "The sins of pastors and sins of members had created distrust within and contempt among outsiders," he later observed. The experience left him discouraged and hungry for a more productive field of work. But the congregation almost doubled in three months, and he was invited to return for the next summer.

"I want to do hard work for God," Walter told a classmate at the seminary. "I want to be a pastor, powerful with men, preaching to them Christ as the man in whom their affections and energies can find the satisfaction for which mankind is groaning. And if I do become anything but a pastor, you may believe that I have sunk to a lower ideal or that there was a very unmistakable call to duty in that direction."[2]

That "unmistakable call" seemed for a time to be for service as a foreign missionary. Walter's sister was appointed a missionary to India, and this spurred Walter to ask for an appointment also. The American Baptist Foreign Mission Society recommended him for the presidency of the Telugu Theological Seminary at Ramapatnam in southern India. Delighted at the prospect, the eager young preacher made ready to go. But the professor of Old Testament at Rochester raised a question as to the "doctrinal soundness" of this young man who so forcefully believed that Christian people needed to apply Christian solutions to social problems. The Society decided it could not take the risk and suddenly withdrew the offer. The First Baptist Church of Springfield, Illinois, which had made overtures to young Rauschenbusch, lost interest on hearing of the Society action.

These were harsh blows. Turned down by the foreign mission agency of his denomination and rejected from consideration as a pastor because of his belief in principles he considered urgently important, Walter Rauschenbusch became seriously discouraged. When the next pulpit was offered him, he accepted it. The call was from a church on the West Side of New York City.

In the Heat of Hell's Kitchen

On June 1, 1886, at the age of twenty-four, the Reverend Walter Rauschenbusch became pastor of the Second Baptist Church, in the big American metropolis. The 125 members could offer him a salary of only $900 a year, of which $300 was needed to pay the rent on a five-room flat. The church building was an old, inconvenient, and ugly structure located on Forty-third Street in the West Side tenement section. There was good reason for the area to be called "Hell's Kitchen" by police and citizens, for some evil was always cooking among its hard-drinking, tough people. After a short time in this pastorate Rauschenbusch wrote to a friend: "God knows I have a little desire to be useful to my fellow men and these few weeks have again taught me that I can do so best by bringing them into living and personal relations with our Lord Jesus Christ."[8]

Here in a neighborhood of wretched, crowded apartment houses, the sensitive bachelor preacher found plenty of opportunities to be helpful to his fellowmen. Here for eleven years he gave his heart and his life to a Christlike ministry of pastoring, preaching, and lobbying for improved social conditions.

Rauschenbusch made a survey of the West Side area to learn firsthand its problems. He observed the ill-ventilated, over-crowded, health-destroying, crime-breeding slums. He vicariously suffered the grinding poverty, the unemployment, the insecurity, malnutrition, and despair of his neighbors, most of them immigrants or first-generation Americans and many of them fellow German Americans. He was especially touched by the plight of the children, and the neglect and temptations that led them into delinquency, called in that day "youthful wickedness." He visited the sick and imprisoned, whether or not they belonged to his Second Baptist Church. He buried the premature dead and challenged his church members to make friends with all the friendless in the spirit of Christ. He preached that the kingdom of God begins with personal religion but includes also concern for the unfortunate and justice for the working man.

Pastor Rauschenbusch lost no time carrying his campaign of civic betterment to the New York City authorities. He pleaded for children's playgrounds (with sandpiles!), fresh-air centers, better sanitation facilities in the tenements, inspection to enforce safety provisions. Many of these proposals for improved conditions were grudgingly granted during those eleven years, for Rauschenbusch became loved and respected by those he befriended. Politicians did not care to offend the friends of anyone so respected—preacher or otherwise. Authorities could not shake him off, for they knew that he spoke for countless thousands of silent citizens who looked to him as their champion.

Rauschenbusch soon heard the rumblings of criticism from fellow Baptist pastors because of his social gospel, but he continued to preach "Thy kingdom come, thy will be done *on earth*."

"These were not the words of an idle dreamer," he thundered. He preached about Amos, the Tekoa herdsman of the eighth century B.C., and he applied the words of Amos' social gospel to conditions in New York City in that day. A butcher who belonged to his church declared, "We have found in Pastor Rauschenbusch more that is Christlike than in any human being we have ever met."[4]

In 1888 the young pastor of robust health came down with a severe attack of influenza, called at that time the Russian grippe. Before he had recovered, and in violation of his doctor's orders, he responded to the call of a church family for help in an emergency. This brought on a relapse that affected his hearing, and he was soon deaf.

In three years' time the membership of Rauschenbusch's church grew to 213. By the sale of the old building on West Forty-third Street, enough money was realized to start a new church building two blocks away with more room, light, and air, at a final cost of $25,000. The cornerstone was laid on October 19, 1889.

Thrifty by nature, Rauschenbusch had agreed to the $900 salary as being commensurate with the financial resources of his congregation. He had simple tastes and his expenses were meager, according to his personal account book, but in 1892 he made a major investment. It was a long-wished-for typewriter. Now he began to put his philosophy and theology into permanent form. He became editor of a weekly paper entitled *For the Right,* which drew favorable editorial comment in the New York *Times.*

The industrial revolution in America had created a vast need for cheap labor. The news reaching Europe brought a flood of workers through the immigration station at Ellis Island to the United States. The immigrants fanned out over the country to build railroads and business houses, to dig metal from the earth, to shape steel products in the mills, and some to till the soil. In good times these immigrants and their children managed, with thrift and enterprise, to get along. When a panic hit, as in the depressions of 1873 and 1893, the new citizens often became the victims of unemployment, with all its accompanying hardships and temptations.

The Baptist pastor vigorously supported the cause of the working men for higher wages and for the right to strike. He declared that the strikes of 1890, when many groups of working men were trying to force employers to grant an eight-hour working day, were justified. During the severe winter of 1894, following the high unemployment that resulted from the hard times of 1893, many of the members of Rauschenbusch's church were forced to give up their tenement flats and move uptown or across the East River for cheaper rents. The pastor-editor denounced the tenement owners for their greed and pleaded with them to improve their buildings and lower their rents. He defended the cause of the streetcar employees of Brooklyn in their strike for higher wages in 1895.

"The prophets believed that this world would be changed into the Kingdom of God here, where he would rule," he declared from his pulpit and in his paper. "The kingdom of God is as broad as humanity, and as big as God himself. And besides, you have the authority of the Lord Jesus Christ in it. That was his idea. That is what he came and died for." And he editorialized about Pilate's washbowl as the symbol of those who shut their eyes to evil social conditions or try to ignore them out of existence.

"When I saw how men toiled all their life long, hard, toilsome lives, and at the end had almost nothing to show for it; how strong men begged for work and could not get it in hard times; how little children died—oh, the children's funerals! They gripped my heart." So Rauschenbusch wrote of the experience.[5]

It was to *persons*, one by one, that he ministered as a pastor. He preached "Ye must be born again," and he visited the elderly, the unemployed, the mentally ill, the delinquent in prison, and the bereaved. To individuals he gave his personal care and devotion. And it was because he identified himself so completely with *persons* that he came to care so much about what an evil social order was doing to them. His belief in the supreme value of human personality led him to crusade for a more just, more co-operative society which would help human beings achieve their full potential as God's creatures. For him, social and personal Christianity were blended.

Rauschenbusch regarded himself as much a Christian evangelist when he proclaimed against cutthroat competition as when he pleaded with individuals to get right with God. He urged his fellow ministers to fight monopolies, thus stimulating the movement that Theodore Roosevelt had launched in his crusade of "trust busting." He was severe in his indictment of the church, using the term, as he often did, to indicate the body of Christian people in the United States: "Its theology is silent or stammers where we most need a ringing and dogmatic message. It has no adequate answer to the fundamental moral questions of our day . . . Its hymns, its ritual, its prayers of devotion, are so devoid of social thought that the most thrilling passions of our generation lie in us half stifled for lack of religious utterance."

The Pastor Becomes Professor

Walter Rauschenbusch acquired a wife, Pauline Rather, in April 1893. She was a Milwaukee schoolteacher whom he had met at a conference of German Baptists in her home church. Pauline became the mistress of the Rauschenbusch pastorium on the third floor of the church house, and a most valuable pastoral assistant to a deaf husband.

In 1897 Rauschenbusch reluctantly left his pastorate and his personal campaigns for social betterment in New York City to become a professor in Rochester Theological Seminary. He was strongly impelled to make this move by the desire to influence the rising generation of pastors to his way of thinking about the kingdom of God on earth. He spent all the rest of his life, twenty-one years, at Rochester, teaching and training leaders for German-American Baptist churches, most of which were still using the German language for worship services. He lived to see these churches become bilingual, and ultimately English-language churches with German-Baptist traditions.

Rauschenbusch taught New Testament interpretation, the natural sciences, civil government, zoology, English—and anything else that was needed and for which there was no other professor at the time. In 1902 he was designated professor of church history for the seminary. He kept his hand in the pastoral ministry by serving as shepherd of a little German-Baptist church on the western edge of Rochester, whose members were all immigrants.

All Rauschenbusch's teaching and preaching were colored and enlivened by his insistence that pastors should lead their churches to the forefront in the struggle for better health, higher wages, safer working conditions, shorter hours with more time for leisure and self-improvement.

Professor and Mrs. Rauschenbusch had a family of five children, of which the father was, in spite of his inability to hear, the life of the party. He had a vital sense of humor and was by nature a fun-loving person. A streetcar in Rochester once knocked him down at a busy intersection. Rauschenbusch picked himself up, brushed the dust off his pants, and apologized to the conductor for obstructing traffic. He wrote a letter of apology that night and sent the company $5.00!

At the seminary, the professor offered a new course on the Devil. It amused him to be told that the students asked one another, "Are you going to the Devil with Rauschie?"

But in the face of the social ills of his time, the preacher-professor was in dead earnest. To his intense sorrow, his father August drank to excess and died an alcoholic. Walter Rauschenbusch had observed that the liquor traffic was the special enemy of the working man, as well as the elderly teacher, and he became a vigorous foe of this business. His "prayer for alcoholics," distributed widely for use in churches and homes, was a poignant petition.

Rauschenbusch was an eloquent pray-er. One of his most potent books, still in use a half century after his death, was *Prayers of the Social Awakening*. He considered prayer his daily food, and he regarded it as vital to the welfare of his country. He said of prayer:

"Perhaps the secret of the decline and fall of nations, or of their rise and power, could more truly be sought in that direction than in wars and trade balances. Perhaps the future of our nation, the future of the white race, the future of humanity is largely contained in the future of prayer. To some extent it depends on the question whether you and I pray. The duty of prayer may be the real 'white man's burden.' "[6]

But prayer for Rauschenbusch was never a rabbit's foot or magic wand for his personal convenience or his church's escape from duty. The year after he moved to New York City he formed a friendship with two other young pastors in the community: Nathaniel Schmidt, pastor of the Swedish Baptist congregation, and Leighton Williams, who gave up law to follow his father, William

R. Williams, in the pastorate of Amity (Street) Baptist Church on West Fifty-fourth Street. These three formed what they termed the "Brotherhood of the Kingdom."

Walter considered it a "society of Jesus"—"a band of men voluntarily associating themselves, with a devotion as great as that of Jesuits, but with clearer and juster opinions and greater freedom for individual action, who should be in a truer and higher sense a Society of Jesus, and who, without subscription to any creed, should endeavor to realize the ethical and spiritual principles of Jesus, both in their individual and social aspects, in their own lives and work, both individually and in co-operation with each other."

The Brotherhood was formally organized in December 1892, after several informal meetings, chiefly in connection with sessions of the Baptist missionary societies. Held at Williams' summer home in Marlborough, New York, in August 1893, the meeting was reported by the local paper in these words:

"A group of Baptist clergymen had met who have organized for the study of Christianity in its social aspects, for the promulgation of more just views of the Kingdom of God, and the application of the principles of the Gospel to the social and industrial systems of the world."

The guest book at the Williams' home showed thirty-one names in 1894, following the initial meeting with less than a dozen participants, and in 1895, forty-five men and women signed the guest book. George Dana Boardman, Jr., who was born in Burma, was one of the Brotherhood that year. Chapters of the Brotherhood were soon formed in Rochester and Boston. It became interdenominational in membership.

The Brotherhood of the Kingdom held its tryst every summer for years. In the Visitors' Book the summer of 1909, Rauschenbusch inscribed these sentiments:

"Only where mind touches mind does the mind do its best work. Where love and confidence draw the bars and bolts of caution and distrust, thought passes easily from heart to heart, and finds ready lodgment. So we grow . . . God bless this hill-top temple of the spirit . . . May it do for others in the future what it did for me in the past."

When the Northern Baptist Convention first met in 1907, its social service activities were organized under the direction of members of the Brotherhood.

Why Reform the World?

Rauschenbusch never expected that his ideas and principles would be immediately accepted by the majority of his fellow Baptist ministers, North or South, East or West, so he was neither surprised nor disappointed at the growing criticisms and denunciations directed his way by his own church leaders. He well understood that from a doctrinal standpoint opposition to the social gospel stemmed from the traditional emphasis placed by Baptists—and by many other denominations—upon the principle of salvation by grace.

"By grace are ye saved!" was the text of countless sermons from the burning lips of evangelists and pastors, seeking the lost. "Not by works, lest any man should boast!" Paul's admonition to the Roman Christians was likewise thundered from the pulpits.

There was genuine fear that anyone who preached a social gospel would do so at the neglect of a gospel of faith, with the result that churches would fill up with unsaved persons who tried to get to heaven by doing good.

Supporting this feeling was a strong background of premillennial belief among Baptists that the world was growing worse and worse, and would continue to grow worse until it would get so bad that the Lord would step in and bring a halt to Time as it is now known. The second coming of Christ was expected any hour of the day or night. In the face of this impending event, the churches were supposed to see to it that individuals were prepared to escape from earth and enjoy the ecstasy of heaven forevermore. The minister's duty was to call men to repentance and to flee from the wrath to come.

In that philosophy it was useless for the church to devote itself to trying to reform the world. After all, the church stood on one side, and the world on the other; and "Come ye apart from them" —lifted out of context—was a convenient and comforting reason for ignoring the wretchedness of humanity or trying to find healing for its social ills.

Walter Rauschenbusch believed in salvation by grace as firmly as did any of his critics. But he sensed more clearly than most of his fellow ministers that changing social conditions in the industrial age made it imperative that churches apply moral and spiritual principles to the solution of the problems of slums, poverty, unemployment, and crime. He wrote:

"To become fully Christian the Church must come out of its isolation. In theory and practice the Church has long constituted a world by itself. It has been governed by ecclesiastical motives and interests, which are often remote from the interests of humanity, and has almost uniformly set church questions ahead of social questions. It has often built a soundproof habitation in which people could live for years without becoming definitely conscious of the existence of prostitution, child labor, or tenement crowding. It has offered peace and spiritual tranquillity to men and women who needed thunderclaps and lightnings. Like all the rest of us, the church will get salvation by finding the purpose of its existence outside of itself, in the Kingdom of God, the perfect life of the race."[7]

Thus Rauschenbusch cut away the dense undergrowth in the traditional Baptist doctrinal forest and showed to his denomination the tall, verdant trees of a religion that takes into account man's responsibility to his fellowmen, and that demonstrates that faith without works is dead.

Believing that he should put his principles of the social gospel into writing, Walter Rauschenbusch began to produce a book which he entitled *Christianity and the Social Crisis*. The pages glowed with the warmth of the author's conviction that the churches were neglecting their social responsibilities and needed to follow the example of Christ in ministering to the physical as well as the spiritual needs of the poor, the troubled, the sick, the unemployed. In late 1906 Rauschenbusch deposited his manuscript with a publisher, and left for a year's study in Germany, intending thus to ride out the storm he knew the book would stir up. When he returned to the States he was amazed to discover that while some Baptists were condemning his philosophy, Christian statesmen were hailing him as a true prophet. Many saw truth in such statements as this challenge to modern Christians:

"The first apostolate of Christianity was born from a deep fellow-feeling for social misery and from the consciousness of a great historical opportunity. Jesus saw the peasantry of Galilee following him about with their poverty and their diseases, like shepherd-less sheep that have been scattered and harried by beasts of prey, and his heart had compassion on them. He felt that the harvest was ripe, but there were few to reap it. Past history had come to its culmination, but there were few who understood the situation and were prepared to cope with it. He bade his disciples to pray for laborers for the harvest, and then made them answer their own prayers by sending them out two by two to proclaim the kingdom of God. That was the beginning of the worldwide mission of Christianity.

"The situation is repeated on a vaster scale today. If Jesus stood today amid our modern life, with that outlook on the condition of all humanity which observation and travel and the press would spread before him, he would create a new apostolate to meet the new needs in a new harvest time of history."

Rauschenbusch continued to write. *The American Magazine* published a Rauschenbusch prayer in each issue from December 1909 through 1911. He produced a steady stream of articles on religious, social, and political subjects. He dared to proclaim himself a "Christian Socialist," long before the Socialist Party of Great Britain became a challenge to the Tories in that country and the term "socialist" had become an epithet among conservatives in America. Professor Rauschenbusch emphatically denied sympathy with the revolutionary approach of Karl Marx. He repudiated entirely the materialism and the atheism of Marxist communism. He decried the autocratic discipline of the revolutionaries.

"Religion is the only power which can make socialism succeed if it is established," he insisted. "It cannot work in an irreligious country."

Rauschenbusch included in his political concept of socialism the public ownership of monopoly services such as gas, water, electric light and power, telegraph and telephone lines, and surface roads. He believed in the extension of education, libraries, museums, parks, playgrounds to promote the welfare of the people. He advocated legislation to shorten the working time and improve conditions for skilled and unskilled laborers, to prevent child labor, and to restrict labor for women. He teamed up with Jacob Riis and others concerned in social betterment to start reform movements that decades later were realized in municipal, state, and national legislation. He considered himself a Republican, of the Teddy Roosevelt variety.

Rauschenbusch toyed with some extreme ideas that have since been abandoned as impractical, such as Henry George's "single tax" scheme which would make property the basis for all taxes and which the industrial age was even then proving unworkable as a means of support for the public services of the government. Doubtless this Baptist crusader also went to some extremes in his opinions as to what socialism could do. He could not have foreseen that developments in American economic life, such as widespread ownership of large corporations by individual stockholders, the organization of co-operatives, and ever-higher taxes to support an ever-expanding government, would distribute profits effectively and at the same time leave industry to function and produce those profits under private initiative.

The Ecumenical Spirit

Responding to a request that he write a paper on "Why I am a Baptist," Rauschenbusch made clear his denominational loyalties and defined distinctive principles of Baptists more effectively than many preachers of his day or since. He wrote:

"I do believe that we Baptists have a magnificent body of truth —free, vital, honest, spiritual, and wholly in line with the noblest tendencies of our age. But we must realize its largeness and present it in all its out-of-door greatness and freshness, and not show people a few dried plants and stuffed animals as exponents of the Promised Land to which God has led us and to which we invite them."[8]

The crusader for social justice stated as his first reason for being a Baptist: "The Christian faith as Baptists hold it sets spiritual experience boldly to the front as the one great thing in religion. It aims at experimental religion. We are an evangelistic body. We summon all men to conscious repentance from sin, to conscious prayer for forgiveness. If anyone desires to enter our churches we ask for evidence of such experience and we ask for nothing else."[9]

His second reason for being a Baptist was equally well defined.

Despite all the criticisms hurled his direction by fellow Baptists, Rauschenbusch said that he liked the social expression of the Christian faith as Baptists know it. "Our Baptist organization, though it is faulty in many ways and though it creaks and groans as it works along, is built on very noble Christian lines and therefore is dear to me." He asserted that the Baptist faith was also dear to him because its churches were Christian democracies, with no priestly class or hierarchy within the ministry, built upon home rule and "declining all alliances with the state."

Rauschenbusch gave as his third reason for being a Baptist his satisfaction with his church's concept of worship, and he added: "In our common worship we shall come closest to the spirit of true Christianity if every act is full of joy in God and his fellowship, love for one another, hatred for all evil, and an honest desire to live a right life in the sight of Christ."

In a spirit of ecumenicity far beyond that possessed by most of his fellow Baptist ministers, Rauschenbusch concluded: "Baptists, in tying to the New Testament, have hitched their chariot to a star, and they will have to keep moving . . . We are not a perfect denomination. We are capable of being just as narrow and small as anybody. There are fine qualities in which other denominations surpass us. I do not want to foster Baptist self-deceit, because thereby I should grieve the spirit of Christ. I do not want to make Baptists shut themselves up in their little clamshells and be indifferent to the ocean outside of them. I am a Baptist, but I am more than a Baptist. All things are mine; whether Francis of Assisi, or Luther, or Knox, or Wesley; all are mine because I am Christ's. The old Adam is a strict denominationalist; the new Adam is just a Christian."

A careful and diligent student of history, Rauschenbusch developed a passionate hatred of war. The Christian Socialist became an articulate Christian pacifist. When war broke upon Europe in August 1914 Walter Rauschenbusch was grieved and dismayed. That the Kaiser of his own ancestral country should have had such a leading part in the tragedy gave him almost unbearable anguish. He pinned a small piece of black crepe on his lapel and vowed to wear it until the fighting stopped.

He kept that vow. When he died on July 25, 1918, four months before the armistice brought an end to the first Great War, he still wore his crepe in mourning for what he considered a monstrous and obsolete way of settling international disputes.

Dr. Harry Emerson Fosdick, who knew the Rochester professor personally, said of him in a short interpretation of his life and work for *A Rauschenbusch Reader:* "Rauschenbusch did more after his death than he ever did in his lifetime. Details of his message might be overpassed in the swift movement of events, but the essence of his message—the social and economic transformation involved in the coming of the Kingdom of God on earth —is an integral part of the Christian gospel wherever intelligence and conscience are alive in the churches."[10]

Proof of that opinion may be found in the fact that all major bodies of Baptists, and most major denominations of various faiths and kinds in the United States, have formed social-action groups to influence public thinking and to enlist public support for social betterment.

Foy Valentine, executive secretary of the Southern Baptist Convention's Christian Life Commission, has said of Rauschenbusch: "It is fitting that Baptists today should seek to become more familiar with the thought and work of this vastly influential Baptist of a previous generation, for the shadow of his ministry at the point of applied Christianity still falls clearly across our own way."

Jitsuo Morikawa, Nisei

"From rags to riches," spiritually defined, is the life story of one Japanese-American from British Columbia. Born near Vancouver, at sixteen the Canadian was a rebellious, bitter Nisei, but he made a decision for God, professed his faith, and submitted to baptism in a Baptist church. He then moved to California for higher education, where he completed a course at the Bible Institute of Los Angeles and graduated from the University of California at Los Angeles. He was ordained to the gospel ministry in 1937. In 1940 he had earned his master's degree in theology at Southern Baptist Theological Seminary, Louisville, Kentucky.

The Reverend Jitsuo Morikawa chose a Japanese-American wife, and he and Hazel served three churches simultaneously in the Los Angeles area, in youth and pastoral work. Then came Pearl

Harbor! In March 1942, 110,000 residents of Japanese descent on the West Coast, by order of President Franklin D. Roosevelt, were forced into "relocation centers." Jitsuo became the Protestant pastor of the Poston (Arizona) camp. He accepted an opportunity eighteen months later to resettle in the Midwest. While World War II was still raging in the South Pacific, the First Baptist Church of Chicago called the alien as its pastor. Morikawa became the senior minister of a white church in the multiracial university community on Chicago's South Side. The church soon became multiracial. Its pastor, who served for twelve years, became a naturalized citizen in 1954.

The American Baptist Convention (later renamed American Baptist Churches, U.S.A.) appointed Dr. Morikawa director of evangelism in 1956. For twenty years he led this major body of Baptists and the National Council of Churches plus the World Council of Churches in the vital function of the church: sharing the Good News of Christ. He and his wife and two sons made their home at King of Prussia, Pennsylvania, with his office at Valley Forge, the national headquarters.

When the famous Riverside Church of New York called Morikawa to be senior minister as interim pastor for one year and to advise in the search for a new pastor, he took early retirement to accept the post. In 1977, during that year of ministry, he was the recipient of the Browning Award for Spreading the Christian Gospel—one of the awards given annually in five major fields of endeavor.

Morikawa is the author of a book, *Servants for a Servant People,* and a brochure, "My Spiritual Pilgrimage"—the speech he made in 1973 at Lincoln, Nebraska, to the Ministers and Missionaries Benefit Board of his Convention. A few statements from that readable booklet deserve to be quoted:

> You can sense what conversion meant: to know my sins were forgiven; and accepted by God, I accepted myself. . . . But also behind this boy saying "Yes" to Jesus was the unsuspected birth of a revolutionary, the birth of a stubborn will which refused to acquiesce to a society which deprived me the elemental rights of citi-

zenship. . . . I was called to a mission to serve God and man . . .

How else can you explain the audacity of a sixteen-year-old boy testifying to the leading Buddhist leader of the community, winning seven young men to Christ in the first six months after his conversion, among them his school teacher twice his age and his brother five years older? How else can you explain the courage of a boy preaching from a crowded street corner at a sensitive age when peer reaction and peer acceptance means more than life itself, but chose to be a "fool for Christ" in the eyes of his peers? . . .

During these forty-five tumultuous years we have seen the church sow seeds of rebirth and reap revolutions: racial, social, political revolutions at home and abroad. For when conversions occur in the human soul from apathy to purpose, from despair to hope, from death to life, from self-rejection to self-affirmation; revolutions for freedom, independence, equality and justice occur in the soul of society, among suppressed races, bondaged peoples, and colonial nations. . . .

So my conversion was a crisis of faith, the pivotal struggle in a human soul as to who prevails: Christ or culture, God or man, Jesus Christ as Sovereign Will or a people's will.

An Itinerant Exhorter

From colonial days to the War Between the States, Negro slaves and freed servants worshiped for the most part with their white masters. They filled the galleries of larger church buildings, or sat in the back benches in the smaller churches, having a devout share from those reserved sections in the services with their white families.

It was generally understood that a slave who wished to attend services in his master's church could do so with the white man's consent, and one who wished to join a church of which his master was not a member could do so on written permission and request of the master. Often white preachers held services regularly on Sunday afternoons for groups of slaves and servants of all ages, sometimes in the sanctuaries of the white churches and more often in the open air in a grove of trees.

However, some Negro preachers led in the organization of separate churches so that they could sing their own hymns, offer their own prayers, and give expression to their feelings of joy or sorrow uninhibited by the overshadowing presence of their white masters.

First such Negro Baptist church was gathered together by a slave preacher on the plantation of wealthy and prominent Thomas Galphin near Savannah, Georgia. The year was probably 1773. The preacher was named Palmer, an itinerant exhorter who had Galphin's permission to come and preach to the slaves on the grounds of the plantation grist mill. Palmer made a powerful impression upon Galphin's Negroes. He baptized several converts in the mill stream, one of whom was David George. This converted slave, who had learned to read and write, recorded that the church was founded with eight members and that he was appointed by white Baptists of the neighborhood to be their preacher. When the British captured Savannah in December 1778, Silver Bluff had thirty members. Hearing that the British promised freedom for the slaves, Elder George fled to Savannah, taking many of his flock with him, and became the bodyservant of a British officer. After the British surrender, another of Galphin's slaves, Jesse Peters, became pastor of Silver Bluff church.

Another slave, George Liele, contributed much to the early Negro Baptist churches in America. Born in Virginia, he was brought to Georgia by his master, Henry Sharp, a Baptist deacon. Liele became an eloquent exhorter, in an unlettered way, and Sharp gave him permission to preach to the slaves of the communities about Savannah. He organized the second Negro Baptist church in the United States, the African Baptist Church of Savannah. Andrew Bryan, a particularly intelligent Negro who had purchased his own freedom, was this church's first pastor under sponsorship of a white Baptist minister, Elder Abraham Marshall.

During the War for Independence, Liele expressed sympathy for the British cause and as a result was imprisoned. When the British forces captured Savannah an English officer rescued the preacher-slave and at the close of the war took him to Jamaica. On that island Liele organized its first Baptist church. It grew to a membership of more than five hundred within a few years. Liele met stiff opposition from the established Church of England and again found himself in prison, charged with sedition. He barely escaped the death penalty and continued his preaching. He organized a missionary society in Jamaica, assisted by Stephen A. Cook, a member of the Jamaica Assembly, who solicited funds in England for the former slave's church activities. By 1842 more than fifty missionaries had been sent out from Liele's society to work in Africa, and about a score others came to the United States to preach among Negro Baptists.

Lott Cary

Other Negro Baptist churches were formed during the last years of the eighteenth century, especially in Virginia, Georgia, and Kentucky, and many examples of exceptional religious leadership by Negroes could be cited. There was Lott Cary, born a slave on a plantation in central Virginia near the close of the Revolutionary War. He was sent to Richmond for work in a tobacco warehouse and in 1807 was converted under the preaching of the Reverend John Courtney. Cary first joined the Richmond First Baptist Church and then the First African Baptist Church, preaching now and then to its congregation.

By 1813 he had saved enough money to purchase his freedom. He continued to preach to his people and became a vigorous advocate of the principal missionary project of his African church, the support of a mission station in Liberia, Africa. In 1821 Cary himself went with his family as a missionary to Liberia under sponsorship of the African Colonization Society. He established the first Baptist church of Monrovia, served as its pastor, and became so influential in the colony that its Assembly appointed him assistant governor of Liberia.

In Alabama in the early 1840s a slave named Ceasar McLemore became such a powerful preacher and such an influence for good among his people that the state Baptist convention purchased him from his master for $625 and "turned him loose" to evangelize the Negro servants. Since the Alabama law did not permit Ceasar to become a freedman, he technically remained a slave of the Baptist convention.

The laws of the states governing the conduct of slaves were stringent and seriously restricted their religious and other group activities. The Slave Code of South Carolina, for example, strictly prohibited Negroes from going to plantations away from home unless accompanied by their masters or by written orders of their white families. The law forbade slaves to meet for schooling or worship, even in company with whites, before sunrise or after sunset. The code provided that only work of a necessary nature was to be done by slaves on Sunday, and another provision "advised" that Negroes should be instructed by their masters in the principles of Christianity. In addition, there was an explicit statement in the law that becoming a Christian did not set a slave free.

In 1801 the Charleston Baptist Association petitioned the South Carolina Legislature to modify some of these provisions, particularly to allow slaves to congregate peacefully at their convenience for worship. This was the time when numerous Baptist leaders in all the southern states were beginning to refute publicly the theory that Negroes had no souls and that both education and religion were wasted on them.

Nat Turner's Insurrection

Such gestures of understanding and conciliation were given a serious setback in August 1831 when a fiery Negro Baptist preacher, Nat Turner, led an insurrection of slaves in Southampton County, Virginia. From his childhood Turner had claimed to hear divine voices urging him to take up leadership among his people. He became mentally deranged, proclaiming in every Negro Baptist church where he could get a hearing that "the bottom rail shall be raised up to the top of the fence," and interpreting that to mean that black people should be raised to a superior position over the whites.

Turner's master and other white citizens looked upon this slave's rantings with amused toleration until the night the tragic insurrection began. Collecting a handful of followers Turner broke into his master's house and murdered all the white family. This was the signal for others of Turner's disciples to gather. Brought to a frenzy by the madman's exhortations, all during that night and through the next day several hundred Negroes attacked their white masters and neighbors. Using knives and other crude weapons they indiscriminately killed sixty-four persons.

Nat Turner and his conspirators were seized and hanged. Tides of fear and prejudice rose all over the southern states and several legislatures quickly passed laws to prohibit any assembling of Negroes, whether for religious or secular purposes. The Virginia Assembly passed an act that forbade Negro preachers to serve their congregations except under supervision of a white minister. Some states went to the extreme of banning all preaching and public speaking by Negroes.

A few years' time with no repetition of the Nat Turner uprising banished some of the fear and softened much of the prejudice against Negro preachers and their spiritual activities.

Richmond's First African Baptist Church

An example of the problems faced by both whites and Negroes in this troubled period of southern history is found in the organization of the first Negro Baptist church in Richmond, Virginia. In 1838 the pastor and members of the First Baptist Church of that city debated its growing difficulty: what to do about its large and expanding Negro membership. The house of worship, located on the corner of Twelfth and Broad Streets, was inadequate to hold the congregation. The pastor of this noted old church, J. B. Jeter, who seven years later became a leader in the organization of the Southern Baptist Convention, came up with the solution. He organized the First African Baptist Church, and according to records of that time, the Negro slaves were delighted. From their small savings and incomes they raised about $8,000 within two years to pay for their share of their new building.[1]

Still, there were legal problems. The laws of Virginia explicitly forbade Negro preachers to serve as religious leaders of their own people, but the white Baptist lawyers who were consulted said that they could be organized for separate worship provided a white minister should always conduct the service. After securing this legal opinion, the Old First Baptist appointed a committee of eighteen men described as discreet brethren to select a white minister. Elder Jeter drew up a constitution for his Negro parishioners and selected thirty deacons from among the African members to conduct the affairs of their church—under strict supervision of the white pastor, Dr. Robert Ryland, president of Richmond College, who served the African church for twenty-five years.

The First African Baptist Church of Richmond prospered in numbers, contributions, and enthusiasm. The plan was considered a true success, and was copied by numerous other larger Baptist churches of the pre-Civil War period. With emancipation came freedom of conscience which Elder Ryland believed was the just privilege of Negro worshipers, Baptist or otherwise.

Reconstruction and Antagonism

Both the American Baptist Home Mission Society and the Board of Domestic Missions of the Southern Convention felt responsibility for Negroes of the South during the years before the Civil War. With the aid of both groups, Negro churches were built, associations were formed, and the beginning of some training for their ministers was made.

However, the tragic Reconstruction Era opened a Pandora's Box of trouble for all the people of the South, white and Negro. White people deeply resented carpetbagger rule by the triumphant Yankees and the preferential treatment given the freedmen. Estrangement between church people of the white race and their former slaves, with separation in the churches, was inevitable. Usually the division took place on the initiative of the Negro church members who recognized that so long as they shared the same places of worship they would rely upon the white members for leadership. Many white ministers and church leaders had conscientiously prepared the black members for spiritual freedom and church management. Among Negro Baptists were many mature, well-disciplined, and effective preachers.

With the end of hostilities, the American Baptist Home Mission Society made various overtures to the southern churches, with some talk of a reunion between Baptists of North and South. Such proposals incensed the former Confederates, largely because they felt the idea was government-inspired and another phase of the occupation.

The Southerners had some reason for this feeling. For example, the Mission Society, meeting in St. Louis in 1865, adopted a resolution presented by the Reverend J. M. Pendleton, a Virginia-born, Kentucky-bred pastor and teacher from Tennessee, that the Society take responsibility for Baptist missions in Kentucky and Tennessee. Pendleton suggested that the Society name as missionaries to that area such "suitable men" as could be found, and he spelled out his idea of suitable men as those of "unquestionable loyalty to the Government of the United States, men who approve the policy of the Government on slavery." Southern Baptists considered Pendleton a carpetbagger on a spiritual plane. Such proposals as his further deepened the sectional estrangement.

In their pride and humiliation, the prostrate Southerners were not ready for reconciliation. Additional resentment developed as the Society began to establish Baptist schools for the colored freedmen, most of whom were totally illiterate and unable to go to northern schools. An institute in almost every state of the old Confederacy was opened by Northern Baptists, who seemed to have unlimited resources for this purpose. The Southern Baptist Theological Seminary, the Baptist colleges, and even the public schools were still struggling for survival, but Negro Baptists were being well provided for. Among Southern Baptists the feeling grew that the American Baptist Home Mission Society, with its headquarters in New York, was far too eager to appropriate the work started by the Southern Baptist Convention Board of Domestic Missions, especially in its program among Negroes.

Sensing this antagonism growing between the races as a result of the war and reconstruction, Negro Baptists stepped up the formation of their own congregations and assumed complete control of their religious affairs, often under the guidance of a representative of the northern Society, even though Southern Baptist leaders co-operated generously to assist their Negro freedmen in establishing their separate congregations and programs.

The National Baptist Convention

Gradually Negro Baptist congregations formed their own associations and state societies. In 1880, under the leadership of the Reverend W. W. Colley, a missionary to Africa who had served under appointment of the Foreign Mission Board, 150 Negro Baptist ministers and laymen met in the largest of the Negro churches of Montgomery, Alabama, and organized the Foreign Missionary Convention. They pledged to co-ordinate the work of southern Negro Baptist churches in sending missionaries to foreign fields.

In that same year William J. Simmons, an outstanding young Negro, born in slavery in Charleston but reared from the age of ten in Philadelphia and graduated from Howard University, was elected president of the Normal and Theological Institute of Louisville, later named Simmons University in his honor. As he watched the organization and success of the Foreign Missionary Convention, Simmons urged the formation of a true national convention of Negro Baptist churches. In April 1886 he sent letters to numerous fellow ministers and educators asking their support for such an organization.

In response to Simmons' invitation, Negro Baptist leaders assembled in St. Louis in August 1886, with about 600 representatives of churches and church groups, and launched the American National Baptist Convention. Elder Simmons served as president of the body until his death in 1890.

Still another organization of Negro Baptists was formed in 1893, the Baptist National Educational Convention. It published literature for ministers and their church members. All three organizations remained separate in their activities.

At the meeting of the Foreign Mission Convention in 1894, Dr. A. W. Peques, a graduate of Bucknell University, proposed that there should be one national organization of American Negro Baptists. One year later, in Atlanta the union of the three groups took place with the formation of the National Baptist Convention of the United States of America. Commenting on this accomplishment by his people of that day, Dr. J. H. Jackson, president of the National Baptist Convention, U.S.A., Inc., at the time of the culmination of the Baptist Jubilee of 1959 to 1964, declared:

"By this step, the ministers and other leaders at that Atlanta convention brought the Negro Baptists into the spiritual and religious mainstream of American life. The Negro Baptist faith had come of age. It had been a slow and difficult process, in part because nothing came easy for my people in those decades following freedom from slavery. In addition, such things come more slowly with Baptists than with any other faith, because Baptists place such heavy emphasis upon freedom of the individual and freedom of his congregation to control their own spiritual affairs. In view of that, it is sometimes hard to build unified action among us. But our elders did the job magnificently at Atlanta."[2]

Membership of the churches affiliating with the National Baptist Convention at its founding totaled approximately one million, in about 8,000 churches, at least one-half of which were in the southern states, and the remainder in the northern and Midwestern areas.

Dr. Jackson in 1940 succeeded the pastor of Mount Olivet Baptist Church, Chicago, upon his sudden death, and continued in the Convention's leadership in 1979. Dr. William A. Jones, Jr., pastor of Bethany Baptist Church, Brooklyn, New York, became president of the Progressive National Baptist Convention at its annual meeting in Los Angeles in 1978.

Booker T. Washington

Another event of great importance not only to Negro Baptists, but to all Negroes of the United States, took place in Atlanta in October of 1895, at the Atlanta Exposition, sponsored by the so-called cotton states of Dixie. It was the speech of a young Negro Baptist educator, Booker T. Washington, head of a nondenominational industrial school for Negroes at Tuskegee, Alabama. In the presence of the governor of Georgia and numerous other important officials Washington delivered an eloquent plea for co-operation between the white and the colored races. He pledged the support of his people toward industrial, educational, and religious progress for the South, and reached a dramatic climax with these words:

"There is no defense or security for any of us except in the highest intelligence and development of all. If anywhere there are efforts tending to curtail the fullest growth of the Negro, let these efforts be turned into stimulating, encouraging, and making him the most useful and intelligent citizen. Effort or means so invested will pay a thousand per cent interest."[3]

President Grover Cleveland sent Dr. Washington a telegram of congratulation. Religious publications of all faiths featured the speech as a high watermark of conciliation in the post-Civil War era. Dr. Lyman Abbott, editor of the *Christian Union* of Boston, asked Washington to write a paper on the exact condition, mental and moral, of the Negro ministers of the South.

Washington wrote the paper, stating that in his opinion there was a great need for education among the preachers of his race, and for more moral, financial, and spiritual responsibility. The paper brought down a storm of condemnation upon Washington's head with demands that he retract, or modify, what he had said.

"I did not utter a word of explanation or retraction," Dr. Washington later recorded. "I knew that I was right, and that time and the second sober thought of the people would vindicate me. Very soon public sentiment began making itself felt, in demanding a purifying of the ministry. I have been told by many of our most influential ministers that my words had much to do with starting a demand for the placing of a higher type of men in the pulpit."[4]

In the forefront of the movement started by Booker T. Washington were leaders of the National Baptist Convention at the turn of the century. Their successors have continued and intensified the program, with insistence upon minimum standards of education and training for their young preachers.

The Negroes Sang

Greatest contribution of early Negro Baptists to the culture of America was their songs and their singing. Just when the Negro in America began to sing, and how his music took shape, is hard to determine, for efforts to collect Negro folk songs were not successful before 1840 and the earliest accounts of Negro song fests were not kept. But it is certain that as soon as the African slaves were disembarked from the trading ships they began the chants they learned in their native jungles.

Professor John W. Work of Fisk University, Negro institution of higher learning at Nashville, Tennessee, has pointed out that Negro Americans came from many tribes of East, West, South, and interior Africa, bringing their customs, habits, languages, and types of music from as many different peoples. "But the general interchange of slaves among the colonies and the uniformity of social conditions partially developed and fostered by Christianity welded them into a somewhat homogeneous group, from which emerged a comparatively uniform body of song."[5]

Almost all the slave songs now in existence were religious in nature. White Baptists of the plantations, along with their Methodist neighbors, were principally responsible for encouraging their slaves to sing religious songs. The Negroes gave the songs, adapted from the singing of the white folks, their own rhythm and harmony. The songs were good to work by as groups of Negroes hoed rows and picked cotton. A leader would line out the chant and the others would follow in unison, moving and swaying to their own voices.

In their cabins or houses the songs were the solace for the hard life they led, and in their places of worship the promise of a heaven where there would be no more toil and sweat was the theme of their most popular songs. They led directly to the composition of the songs later called spirituals.

For a time after emancipation Negro singers preferred to sing the more sophisticated church music. The songs of the slavery days seemed best forgotten. Then the need for funds for Fisk University, founded as a freedmen's school in 1866, prompted the organization of a group of students to sing Negro spirituals. Their concerts, which began in 1871, introduced this type of religious music to all America and then to many countries of Europe, creating for it a hearty popularity. The school's chorus became known as the Fisk Jubilee Singers, and their songs were sung in Negro churches all over the nation. Their effect was described by Howard W. Odum and Guy B. Johnson of the University of North Carolina in *The Negro and His Songs:*

"All of the Negro's church music tends to take into it the qualities of his native expression—strains minor and sad in their general character. The religious 'tone' is a part of the song, and both words and music are characterized by a peculiar plaintiveness. The Negroes delight in song that gives stress and swell to special words or phrases that for one reason or another have peculiar meanings to them. For the most part, all religious songs are 'spirituals' and easily merge into satisfying melodies when occasion demands . . . In addition to the tune in which the hymn is written the Negro puts his own music into the singing, and his own interpretation into the words. This, together with the 'feeling-attitude' which is unconsciously his, and the satisfaction which he gets from his singing, places Negro church music in a class of its own."

After Negro Baptists began to worship apart from their white neighbors, their choirs North and South trained young voices to sing with pride in their Afro-American musical heritage. The nation was enriched by the contribution of professionally competent Negro musicians and their concerts.

Roland Hayes

One of the soloists with the Fisk Jubilee Singers, Roland Hayes, was the first Negro Baptist musician to achieve worldwide acclaim. Born June 3, 1887, in Flatwoods (now Curryville), Georgia, one of seven children of a father who was proud to be "a good part Indian" from Missouri, and a Negro mother, Roland was reared in the Mount Zion Baptist Church, which his mother helped to establish the year he was six. He often related that as a child he drank in all the music he heard—in the woods and fields, in the cabin, at the church and the singing school, and sometimes on the dusty road.

As a renowned concert singer, Hayes learned from those who had known his family that he was descended from Aba 'Ougi, a high-born chief of the Ivory Coast, who was ambushed in Africa and auctioned off in Savannah about 1790. Renamed Charles, this handsome giant of an African never allowed his owner to become his spiritual master. He was put to work on the Weaver plantation near Jonesboro, Georgia. He demonstrated such skill in leadership that he was soon made overseer. His fellow slaves looked to him for counsel and consolation, and this natural ministry led him to the role of pastor and evangelist of the slaves on that and nearby plantations.

Charles's owner was not sympathetic with his slave overseer's Baptist religion, so to call a meeting for prayer and Bible teaching in a familiar ravine or marsh, Charles would give the word to "steal away!" and the summons soon passed from plantation to plantation. The big slave preacher composed a chant which told the story of the crucifixion, around the theme "He never said a mumberlin' word." Great-grandson Roland Hayes mastered a spiritual based on the call "Steal Away!" and another on the tragedy of the crucifixion and sang them in hundreds of concerts all over America and in Europe.

Roland's widowed mother hoped that her shy, thoughtful son would grow up to be a Baptist preacher but was satisfied when she saw him develop his great talent for singing. Often the preacher at their church would sing his sermon, and Roland absorbed it, note for note, so he could repeat it as he worked in the field. At Fisk he worked to pay his way, and his voice won him a scholarship in a Boston conservatory. His first paid performance outside Boston was at Howard University, Washington, where he was given $35 for a solo in *The Messiah*.

Hayes took pride in indigenous Negro music. He abhorred any burlesquing of the spirituals. He declared that his purpose was "to restore the music of my race to the serious atmosphere of its origin and help to redeem it for the national culture."

Following a concert in New York, Heywood Broun said in his column in the New York *World:* "Roland Hayes sang of Jesus . . . I saw a miracle in Town Hall. Half the people were black and half were white, and while the mood of the song held, they were all the same. They shared together the close silence. One emotion wrapped them. And at the end it was a single sob."

After Hayes had sung a concert in New York one evening, he met a young woman, a cousin who had migrated from Georgia to the city, who had come backstage to congratulate him. He married this cousin, and the child born to the Hayeses was named Africa Alzada. Hayes bought the land in Georgia that his family had worked as slaves and developed it as his heritage. He announced that he proposed "to use Negro money to build Negro reputations." He brought promising young artists—writers, poets, painters, musicians—to his farm where they could live close to the soil and be tested in their vocations. The best of these Hayes would send to Boston for study, and the Hayes home in Brookline served as a youth hostel for them. The few who showed the greatest promise he would send to France, where a villa that Hayes acquired was their home while they studied.

In 1921 Hayes had the honor to sing in Buckingham Palace before King George V and Queen Mary. He included in the concert his African forefather's story of the crucifixion. The irony of the situation lay in the fact that Hayes's great-grandfather was brought by British traders to America and sold into slavery in a state named for George II.

After his command performance the Negro American singer thoughtfully cabled his mother that he had just sung before the King and Queen. Her reply to this great news came by mail with the injunction: "Remember who you are, and give credit to where it is due."[6]

Hayes died on the last day of the year in 1976.

An Ambassador of Good Will

Carefully and patiently through the years since World War II many Negro Baptist leaders have devoted their efforts to establish better relations between the races in the United States, North and South. Before the civil rights movement was thrown into the political arena these men and women of good will were working at the task of creating understanding of the growing problems of Negro families and how both races could work together to solve them.

Such an exponent of good will was the Reverend Charles E. Boddie. Born in New Rochelle, New York, one of eleven surviving children from a total of twenty in the home of the pastor of Bethesda Baptist Church, Charles completed high school in his home town, college at Syracuse University, seminary at Colgate Rochester Divinity School, and graduate school at the University of Rochester. For his master's thesis "Chuck" Boddie dealt with the relation of a Negro church to its community. His admiration for his pastor-father was revealed in his biography *Giant in the Earth.*

Boddie served the American Baptist Foreign Mission Societies, first as a personnel secretary, visiting colleges, speaking in student assemblies, meeting missions volunteers, and guiding young people to vocational decisions; later in public relations, which permitted a six-month global tour of Baptist missions. With his imposing platform appearance, eloquence, and good humor, Boddie was in great demand in American Baptist and National Baptist churches and in summer assemblies for lectures and conferences on interracial problems.

Chuck Boddie's appearance at a convention of white Baptist students on the campus of a state college in Missouri while the civil rights issue was stirring emotions was typical of his method. He arrived just in time to be escorted to the meeting by a woman known to the group. The audience had not expected the Negro visitor, and some students showed little interest when Boddie was invited to say a word.

Graciously he thanked his hostess and the program director for the opportunity to meet fellow Baptists. He made an incisive comment about the Bible passage just read, and mentioned a certain Negro spiritual that was inspired by that passage. Backing up to the piano, the speaker gave the stool a brisk turn, sat down, played a few chords as he continued to talk, grasped one end of the piano with both hands and pulled it around to an angle that gave him a view of his audience, and then, with shoulders slightly hunched, in a throaty baritone he launched into the strains of a spiritual. Once he had sung it through, Chuck Boddie nodded for the students to sing with him and the whole group responded with obvious delight.

From that moment Boddie's appearance at that campus was a complete success. The dignity of his bearing, the total absence of the stamp of caste of the Negro people, and the calm logic of his appeal for interracial understanding totally dispelled all hostility. After the program Boddie was detained by students eager to question him and was followed from the building by half a dozen who wanted to discuss further the issues he had raised.

In 1963 Charles E. Boddie became president of the American Baptist Theological Seminary in Nashville, Tennessee, an institution founded jointly in 1924 by the Southern Baptist Convention and the National Baptist Convention, Inc., to train Negro Baptist ministers and religious workers. Southern Baptists provided the buildings and National Baptists the furnishings. The governing board was made up of representatives of both conventions. When President Boddie was inaugurated he announced that it would be his purpose in the seminary "to help Negro preachers to understand the need to baptize their brains." As of 1979, Dr. Boddie was still the president.

After the death of his first wife, Dr. Boddie, native of New York, ably assisted as seminary president by his second wife Mabel, native of Alabama, is comfortable in an educational institution which traces its origin to Roger Williams University.

Baptists of the North launched a movement on behalf of freed slaves after the Civil War. Their National Theological Institute brought into being several fine schools to provide spiritual and educational training across the South. Roger Williams University, founded in 1866, merged in 1927 with a college in Memphis; it had graduated such stalwarts as the late Mordecai Johnson. Adjoining its campus in northeast Nashville, Tennessee, was the new American Baptist Theological Seminary. Nearby are Fisk, Meharry Medical, and Tennessee Agricultural and Industrial Institute.

Chuck Boddie takes his cue from Paul's word to the Corinthians when he states his ambition to be "a steward of God's grace in the ministry of reconciliation" among Baptists and all people.

Listed by *Ebony* magazine, a monthly which portrays black-American life in America, among the "100 most influential Black Americans" of 1977 were seven Baptist clergymen and one woman who is a Baptist. One of the ministers is the only American to have served two different bodies of Baptists as president. Dr. Thomas Kilgore was president of the American Baptist Churches, U.S.A., in 1970, and became president of the Progressive National Baptist Convention, Inc., in 1977.

The list named Coretta Scott King, the widow of Martin Luther King, Jr., Walter Fauntroy, Benjamin Hooks, Jesse Jackson, Joseph H. Jackson, James C. Sams, and Leon H. Sullivan.

XVII

THE GREAT VARIETY OF BAPTISTS

The Dubious Honor

Baptist historian Norman W. Cox, discussing in 1959 the thirty different bodies that bear the Baptist label, remarked somewhat sardonically: "For three centuries American Baptists have been exercising their deeply cherished privilege of separating themselves from the fellowship of other organized groups as their choice decided them."[1]

Their choice among Baptists has given them the honor, however dubious it may be considered by many within and without the worldwide denomination, of establishing more independent bodies than has any other religious group in the United States—or the world.

Controversies over such subjects as the virgin birth of Christ, the nature and purpose of baptism, admission of members from other churches, the practice of open or closed communion, Landmarkism, Sunday schools and missions, the millennium and evolution—all have stirred congregations and associations of Baptists at one time or another. Some of these have evoked such emotional upheavals that a large branch of Baptists has from time to time splintered off the main trunk and formed a new body.

A study of these splits reveals that the causes were principally of two kinds: honest doctrinal differences and personality conflicts. The first type usually had strong spokesmen who debated the issues and who inevitably attracted some disciples for each side of the debate. The second type invariably appealed for support on biblical grounds and with spiritual truths to sanction one man's claim to leadership. Even a good theologian would find it difficult to distinguish between doctrinal disputes and power politics in the denomination.

One favorite topic of disputation among ultra conservative Baptists is the doctrine of the millennium, dealing with the second coming of Christ. One mention of the millennium in the Book of the Revelation, taken literally, gave rise to arguments about the rule of Christ on earth—whether it would be for a thousand years before his final ascension or a thousand years after. The term spawned some unholy concepts and quarrels. Often a preacher's reputation rose or fell according to his reply to the question, "Are you a premillennialist or a postmillennialist?" To sidestep the issue, shrewd Baptist ministers might answer: "I am neither. I am *promillennialist*—I'm for it, whenever it comes!"

Premillennialism/Zionism

Many wars have erupted in the Mideast between the new nation of Israel, carved out of Palestine by the United Nations in 1948, and the ancient country of Egypt and her allies. As of this writing, the governments of Egypt and of Israel seem close to agreement on a treaty of peace. The circumstances have prompted many Baptist ministers and biblical students to emphasize their belief that "possessing the land," which Israel claims, is in fulfillment of divine prophecy, especially as found in the Book of Revelation. Dr. Timothy P. Weber, assistant professor of church history in the Conservative Baptist Theological Seminary, Denver, Colorado, explains this doctrine:

> According to the premillennial reading of biblical prophecies, at the end of the church age, God will restore the state of Israel in Palestine. Once this is accomplished, a whole series of predicted events will come to pass: Antichrist will be revealed, powerful kings of the North and South will attempt to destroy the Jewish state, Antichrist and powerful kings from the East will converge in Palestine for the Battle of Armageddon, Jesus and his saints will return to earth to defeat the

forces of evil and establish the millennial throne in Jerusalem. . . .

All this means of course that premillennialists have always taken a lively interest in the return of the Jews and the establishment of a Jewish state in Palestine. Even before Herzl founded the Zionist movement, premillennialists were calling for the setting up of a Jewish homeland. Some premillennialists even became firm supporters and enthusiastic participants in the Zionist movement; and virtually all have been unyielding supporters of Israel since 1948. Jewish leaders in the United States and Israel have always recognized that they can count on "evangelical" support—most of which is rooted in premillennialist beliefs about the importance of Israel in biblical prophecy.

Dr. Duke K. McCall, president of the Southern Baptist Theological Seminary, Louisville, Kentucky, criticized what he calls "The non-negotiable spirit" in life today in these words:

Whether the issue is school integration, labor contracts, women's rights, air quality, zoning, or settlements in the Sinai, the present mood seems to be that there must be an absolute victor who wins every marble or the matter cannot be settled. This absolutist approach puts jagged edges on all human relations and assures that somebody will get badly hurt.

Israel passes laws to make it possible for any court to convict Christian missionaries if, through their witness, a Jew accepts Jesus as the Messiah. No freedom of choice is left a young Israeli in the realm of religion.

This is the denial of a basic civil right, but there has been little attention paid in our Baptist papers to the outcry of Christians in Israel (including Baptists). Unswerving, absolute support of Israel is the demand of many Christians who equate the present Israeli state with biblical prophecy. To believe the Bible is one thing. To identify the Begin government as the object of biblical prophecies is a nonsequitur. I can pray and hope for the Jewish people, but the treatment of the Arab refugees was, and is, immoral.

It is time for some "sweet reasonableness" to be introduced into this situation. As a Christian I care deeply for the future of Israel and the welfare of the Jewish people, but the teachings of Jesus make it necessary for me to care deeply for the welfare of the Arab people also. They, too, are the children of God in the redemptive purposes of Jesus Christ.

They Thrive on Controversy

Within the thirty identifiable Baptist groups in the United States, according to the Baptist World Alliance, there were about 97,000 churches with more than 23,000,000 members in 1979. Largest was the Southern Baptist Convention, followed numerically by the two largest conventions of black Baptists, then by the American Baptist Churches (formerly the American Baptist Convention). These four alone totaled about 78,000 churches with some 19,900,000 members.

A second group is made up of the so-called old-line Baptist bodies, most of them small, that go as far back in their history as the tiny remnants of the General Six-Principle Baptists, 1653, and the Seventh Day Baptist General Conference, 1671. There are those that trace their beginnings to the eighteenth and nineteenth centuries, such as the Primitive Baptists and the United Free-Will Baptists. This group totaled 2,524 churches with about 250,000 members in mid-1965.

A third group comprises the two major Baptist bodies formed especially to serve Baptist immigrants and their descendants from Germany and Sweden, the North American Baptist General Conference and the Baptist General Conference respectively.

The fourth collection of Baptist bodies includes all those that came into being during the twentieth century. For the most part they broke away from the major bodies because some outstanding leader became dissatisfied with the parent organization and pulled away, taking with him a sizeable number of his own loyal followers into pastures that he designated as greener and better watered with scriptural truth. Outstanding examples of these, as we shall see, were the Landmarkers who believed in unbroken Baptist succession, the Fundamentalists who believed in literal interpretation of the Bible, the Negro Baptists who split away from the National Baptist Convention, Inc., and the Bible Baptists who split away from the Fundamentalists—all led by one or more men of unusual power and persuasiveness. Since 1905 at least six such bodies with memberships of more than 100,000 and up to almost a million have been launched.

Countless battles have been fought as the swords of belief and interpretation of the Scripture have clashed among Baptists during the more than three centuries of this nation's history. But for the indomitable Baptists this merely proves the point that freedom of conscience, most priceless heritage of all human liberties, may as well be exercised. It proves, Baptists contend, that there is room within their great fellowship for all sorts of differences of opinion—provided these fundamentals are always retained: salvation through faith, believers' baptism by immersion, the autonomy of each congregation, separation of church and state, complete freedom for individual and collective worship.

Within those guidelines the differences among Baptist leaders have flared. Some of the differences seem petty indeed—such as when the millennium will dawn, how long an officer should serve in a Baptist convention, and whether there will be a bodily resurrection of the dead. But in support of the fundamental Baptist distinctives all who bear the name Baptist would rally as one, as they have rallied in the past. Therein lies what Baptists consider a major contribution from their fellowship in shaping the course of American history.

Baptist preachers have stood toe to toe and slugged it out, verbally, over whether there should be open communion, meaning a sharing at the communion table, using the symbols of bread and wine, with Christians of other denominations. Then the disputants have sat down in complete accord to lay plans for their next associational meeting. Baptist leaders have quarreled vigorously over the place of boards and commissions within their respective fellowships, then showed up at their state capitol to stand shoulder to shoulder in solid array to oppose bills to permit gambling or to sponsor legislation against that common foe, the liquor traffic. Two Baptist deacons within the same congregation have argued heatedly over whether Christ's return to the earth is imminent, then in revival time knelt on either side of a penitent sinner, clasping their hands behind his back as they "prayed him through" to salvation.

Baptists have thrived upon controversy, at least to creating interest and excitement in their state and national conventions. It is not unusual for a Baptist delegate or messenger, returning from an important convention, to enter into a conversation with a fellow member of his congregation who was not so fortunate as to make the trip, which runs as follows:

"How was the convention?"

"Rather slow. Not a single fight this time!"

Even in the troubled field of relations with other Christian bodies there are acute differences of opinion among Baptists. Shall we join the local Council of Churches? No! say some of the Baptist congregations. Yes! say others in the same town or city. Then both groups meet and sing "Blest Be the Tie That Binds" in their associational meetings.

In a small Ozarks community in the early years of this century, debates between Baptist and Campbellite (Christian) preachers were scheduled, pitting the champion of one group against that of the other. One such debate, set for a Sunday afternoon in the Christian church, had to be postponed because on Saturday morning the building burned to the ground. Immediately, the Baptist pastor and his congregation invited the Christian church congregation to hold their worship service in the Baptist sanctuary prior to the Baptist service. And the Baptist congregation, forgetting all about the proposed debate, heartily welcomed their Campbellite brethren.

The Gentle General Baptists

Scattered through the states of the Midwest and South are the people called *General Baptists*. If asked: "Where did your fellowship begin?" they will answer:

"We go back to the first Baptist churches, organized by John Smyth and Thomas Helwys in England and Holland. Before that, we have the heritage of the Waldenses and the Anabaptists."

Roger Williams, founder of the first Baptist church in America in Providence, Rhode Island, and staunch champion of religious liberty, held to General Baptist principles. General Baptists have been in the front ranks of the forces struggling for freedom of conscience and worship in Europe and America.

These Baptists have always been strongly free-will in doctrine, as opposed to the Calvinist principle of predestination held by the so-called Particular Baptists. Almost overwhelmed by the Calvinist Baptists of the Eastern states during the eighteenth century, General Baptists emerged as strong contenders in communities of the frontier areas. In 1823 their leading preacher, the Reverend Benoni Stinson, organized a General Baptist church in Evansville, Indiana, and this congregation is still considered the Mother Church of modern General Baptists.

Benoni Stinson was born in December 1798, the son of a hard-drinking, abusive man, a veteran of the Revolutionary War who lived first in Georgia and then in Kentucky. Young Benoni settled in Wayne County, Kentucky, and on November 1, 1821, was ordained to preach. An eloquent speaker and exhorter, Stinson spread his gospel of free salvation over wide areas of Kentucky, then into Indiana. An early historian of the General Baptists related:

"The idea that a young man with but little beard on his face could gather such crowds to hear him preach, and then hold them enchanted with his peculiar eloquence, grated somewhat harshly upon the sensibilities of some of the older Elders, especially the Calvinist portion of them."[2]

Stinson organized the General Baptist churches of southern Indiana into Liberty Baptist Association. A home mission program was launched and a publication, the *General Baptist Herald,* was founded. Weathering the Civil War days, General Baptists grew in numbers, churches, and associations, and in 1965 they had approximately 900 congregations with about 100,000 members. They serve mission fields on the islands of Guam, Saipan, and the Philippines.

While General Baptists stand firmly on the usually accepted fundamental principles of Baptist belief, they offer three distinctives not always accepted by others who bear the Baptist name.

First, General Baptists practice open communion. They admit to the Lord's Table, the ordinance of remembrance of Jesus' breaking the bread and drinking the wine of the Feast of the Pass-over with his disciples, all who profess to be Christians and desire to fellowship with other believers.

Second, they believe in apostasy, commonly called "falling from grace." In this respect their doctrine closely parallels that of the Methodists—a matter that does not disturb General Baptists in the least. They modify the doctrine of "once saved, always saved" by the principle that sin can cause a change of relationship between the individual and his Savior, and that a soul may thus be lost.

Third, local General Baptist churches do not ordain ministers and deacons, but assign that responsibility to a presbytery which may include ordained ministers and deacons of several churches within an association.

In the church covenant followed by General Baptists are these significant words: "We will be Christlike in all our deportment. We will be tender and affectionate toward each other; we will be careful of each other's reputations, thinking no evil and backbiting not with our tongues; we will return good for evil; we will be just and honest, truthful and honorable, in all our dealings; we will do unto others as we would be done by; we will be meek, loving, and forgiving, as we desire and hope to be forgiven."[3]

Primitive Baptists: Like Their Fathers

In a farming area not far off U.S. Highway 82 which runs from Brunswick to Waycross in southeastern Georgia there is a wooden church building. It houses one of the oldest Primitive Baptist churches in the United States, High Bluff, having been founded in 1836. The outer walls are darkened and cracked, for the building has never been painted. Paint would indicate human pride, and pride is a sin in the eyes of good Primitive Baptists.

There are no glass windows in High Bluff meeting house, only openings with hinged wooden shutters that can be swung back to let in light and air. The benches that serve as pews are rough and unpainted. The pulpit stand is of pine boards. A table in front of the pulpit holds only a bucket for drinking water with a dipper for common use.

Service in High Bluff is held once a month, with a preacher

from a rural community near Brunswick "bringing the sermon." No Sunday school, youth meetings, or other services are held, except for a "yearly meeting" that brings several Primitive Baptist ministers together for sermons that begin in the morning and follow one another until late in the afternoon, with noon "dinner on the ground." Many of the men and women and the few young people who worship at High Bluff are sons and daughters of families that worshiped there long years ago and whose mortal remains lie in the peaceful cemetery close by. Some members are business and professional men living in Waycross and other southeastern Georgia cities. Many of these pause in their cars before arriving at the grounds to take off their neckties if perchance they put them on that morning from force of habit, for such evidence of worldliness is taboo in this Primitive Baptist fellowship.

The sermon begins quietly, and works up to a louder and yet louder pitch as the Spirit takes stronger hold upon the messenger of the Lord. It may run for as long as an hour and a half, and for about that long afterward, the members will stand around or sit and visit in friendly fashion.

Such is the worship service of the Primitive Baptists in the piney woods of Georgia, and to some extent it is typical of all their services. Primitive Baptists still have no home or foreign mission work, no denominational ties or activities, no Sunday schools or youth societies, holding that all such are the invention of men and have no biblical origin.

While they have traditionally opposed Sunday schools and other teaching and training services, some of the more progressive Primitives (almost a contradiction in terms) are yielding on these points. Sunday schools have actually been established in several Primitive Baptist congregations in the Savannah, Georgia, area. More reforms may be expected—unless the elders decide it would be better for their fellowship to become extinct than to bring it into the march of Baptist progress.

Landmarkers Hold the Line

In 1852, an earnest Baptist evangelist, James R. Graves of Nashville, Tennessee, came to Bowling Green, Kentucky, at the invitation of the Baptist pastor of that town, the Reverend James

Madison Pendleton. Elder Graves had embraced some principles not generally accepted by Southern Baptists, and he proceeded to convert his host, Elder Pendleton, to his unorthodox way of thinking.

In brief, the doctrinal points emphasized by Graves were these: Baptist churches have descended in an unbroken line from the early Christian churches. As we noted in our early mention of the "Landmarkers" this idea assumes that one church organized another, and another, in a line of succession, even though the line fades out during several periods of history. Carried to its logical conclusion, no Christian body can be considered *the true church* unless it has a lineal descent from the early Christian churches, all of which were Baptist churches. Thus Baptist churches are the only true churches of Christ; other Christian bodies cannot be true churches, according to this theory.

In 1851, in the rural Big Hatchie Baptist Association in Tennessee, Elder Graves sponsored a resolution which contained this doctrine and which declared that Baptists have no scriptural authority to recognize a non-Baptist minister or permit him to occupy a Baptist pulpit. As a final line of demarcation, Graves's resolution asserted that peoples of faiths other than Baptist should not be addressed as brethren.

In the *Tennessee Baptist* for September 1, 1855, Elder Graves proclaimed: "But the members of no one church have the right to come to the table spread in another church, though of the same faith and order; for each church is independent."

This carried the doctrine of close communion to its ultimate extreme, and made of it an ordinance only for the members of each single congregation. Elder Pendleton, convinced that these fine points of Baptist exclusiveness were scriptural, wrote a paper entitled "An Old Landmark Re-Set." The word Landmark gave the nickname to this body of Baptists.

While the Landmarkers never carried the authority of the local church over baptism quite to this extreme, they did hold, and still do, that a baptism by immersion performed by one who is not a Baptist cannot be accepted within their fellowship.

The Landmarkers' severest attacks came upon the Southern Baptist Convention's Foreign Mission Board. To make the missionaries answerable in any way to an agency of the denomination, rather than to an individual congregation, was entirely un-scriptural, the Landmark leaders contended. In the *Tennessee Baptist* for September 4, 1858, Elder Graves explained his position:

"We do not believe that the Foreign Board has any right to call upon the missionaries that the churches send to China or Africa, to take a journey to Richmond to be examined touching their experience, call to the ministry, and soundness of the faith. It is a highhanded act, and degrades both the judgment and authority of the Church and Presbytery that ordained him, thus practically declaring itself above both."

The first association of Landmark churches was organized in about the year 1899 in Texas. Another was formed in Arkansas in 1902. By 1905 there were enough Landmark associations, principally in the southern states, to form the Baptist General Association, under leadership of the Reverend Ben M. Bogard. In 1924 the name was changed to the American Baptist Association.

Differences of opinion developed within the fellowship over representation of the churches in annual meetings of the Association. The matter came to a head in 1949 over the question of seating only messengers from churches they represented. Held over for discussion at the next annual convention in Lakeland, Florida, the question split the fellowship. At a convention in Little Rock, Arkansas, in May 1950 a new body of more than 800 messengers was formed and named the North American Baptist Association.

The parent body has grown and spread to twenty-four states and the District of Columbia. True to its ideal of the supremacy of each local congregation, several Bible institutes teaching Landmark principles are sponsored by larger churches in states from Florida to Kentucky and California.

The newer Landmark body launched into vigorous programs of enlistment and expansion, emphasizing Sunday schools, young people's training unions, and church publications. Foreign missionaries sponsored and supported by individual churches are serving both Landmark bodies in Latin America, Europe, and Asia.

In Arkansas, where both branches of the Landmarkers are

strongest, the attitude of Baptist tolerance and generosity was expressed thus by the Reverend Don Hook, pastor of the First Baptist Church of Malvern:

"It seems doubtful if very many of their churches will ever cooperate with any of our conventions. But we are brethren in the Lord and pray for God's great and wonderful blessings upon them as they continue to spread the gospel of the kingdom."[4]

The Sabbatarians

Outstanding among the minority Baptist bodies of the United States are the *Seventh Day Baptists,* who are in all respects in full fellowship with their majority brethren of the denomination except one vital matter: For them the seventh day is for rest and worship. Firmly unmovable, the Seventh Day Baptists hold to the principle that the Founder of Christianity did not authorize any change in the historic commandment given to the Chosen People of Old Testament times: "Six days shalt thou labor and do all thy work; but the Seventh is holy unto the Lord." Saturday, the seventh day of the present calendar, is therefore the true day of worship for Seventh Day Baptists.

Their forebears go far back in American history, for Seventh Day Baptists founded a congregation in 1672 at Newport, Rhode Island. Immigrants from the British Isles, and a few from the Continent, who held to the seventh-day worship augmented their early churches, principally in New York, Pennsylvania, and New Jersey. Through the years the fellowship grew and several regional associations were formed to assist local congregations and encourage their holding fast to the historic principle.

Seventh Day Baptists have always been both missionary and ecumenically minded people. They have sent their missionaries to many areas of the world. Without any thought of yielding on their seventh-day worship they have co-operated with local and nationwide interdenominational movements. The Seventh Day Baptist General Conference is an active, fully participating member of the Baptist World Alliance.

Baptist Sabbatarians in America claim 5,284 members in only seventy churches in the late 1970s, but a World Federation of Seventh Day Baptists recognizes member churches in Brazil, Burma,

Central Africa, England, Germany, Guyana, Jamaica, Holland, Mexico, New Zealand, and the United States.

The Free Will and Other Baptists

Largest of the minority Baptist bodies that took root in the soil of the post-Revolutionary War period are the *Free Will Baptists*. They organized their first so-called quarterly meeting, an association of their congregations, in 1783 in New Hampshire. Contrary to the Calvinist theory of salvation only for those so predestined, Free Will Baptists taught what they called the threefold doctrine of "free grace, free will, and free salvation."

By 1800 the movement counted a total membership of about 25,000. In 1827 the General Conference of Free Will Baptists was formed, and its churches had spread into most northern states by the outbreak of the Civil War. The issue of slavery divided the fellowship, as it did the major body of American Baptists. The churches of the northern conference merged with the Northern Baptist Convention in 1910. A general reorganization took place in 1935, resulting in the present National Association of Free Will Baptists. Its 203,000 members in 2,275 churches support a Bible college and two liberal arts colleges in the States.

One cherished ordinance of the Free Will Baptists is the ceremonial washing of feet during the worship in literal obedience to the example set by Jesus as he performed this humble service for his disciples. As their name indicates, the Free Wills are strongly Arminian in doctrine. The denomination maintains home and foreign missionary work.

Enriching the diversity of Baptist life in the United States are many other separate bodies that originated before the turn of this century. A few of these are increasing in churches and membership, but most are barely holding their own or are moving slowly and surely into the shadows of extinction. Unable to compete with the larger denominations, white and Negro, and lacking the challenging appeal needed to recruit educated young people to their doctrinal banners, these bodies, living evidences of Baptist independence, exist largely on the glory of their past battles, with the memory of the victories and defeats.

There are the *United Baptists,* organized in Virginia and Kentucky in the late eighteenth century, united as a small association of churches but divided among themselves as to predestination, close communion, and the ordinance of foot washing.

The *Separate Baptists,* descendants of the "separatists" of England and the early American colonies, also add the ceremonial washing of feet to the ordinances of baptism and the Lord's table.

The *Duck River Association of Baptists* harks back to 1825, and a few of their churches persist in areas of the South, kindred in spirit and worship to the Regular Baptists.

Many ethnic Baptist groups swell the total of the fellowship in the United States: Finnish Baptist Union of America, French Baptist Conference, Hungarian Baptist Union, Italian Baptist Association, Polish Baptist Conference in the U.S.A. and Canada; Roumanian Baptist Association and the Czechoslovak Baptist Convention in America.

Scattered churches, or associations of churches, make up a few more congregations of minority Baptists, clinging to a heritage of beliefs which they cherish above all things, including the most cherished tenet of all indomitable Baptists—complete freedom of conscience and worship. For *that* principle they would all rise at the trumpet call and join their brother Baptists—even those they consider in error on certain points—in the fight against the common enemy.

J. Frank Norris, the Most Successful Lone Wolf

With the twentieth century came several major upheavals within Baptist ranks. One cause was the Darwinian theory of evolution, slowly but surely pervading the teaching of science. It seemed to many religious leaders, Baptist and otherwise, to conflict with the Genesis account of creation and thus to cast doubt upon the verbal infallibility of the Bible. This brought vigorous attacks upon schools and colleges teaching the theory of evolution, and the war against Darwinism grew in intensity. It slowed down for damning the German Kaiser and shouting for victory in World War I and began again at the war's ending, with fundamentalist leaders in full cry.

Several strong personalities became divisive influences among Baptists. The beginnings of one controversy can be traced to 1906 when a lean young Texas preacher took over the pastorate of a small Baptist church in Dallas. He assumed business management of the state denominational paper, *The Baptist Standard,* and soon afterward became editor. He began a sensational journalistic campaign against racetrack gambling in Texas. In 1910 he moved to Fort Worth as pastor of the First Baptist Church.

Thus began the crusading career of the Reverend J. Frank Norris, the man chiefly responsible for founding the so-called Baptist World Fellowship. No man in the entire story of the Baptists was more constantly at odds with his own denominational leaders, nor played the lone wolf with higher degree of success. He gloried in the reputation he acquired as the country's most noted religious hunting dog, scenting out the hiding places of what he considered unorthodox birds roosting under Baptist shelters.

In 1917 Norris launched his local church paper called the *Fundamentalist* to give voice to his emphatic, often caustic, criticisms of the Southern Baptist Convention. Next he teamed with the Reverend W. B. Riley of Minneapolis to sponsor a conference on prophecy in Philadelphia, which led to the formation of the World's Christian Fundamentalist Association in 1919.

Because of Norris' sensational preaching and his vicious attacks upon fellow ministers, his one-time sponsor, Dr. B. H. Carroll, withdrew his membership from the Fort Worth church. One special target of Norris' verbal barrages was Dr. Joseph Martin Dawson, pastor of the First Baptist Church of Waco and a member of the board of trustees of the largest Baptist-sponsored school in the world, Baylor University.

Norris changed the name of his paper to the *Searchlight* and began to expose what he termed the secret cabals against scriptural truth fostered by such men as Dawson and Dr. George W. Truett, pastor of the First Baptist Church of Dallas, and for that matter to expose the heresies being taught at all Southern Baptist colleges and seminaries.

Specifically, Norris charged that Darwinism, prompting what he described as an "allegorical view" of Genesis, had crept into the curriculum at Baylor. Dawson won approval of an investigation of the charges by the Texas Baptist General Convention, which cleared the school of any heresy. But Norris next moved to crusade against that bastion of orthodoxy, the Southern Baptist Theological Seminary, his own alma mater.

"While this publicity met resentment from many Baptists," Dr. Dawson observed, "it won large audiences and many accessions to his church. So quick was the growth, [that] demand for a new edifice rose to a clamor. One night the old church burned down. Norris was indicted on a charge of arson, but upon standing trial he was acquitted. The local Baptist association expelled him, but the adverse action only caused him to intensify his efforts for complete vindication."[5]

J. Frank Norris also had to seek vindication in another episode. A Fort Worth citizen whom he had offended came to the church office to have a talk with the pastor. No one heard their conversation, but a pistol shot rang out. When a church employee rushed into Norris' office, the preacher was holding a smoking gun in his hand. His visitor had been slain on the spot. Norris explained then —and later in court—that the visitor had reached toward a pocket, and thinking the man was reaching for a gun, Norris had seized his own pistol, kept handy in a desk drawer, and had fired in self-defense. No gun was found on the slain man. When the jury announced an acquittal, supporters of Dr. Norris began a revival service right in the courtroom. It is certain that Norris never recovered from the emotional strain of the tragedy.

In May 1923 Norris and his principal fundamentalist associates, W. B. Riley and T. T. Shields, organized the Baptist Bible Union of America. A man of tremendous magnetism and platform ability, Norris began winning young Texas preachers in a campaign to take over the Texas Baptist Convention and the Southern Baptist Convention. He set up his own theological seminary, the Fundamental Baptist Bible Institute, at Fort Worth, and by 1934 had gained enough followers to organize the Premillennial Baptist Missionary Fellowship for independent mission enterprises.

At every annual session of the Southern Baptist Convention, Frank Norris held a rival meeting in the same city. A man hired by Norris would be seen walking about on stilts with sandwich boards announcing the time and place to hear the editor of the *Searchlight* expose "the heresies of the Southern Baptist Convention."

In 1935 Norris accepted the pastorate of Temple Baptist Church in Detroit, in addition to his pastorate at the First Baptist Church in Fort Worth, and commuted by plane between these pulpits. He agreed that his associate, the Reverend G. Beauchamp Vick, would serve as joint pastor in the Detroit church. Dr. Vick lived in Detroit and had been an associate of several fundamentalist evangelists, including Mordicai Ham, for several years. Dr. Vick had built up the Temple church in Detroit to become the greatest Baptist congregation in that city.

Dr. Norris persuaded Vick to come to Fort Worth and serve as president of the seminary sponsored by the First Baptist Church. Dr. Vick, well trained in church and institutional funding, moved promptly to separate the finances of the seminary from the First Baptist Church—a move that met vigorous opposition from Norris. In 1947 the World Baptist Missionary Fellowship was organized, with the Reverend William E. Dowell, pastor of High Street Baptist Church in Springfield, Missouri, as president.

Accepting the pastorate of the Detroit church gave Dr. Norris the opportunity to attack the Northern Baptist Convention as he did his old southern brethren. The Fort Worth Baptist firebrand often came to Waco to conduct revival meetings, in which he castigated Pastor Dawson of Waco's First Baptist Church as a menace to Baptist orthodoxy. He would denounce "Dawsonism" at his meetings and have his searing *Searchlight* deposited at every doorstep in town.

When the Reverend Everett Jones, rector of Waco's St. Paul's Episcopal Church, and Methodist Edmond Heinsohn of Southwestern University's church joined Dawson to form an association for discussion of theological and sociological questions, Norris denounced Dawson as an enemy of Baptist doctrines. When Dawson preached in Waco's liberal synagogue, presided over by Rabbi Macht, he was branded by Norris as intolerable. When Congressman Walter H. Judd, a former Congregational missionary to China, spoke in Dawson's church to the Waco United Church Women, Norris declared this action was an overture to "the insufferable Federal Council of Churches."

In 1938 Frank Norris had founded the World Fundamental Baptist Fellowship. It became the World Baptist Fellowship in 1950, when the founder, ill and almost blind, lost his grip on the organization and new leaders supplanted him.

The Baptist Bible Fellowship

Dr. J. Frank Norris' health began to deteriorate in 1948, and with ill health came a dictatorial attitude on his part toward his closest associates. He accused some of misappropriation of funds, others of mismanagement, and many of being "traitors" to his cause.

After a stormy meeting in Norris' church on May 23, 1950, about 150 fundamentalist ministers and laymen, who had for years supported Norris, broke with him completely. The next day they held a meeting in the ballroom of the Texas Hotel in Fort Worth and approved a motion that "we organize a separate, new, independent, fundamental, premillennial, old-fashioned Baptist missionary fellowship." They named the new organization "Baptist Bible Fellowship" and chose Dr. Dowell as president.[6]

The founders of the Fellowship also decided to launch a new school, the "Baptist Bible College," with Dr. Vick as president and Dr. Dowell as chairman of the faculty, and to locate the college in Springfield, Missouri. They agreed to issue a weekly publication, the *Baptist Bible Tribune,* and the Reverend Noel Smith, formerly editor of the *Fundamentalist,* was elected editor. Others who became prominent leaders of the Fellowship were Fred Donnelson, director of missions, R. O. Woodworth, Wendell Zimmerman, John W. Rawlings, Charles McDowell, and Scotty Alexander.

Within a few months of its founding, the Baptist Bible Fellowship had enrolled more than one hundred churches, some of them formerly affiliated with the Southern Baptist Convention. By 1966 the number had grown to about 1,600 churches, and in 1979 the number reached approximately 3,500, in every state of the Union and in fifty-four foreign countries, with a total membership of about 1,500,000. Its doctrinal principles were summarized by Dr. Dowell:[7]

"The Baptist Bible Fellowship stands firmly for the Bible as the infallible, inerrant word of God; for the Bible account of creation, the fall of man through sin, the Deity of Christ, the virgin birth of Christ, Christ's sinless life, His substitutionary death for sin, the efficacy of His blood, His triumphant resurrection, His work of intercession at the Father's right hand, salvation by Grace, eternal security, and the premillennial return of Christ. Our Fellowship believes firmly in separated living of Christian people; and the doctrine of the autonomous local church, an organization founded by Jesus Christ, empowered on the day of Pentecost and commissioned to preach the gospel to the whole world."

The three divisions of the Baptist Bible Fellowship are the Missions Office, the college, and the *Baptist Bible Tribune*.

"World missions sponsored by autonomous churches" is the description used by Fellowship leaders for its mission work. By 1979 there were 500 adult foreign missionaries serving the Fellowship in many areas of the world. Each missionary or missionary couple must secure his or her own support from churches willing to pledge contributions sufficient to underwrite the funds needed.

Baptist Bible College is a training school principally for preachers, missionaries, and other church vocations. In May 1978 the college graduated 536 students. More than 4,000 pastors, missionaries, alumni, teachers, and students attended the week-long commencement events that featured conferences, the graduation exercises, and the kickoff for a fund drive to raise $675,000 for college expansion. The college enrollment for the 1978–79 term totaled 2,203 men and women. They came from all fifty states and twenty-five foreign countries. Many Baptist Bible Fellowship churches sponsor Christian elementary schools, and the teachers for those schools primarily receive their training at the college. Training for teachers of secondary grades is being planned for the next two years.

The *Baptist Bible Tribune* circulates in every community where there is a Fellowship church, and in 1979 the weekly reached a circulation of about 25,000.

During Dr. Vick's presidency of the college, at each graduation exercise he would make a final charge to the members of the senior class about to receive degrees. In an emotion-packed speech he would recite the fundamental doctrines of this Fellowship. He would begin each sentence with: "If you believe—"

"If you believe that God made the heavens and the earth . . . If you believe that on the sixth day he created man in his image . . ." and so on. When the list was complete, Dr. Vick issued his dramatic challenge: "If you believe all this, without reservation, stand to your feet!"

Those who stood received their diplomas. No student of Baptist Bible College failed to stand. President "Bill" Dowell continues the substance of this annual challenge.

Fundamentalists Go Their Way

The Northern Baptist Convention, meanwhile, was harassed and torn by dissensions of other fundamentalist leaders. Since its founding in 1907 the battle between so-called modernists and the fundamentalists had grown in intensity and bitterness.

The contest had its roots in the soil of the heated debates over the theory of evolution. On one hand were the supporters of the theory, many of them teaching in high schools, colleges, and universities all over the nation. On the other side were religious leaders, Baptist and otherwise, who saw in the theory a threat to the acceptance of a literal interpretation of the biblical account of the creation of the universe and man.

Devout scientists had no difficulty with the theory of evolution. For them, it enormously expanded their concept and appreciation of a divine Creator in time, space, and method of creation. Yet such interpretation of the theory in church-sponsored schools and seminaries brought prompt denunciations and charges of heresy from fundamentalist leaders.

With World War I out of the way and the nation getting back to what Baptist candidate for the presidency, Senator Warren G. Harding, called normalcy, Baptists were free to carry on the fights that had been deferred for unity in winning the war and making the world safe for democracy. So from 1920 until 1932 a continuous battle was waged within the Northern Baptist Convention against the modernists. Dr. Shailer Matthews of the Chicago Divinity School, a Baptist-sponsored institution, and Dr. Harry Emerson Fosdick, noted Baptist of New York City, were two shining targets for the arrows of the fundamentalists, who accused them of teaching and preaching scientific and social theories that undermined faith in the traditional Baptist interpretation of the Bible.

The attack was led by the Reverend W. B. Riley of Minneapolis, Dr. John Roach Straton of New York, and the Reverend Robert T. Ketcham of Chicago. Just how bitter the fight became was revealed by Dr. William B. Lipphard, editor of *Missions,* in his biography *Fifty Years an Editor.* Like all other Northern Baptist agencies, the Foreign Mission Society came under heavy attack. The secretary to the Society's executive, under pretext of staying to work overtime at her office, systematically searched the files and copied from confidential letters of missionaries overseas many sentences and paragraphs to prove that the Society was "modernist" and therefore unorthodox. She presented this evidence to the Society in the presence of her boss, after revealing it to those who had asked her to perform this service. Her perfidy cost her only her job.

Unable to gain control of the Northern Baptist Convention, in May 1932 a group of fundamentalist leaders met at the Belden Avenue Baptist Church in Chicago and organized the General Association of Regular Baptists. With Dr. Ketcham as general secretary, the new fellowship specified the New Hampshire Confession of Faith as its official doctrinal position, with additional strong emphasis upon belief in the premillennial return of Christ to the earth. In addition, the General Association asserted its belief in other fundamental principles of many Baptists, including the virgin birth of Christ, the vicarious atonement, believer's baptism by immersion, and the complete autonomy of each congregation. The General Association of Regular Baptists had grown to about 1,000 churches by 1979, with aggregate membership of approximately 150,000.

Meantime, another fundamentalist movement was launched at a meeting of the Northern Baptist Convention in Buffalo, New York, in June 1920, the Fundamentalist Fellowship of the Northern Baptist Convention. The founders' plan was to remain in the Convention and leaven its lump with fundamentalist principles. Years of struggle followed as the leaders of the movement tried to gain control of the Northern Baptist Convention. Finally, at the annual meeting of May 1947 in Atlantic City the fundamentalists decided to break away and the Conservative Baptist Association of America was formally launched—strongly premillennial in doctrine, strictly literal in interpretation of Scripture, and passionately evangelistic.

Some Negro Baptists Differ

From the beginnings of the twentieth century, dissension also tore at the ranks of the National Baptist Convention. Headquarters of the foreign mission work were moved from Richmond to Louisville, with the plea that this central location would be more convenient for all Negro Baptists of the country. Leaders of the convention in Virginia, backed by those of the Carolinas and some other eastern states, strongly dissented. They withdrew to establish the Lott Cary Missionary Convention, chartered as a society to further among Negroes the cause of foreign missions.

A still more serious breach occurred in 1915, occasioned by a controversy over the ownership and control of the Convention's Publishing Board at Nashville, Tennessee. The secretary of the publishing agency, Dr. R. H. Boyd, by agreement with the Board had carried on the publishing of Sunday school and other literature as his own private business. At the meeting of the Convention in 1915 a move was made to bring all agencies serving the Negro Baptists into control of the Convention. Dr. Boyd was asked to give an account of the finances of the publishing work on the ground that it was a part of the activities of the Convention and must be under its direction. Boyd refused to comply, contending that since he had invested his own funds in the venture and had built up the business by his personal efforts the control should remain with him.

A lawsuit was decided in Boyd's favor, but the controversy resulted in the formation of still another convention, the National Baptist Convention of America. About one-third of the churches of the old Convention went with Boyd and his supporters to create the new body. It was a split in a religious organization unique in the story of such divisions in that no doctrinal differences whatever were involved. Personalities and personal loyalties drove the wedge.

In October 1960 the president of the American Baptist Convention, C. Stanton Gallup, asked a fellow Baptist layman (the coauthor of this work) to give his greetings to the annual session of the National Baptist Convention of the U.S.A., Inc., meeting in Philadelphia. When the layman arrived at the convention hall, the session was in turmoil. The huge auditorium was filled with Negro men and women delegates, but no program was in progress. The platform was crowded with men, divided into two groups, each group attempting to get control of the floor and the organization.

The microphone had been disconnected. At the speaker's stand was a delegate, follower of the Reverend J. H. Jackson, of Chicago, who for eight years had been president of the Convention and was then a candidate for re-election. Surrounding the delegate were the incumbent's supporters. Back of them, and around them, were the partisans of a rival candidate for the high office, Dr. Gardner C. Taylor, pastor of a large Brooklyn church and president of the Protestant Federation of Churches of New York City.

The visiting layman dragged a table to the space beneath the platform, mounted it, and began to speak. A hush fell upon the audience. The struggle on the platform subsided. The speaker brought the fraternal greetings, then launched into a plea for unity of all Baptists in the common task of building better race relations, maintaining separation of church and state and sending the gospel to the ends of the earth.

"That's right! Amen!" a chorus of voices sounded from the audience, echoed by many on the platform. The shouts of approval increased during the visitor's impromptu speech. When he finished, the convention song leader stepped to the front of the platform and began the hymn so dear to Baptist hearts, "I am Bound for the Promised Land." The audience rose and picked up the words and tune in a mighty chorus.

Unfortunately for that great fellowship, the tie that bound its churches was not strong enough to prevent a split. From that Philadelphia convention there emerged the Progressive National Baptist Convention, composed of churches whose leaders desired to replace the president. Dr. Taylor became the president of the new fellowship, composed of about 12 per cent of the churches formerly in the parent convention. Many of the churches of the Progressive group are aligned also with the American Baptist Churches in a dual affiliation.

At the 1978 convention of the National Baptist Convention, U.S.A., Inc., the organization could count 6,500,000 members. This ninety-eighth annual gathering of the Baptist body, second only to the Southern Baptist Convention in membership, was held in the Louisiana Superdome in New Orleans. For the twenty-fourth year, Dr. Joseph H. Jackson, pastor of Chicago's Olivet Baptist Church, was elected president.

About 25,000 black clergy and their wives, and a large number of lay men and women, attended the five-day meeting. Dr. Jackson cautioned the messengers against what he called "blaming others for one's failures." The veteran Baptist minister declared:

"There is a mistaken notion about the meaning of freedom. Some believe that freedom means the lack of restraints. The person who desires freedom seldom blames himself for not getting what he sees as his full share of freedom. Just as important as the constant yen for freedom is the knowledge that freedom carries with it certain responsibilities, certain obligations, certain burdens."

Meeting in New Orleans at the time of a strike of schoolteachers in the city, the messengers adopted a resolution, proposed by Dr. Jackson, stating: "The right of teachers to strike should be subordinate to the responsibility of teaching children. The program of unions should be secondary to the high educational function of teachers."

The other large convention of black members, the National Baptist Convention of America, sometimes called the "Unincorporated National Convention," in 1979 represented 12,000 churches, located in most of the fifty states, the District of Columbia, the Bahamas, and Bermuda. It had enrolled approximately 3,500,000 members.

The Reverend J. C. Sams, a Jacksonville, Florida, pastor, served as president of the convention and the organization's chief executive. A foreign-mission board guides mission work in Liberia, Jamaica, Panama, and the Bahamas. The convention also has boards for home missions, Training Union, education, publishing, and evangelism.

There are also commissions on orthodoxy, social justice, the Christian ministry, the armed forces chaplaincy, transportation, and benevolence.

The NBCA is a member of the National Council of Churches, the World Council of Churches, the North American Baptist Fellowship, and the Baptist World Alliance. Its publishing board has a co-operative relationship with the Sunday School Board of the Southern Baptist Convention.

XVIII

THE BAPTIST WOMEN

Ann Hasseltine Judson

The development of women's work in Baptist churches was much more rapid in America than in England. The more conservative atmosphere and the love of tradition in Great Britain were not the only factors that accounted for the difference. The Baptists of the new world had a glamorous heroine. She had gone with her husband to the opposite side of the globe to help him convert the heathen.

No more striking contrast could exist than that between Dorothy Carey, wife of William Carey of London, first Baptist foreign missionary, and Ann Hasseltine Judson. Dorothy lacked her husband's world outlook. She was a homebody, thoroughly content to cook and sew and raise children. She did not share William's sense of a call to lifetime service.

Mrs. Carey never accepted India. She loathed its heat and filth and poverty, its crocodiles and tigers, its strange sounds and vile smells. She became morbidly homesick. Carey gave her the best possible care until her death in 1807.

In contrast, Ann Judson was a true missionary. The day after her wedding, as she stood all decked out in her new scoop bonnet and her going-away outfit in the Salem meeting house, she shed no tears. Impulsively, the young woman known as Nancy left her pew to kneel beside her husband for the laying on of hands in the ordination service. It mattered not to her that her name was not on the docket as one sent officially to the faraway land. She was answering a divine call, just as was Adoniram. She anticipated life as one long honeymoon following a four months' wedding trip on the high seas with the one she called "the most faithful and affectionate of husbands."

At the end of the voyage, when she and her husband agreed to renounce the support of the American Board of Commissioners for Foreign Missions and trust God to care for them until the Baptists adopted them, Ann Judson did not panic. Always, her letters to her family and the mission board, published in missionary magazines, made exciting, poignant, family-altar fare. In terms of public relations, Ann Judson was an unlimited asset to the promotion of women's work in the Baptist churches from the rockbound coasts of Maine to the Gulf beaches of Alabama. The image of that exquisite American woman in "Burmah" did more to galvanize Baptist women in the United States into action for the support of missions than all the pulpit poundings and appeals to the Almighty put together.

Luther Rice, the bachelor, loved Ann and Adoniram, and during all his travels in behalf of foreign missions he painted the word portrait of the beautiful Ann Hasseltine Judson with all the power of a rich vocabulary.

As early as 1800 Mary Webb and other Baptist women in Massachusetts had joined with Congregationalists to create the Boston Female Society for Missionary Purposes. Their offerings were at first designated for the Congregational Missionary Society, but when the Massachusetts Domestic Missionary Society was formed for Baptist mission projects, each member was permitted to give to her chosen cause.

Mite societies and cent societies were thus formed in churches all over the Eastern seaboard. Taking their name from the two-mite widow whom Jesus commended for her generosity, these groups of women met faithfully for prayer and contrived to earn small sums of money with their chickens, butter, pies, knitting and sewing, in order to give to missions. The records of Baptist associations in New England regularly showed sums of money from these women's societies, revealing their concern for the expansion of churches to the "far west" of New York State, Ohio, Kentucky, and even to the Missouri territory.

Helen Barrett Montgomery

For the year 1811, the Boston Female Society for Missionary Purposes adopted a new policy by giving all the money raised to the "translation of the Scriptures carried on so extensively and successfully by the British Baptist missionaries at Serampore in Bengal." The next year, when one of their very own daughters left for the Far East, the impulses to give were increased a hundredfold.

The records of the organization of American Baptists in the Triennial Convention in 1814 list the names of thirty-three delegates, all men, but women were present in spirit, and the news of the remarkable achievement was the talk of the day among truly consecrated, Christian missionary-minded women. They thanked God for the ready-made Baptist foreign mission enterprise.

After the southern states seceded from the Triennial Convention in 1845 and the nationwide organization revised its agenda and roster, it adopted the name American Baptist Missionary Union. One of its missionary wives in Burma urged her sister in Newton Center, Massachusetts, to get American women to band together in societies to serve as auxiliaries to the Union. This suggestion led directly to the formation in 1871 of the Woman's American Baptist Foreign Mission Society in Boston. Six years later, the Woman's American Baptist Home Mission Society was launched there.

Nobody was fooled by the term "auxiliary," and nobody believed the women were going to content themselves with fund raising. They had ideas about how the mission boards should operate, and they wished to influence some decisions. For a time, the societies devoted themselves to Bible study and missions, reading missionary letters aloud, studying the news from the mission fronts, and praying for lost souls.

Such a program had the immediate result of stimulating consecrated giving, and women whose hands were occupied with milking and churning, baking and canning, raising children and caring for elderly relatives felt satisfaction in being missionaries vicariously. But every message from the wives of missionaries appealed for qualified single women who could give full time to missions. Was it fair for the mission boards to appoint only men?

Were they denying God-called women with special training and skills the right to spend their lives in service? Were these board members depriving the home and foreign mission enterprise of the talents of women doctors, nurses, teachers, and evangelists who could minister to women and children as no man ever could?

Before the directors of the two mission Societies could be persuaded to forget their prejudices against females, the auxiliaries saw the opportunity to appoint women who had appealed in vain for the chance to be missionaries.

One of the most brilliant presidents of the Woman's American Baptist Foreign Mission Society distinguished herself by translating the New Testament from Greek into Modern English. Helen Barrett of Philadelphia, the daughter of a Latin and Greek teacher named Adoniram Judson Barrett, acquired from her father both a love of missions and a love of languages. She mastered Greek at Wellesley under its president, Alice Freeman, later Mrs. Palmer. She became the wife of a businessman, William A. Montgomery of Rochester, New York, who grew wealthy after backing financially the inventor of the self-starter for autos. Helen Montgomery made many substantial gifts to missions. She traveled around the world to see where her money was being used, and with the influence of her traveling companion, Mrs. Henry W. Peabody, she promoted the idea of a day of prayer for world missions. This annual event, inaugurated in 1919, became The World Day of Prayer, promoted by United Church Women, whose name was changed to Church Women United.

One of Helen Montgomery's lasting contributions was made in response to her concern for the dearth of Christian reading matter for new converts and members of the younger churches around the world. She started a movement that resulted in the Committee on World Christian Literature, and she gave the first $25,000 for it.

For many years Mrs. Montgomery worked on the translation of the New Testament from the original Greek. It was a monumental labor of love on the part of this scholarly Baptist woman. Officials of the American Baptist Publication Society, anticipating its centennial celebration, in 1924 brought out Helen Montgomery's version, calling it The Centenary Translation of the New Testament.

It is the only one in existence produced solely by a woman scholar.[1]

A dynamic Sunday school teacher for forty-four years, a popular lecturer year after year at the Northfield and Chautauqua summer conferences, and a prolific writer of mission texts, Helen Barrett Montgomery was given four honorary degrees, including a Doctor of Laws by her alma mater.

A woman of rare good humor, Mrs. Montgomery sometimes quoted from the minutes of an early Baptist church which related that a woman member was brought before the church to be disciplined, but was dismissed with this verdict: "After considerable conversation on both sides, the church imputed some part of her misconduct to ignorance—she being a woman." Northern Baptists, more readily than Southern Baptists, recognized the equality of the sexes, and Mrs. Montgomery was the first woman to be elected president of the Northern Baptist Convention, serving during 1921–22. Later this body of American Christians authorized the ordination of theologically educated women.

Must a Delegate Be a Brother?

Baptist women of the South had to resort to indirect methods to achieve the same results that northern women achieved by direct action. At every turn they were confronted with the traditional southern mixture of false chivalry and piosity. Fear of the problems that greater freedom for women might create plagued denominational leaders. Baptist ministers in the South took literally the injunction of the Apostle Paul to the early Christians at Corinth: "Let your women keep silence in the churches." They considered that it was proper for the women to pray silently and give liberally for missions, but that no real lady would presume to know anything about business matters and certainly women could have no voice in the administration of a mission board.

The most newsworthy event at the fortieth anniversary session of the Southern Baptist Convention in Augusta in 1885 was the appearance of two Baptist women from Arkansas, officially appointed as messengers, who asked to be seated. Alarmed at this development, the Convention appointed a committee of five men to deal with it. The committee could find nothing in the constitution barring women messengers—for the very good reason that in 1845 no one imagined the question would ever come up. The Convention duly voted to change the wording of the constitution, substituting *brethren* for *members,* thus signifying unmistakably that messengers were considered to be of the male species only. The 1885 session then made this concession:

"We think it important that there should be Women's Central Committees established and fostered by State Conventions, or Associations, with the co-operation of the Boards of the Conventions . . . Let such funds be credited also to the General State Convention or Association. Then let these moneys be represented in this body by delegates chosen, if they prefer, by the local societies, upon the same basis and conditions specified for all other moneys reported."[2]

The women accepted the challenge of working through their state conventions, yet every development strengthened their determination to have their own organization. They did not favor a competing mission society. The cause of missions, they reasoned, would be better served if they could create a true auxiliary to the Convention. Playing second fiddle is no disgrace, they reasoned, if you play it to the glory of God and the first fiddle is in tune. Thus adroitly, the women talked and planned for creating something for missions that would advance the education of women and young people, recruit personnel and mobilize financial resources for the two mission boards.

At the Southern Baptist Convention in annual session in Louisville in 1887, the women met in a separate church and heard two of their most articulate spokesmen, Miss Annie W. Armstrong of Baltimore and Mrs. M. E. McIntosh of Charleston, propose a national organization of Southern Baptist women. The resolution included the following:

"Resolved, that the above is not to be construed as a desire upon the part of the ladies to interfere with the management of the existing Boards of the Convention, either in the appointment of missionaries, or the direction of the mission work; but is a desire, on their part, to be more efficient in collecting money and disseminating information on mission subjects."

During that year twelve state Baptist conventions appointed women to represent them in plans "to be more efficient in collecting money" and informing the people of the churches, young and old, about the importance and the projects of Baptist missions.

The 1888 meeting of Southern Baptists was held in the Old First Baptist Church of Richmond. The women selected as delegates to complete plans for their national organization met not far away in the Broad Street Methodist Church. The brethren attended to the usual business of the Convention through reports and model sermons, each with an ear cocked in the direction of the Methodist church house.

"You never can tell," said one of the pastor-messengers nervously, "what the women might take to praying for, if left to themselves!"

As he doubtless suspected, the women were not going to be content merely to pray. They were organizing. They formed the Executive Committee of the Woman's Mission Societies— Auxiliary to the Southern Baptist Convention, and the words of their constitution, as adopted then, have stood all down the years as they were written, with slight revisions: "First, to distribute missionary information and stimulate effort, through the State Central Committees; second, to secure the earnest sympathetic cooperation of women and children in collecting and raising money for missions."

In 1890 when the name of the organization was changed to Woman's Missionary Union, contributions from the women totaling more than $45,000 helped not only in home and foreign mission work, but also in educating ministers and in publishing Sunday-school literature and Bibles.

On the twenty-fifth anniversary of the Woman's Missionary Union in 1913, women appeared for the first time on the platform of the Convention in front of all the men and gave a report of their stewardship as an auxiliary. They have given a formal report to the Convention at every annual meeting since.

The Privilege of Taking Notes

When the fall term opened at the Southern Baptist Theological Seminary in 1904, four young Baptist women, desiring to be better equipped as missionaries, applied for admission as students at the institution. The seminary faculty gave the matter careful and prayerful consideration. Arguments were presented for and against the proposal, with opponents standing firm in their opinion that the presence of young females in the classrooms would completely demoralize the young ministerial students intent upon theological studies. Finally a compromise was reached whereby young women students were granted the privilege of taking notes on the classroom lectures, provided they remained out of sight in the hall and did not expect credit from the seminary.

The affair spurred Baptist women of the South to establish their own Missionary Training School in 1907, located at Louisville, not far from the seminary so that theological professors, completely immune to feminine charms, could come and give lectures to the young women in their own classrooms.

In the 1916 session of the Southern Baptist Convention, following an introduction by the corresponding secretary of the Southwide women's organization, a woman gave the running narrative for a stereopticon program. This second intrusion of women into the convention program seemed justified by the nature of the pictures. It was a report of the Woman's Missionary Union Training School in its first nine years of service to young Baptist women.

After the seminary removed all barriers to women students in 1940, the Training School changed its curriculum and became the Carver School of Missions and Social Work. The name was in honor of Dr. William Owen Carver, the Southern Seminary professor who as early as 1904 most actively encouraged women to learn about missions, systematic theology, and even Greek and Hebrew. He inaugurated a course in Christian missions, the first in any theological institution in the world, and also persuaded the faculty to allow him to conduct a course he called Christian Missions and Comparative Religions, which was considered a radical departure from traditional Baptist teachings. On the advice of management consultants retained in the 1950s for a complete study of the operations of Woman's Missionary Union, the organization abandoned its effort in the academic field and Carver School merged with Southern Seminary.

By the 150th anniversary of the Triennial Convention in 1964, women outnumbered men two to one in the missionary force of the Baptists. In actual maintenance of a mission program, at home or abroad, Baptists sent two women for every man appointed: His wife, who was a missionary homemaker as well as teacher, nurse, or reporter; and a professional assistant who gave full time to the ministry in a hospital, school, mission headquarters, or field work. All three were on the payroll and all three consider themselves evangelists, witnessing to the love of God through their specialties, including that of homemaker. By far the greatest number of volunteers for missionary service are young men and women who have come up through the missionary organizations of their churches. The Woman's Missionary Union, the American Baptist women, and corresponding groups in other Baptist fellowships generally have sponsored youth groups in weekday missionary education that introduce young people to the heroes of the world mission enterprise, the national Christians who have made good, and the challenge of being a missionary in every occupation.

Women have not neglected the duty to give money. The appeals of an overworked missionary in China, Miss Charlotte Moon of Virginia, unwilling to take home leave until she had someone to fill in for her, inspired the women of the South, in 1888, to take a special offering for foreign missions at Christmas. The newly organized Woman's Missionary Union gave enough to enable the Foreign Mission Board to send three recruits to relieve the missionary. "Lottie" Moon got her vacation. By vote of the Union, the appeal was made a second year, with a week of prayer for foreign missions to precede the offering.

Soon the significance of this bonus for missions led the women to offer, and the Foreign Mission Board to accept, some suggestions for the disbursements of the funds. There were certain projects on foreign fields that were cherished by the women but overlooked by the boards. This offering served as leverage to secure support for these specials: a baby home here, a mobile medical clinic there, more money for children's literature for one country, an additional worker for a Good Will Center in another.

In the Southern Baptist Convention this working relationship between the women and the board that administered the program doubled the convention's foreign mission revenue. The plan resulted in an annual Christmas offering budget, agreed upon in consultation between the women and the board, and this in turn set a goal for the offering each year. The goal has been increased year by year and always achieved until 1977, when the gifts totaled almost $32 million but only 94 per cent of the goal for the Lottie Moon Christmas Offering. Yet it was 11 per cent more than the previous year's Christmas offering for foreign missions. With courage and zest, the women dared to set the 1978 goal at $40 million —about half of the budget of the Foreign Mission Board, which receives and dispenses the funds.

The success of the foreign mission offering, named for Miss Lottie Moon of China who first proposed it, suggested that a similar offering be made for home missions, this one named for Miss Annie Armstrong, who was one of the organizers of Woman's Missionary Union. The women chose the month of March for the home missions emphasis and bargained with the Baptist Home Mission Board for the right to help budget the money contributed for this offering. In the 1970s it was designated as an annual Easter offering, and in 1978 the goal of $13 million for home missions was reached long before the deadline.

Emphasis is placed by Baptist women upon the "seasons of prayer" for missions—foreign and home; the women believe that the money is incidental to prayer but go together, and the boards count on both.

While Southern Baptist women chose to achieve their goals for missions through "the system," Northern Baptist women decided on a different plan. In 1871 they organized the first regional Woman's American Baptist Foreign Mission Society, and merged three regionals in 1914. In 1877 they organized the Woman's American Baptist Home Mission Society. In this way the women of northern churches could appoint professional women for missions overseas or in America and support them by their own efforts.

The Baptist Board of Foreign Missions in the United States became the American Baptist Foreign Mission Society in 1910. The two Foreign Mission societies and the two Home Mission societies merged in 1955 into two societies.

Juliette Mather

Baptist women in the several bodies of the Baptist denomination have been more willing to brave frontiers of thought and action than those in primary positions of leadership. At the celebration of the ninetieth anniversary of Woman's Missionary Union, auxiliary to the Southern Baptist Convention, the honor guest was eighty-two-year-old Juliette Mather.

Over the birthday cake with ninety candles ablaze, the sprightly woman, who retired after fifty-seven years on the staff, dared to name women's natural aggressiveness as "pushability." It was the women's organization of the churches, she asserted, that first launched the well-established projects now on the Convention agenda: Vacation Bible school, co-operative ministries with blacks, mission work among language groups, social-work centers, volunteers in missions, Baptist Student Union on college campuses, student summer missionaries, and the use of Ridgecrest (North Carolina) as a conference center.

Most of the Southern Baptists had little knowledge of the Mather family. Related to, but not directly descended from, the famous Massachusetts preacher Cotton Mather, the Mathers of Granville, Ohio, produced Asher, who was a missionary to Assam until disease took him; Kirtley, Harvard University geologist, who died in retirement in 1978; William, a pastor who retired to Florida; Ruth, missionary to China and later Burma, now retired to Florida; Harriet, for years the superintendent of nurses at the New Orleans Baptist Hospital; and Juliette, the tiniest of the sisters.

On the staff of Woman's Missionary Union as youth leader from 1927 until she was made editor of publications, Miss Mather invited to the Ridgecrest platform, for the ten-day program of Bible study, inspirational addresses, and recreation, Christian men and women of other than Southern Baptist background.

In 1941 the war in Europe and the worldwide international crisis created tensions that made some speakers wary. A Baptist journalist and cartoonist from a Quaker family, Charles A. Wells, world traveler and popular lecturer in northern states, had been introduced to Southern Baptist young women at their missions conferences in previous years.

Mr. Wells was booked for the student conference just before Miss Mather's young women were to meet. When he appeared for his series of lectures, he was pulled aside by the conference leader and asked to avoid any mention of pacifism. Somewhat surprised at the request, Wells nevertheless assured his host that he would be discreet and not embarrass the executive.

When the students departed and the teenage girls arrived on the Assembly grounds, Wells took the initiative to allay the anxieties of the conference leader of the young women. He said he was well aware of the change in emotional climate. "I understand what this war situation means to you denominational executives," he said. "I'll play down the peace talk."

Miss Mather caught the inference and responded with brown eyes flashing. "You'll do no such thing!" she declared. "We want the kind of message that only you can bring these young women in times like these."

Acting on orders, Wells talked of Christ and world need, even on the eve of World War II. Juliette Mather was one of many women who carried and waved the ensign with the slogan "No thought control here." Charles Wells continued to be invited to speak and hold conferences in Southern Baptist gatherings until he retired. He died of a heart attack at his home, Echo Farm, Washington Crossing, Pennsylvania, in May 1976.

Juliette considers the electronic-media impact as the newest frontier, and as usual she was thinking ahead of those in places of responsibility. As she put it in 1978, "I want the Bold Mission Thrust to be a grand success in lifting Southern Baptists out of themselves into a new lifestyle. You (women) may have to be the center for this."

Nannie Burroughs: Woman with a Dream

Among the delegates from the National Baptist Convention to the first meeting of the Baptist World Congress in London in 1905 was an intelligent, energetic young Negro American named Nannie Helen Burroughs. She had served for five years as corresponding secretary of the women's organization of this Convention and was rapidly becoming the best-known and most highly respected Negro Baptist woman in America.

An afternoon session of these Baptists from many parts of the world was held in the open air in Hyde Park with more than 18,000 persons in attendance. Selected as one of the speakers, Miss Burroughs captivated her audience with her eloquence and wit. In the London *Mirror*'s account of the speech were these words:

"Undoubtedly the most popular speaker of the afternoon was Miss N. H. Burroughs, Negress. She was a handsome woman, dressed in a gray gown with touches of green that harmonized well with her bronze skin; the flashes of humor which characterize the American Negro showed now and again her brilliant white teeth as she smiled in sympathy when a laugh rang out over the crowd, and as she told one tale that greatly amused them."

Miss Burroughs had a vision. She would found a school for Negro girls in Washington. It would be a school, as she later wrote, "that would give all sorts of girls a fair chance to help overcome their handicaps of race; a national school for girls—not just a Baptist school, but one that would serve young Negro women of all creeds; one that is created and supported by Negro-American women for themselves; one that will train leaders for our race."[3]

Nannie Burroughs was born of slave parents in Virginia. She remembered both her grandfathers as belonging to that small class of ex-slaves who achieved some distinction after emancipation. One owned a Virginia farm and made a good living from the soil. The other was a skilled carpenter and helped rebuild the town of Orange after the war. Nannie's widowed mother brought her to Washington so she could have a good school. Nannie graduated from high school with honors, having specialized in domestic science and in business. She expected to be named assistant to the domestic science teacher, but another girl, one with more "pull," got the appointment. It was a severe disappointment, but it taught Nannie Burroughs a lesson. As she later told it, "If you find one door shut, push on another one!"

She pushed open the door to a job with the foreign missions office of her denomination at Louisville, Kentucky. She taught a Sunday school class, and was soon speaking in Negro churches all over Louisville. But she did more than talk. She brought Baptist women together and organized the Woman's Industrial Club. The club rented a house and served inexpensive, nourishing lunches for Negro workmen. At night Miss Burroughs conducted classes in cooking, sewing, and housekeeping. She taught her pupils how to do "everyday things needed in the home"—personal hygiene, care of children, sanitation, laundry work, personal grooming.

An influential white woman of the city came to Miss Burroughs' office and asked how she was financing the school. "We club members pay a dime a week toward the expenses, and we make pies and cakes and sell them," Miss Burroughs replied.

"Don't give your lessons away any longer," the visitor urged. "People value what they pay for, and if they can't pay more than a penny, let them pay that. I'll pay you regularly for every pupil you have, so you can help equip the school and enlarge your ministry." And there Nannie Burroughs learned a second important lesson: *People value what they pay for*. The cooking and housekeeping school grew so fast and so large that Miss Burroughs had to hire a staff of teachers.

She never lost her dream of a school for Negro girls in Washington. In 1907, two years after her trip to London and the Baptist World Alliance, the energetic young Negro woman spent her summer vacation in Washington. With a borrowed horse and buggy Nannie Burroughs drove all around the northeast part of the city. She found a vacant, dilapidated, eight-room house on an eroded hill, with a good view of the neighborhood, and decided that was the place for her school. The house and the six acres of good earth around it were priced at $6,500. Nannie Burroughs promptly bought the property, promising to pay $500 in ten days and $500 twenty days later, the rest over a period of years. She hurried back to Louisville to raise the first payments. She later explained: "You see, I had prayed about this thing for a long time. I felt God wanted me to go ahead. I knew if I did what I could and trusted him, God would see it through. And he did."

Miss Burroughs remained in Louisville until the Washington property was paid for, with enough money left over to do the repairing and remodeling, then she claimed the school site. She opened the institution in October 1909, with eight pupils, as the National Trade and Professional School for Women and Girls, Inc. The property was vested in a self-perpetuating board of trust, the majority of whose members were women. It can be used only for educational purposes.

Nannie Burroughs called her institution "The School of the Three B's: the Bible, the Bathtub, and the Broom." In the printed material advertising the school Miss Burroughs explained: "The *Holy Bible* as a guide and inspiration to every day spiritual living. The *bathtub* symbolizes personal cleanliness in order to make acceptable social contacts. The *broom* is for cleanliness of environment and community acceptance."

"Get the Alley Out of the Negro"

World War I gave the school its most severe test. A hard freeze in the winter of 1917–18 put the school pump out of commission. Every drop of water used at the top of that steep, icy hill had to be carried from neighborhood wells during the rest of the winter. Coal companies dumped the fuel at the base of the hill, and the students carried it to the school's fireplaces. Miss Burroughs later wrote:

"I just explained to the girls that it was really our service to our country to manage our problems ourselves while our men were fighting the nation's battles overseas. So we did. We carried coal and water, tended our pigs and chickens, cooked, cleaned, and did our school work in a cheerful, happy spirit. I think the 'hard' years were the best ones. They built more character. Souls grow under hardships."

In 1920 Miss Burroughs and the board of the National Trade and Professional School launched a campaign to raise $125,000 to care for needed expansion. The campaign was successful, and the school entered the period of its greatest growth. Its enrollment each year has regularly included girls from a score of states, Haiti, Liberia, and the West Indies.

Miss Burroughs' reputation as a leader of Negro women brought many distinguished visitors to her office. One of them flattered her with an invitation to participate in a "slum clearance" program. She listened carefully to his proposal.

"I'm sorry; I can't help you!" she said firmly.

"What? You mean that you refuse to help get these niggers out of the alleys?"

"I mean just that," Miss Burroughs responded. "My business is to help get the alley out of the Negro. There are many humble people, both black and white, who cannot afford any better housing than what they have. It is important for them to realize that they can keep it clean and homelike until they can do better." And she bade her visitor good-by.

When the "votes for women" crusade swung under way Nannie

Burroughs was interviewed on the subject: "Sure, I'm for woman suffrage. The Negro woman needs the ballot to get back by the wise use of it what the Negro man has lost by the misuse of it. She needs it to redeem her race."

Nannie Burroughs was noted for her sayings, her bits of homespun philosophy which she made a part of the teaching of the school. One of her best-read pamphlets was titled "Twelve Things the Negro Must Learn to Do for Himself," in which she urged: "The Negro must learn to put first things first—education, character, a trade, and home ownership. He must stop expecting God and the white folks to do for him what he can do for himself; keep himself, his children, and his home clean; learn to dress more appropriately for work and for leisure; make his religion an everyday practice; wipe out mass ignorance; stop charging his failures to his color, and to white people's attitudes; overcome his bad job habits; learn how to operate business for all the people; come down out of the air and be more practical; and stop forgetting his friends."

"Use what you have!" Miss Burroughs constantly admonished her students. She showed them how to make cushioned chairs from empty wooden barrels. "Put yourself on the program!" meant take every opportunity to become involved.

Miss Burroughs remained the president of the Auxiliary to the National Baptist Convention, Inc., for fifty years. For that half century this woman was the voice for progress not only of the women in her denomination but of all Negro women in America. It was a proud day for Nannie Helen Burroughs when on a Sunday in July 1956 she presided at the dedication of a new dormitory at the National Trade and Professional School for Women and Girls, Inc. Dr. Mordecai Johnson, president of Howard University, was the speaker. Miss Burroughs, now Dr. Burroughs by courtesy of Shaw University, Raleigh, North Carolina, personally presented her fellow Baptist and fellow educator. The building could have been dedicated some months before, but Miss Burroughs would not permit this until she had raised the $200,000 needed to pay all its bills. "I am not going to turn this building over to God with a debt on it!" she said.

The Nannie Helen Burroughs School, Inc., at 5001 Grant Street, N.E., Washington, D.C., is still in operation. After the death of the founder in 1961, the Progressive National Baptist Convention bought the property and revamped the institution as a private elementary school for prekindergarten through the sixth grade. Dr. S. S. Hodges, executive secretary of the younger organization of black churches, covets for the new school the same spirit Miss Burroughs gave it in her day.

The Reverend Mrs. Barr

Martha Mathews Barr in 1975 became the highest-ranking woman among American Baptists: associate to the executive secretary at the national headquarters in Valley Forge. Daughter of a veteran pastor who retired to the Ozarks of Missouri, Martha was ordained by the South Avenue Baptist Church, Rochester, New York, after graduation from William Jewel College and Colgate Rochester Divinity School.

The Reverend Mrs. Barr is as much at home in the pulpit as she is at her desk as Deputy for National Operations. On a June day, 1978, in Alexandria, Virginia, wearing a simple street dress, she conducted a memorial service for her brother, the Reverend Hubert Clyde Mathews, Jr., long-time missionary to American Indians in Nevada, drafted by the Department of Health, Education, and Welfare for a more extensive service to the first Americans.

Tearlessly, with complete poise, Mrs. Barr looked out across the flag-draped casket to a dimly lighted room full of friends— "red men," blacks, and whites. After a Psalm, a couple of verses from the New Testament, and a spontaneous prayer, she announced: "This is a service to mourn for our loneliness." She introduced one of Clyde's associates, who had asked for the privilege of "sharing," and stated that anyone else who wished to speak could feel free to come forward or to stand where he sat.

Testimonials to the ministry of the deceased, dead of a heart attack at fifty-seven, filled an hour. Dr. William Barr, a university professor, sat in the second pew with the couple's ten-year-old daughter and seven-year-old twins. Clyde's widow and their three grown children occupied the front pew. The service was closed with a simple prayer of thanks for the life of Clyde Mathews.

Dr. Robert C. Campbell declared (when he appointed Mrs.

Barr one of four assistant general secretaries at Valley Forge): "In a sense she will act as my 'alter ego.'"

In the news release Dr. Campbell was reported to have said of Martha Barr: "Here is a perfect example of systemic injustice—Martha has had no problem securing positions on the basis of her qualifications, but they were always short-term assignments probably because she was a woman. I hope that by putting such key people in positions of denominational leadership, we can modify the system and open it up to persons regardless of sex, race, and national origin."

Of her appointment, Mrs. Barr declared: "God's call to be a servant of Jesus Christ has led me into a variety of experiences. I am grateful for this new opportunity for ministry in the church."

Carolyn Weatherford, Executive Director

Ordination of women is not the basic issue of churches today, asserted the head of Woman's Missionary Union of the Southern Baptist Convention, Birmingham, Alabama. The only woman among fifteen speakers invited to a seminar on Christian lifestyle, called by the Christian Life Commission of this largest body of Protestants in the world, she declared:

"We waste a lot of time debating the merits of the idea of ordaining women to be deacons or preachers," and then stated: "More basic is whether or not God calls women to serve Him through the church."

Women's lifestyle began to change the day in 1955 when a black woman named Rosa Parks of Montgomery, Alabama, refused to move to the back of the city bus, Miss Weatherford reminded her fellow Baptists, most of them Southerners, most of them male. That action started a movement, she said, for which Baptists and others were unprepared, because "we haven't helped people evaluate what's happening in society."

Changes in religious circles have also caught church leaders by surprise. "Spiritual leaders can provide support for women who are thwarted in what they believe to be God's will and purpose for their lives."

Women deserve a chance to serve in leadership roles, the WMU executive believes. She cited the fact that 1,053 persons were elected by the Southern Baptist Convention to membership on boards and commissions for fiscal year 1977–78. "Only 114 of these were women, and Carolyn Weatherford was four of them!" she proclaimed. "And this year only eight of the 52 members of the all-powerful Committee on Boards are women. The percentage is not likely to change."

That seminar led to a larger meeting: the "first consultation on Women in Church-Related Vocations," a three-day conference four months later in Nashville, Tennessee. It brought 300 laywomen and laymen, Seminary professors and presidents together to talk. Eleven of the Convention agencies sponsored it.

"Work through the denominational political system," the agency heads admonished them. "You can urge the appointment of more women as trustees of our agencies."

Miss Weatherford reminded them that "the climate toward more women trustees is changing but not very fast," and she cited the membership of the Convention's Executive Committee: six women out of 69 members. Yet four of the agencies (the two mission boards, the Historical Commission, and the Christian Life Commission) have boards of trustees of which at least 20 per cent are women.

"The competition is keen to serve on committees and boards," the president of the Baptist Sunday School Board acknowledged. "Make your wishes known to your two state representatives to the Committee on Boards."

Symposium moderator Harry N. Hollis, Jr., of the Christian Life Commission mentioned the movement: "a revolution for genuine freedom for women and for men that will not be stopped and ought not to be stopped. The question is whether we are going to sense that this revolution is a part of God's timing for humanity and that we can help shape the revolution for good."

Southern Seminary Professor Andrew Lester of Louisville (Kentucky) offered the opinion: "Men have almost no experience relating to women in the role of minister, which creates problems concerning normal sexual attraction." He dealt with the psychological areas of competition and authority.

The Bible presentation brought out the contrast between Jesus and Paul in their attitudes toward women. Frank Stagg, coauthor with his wife, Evelyn, of *Woman in the World of Jesus,* reminded the consultants "Jesus appeared first to women after the resurrection . . . We must reaffirm the lordship of Jesus Christ who liberated women when he liberated the human race."

Female employees of the publishing house and of the Annuity Board of the Southern Baptist Convention were conspicuous in their absence from the Consultation. Spokesmen for those two agencies stated they could not participate due to "legal reasons peculiar to those agencies." A research project which preceded the Consultation showed that some 70 per cent of the current women's work force in the dozen agencies serve with a definite sense that "God has called me to this specific job." The project also revealed that 63 per cent of women employees believe "no man would do what I do for the same pay."

An unscheduled meeting held after the project was reported challenged its findings. Some fifty women declared it did not fully represent the views of women in the Convention.

The controversy will continue. Southern Baptists have no exact record of the number of ordained women, but the guess is somewhere between forty-five and fifty; some Baptist bodies have none.

By June 1978 the American Baptist Churches of the U.S.A. claimed 157 women ordained to the ministry, a small percentage of the 8,566 clergymen but the third highest proportion of women clergy among ten major Protestant denominations. The United Church of Christ had the most: 400 out of 9,607 ministers.

Mrs. George R. Martin

The patterns of women's work in the Northern and Southern Baptist Conventions were followed with little variation by the two National Baptist bodies and the smaller Baptist fellowships. Until the mid-twentieth century, all the Baptist women's societies or unions existed side by side, having little if any contact with one another, except for an occasional exchange of literature and ideas, some reciprocal speaking engagements, and appeals for help from the weaker organizations.

It was the chairman of the women's committee of the Baptist World Alliance, Mrs. George R. Martin of Norfolk, Virginia, who first conceived the idea of continent-wide Baptist women's fellowships. A former president of Woman's Missionary Union, Auxiliary to the Southern Baptist Convention, Mrs. Martin made the proposal to the Baptist World Alliance executive committee, at its meeting in London in 1948. She asked the committee to let her organize the women of all Baptist bodies affiliated with the Alliance, by continents all over the world. The men were skeptical but they could not refuse to let this aggressive leader try her project.

Mrs. Martin began the task of bringing Baptist women together across national boundaries. She traveled on every continent, visiting the missionaries, meeting the national women leaders, pleading for international co-operation, building stronger ties from country to country. In 1952 she triumphantly announced the formation of the European Baptist Women's Union. A year later the North American Baptist Women's Union came into existence. By 1956 Mrs. Martin had effected women's unions in Australia, Latin America, and Africa. Finally, the Baptist women of the Orient were assisted in organizing the Asian Baptist Women's Union. Mrs. Martin had forged in one decade what she called the "chain of fellowship." Thus Mrs. Martin enlisted thousands of women leaders, in many nations and speaking many different tongues, in awareness of one another, in understanding of mutual needs and accomplishments, and for inspiration to strengthen the churches worldwide.

Then Mrs. Martin prevailed upon the executive committee of the North American Baptist Women's Union, by far the strongest, most affluent, and most numerous, to pay the travel expenses for women from other continents to the Baptist World Congresses. The project began with the tenth Congress, meeting in Rio de Janeiro, Brazil, in 1960, with Mrs. Martin's plea:

"Every part of the globe ought to be represented by Baptist women. If you are Chinese-minded, you can bring one woman from Hong Kong or Taiwan for $1,700. If you are Indian-minded, you can do it for $1,600." Reduced to those terms, Baptist women of the United States and Canada made possible the attendance of a score of women from other continents.

"It takes women to make a successful meeting," said Mrs. George Martin.

Akiko Endo Matsumura, B.W.A. Vice-President

"I have met and spent an enjoyable evening with Akiko Matsumura . . . In perception, forthrightness of speech, leadership qualities, and personal character, I would say she comes across as more of a charismatic Baptist leader of internationalist stature than as a mere Japanese Christian leader. She is a marvelous person with great depth of understanding of both Eastern and Western Christians, and Christianity. It was a memorable evening, perhaps gala; as tired as she was after four days in a bilingual conference, three speeches, and chairing other sessions of the conference, she brings a 'presence' and warmth into a group."

So stated the American director of operations for International Human Assistance Programs, Inc. (formerly American-Korean Foundation), who with his wife entertained the president of Asian Baptist Women's Union for 1973–78 when she was in Seoul for the Convention. A mutual friend in the States introduced Akiko Matsumura to Dr. and Mrs. Carroll B. Hodges, on duty for five years in South Korea. A retired Army colonel, Hodges had once been on the staff of Adjutant General in the U. S. Army. He had earned his doctorate in the University of Munich during a stint of duty in Germany. Hodges knows human character. His wife, Harriet, shared his high opinion of their Japanese guest.

Who was the guest?

Of Samurai heritage, daughter of a well-to-do businessman in Tokyo, Akiko Endo reached high school graduation by genuine discipline and expected to enter a university as her two brothers and her sister had done. When her father doubted her ability to make use of further education, she settled for a business course. In the crowded corridors at the YMCA, she encountered a kindly American woman, Dorothy Carver, who offered her a chance to improve her English in exchange for tutoring in Japanese conversation.

The arrangement led to Bible discussion, and the Scriptures, which were taboo in a strict Buddhist home, intrigued the intelligent young Japanese student. When her father forbade her to continue, she declared her right to discover truth for herself and accepted the penalty: homelessness.

The Baptist missionary found an opportunity for her protégée to enter Kwassui ("Living Water") Junior College, a Methodist institution at Nagasaki, and Akiko took it. She later applied for a scholarship in America and was accepted by the Baptist W.M.U. Training School in Louisville, Kentucky. She was denied a passport.

Wartime restrictions limited Endo *Sensei* at Kwassui, but she had no other place to live and she taught whatever courses the administration assigned. Her only sister died of tuberculosis during the war; one brother was severely wounded in battle in China. A message finally reached her from a proud but contrite father: "Please come home. At times like these, families need to be together." Akiko had the grace to return to Tokyo. She escaped the atomic bomb on Nagasaki, but in the foxholes during the bombings of her home city, she did a lot of soul-searching. What is life? If God is real, as the Bible portrays, had He a plan for her life? If she survived the war with Christian America, could she find a Christian vocation as a teacher or youth leader?

Her missionary friend, who had become the wife of Dr. Maxfield Garrott, Baptist missionary on duty in Japan before Pearl Harbor, was evacuated to Hawaii. Dr. Garrott was imprisoned but later repatriated. In 1947, by a surprising turn of events, the scholarship Akiko had forfeited in 1941 was offered her, and she was one of the first Japanese nationals to be granted a passport, after war's end, to study in the United States. In her spare time she began to master the Greek language. She was graduated from the Training School in 1950.

Only sixteen Japanese congregations of Baptists related to the Southern Baptist Convention survived the war. Membership was about 500. A small group of leaders met in Fukuoka in 1947 and organized the Japan Baptist Convention. Akiko became their youth leader upon her return from America. She produced a book for American mission study, entitled *Ring in the New*. She began to do some translating and wound up with a contract from the United and Foreign Bible Societies to help produce a modern translation of some books of the New Testament.

Shuichi Matsumura, a dynamic labor leader, became a Christian, and he was chosen to lead the Convention. Akiko worked closely with him in evangelistic responsibilities among women and young people. When he lost his wife, Miss Endo accepted his proposal, became his partner in the Tokiwadai Baptist Church pastorate and helped rear his three motherless children.

When the Convention celebrated its thirtieth anniversary in 1977 with 174 churches and 72 missions, having a total of 25,000 members, the Foreign Mission Board announced the Japan Baptist Convention had become self-supporting. Akiko had a major influence in that thirty-year achievement.

Mrs. Matsumura's fluency in English opens opportunities denied many Japanese. She was invited to the quadrennial meeting of the Asian Church Women's Conference following her duties as president for five years of the Asian Baptist Women's Union. The theme "Called to Change; Committed to Serve" was in line with the World Council of Churches' and the National Council of Churches' emphasis on social and political issues. The Baptist speaker decided her message should interpret the theme in biblical and theological terms "with some practical applications."

Akiko's typical reaction to ecumenical opportunity: participate but contribute the unique interpretation of the Evangelical faith.

XIX

TO THE ENDS OF THE EARTH

The Common Baptist Contribution

Onto the pulpit stage of the First Baptist Church of Dallas, Texas, on a summer's Sunday morning strode an athletic figure, impeccably neat in a white suit and white shoes, a striped necktie, and an air of supreme confidence in himself as the leader of this big downtown congregation.

Dr. W. A. Criswell, successor to a minister revered by Baptists all over the world, Dr. George W. Truett, was flanked by two associates on each side, also dressed in white. The five men knelt in silent prayer during the organ prelude, while deacons in the several front pews bowed their heads. The great audience was suddenly quiet.

The pastoral team rose from their knees, and the music director announced a well-known hymn. Another Sunday morning service in air-conditioned comfort began in the largest white Baptist church in the world. Dr. Criswell's sermon was clear, articulate, and basically biblical in its approach to Baptist convictions. He spoke to a congregation in a church with more than 13,000 on its roll, and a financial program of well over a million dollars annually.

Dr. Criswell spoke the language of that congregation, whether of his wealthiest member, H. L. Hunt, the late multimillionaire Texas oil and industrial king, or the truck driver who sat with his wife and their five children not far from Mr. Hunt. Billy Graham's name is on the roll of that church, as are the names of many lay men and women, office workers, skilled laborers, widows living on social security checks. The First Baptist Church of Dallas is a cross-section of the life of that city.

Except for the differences in time zones more than 30,000 other Baptist congregations were meeting that Sunday morning in communities all over America, from the Abyssinian Baptist Church in Harlem, New York City, up to Maine, down to the crowded Baptist churches in the Old South, over to the great Baptist Temple of Los Angeles and everywhere between, in churches great and small.

All these churches have in common more than the Baptist name. They have, and will have so long as they exist, more in common than a set of beliefs that, despite many differences, bind them together in mutual concern and helpfulness. They have in common the knowledge of, the satisfaction from, and the pride in what they consider a great contribution by the many bodies of their denomination to the spirit, life, and progress of the United States, especially since the beginning of the twentieth century. That contribution, say the Baptists, is this: the development and maintenance of moral and spiritual values that have resulted in respect for law and order, regard for property and personal rights, knowledge of the importance of sobriety, industry, and thrift, and an ever-increasing Christian social concern.

They have accomplished this, say the Baptists, by decades of teaching their youth in Sunday schools, training organizations, and programs of character development, with church-sponsored recreation and social life. By precept upon precept, by the example of the elders, by parents who have relied upon the backing of their church leaders, the lessons have been taught.

In summary, Baptists contend, they have created generations of citizens who know what is right and what is wrong, and who are conditioned to do what is right and avoid what is wrong; and while human error must always be reckoned with, the result of the contribution of Baptists of America, white and Negro, has been to make the importance of moral and spiritual values the guiding light in their own personal lives and in the lives of those who make up their communities and the nation.

Baptists confidently hold that their contribution to good citizenship helped lay the foundation for pride in America and her institutions, for patriotism that placed God and country above self in two great world wars, and at the same time opened the way for the development of a spirit of brotherhood that has launched the American people in a quest to bring an end to wars and to build a just and lasting peace based upon freedom and justice.

Before the twentieth century the major emphasis of Baptist preaching and teaching was upon doing right in order to reach heaven and avoid hell. Jonathan Edwards' famous sermon "Sinners in the Hands of an Angry God" still added fire and brimstone from many a pronouncement in Baptist pulpits. Since the twentieth century began, the emphasis of Baptist preaching, teaching, and training has been upon the necessity for righteous living to help usher in the kingdom of heaven on earth.

Every Baptist fellowship, whatever its name, has both contributed to this heritage and benefited by it. Not one Baptist would claim that the creation of respect for the right and rejection of the wrong has been the exclusive accomplishment of his church and spiritual leaders. All would unite in giving credit to other major denominations in America and express pride that each could have been a member of a spiritual team that strengthened the sturdy structure of liberty, justice, and morality in America. At the same time other denominations would give credit to Baptists for their undeniably effective leadership.

The Northern Baptist Convention

An event of outstanding importance for Northern Baptists began shaping up at the turn of the century and came to its conclusion in 1907—the founding of the Northern Baptist Convention. It gave to Northern Baptists the same type of organizational base as existed among all other major Baptist bodies, and brought them into the mainstream of denominational efficiency.

Centripetal forces had been drawing closer together the major agencies of the Northern Baptist churches since the early 1890s. One such force was the obvious need for some efficient administration of a religious body of national importance, rather than to continue to operate through separate and independent boards. Previous moves brought the "May anniversaries" of the American Baptist Missionary Union, the American Baptist Home Missionary Society and the auxiliaries of these boards, and the American Baptist Publication Society to meet on consecutive days. Northern Baptist leaders approved of this since they could at least attend all these meetings without extra travel. But still the financing of the various activities was separate. The control of each was independent of the others, as it had been from the beginning of the Triennial Convention. Co-ordination of both the support and the growing activities at home and abroad was badly needed.

Another force, unseen but quite powerful, was at work. It was the obvious success of the Southern Baptist Convention centralized organization. Without saying too much about it from public rostrums, Northern Baptist ministers and laymen discussed the matter at every anniversary meeting of their societies. Some would mention that the Southern Baptists were forging ahead in publishing church literature. Others would refer to the fact that Southern Baptists were fast gaining in the number of foreign missionaries, although the Foreign Mission Society had been in existence since the time of the Judsons. "How can we account for Southern Baptists organizing new congregations far ahead of those sponsored by our Home Mission Society?" was sure to be asked.

Various reasons were given for Southern Baptist growth such as warmer weather in the South which encouraged greater church attendance and greater evangelistic fervor of the ministers, but these explanations did not satisfy alert Northern Baptist leaders. The true reason was apparent to them. It lay in the centralized organization that assisted the entire Southern Baptist fellowship.

At the May meetings of 1896 the representatives of the societies called for the appointment of a Commission on Systematic Beneficence. After five years of deliberation and study, this Commission recommended that the societies no longer compete for funds but make a joint appeal to the affiliating churches for support; that the same delegates be seated at all meetings of the societies; and that the officers of the three bodies begin to co-ordinate their work.

These steps led directly to the long-awaited one—the recommendation of 1906 that at the May anniversaries the mission societies and the Publication Society come up with a plan for unified denominational control. In 1907 the plan was adopted. The historic step was taken at a joint meeting of the bodies in Calvary

Baptist Church, Washington, D.C. Three sets of hands were clasped as the presiding officer, Governor Charles Evans Hughes of New York, pronounced the Northern Baptist Convention duly formed.

Two years later the denomination was incorporated, with its purpose chiseled into the stone of legal recognition: "To give expression to the opinions of its constituency upon moral, religious, and denominational matters, and to promote denominational unity and efficiency in efforts for the evangelization of the world."

The door of invitation was flung wide open by the bylaws, which provided that membership in the Northern Baptist Convention should include "all Baptist churches in the United States which co-operate in its work." Co-operating organizations, such as Baptist state conventions and Baptist city societies, were welcomed under the wide roof of affiliation.

Luther Wesley Smith—Northern Baptist Crusader

At the start of each week, in the decade before World War I, a family of Baptists living in Roxbury, Massachusetts, would ask:

"What is it that we can give up this week so that in addition to our tithe we may have a worthy part in spreading God's kingdom?"

Sometimes the family would decide to give up meat. The next week they would deny themselves butter, perhaps, or dessert in order that they might contribute more to feed the hungry people of the world. Such was the family of the Reverend and Mrs. Wesley Alonzo Smith, and in that family a son, Luther Wesley Smith, was reared. His devout parents dedicated him to God's service at his birth. They named him Luther, in response to their Protestant feeling about the great Reformation under Martin Luther, and Wesley, out of respect for the great Evangelical revivalist, John Wesley.

The boy grew up with the knowledge that he had been consecrated to the Christian ministry. Following his service in the U. S. Navy Luther entered Harvard University and was graduated, *cum laude,* in 1923. As a student he mastered the clarinet and played in the Boston Symphony.

Young Smith's first pastorate was the First Baptist Church of

Columbia, Missouri, where he ministered for eleven years. He served the students of the state's university as well as the townspeople in the heart of Missouri. Dr. Ben Browne relates:

"Luther Wesley Smith sent student teams flying all over the state in a crusade to raise $120,000 for a Student Christian Center. With abandon he threw himself into the pursuit of contributions. When he called on an industrial magnate for a gift, the manufacturer tried to hire Luther at a salary of $25,000 to head his shoe business. Luther refused, but left with a fat donation. One of Luther's ebullient student teams parked in the wrong place and was hailed into court by the police. Luther Smith appeared before the judge to plead for his overzealous followers. By the time Smith finished his plea, the judge set the boys free, apologized to Smith, whipped out his pen, and wrote a large check for the student center."

Next came a pastorate of four years in Syracuse, New York, at the First Baptist Church. He and his bride, Harriet Vaughn, an honor graduate of Mount Holyoke College where she majored in Bible, had begun to attract favorable attention. In 1937 the Northern Baptist Convention appointed Luther Wesley Smith chairman of the American Baptist Youth Movement Committee, through which he organized a new nationwide youth program for 7,000 American Baptist churches.

The following year Dr. Smith was elected executive secretary of the American Baptist Publication Society, founded in 1824, now located in Philadelphia. Three years later he took on an additional assignment: executive director of the American Board of Education. Under his leadership of this board, all phases of the Northern Baptists' program of education and publication in churches, schools, colleges, and seminaries were co-ordinated and supervised. More than forty-five educational institutions were involved in this correlation, and work with students was sponsored in 125 college and university campuses.

From 1939 to 1956 Dr. Smith served as a member of the executive committee of the Baptist World Alliance. During World War II he represented his denomination on the executive committee of the General Commission on Chaplains in the Armed Services.

During the war period, Luther Wesley Smith also lead a campaign which raised $5,500,000 for Christian higher education. At the end of the war, this Northern Baptist leader was drafted by his denomination to head the World Mission Crusade, which brought in $16,000,000 for world relief, and for the rebuilding of bombed-out Baptist churches, hospitals, and schools in Burma, China, Japan, and the Philippines, and for church work in the United States and Central American countries.

One of Dr. Smith's friends was passing through Philadelphia on a Christmas Day and called the Smiths' home to exchange season's greetings. Dr. Smith insisted that the visitor come to the house for dinner. The friend accepted and shared the Smith family Christmas feast—of graham crackers and milk! They had agreed to give up roast turkey and other Christmas goodies, to donate to the World Emergency Fund the money they would have spent on self-indulgence.

Dr. Smith founded the National Baptist Scholarship Fund and was one of several Protestant leaders to plan and secure completion of the translation and publication of the Revised Standard Version of the Bible. This Protestant version has since been approved by the Vatican for use in the Roman Catholic Church. In 1949 Dr. Smith was one of the founders of the National Council of Churches.

In line of duty Dr. Smith came to know a Chicago Baptist layman, James L. Kraft, who built a successful business in manufacturing and distributing cheese products. It was Mr. Kraft who backed Dr. Smith in the search for a national conference center, and the eventual purchase of Lawsonia on the eastern shore of Green Lake in Wisconsin. The vacation center developed by a Chicago newspaper editor became Green Lake Baptist Assembly, one of the most beautiful and most extensive Christian conference centers in America. It is used not only by American Baptists but other religious groups and national character-building agencies. After it was well established, Dr. Smith remained adviser to its governing board for the remainder of his life.[1]

In 1953 Dr. Smith suffered the first of several heart attacks. Despite his illness, with the loyal support of Harriet and their three children, he continued to carry on most of his responsibilities until retirement in 1964. They enjoyed their home at Ardmore, Pennsylvania, until it was necessary to move to a warmer climate, and it was at Palm Shores, the American Baptist Retirement Home in St. Petersburg, Florida, that he passed away March 27, 1971.

A memorial service was held for Luther Wesley Smith in the American Baptist Church of the Beatitudes, St. Petersburg. His ashes were interred on the beautiful grounds of Green Lake Assembly, and in the garden of the home for retirees where he spent his final years is a tree, lovingly planted and tended by his wife.

The trees of Baptist organizations, representing the Southern and the Northern Baptists, the Negro Baptists, the German, Swedish, General, Seventh Day, and smaller bodies of Baptists, grew to a mighty forest of churches, memberships, and church-related activities during the first two thirds of the twentieth century. Baptist leaders declare that the progress of the various bodies in their denominational fellowship was no accident. It came about, they maintain, as result of these major factors: a continuing, increasing effort to proclaim the gospel message to the ends of the earth, through ministries of modern physical and social, as well as spiritual, techniques; methods of organization which made possible the teaching and training of a maximum number of members of their churches, from childhood through adult life; programs of information through local, state, and national Baptist publications; continuous evangelism to enlist new members for the churches; encouragement of social and recreational life centered in the local churches; social concerns with respect to problems of modern life, such as institutional ministries, civil rights, and urban living; public witness through radio and television; co-operation among various Baptist bodies for fellowship and mutual assistance, and to maintain Baptist distinctives, such as personal religious liberty and separation of church and state.

Interest and activity in foreign missions first drew Baptists together in a true denomination, and all their bodies in America except the fast-disappearing predestinarians have pumped their life blood into the cause of proclaiming the gospel to people in other lands with other cultures and speaking many tongues. Starting with the Judsons the names of these Baptist crusaders are legion, but a few examples are typical of their dedication, courage, and accomplishments.

General Hawthorne, Solomon Ginsburg, and the Enetes

At the end of the Civil War, Southern Baptists had missionaries in China and in West African Nigeria. A Confederate officer of that war, General A. T. Hawthorne of Texas, was a poor loser. He preferred to leave America than to live under Yankee domination, so he went to Brazil. On a visit back to his native state he became a convert under the preaching of an evangelist and promptly requested the Baptist Foreign Mission Board to send missionaries to his adopted country. Young William B. Bagby and his bride of three months responded. They helped to establish the First Baptist Church of Rio de Janeiro, with F. F. Soren an early convert. Five of the Bagbys' nine children became missionaries. A son of Soren became the tenth president of the Baptist World Alliance in 1960.

There was Solomon L. Ginsburg, who followed the Bagbys in Brazil. Born in Poland, but expelled from his devout Jewish family when he became a convert to the Christian faith, Ginsburg lived in England for a time, holding various jobs, then moved to Portugal where he learned the language, and finally emigrated to South America.

After Ginsburg began to work with the Baptists he married a young missionary to Brazil, Emma Morton of Kentucky, and fathered a large family of girls. His work in distributing gospel tracts and preaching where the Baptist witness had never been heard got him into a great variety of scrapes, which involved serving time in jail and being bodily ejected from Rio for his preaching the Baptist faith. He was often bombarded with rotten fruit, bad eggs, and stones and publicly reprimanded as an apostate Jew.

Solomon Ginsburg continued to travel up and down the Brazilian seacoast by train, oxcart, ship, streetcar, and on foot, giving out the leaflets printed by the Baptist publishing house in Rio, talking to anyone who would listen—Catholic priests, farmers, peddlers, policemen, fellow prisoners, women of ill repute, schoolchildren. He preached in any square or auditorium where he could gather a crowd. He acquired a portable organ that he could set up quickly, and his hymn singing to his own accompaniment drew crowds if nothing else could.

For a time Ginsburg worked for the Baptist publishing house, delighted to be able to help create an evangelical literature for Brazil. He served as secretary for the Brazilian Baptist Home Mission Board, thereby widening his ministry even further. He gave thirty-five years of his life to help lay a foundation for the strong evangelical community in Brazil. Flamboyant, indefatigable, courageous, the Christian Hebrew left converts in every community he visited. He died in 1927.

Like the Judsons who were married, appointed, and given a fond farewell all within a few days a century earlier, the Rev. William W. Enete of Louisiana and his Missouri bride, Crystal Armstrong Enete,[2] fellow students in the seminary in Louisville, were married, were appointed for overseas service, and then disembarked for Brazil all in the summer of 1924.

Rio de Janeiro was their base for thirty-six years. "Billy" was an expert in Vacation Bible school methods, preparation of books and materials, and leadership. Crystal, an artist, worked for the Brazilian Baptist Publishing House as illustrator, and taught in the Women's Training School.

Missionary Enete, a ventriloquist, used his "helper," a well-dressed dummy he called "Sammy," to publicize the schools, services, and revivals. The Billy-Sammy act drew crowds of eager Brazilians in city or village, and filled the church buildings for the evangelistic event. Where prejudice against Protestants was strong, the voice of Sammy was hard to resist and opposition often vanished.

Crystal used her skills as an artist wherever bare walls of the baptistry in a Baptist church offered the opportunity. She painted many a river scene in Brazilian churches.

The Enetes reared their four children in Brazil. They reached retirement age but returned as volunteers for eight years to penetrate neglected areas of the interior. The missionary ventriloquist evangelist died in Texas in 1967; as of 1979 the missionary-artist was a popular speaker in schools of missions and women's meetings in the States. "Sammy" lives in the memory of mature Brazilians who were introduced to the God of love, life, and laughter represented by "Uncle Billy."

Japan, Italy, Cuba, and Burma

As early as 1860 Southern Baptists, responding to the news that a treaty with Japan permitted entry to American missionaries, appointed a couple to begin work there. The ship on which these missionaries sailed disappeared in the Pacific with all on board, and it was not until 1889 that the Foreign Mission Board commissioned another couple, who located at Fukuoka. In 1872 the American Baptist Foreign Mission Society launched a mission in Japan, and continued with little interruption for a century. At the entry of the United States into World War II there were about forty-five Baptist missionaries in Japan. At General Douglas MacArthur's urging that Christian missionaries be sent to Japan, in the following twenty years after the war Baptists increased the number of their missionaries there to about 360.

In 1870 Baptists of America heard with interest that the triumph of King Victor Emmanuel over the papacy in Italy opened the door of that country to Protestant missionaries. The Reverend George Boardman Taylor, son of the Reverend J. B. Taylor, who had served for twenty-five years as executive secretary of the Foreign Mission Board, was appointed missionary to Italy. Since then, missionaries of both Southern and Northern Baptists have served in several countries of Europe.

Sympathy for Cuban refugees during their struggles for independence from Spain inspired Baptists in Florida and other southern states to urge their churches to send missionaries to that island. In 1886 the Home Mission Board opened a mission in Havana, and later a deal was made for purchase of the Jané Theater, near the capitol building of Cuba, to serve as the Baptist temple. The Reverend Moses Nathaniel McCall was the first Baptist missionary to Cuba, serving there all the rest of his life. After Cuba won independence, the Southern Baptist Home Board and the Northern Baptist Home Mission Society entered into a comity agreement in 1898 to share responsibility for evangelizing Cuba. Northern Baptists took the eastern half of the island and Southern Baptists continued to develop their mission churches in the four western provinces and the federal district. Before the Castro regime, the Havana *Templo Bautista* property was valued at

$2,000,000 and the Baptists were eager to dispose of it in order to move out from the city and expand. Under the dictatorship, this proved impossible.

From 1910 to 1940 the Reverend and Mrs. Paul R. Hackett served as Northern Baptist missionaries in Burma, with headquarters at Moulmein. Building on the foundation laid by the Judsons and other Baptists in that Buddhist country, the Hacketts sponsored the founding of Christian churches, schools, and hospitals. A son, William D. Hackett, served as an agricultural missionary, teaching the Burmese farmers how to produce more crops to overcome the chronic hunger of the masses. On orders of the Burmese government that all foreign missionaries had to leave the country by the end of July 1966, Bill Hackett was one of the last to say good-by to the people whom for more than half a century his family had served.

Both Bill and his wife, Marion, were ordained, during their quarter of a century in Burma, by Baptists who were grateful for their service. Instead of returning to Missouri or Massachusetts for life, they became "missionary transplants." Bill joined the faculty of Chung Chi College in the New Territories of Hong Kong, teaching agriculture and an assortment of other courses. Then Hong Kong Baptist College in Kowloon, a twenty-year-old Christian school, offered the couple an irresistible opportunity. Not only do they teach numerous courses in sociology and religion for many of the 3,300 students, but Bill ministers to refugees from Burma on Macao, on Chu Lap Kok island, and in other areas.

Dr. Hackett pays a visit to Burma once or twice a year, delivering gifts of scarce items his Baptist friends need: spare parts for cars, film and tape, common household needs, and news from the free world.

"Mother George" in Liberia

The Republic of Liberia has been the special concern of the Foreign Mission Board of the National Baptist Convention, Inc., largest Negro Baptist body. Mrs. Eliza Davis George, appointed for service to Liberia with her husband early in the twentieth century, survived him and stuck to her post. "Mother George" to a whole generation of the Sarpo people near Greenville, Liberia, the Negro-American missionary used all her ingenuity and her consecration to the service of neglected people to provide education where there was nothing but illiteracy and superstition, to encourage personal hygiene where there was filth and disease, and to promote holy living where she found slavery to fear and false gods.

A missionary of the National Baptist Convention, she kept in touch with American friends who believed in her and the cause to which she had dedicated her life. The Vice-President of Liberia, William R. Tolbert, Jr., later to become the eleventh president of the Baptist World Alliance, and still later President of Liberia, became a close friend to Mother George. In 1962 the Baptist Foreign Mission Board brought her to the Southern Baptist Convention in Kansas City for recognition of service well done.

After fifty-five years in Liberia, Mother George celebrated her one hundredth anniversary January 20, 1979. Her "spiritual son," Augustus Marwieh, relieved her of heavier responsibilities when she turned eighty-six, but she still wears the title "Grand Commander for the Redemption of Africa," awarded her by the late President, William V. S. Tubman of Liberia.

Since World War II a special project of the National Baptist Convention has been to establish and maintain in Liberia the Carrie V. Dyer Memorial Hospital, which became the key health center for the entire country. Highly skilled doctors and nurses, sent by American Negro Baptists, minister to all classes of the Liberian people. In 1959 the National Baptist Convention, Inc., inaugurated a new type of missionary service. Encouraged by the government of Liberia, the convention's Foreign Mission Board sent several teachers and farmers with their families from the United States to Liberia where they established communities in the rural districts and set up their homes as citizens of the Republic. As the result of the work of American Negro Baptists and their converts in Liberia, in 1965 there were 1,200 Baptist churches in that country, with 18,000 students in their mission schools.

At the 1965 Baptist World Congress, reports showed that Baptists of the United States had missionary work and churches, increasingly being led and manned by nationals, in every one of the 118 countries listed at that time as members of the United Nations.

"Chief of the Medicine Men" in Nigeria

Gradually but surely in the first three decades of the twentieth century, Baptist foreign missions contributed something more than preaching to secure Christian—and Baptist—converts. New dimensions were added to this denominational activity when missionaries, representing all the major Baptist bodies, white and Negro, were selected and sent out because of their skills in medicine, nursing, agriculture, school administration, and later engineering and architecture.

Of increasing concern among Baptists has been the mission of healing, of which the late Reverend George Green, M.D., was an exponent. A citizen of Great Britain who emigrated to Canada, young Green worked his way through school as a bookbinder in Montreal and at Woodstock Baptist College, then earned a degree from the Medical College of Virginia. He became Southern Baptists' first medical missionary to the British Crown Colony of Nigeria, West Africa. He was licensed to preach by his Canadian church and ordained to the ministry by the First Baptist Church of Richmond, married a nurse from Norfolk, Virginia, and the couple was appointed, as their commission stated, for "medical work as an auxiliary to evangelism" in Southern Baptists' second oldest mission field.[3]

Dr. Green's first operation was performed on his dining table straightening the leg of a four-year-old girl who as an infant had been badly burned. When the crippled child was seen walking, skipping, and jumping like other children, fear of the foreigner vanished and sick people were brought in from miles around. The blind, the leprous, the lame, smallpox patients, men with hernia, snake-bite victims, women in advanced labor, children with worms and fever—all expected healing at the hands of the white doctor and his wife.

The mortality rate among missionaries in the tropics was almost as high as among the natives. Dr. Green had several responsibilities in addition to preaching and healing. As treasurer of the mission, he was administrator, and made a circuit once each year of all the churches and mission outposts in Nigeria. On these excursions, which lasted several weeks, he made scientific observations and recorded them: temperature, humidity, vegetation, soil, water, insects, fish, and fowl.

Realizing the need for a great supply of vitamins in the diet, Dr. Green appealed to the U. S. Department of Agriculture for advice on how to grow citrus fruits, and established a regular exchange of information about yams and other African vegetables.

In 1924 Dr. Green, his wife, and four daughters obtained their American citizenship, but when the British Empire celebrated the twenty-fifth anniversary of the crowning of King George V and Queen Mary, Dr. and Mrs. Green were two of the four Baptist missionaries in Nigeria who were honored with Jubilee medals in recognition of their service to British subjects. Due to the efforts of the Greens, a Baptist hospital was established at Ogbomosho in southern Nigeria. Dr. Green aided the staff of Ago Ireti (Camp of Hope), a colony of 650 men, women, and children ostracized because of leprosy but receiving medical treatment and care. The Motherless Children's Home, which housed youngsters whose mothers had died in childbirth, was another of Green's projects, as was also the Nigerian Baptist Theological Seminary.

Dr. George Green retired after thirty-seven years as medical missionary, but returned to Nigeria to receive honors at the centennial celebration of the African mission. Before his departure for home the Council of Ogbomosho conferred on him the chieftainship of Ba'nisegun, which means Chief of the Medicine Men.

William L. Wallace—Martyr for Freedom

One day in the fall of 1934 the superintendent of the Stout Memorial Hospital in China's ancient city of Wuchow, Dr. Robert E. Beddoe, wrote a letter to his friend and fellow Baptist Dr. Charles E. Maddry, secretary of the Baptist Foreign Mission Board at Richmond, Virginia, in which he said:

"We have a long and noble history here at the Stout Memorial Hospital, and Southern Baptists can be proud of what has been done in the name of the Lord Jesus Christ. But we must have another missionary doctor, a surgeon who can come in and do things I have not been able to do since my eyes gave way so many years ago. I repeat. *We must have a surgeon.* I appeal to you, in behalf of all the suffering which you yourself are aware of here, find us a surgeon."[4]

By an astonishing coincidence, a young Baptist doctor doing his surgical residency at General Hospital in Knoxville, Tennessee, William L. Wallace, wrote a letter to Dr. Maddry that arrived almost in the same mail as Dr. Beddoe's from China. In it Dr. Wallace, son of a physician well-known and respected in Knoxville, told of his education and present position, and said: "Since my senior year in high school I have felt that God would have me to be a medical missionary, and to that end I have been preparing myself . . . I must confess that I am not a good speaker nor apt as a teacher, but I do feel that God can use my training as a physician. As humbly as I know how, I want to volunteer to serve . . . I will go anywhere I am needed."

Within a few months Dr. Wallace was on his way to China and to the hospital at Wuchow. Like all missionaries in a strange land, he had to master the language and become acquainted with the customs and needs of the community. His years of service in China can be summed up thus: He was an efficient, tireless physician and surgeon, totally dedicated to the task of physical healing and of impressing his patients with the importance of their religious faith. His fame as a surgeon brought people in need of treatment from as far away as hundreds of miles. He performed operations that many of his patients were persistent in believing were miracles. He became one of the most respected and best loved of any man of any race or calling in that area of China.

Dr. Wallace made friends and worked closely with all the missionaries of his area. He had many a Sunday dinner with the Christian and Missionary Alliance group at their compound in Wuchow. The nearby Catholic Maryknoll Mission had long depended upon the Baptist hospital for their medical services. Now to the surprise of the priests and their associates at the mission Dr. Wallace came often to their quarters to follow up his Maryknoll patients' care and well-being. He refused all their efforts to pay him. "Let us just be friends in the Lord's service," he would say.

In the fall of 1943 the governor of Kwangsi Province, H. Wong, was brought to the Stout hospital suffering acutely from a ruptured appendix. The high official had been treated at a government hospital, but the doctors there, fearing loss of face if they should lose such an important patient, sent him to Dr. Wallace. Peritonitis had set in, and the case seemed hopeless. Wallace performed the operation, then brought in a cot so that he could stay close by Governor Wong's bed. His skill and attention saved the governor's life—and spread the doctor's fame further over China.

By the time the Communist advance reached South China, many missionaries, Catholic and Protestant, had been transferred to other safer fields of duty, but Dr. Wallace, now superintendent of the Stout Memorial Hospital, insisted he must stay. He felt that his medical services were so badly needed that even the Communists would appreciate his work. In this he was mistaken. Persecutions and harassments took the form of exorbitant taxes on the hospital, needless inspections, and accusations against Dr. Wallace and his staff for being "Yankee spies." Under threats to close the hospital, Wallace was forced to send ten nurses in uniform to take part in an allegedly spontaneous parade to show his support of the new People's government. The doctor and his staff watched with horror as the trials by mob took place.

On the evening of December 18, 1950, Dr. Wallace made the rounds of his hospital wards with his head nurse, Miss Everley Hayes, who had joined his staff as a missionary. As they checked the patients the doctor noted that a young Communist soldier whose appendix he had removed was making good recovery. Dr. Wallace made some notations for his nurses and retired.

At three o'clock that morning there was a loud banging on the hospital gates. An attendant cautiously approached the gate.

"Open up! We have a sick man here who needs help!" a voice called out. The attendant opened the gates—to be confronted with the bayonets of Communist soldiers. The officer in charge of the raiding party told Dr. Wallace that he was under arrest for treasonable activities, including the hiding of firearms in the hospital. He denied the charge and his voice was drowned out by the cries of his staff members that the accusation was a lie.

"He is our friend! He is a friend of the Chinese people! He has treated our sick! He is like a father to all of us!" chorused the voices.

"You will soon see!" declared the officer. "Search his room!"

Several soldiers hurried away, taking the personal attendant with them. One of them pulled up the mattress of Dr. Wallace's bed, reached under, and pulled out a pistol.

"But Dr. Wallace never had a gun!" the attendant said. A sharp blow across the mouth silenced him.

When the officer placed the gun before him, Dr. Wallace denied he had ever seen it. His words were wasted as the raiding party put everyone under arrest.

"We know that you are the principal spy for President Truman and the Americans here in South China!" the officer shouted.

Dr. Wallace was imprisoned, along with several of his staff. At his public trial he was brought before a small table piled high with guns, radios, opium, and other articles which the prosecutors accused him of stealing. He heard the charges shouted at the small group of people who had assembled.

"He is a spy! He is an incompetent surgeon! He has maimed and murdered our Chinese people. He has performed obscene operations. Should he be punished?"

Wallace looked down into the grim, immobile faces of the people before him, and saw a sight that enraged his tormentors. Not a fist was raised. Not a voice was lifted against this man who had been the friend and doctor to everyone there. Every person remained silent.

Back to his cell—and to days and nights more of questionings and attempts to force the doctor to confess to crimes he had not committed. The story of what happened then has been graphically told by his biographer, the Reverend Jesse C. Fletcher, who obtained much of his information from Nurse Everley Hayes and from two Catholic priests who were imprisoned in nearby cells:

"The Communists plainly intended to brainwash their victim into an open confession, to have him repudiate publicly all that he was and all he had stood for. They thought their goal was within reach, but the tough spirit would not capitulate so easily, and his protests rang through the night.

"The guards, driven by fear or perhaps guilt, came to his cell in the night with long poles and cruelly thrust them between the cell bars to jab the doctor into unconsciousness. Somebody figured wrong. For one night the battle was over, and though no one heard Bill Wallace cry 'It is finished,' he offered up his spirit and brought his ministry and mission to a close. Quietly his soul slipped from his torn body and his exhausted mind and went to be with the One he had so faithfully and unstintedly served through the years."[5]

Next morning the guards announced that Dr. Wallace had taken his life. They brought the two priests from their nearby cells to show them that the body of the doctor was hanging from a beam by a quilt—a feat he could not possibly have managed by himself. The priests were asked to certify that he had committed suicide. This they refused to do. Dr. William Wallace had found his life by losing it in loyalty to the service of healing.

Brayton Case—Farmer Extraordinary

Among Baptist missionary specialists were the dedicated farm experts, in the forefront of those who definitely influenced the United States government in post-World War II to launch its program of foreign aid and the formation of the Peace Corps.

Outstanding exponent of this type of foreign missions was Brayton Case, son of the Reverend and Mrs. John E. Case, American Baptist missionaries to Burma. Born there and reared among the pagodas, palm trees, rice fields, poverty, and Buddhist festivals of the Burmese people, Brayton as a lad became curious as to why so many of the people were so poor. Why, he asked his missionary father, could he count the ribs on his Burmese playmates and they could not count his ribs? His father explained that most Burmese children were not well and were physically poor because they did not get milk to drink; they ate almost nothing but rice, and never had enough of that. Many times Brayton had seen Mama Hla Sein, the Burmese woman who worked in their home, go to the rice pot, take out a handful of rice, chew it herself and thrust it in the mouth of her crying baby.

The elder Case explained to his son that much of the poor condition of the people they served as Christian missionaries was due to the religious teaching that one must accept misfortune and poverty as his fate in life, and if he is patient enough he might be a very wealthy man, and even a king, in another existence.

When Brayton was fourteen, the Case family moved back to the home community of Newton, Massachusetts, where the youth finished high school. He studied at Brown University and then specialized in agriculture at the University of California, but he never forgot the bamboo houses in the village of Burma, the gentle, poverty-ridden people, the language he learned as a child among their black-haired, turbaned children.

Standing beside an irrigation ditch on a ranch in California one day, Brayton Case saw the needs of ten million farmers of Burma so vividly that he said to himself, aloud: "I have got to help them!" Then and there he decided to be an agricultural missionary.

Convincing the American Baptist Foreign Mission Society that they should support a missionary in Burma who would not only preach but teach farmers how to plow and grow more rice and other crops was a task. Case accomplished it by telling the members of the Society:

"I cannot return to Burma and say, as the apostle James put it, 'Fare ye well; keep yourselves warm and well fed,' then preach about the lilies of the field and the birds of the air, about bread and water and light and truth, while my congregation goes out to dig in the earth with a crooked stick and raise one inferior crop of rice a year. I must share with the people of Burma what I know of modern science applied to their peculiar problems and opportunities. I shall do it in the name of Christ."[6]

Brayton Case won the Society's approval and sailed back to Burma in October 1913. The welcome he received in Rangoon and everywhere along the Irrawaddy River was that of a favorite son come home. Along with his routine mission work, he set out a vegetable garden to test his ideas about Burma's soil and climate, and surveyed the country to find the best spot for an agricultural experiment station, and later a school. Pyinmana, a city halfway between Rangoon and Mandalay, looked good. It had fertile land and was located between the wet and the dry areas of Burma. And it had a good name. Pyinmana means "Lazy Man Rest Not."

Beset with loneliness, Case wrote to the Society: "There is a great calm in the old mission house. I sit down alone at the round table at mealtimes . . . I look about the great white room, and the silence is oppressive. The books and pictures are very acceptable, but I wish some of my faraway friends were on the opposite side of the table."

Case found a friend not so far away, Lena Tillman, sent by the Society to Burma as a missionary teacher. In January 1917 they were married, and together worked at the task of teaching Burmese farmers how to produce better crops, poultry, and livestock. In 1923 they fulfilled their dream of an agricultural mission school. It opened with four teen-age farmers. These students lived in an old Buddhist monastery and worked in the mission fields every other day, for one *anna* (two cents) a day. On alternate days they were in the classroom learning about farming. Before the year was out the school had sixty students. When the youths realized that their schoolmaster was teaching them how to get the most out of the soil by hard work instead of by magic, a few dropped out. But the majority showed an eagerness to learn and willingness to work.

At the Pyinmana school the students learned first how to make a living with the hoe and *dah* (a huge knife), how to work a yoke of oxen. Then they were given the care of a herd or flock of animals. Finally they learned how to use and repair power machinery. They were taught not only about soil and tools, about sugar cane, fruit, vegetables, and finer rice, but from *Saya* Case and Lena they learned about the Christian's God who made things grow and yield food for them. Whenever he could spare a day, Case went out into the countryside, at first in the Pyinmana community and then over much of Burma, teaching the same lessons to the farmers and their families.

When the Cases returned from their first furlough in the States they brought a batch of assorted chickens and ducks and several blooded pigs. Case attended every Baptist associational meeting he could to tell the church people about Pyinmana. Striding into the village that was host to such a meeting, he carried a fat Berkshire pig under one arm and a plump Barred Rock hen under the other. At the corner of the bamboo platform under the grass arbor built for this meeting he tethered the "Christian pig," then crossing to the opposite corner, he tied up the "Christian hen." A helper placed charts on the screen behind the speaker's stand.

"A GOOD PIG IS A FRIEND OF BURMA," announced one. "HOW TO MAKE HENS LAY GOLDEN EGGS," said another.

When the moderator introduced the missionary for the main address, Brayton Case would step to a corner of the platform, pick up the squealing pig by his hind legs, and listen smilingly as the animal gave a soprano solo, to the delight and amusement of the congregation. Case would then recount the story of that young porker: who his sire was, how much he weighed, and how good his pigs all tasted; who his mother was and how many litters she bore. Leaving the pig at his corner Case would walk across to the Christian hen and while she made appropriate noises he would tell the people about her: how many eggs she could lay in a year, and how many fine children she had produced.

After that the missionary-farmer would pick up a handful of rice and tell the engrossed listeners how it was planted in straight rows after the field had been plowed deep and harrowed well. He would stand a stalk of sugar cane up beside him and show that it was twice his height; a sampling would prove that it was twice as thick and juicy as the common variety. Case would then sell the seed and animals at token prices, including all in the boxes and crates stacked outside. He would demonstrate his farm implements in the same way, often plowing several furrows to show how much better a steel plow point was than a sharpened stick while his audience ran shouting and gesticulating after him.

The Bo Case Bean

Brayton Case found that 70 per cent of the arable land in Burma grew rice, and that Burmese farmers worked only about four months of the year growing the crop. "For eight months they would sit down, fold their hands, and wonder what sins have predestined them to be poor," he wrote. Case would gather the rice growers in groups and tell them:

"Brothers, if you work only *one third* of the time how can you expect to have plenty to eat *all* the time? Almighty God himself cannot bless a lazy farmer. Get busy—cut down the weeds in your back yards swarming with mosquitoes which give you malaria fever. With a hoe make a garden which will keep your curry pot full of vegetables the year around. Raise beans and peas. By working part of the time you now waste, you and your family will have plenty to eat!"

Early in his career in Burma the farmer-missionary won the affectionate title of *Bo,* meaning chief, from his associates and admirers. On one of his field trips far into the hills he awoke one morning to hear a woman in the kitchen say, "It is very good to boil and eat Bo Case." He wrote in his diary that he thought best to clear out quickly and quietly, until the kitchen woman's conversation revealed that she meant the bean, which they had named the *Bo Case Pe* and which she was preparing for his breakfast.

The annual ten-day workers' institutes held at the school brought together 75 to 100 adults to instruct them in Christian principles for village life. A missionary nurse presented demonstrations on health, nutrition, and sanitation. A baby show was sometimes held. Some new gadget, like a fireless cooker made from a rice-storage basket, was displayed. The special speeches made at the institute usually appeared in a daily paper, *The New Light of Burma,* so that they reached many more people than the school could hold.

Case would relate with amusement how one Burmese farmer-preacher reported the events of the institute to his wife back home: "We learned about Corinthians and cabbages and preaching and pigs. Such big cabbages, peppers, and tomatoes! They must treat them with medicine. Corn sweet as sugar. Wonderful rice so big and even, just like rows of peacocks heads. How does Bo Case make it grow that way?"

In the early 1930s the Burmese government, recognizing the value of the Pyinmana school and Case's teachings in the improvement of the national economy, granted an annual sum of money for his demonstration farm.

Lena Tillman Case did her full part in the education of countless thousands of farm families of Burma in better methods of producing the much-needed food. She helped to organize a Co-operative Fresh Egg Association. She lectured to the farmers' wives and daughters. "To transform a people, the women and homes must be reached as well as the men and the fields," she wrote to her friends in the Society. Lena Case helped her husband establish a child-welfare clinic. She planned a homecrafts school—and Baptist women of America built it as a memorial to her after she was taken by death from cancer in 1939.

During World War II, Case organized the Vegetables-for-Victory movement, with the full backing of the Burmese government. Eventually Pyinmana was bombed and the Americans were forced to retreat. The missionary served as guide and interpreter for American troops crossing the mountains into India.

On Christmas Day 1943 Bo Case was the honored guest of some Christians of the Kachin tribe, in a ten-house village near the Indian border. His Christmas message to the people who had come over jungle trails for miles around was followed by three hours of song and pageants. At the close of the festival a leader of the people presented Case with a sum of money with the remark: "We have raised it ourselves and want you to take it to help rebuild the Christian work in Burma." It amounted to nearly $25.

When the 1944 monsoon season ended, Case asked a British navy unit to give him a lift across Lake Indawgyi so that he might take a stock of seed to a remote part of the country. Something went wrong with the craft and it sank in the middle of the lake. All on board were rescued except Brayton Case, who disappeared never to be seen again. This American Baptist died as he had lived —taking food and the gospel of love to the hungry.

Such was the ministry of the Reverend Brayton Case, missionary-farmer extraordinary, and the woman who came to sit opposite him at the round table in the mission house. His methods of teaching better farming were copied by agricultural missionaries of all denominations, and became the model for agricultural representatives of the United States government in every area where this type of American aid has gone.

Gaines S. Dobbins—"Mr. Southern Baptist"

"Bold Mission Thrust," the program announced and adopted by the Southern Baptist Convention in its 132nd year, was new to the 18,000 messengers attending the Kansas City annual meeting, but only in the choice of words.

The Convention's slogan of the 1930s, "The Evangelization of the World in our Generation," was aborted by World War II and its aftermath. By 1977, after the nation's bicentennial celebration, the leaders of the largest body of Baptists in the world offered the same goal in a three-word slogan.

If it could be personalized in one man, that man was Professor Gaines S. Dobbins who had lived it and taught it for sixty years. Missions was the central emphasis of his life's work, from the writing of his doctoral dissertation at Southern Seminary in 1914 to his last day in September 1978. Identified for thirty-five years with Religious Education and Church Administration, he defined them both as effective witnessing.

The 1978 summer issue of *Review and Expositor,* published quarterly by the faculty of Southern Baptist Theological Seminary, is titled "Religious Education: Festschrift for Gaines S. Dobbins." The managing editor stated the reason: "Dr. Dobbins has led Southern Seminary and Southern Baptists in fashioning an adequate concept and practice of ministry in a surprising number of areas: education, journalism, administration, pastoral care, worship, evangelism and many more."

Dr. Dobbins, a nonagenarian, was enthusiastic about the concept of a Missions Service Corps proposed in 1975. He had advocated it for years. "With clergy and laity working together, the world can be reached for Christ," he declared in the February 1977 issue of *The Baptist World.* "By the year 2001, world population will have doubled," he reasoned, "and a multiplied force of ordained clergy and appointed missionaries will be all but helpless in the face of insuperable difficulties of Christianizing the multiplied masses of unsaved."

Even at ninety-two, Dr. Dobbins was eager to volunteer. "Jesus did not say, 'Ye shall be witnesses unto me until you are sixty or seventy or ninety years of age'; he said simply, 'Ye shall be witnesses . . .' (Acts 1:8) In the greatest business in the world there is no retirement age. When we enlisted as disciple winners, it was for the 'duration,'" he contended.

Born and reared in Mississippi, at eighteen, Gaines Dobbins became a master printer, Associated Press correspondent for southern Mississippi, and editor of a weekly newsmagazine. "I had become hardened against religion by the irreligious men with whom I had been working," he admitted. "I prided myself on being agnostic."

His Latin professor at Mississippi College made the difference. After graduation from that Baptist school in 1908 he entered the Louisville seminary, expecting to remain a year, then go to a school of journalism. "Never in my wildest dreams had I thought of myself as a member of the Seminary faculty," said Professor Dobbins late in life. He married his Mississippi sweetheart, May Riley, on Christmas Day, 1909, and, largely due to her influence, they spent their life together "in the ministry." Their two sons, Riley and Austin, are worthy survivors of the couple.

A phenomenally disciplined man, Dr. Dobbins could be stubborn as well as gentle. He forfeited a doctor's degree from the University of Chicago in 1925 for his refusal to revise his dissertation to modify its conservative ("Southern Baptist") viewpoint. He did a rewrite job on the scholarly treatise and published it in 1941 under the title *Can a Religious Democracy Survive?* It was one of thirty-two books he authored in a lifetime. He had submitted to Broadman Press a book manuscript titled *Bold Mission Thrust—Guidelines to the Consummation of Christ's Commission* and had another book manuscript in production on the day of his death.

"Retirement to inactivity," he once said, "has little appeal to a healthy man habituated to work." He retired in 1956 from Southern Seminary as first dean of the School of Religious Education, spent ten years at Golden Gate Baptist Theological Seminary, at Mill Valley, California, as Distinguished Professor of Church Administration, served as chaplain for six years at one of Birmingham's largest nursing homes, then taught a year at Boyce Bible School in Louisville.

When Dr. Dobbins was named interim president of the Seminary in the crisis of the sudden death of its executive, many changes were made, one of which was the admission of blacks to Seminary classes on the same basis as whites—a full year before the Supreme Court announced its decision to desegregate the public schools.

Between terms, and in response to appeals from the Baptist World Alliance and the Baptist Foreign Mission Board, Gaines Dobbins was a visiting professor at Baptist seminaries in all the countries of the world.

Hard-pressed students made jokes about "Dobbinology" but they never doubted its results in terms of vital churches and dynamic leaders.

XX

THE BAPTIST ASSEMBLY LINE

A Genius for Organizing

Few Baptists have missed hearing—some many times over—a pastor, evangelist, or denominational worker tell the story of the man out walking with his small son in the country who, seeing an occasional insect, slashed at it with his cane. The man and boy passed beneath the branch of a tree from which hung a large nest of hornets.

"Hit them, Daddy!" the boy implored.

"Oh no, son," the father responded firmly. "They're organized!"

In every Baptist church in the land, in all the fellowships, with some variations for doctrinal emphasis, the denominational genius for organizing is apparent. It has brought the functioning of Sunday schools, youth training groups, women's societies, brotherhoods, and all the many auxiliary bodies to machinelike precision. Graded classes, graded lessons, opening and closing exercises, uniform literature, diplomas, certificates, awards, convention procedures—all have been standardized and are turned out on the assembly lines of Baptist organization. All have been studied, and some copied, by leaders of other denominations.

Baptist organizational life took deep root in the soil of a determination on the part of pastors and church leaders generally to teach and train their children and youth so that they could participate in church activities. Although Baptists repudiated infant baptism, most Baptists after the decline of strict Calvinism eagerly supported Sunday schools and youth training agencies, so that everyone could play his proper role when he came into membership in the church.

The early Baptist churches were simple organisms, led by pastors and guided by deacons and elders. By the twentieth century they were on the way to becoming highly complex, with organizations for all ages and groups, designed to teach every member of a family to take part in the democratic process of choosing candidates for offices, voting on church policies and projects, and conducting orderly meetings.

In their organizational activities Baptists have not hesitated to appropriate what they considered the best in other religious bodies, adjusting them to Baptist needs. This was especially true in Sunday schools and youth work. Baptists observed that Sunday schools in many other churches used the best qualified teachers for the classes; this started in motion a plan of organized teacher training. They found that young people in Presbyterian Christian Endeavor Societies and Methodist Epworth Leagues thrived best when the young people themselves participated; this led to the group system in the Baptist Young People's Union, by which every member was given a chance to speak. Baptists saw awards given in other churches for persons completing studies in the Bible; why not standards of excellence for *all* Baptist groups, so that by attaining the standard the whole group could get an award? The standards of excellence were adopted, and they brought Baptists of all ages happily straining to attain higher goals.

Scores, hundreds, thousands of leaders, North and South, men and women, white and Negro, moved in the van of twentieth-century Baptist organizational life. Countless ministers, missionaries, editors, writers, teachers, planners contributed to the massive structure of Baptist programs that brought this denomination's membership in the United States over the 30,000,000 mark by 1979.

One family can be used as an outstanding example: the Leavells of Oxford, Mississippi. There were nine boys in the Leavell household, sons of merchant George Leavell. As a boy George saw Yankee soldiers burn his family's house, barn, and cotton gin with the cotton in it. Surviving the war, he married Corra Berry, daughter of Confederate Major Nathan W. Berry whose wife was related to Mary Ball, mother of George Washington. All their sons graduated from the University of Mississippi.

In the First Baptist Church of Oxford, George Leavell was at times deacon, church clerk, treasurer, Sunday school superintendent, and founder and leader of a mission Sunday school at the edge of town. As the boys came along two and three years apart, each began his attendance at Sunday school and church services as soon as he could be lifted from the cradle. As he grew up, each was given some place of responsibility in the work of the church, including teaching a class at the mission Sunday school on Sunday afternoons. Four of the Leavell sons, James, Leonard, Clarence, and Roland, became Baptist pastors. The latter, after years in the pastorate, served the Home Mission Board as secretary of evangelism, then became president of New Orleans Baptist Theological Seminary. Two served as missionaries in China, George as a physician and Ullin as a teacher. Clarence served as state Sunday school secretary and educational director, and Arnaud was a dentist and an active Baptist layman.

The oldest son, Landrum P., and the middle son, Frank H., made significant and lasting contributions to the organization of Sunday schools, youth training and student fellowship organizations in the Southern Baptist Convention, and from that body to all Baptists in the United States. From its organization in 1891 the Baptist Sunday School Board had proved a complete success. It quickly won the literature orders of most Southern Baptist churches and began organizing a church school for every congregation that lacked one. A businessman of Baldwyn, Mississippi, Arthur Flake, in 1899 organized the first Baptist Young People's Union in his state, and in 1903 organized the Union's first state convention. He proposed to Mississippi Baptists that the time had come to hire a state director of Sunday school work and that Landrum P. Leavell be that director.

Leavell worked so efficiently as organizer of both Sunday school and training unions in Mississippi that the Sunday School Board made him its southwide field secretary. In 1907 he brought out the first handbook, *The B.Y.P.U. Manual,* recognized among Baptists as the authority for the organization and functioning of youth training groups. In 1918 the board created the B.Y.P.U. Department, with Leavell as its secretary and editor. In this position Landrum Leavell demonstrated to all Baptists how to inspire young people to dedicate their talents to Christian service.

Meanwhile, state Baptist conventions all over the South were following the example of Mississippi and organizing Sunday school and youth work under full-time directors. Frank H. Leavell served Georgia Baptists for nine years as their B.Y.P.U. secretary, then in 1922 became secretary of a new commission of the Southern Baptist Convention to direct a denominational student ministry. In 1928 this commission became the Department of Student Work of the Baptist Sunday School Board, enlisting students in Baptist and other colleges and universities in campus religious activities.

Arthur Flake continued to specialize in both Sunday school and Baptist Young People's Union promotion, through his writings, lectures in summer assemblies, and demonstrations in selected churches. From 1920 to 1936 he edited the *Sunday School Builder*. In this magazine, and in his book *Building a Standard Sunday School,* Flake initiated for Baptists, and for any other denominations whose leaders cared to borrow his ideas, all the details for successful Sunday school work.

In the Baptist genius for organizing lay the custom of seizing upon bright young church workers and bringing them into positions of responsibility in the denomination, and this secured for Southern Baptists the services of the late Jerry E. Lambdin, for thirty-five years as the board's director of church training. Lambdin extended the youth work to include adults under the slogan "The Training Union is a family affair."

All Baptist bodies in America have departments or activities of Sunday school, youth, and student work. All publish church literature. All have women's organizations for missionary activities at home and abroad. Their laymen assemble in brotherhoods, and their stewardship commissions promote the support of local, state, and convention-wide programs. All have established some annuity plans to care for their retired ministers and missionaries.

While some among the great variety of Baptists do not call their agencies boards or commissions, all Baptist leaders have found that in the era of complex modern living some recognized organizations are essential to the very existence of their churches and their influence upon American life.

All Baptist fellowships co-operate with the United States Government in providing chaplains for the military services. They consider the chaplaincy an extension of the ministry of the local church. At the Jubilee celebration of Baptists in 1964, Major General Robert P. Taylor, chief of chaplains, himself a Baptist, declared: "The chaplaincy is rooted in the Great Commission as we strive to minister to all men in uniform, at all times and in all circumstances. The military chaplain is inspired by the conviction that spiritual strength is the ultimate power in the world."

The larger bodies of Baptists have expanded their ministry to include hospital, institutional, and industrial chaplaincy.

Big Business of Publishing

The Baptist Sunday School Board, under the leadership of the Reverend I. J. Van Ness, who succeeded Frost as secretary and served for thirty-five years, became the greatest of all single Protestant agencies in America, in its output of literature, income, and employees.[1] In 1901 its net sales of printed material totaled $72,468; at the Baptist Jubilee meeting in 1964 these sales topped $20 million. Total assets of this board for the same period grew from $15,819, to $19 million and included two large office buildings in Nashville, Tennessee. In 1920 the employees of the board numbered 115; by 1978 the number had increased to more than 1,500. Graded curriculum materials, both monthlies and quarterlies, published by the Board, need 1,800 free-lance writers a year.

Activities of the huge Baptist agency, in addition to its publishing and distribution of literature and books, and its departments of Sunday school, youth and student work, had expanded to include the operation of 58 bookstores, supervision of summer assemblies, programs of church music, family life, church-related family guidance, church administration, tract distribution, church architecture, church libraries, church recreation, research and statistics, special ministries, and co-operative work with state conventions, besides providing a lion's share of the operating expense of the Southern Baptist Convention.

The Home Mission Board of the Southern Baptist Convention experienced a comparable growth from its early days. With its major interest in encouraging the founding of new churches, this agency reported that in 1964 the 4,126 Baptist churches existing in 1845, the year of the founding of the Convention, grew to 27,634 in 1921 and to 33,388 at the Jubilee year. Total number of churches affiliating with the SBC reached 35,000 in 1979, with a value in property of $7,605,192,513, and total gifts of $1,900,000.

Leaders of other Baptist bodies have pointedly made clear that they were not trying to match this biggest brother's accomplishment in members and money. However, all have given serious study to Southern Baptist agencies and methods and have adapted many of them to their needs.

Early in its history, the American Baptist Publication Society of Philadelphia adopted the name "Judson Press"—an obvious choice for an institution located in the city where Baptists of America first gathered to mobilize resources to support Adoniram and Ann Judson in Asia.

Years after the Baptist Sunday School Board was established in Nashville, a book editor was named but what name could they give the publisher of books? The late John L. Hill coined a name.

On a train approaching Greenville, South Carolina, in July 1933, as he was shaving in the small dressing room of the Pullman car, he was pondering the need for a name and he remembered the two men of the short-lived Southern Baptist Publication Society: John A. Broadus, secretary, and Basil Manly, president. If he put the two first syllables together, he would have a name that is easy to pronounce and would honor two important Baptist leaders.

The Board at its next session was introduced to "Broad-Man" and promptly adopted the name "Broadman Press" as the imprint for general religious titles and children's books. For books of specialized purpose, such as study courses, mission study, and the like, the imprint is "Convention Press."

Baptist Seminaries

Appreciation for a trained ministry grew among Baptists of America during the nineteenth century, as worshipers turned increasingly away from a desire to hear an emotional harangue and favored more thoughtful, well-ordered sermons on man's relationship to God and to his fellowman. Baptist seminaries, academies, and colleges were planted with the westward expansion of the nation.

To match what Baptists of the North were doing in educating ministers at Newton Theological Institute in Massachusetts, four Baptist preachers in the South in the 1850s founded a theological seminary at Greenville, South Carolina. They were James P. Boyce, son of a wealthy cotton broker and banker of that state; John A. Broadus, former teacher of Latin and Greek in the University of Virginia; Basil Manly, Jr., whose father was pastor of the First Baptist Church of Charleston and later president of the University of Alabama, former student at Newton Theological Institute and a graduate of Princeton University; and William Williams, teacher and language scholar.

Elder Boyce, the leader of the group, proposed to the Southern Baptist Convention that it sponsor such a seminary, and promised to raise $100,000 for the school if Baptists in other states would secure a like amount. A persuasive money raiser, Boyce traveled over South Carolina and collected the $100,000. The additional amount was subscribed and the Southern Baptist Theological Seminary opened its doors at Greenville in the fall of 1859, with twenty-six students enrolled. All four of the founders taught classes, comprising a faculty as learned as that of any other institution in America, at that time.

With supreme confidence in the justice of the Confederate cause, and therefore of its invincibility, Boyce invested all the seminary funds in Confederate bonds. By 1863 not a student was left and the institution closed. Both Boyce and Broadus became chaplains in General Lee's army. In 1865 the four founders met to decide what to do about their school. The bonds were worthless. "The seminary may die, but let us die first," Boyce proposed.

They opened the seminary again. Only seven young ministers enrolled. During the term a delegation of Baptist ministers came to visit the institution. They found Dr. Broadus, a Greek and Hebrew scholar of note, expounding the Bible from its original texts —to one student only, a young man totally blind. The carefully prepared lectures to that blind student were later put together by Dr. Broadus in a volume that became a standard work in Baptist seminaries, *The Preparation and Delivery of Sermons*.

After a few years of struggle during the Reconstruction Era, the seminary was moved to Louisville, Kentucky. In its first year there the institution enrolled ninety-six students. Dr. Broadus, who succeeded Boyce as president, collected $60,000 in one trip to New York, $25,000 of which was donated by the Baptist oil king, John D. Rockefeller. In the 1930s the seminary moved from its cramped quarters in downtown Louisville to a campus of fifty-three acres covered with beech trees. The seminary's board hired a firm of architects who studied Baptist history and decided that brick in early American architecture most truly reflected the simple faith and the cultural origin of the denomination. By mid-century the Southern Seminary had become one of the largest and most authentic examples of that style of architecture now in existence, and established a trend which is apparent in new Baptist church buildings from the Atlantic to the Pacific.

The greatest contribution of the Southern Baptist Theological Seminary to the education of young ministers in its early days was the adoption by Boyce and his faculty of an elective system, by which a student could study the Scriptures in English as well as in Hebrew and Greek, with an application of spiritual teachings to problems of modern church life—innovations considered most radical at the time.

Controversies marked the history of this school for Baptist ministers, as they did numerous other institutions of higher learning. One of the first students, Crawford H. Toy, in 1869 became its fifth professor and taught for ten years. A careful student of science as well as theology, Toy accepted Darwin's theory of evolution, and was forced to resign from the faculty—continuing his teaching career at Harvard University. Professor Williams indicated that a Baptist church should receive members from other denominations if they had been immersed by any Christian minister, and for this he was driven from the school. William H. Whitsitt, third president of the Seminary, in 1880 did some summer research in England, and wrote a paper in which he asserted that perhaps the practice of immersion began with British Baptists, around 1641. A storm broke about his head in view of his questioning what was known as immersion succession. Landmark Baptists were especially vocal in demanding Whitsitt's theological scalp. State Baptist conventions passed resolutions condemning him, and he too was forced to resign.

Moving into more liberal eras, Southern Baptist Theological Seminary gave shelter to such outstanding scholars as A. T. Robertson—"Doctor Bob" to all his students. While teaching at the Southern Seminary, Robertson produced forty-four books. Many of these were translated into foreign languages for use in theological schools, and many became standard textbooks.

Dr. Bob was a staunch advocate of Baptist independence, and this attitude was well illustrated one Sunday morning when he was invited to preach at a large city church accustomed to more formality than Dr. Bob practiced. As he was preparing to enter the sanctuary his host pastor, dressed in a ministerial robe, handed Robertson a robe.

"Do I *have* to wear this?" Robertson asked.

"No, it is not compulsory," the pastor answered.

"Well then," responded Dr. Bob, "if I don't have to wear it, I will!"

In addition to the century-old Southern Baptist Theological Seminary at Louisville, the Southern Baptist Convention maintains five other seminaries: Southwestern at Fort Worth, Texas; New Orleans at New Orleans, Louisiana; Southeastern at Wake Forest, North Carolina; Golden Gate at Mill Valley, California; and Midwestern at North Kansas City, Missouri.

Six seminaries are affiliated with the American Baptist Churches. The oldest was Newton Theological Seminary, at Newton Centre, Massachusetts, which combined with Andover to become Andover-Newton in 1931; the University of Chicago Divinity School, Chicago, Illinois; Colgate-Rochester Theological Seminary, Rochester, New York; Eastern Baptist Theological Seminary, Philadelphia, Pennsylvania; Central Baptist Theological Seminary, Kansas City, Kansas; the Northern Baptist Theological Seminary, Lombard, Illinois; Virginia Union University, Richmond, Virginia; American Baptist Seminary of the West, with campuses at Covina and Berkeley, California; and Morehouse Theological Seminary, Atlanta, Georgia.

Uniformly, all Baptist seminaries have lifted their standards for a trained ministry, requiring a bachelor's degree from an accredited college and three years of seminary work—a far cry from the days when many Baptists feared that education would wean the preacher away from heartfelt religion!

In 1978, the International Baptist Theological Seminary, founded in 1949 at Ruschlikon, suburb of Zurich, Switzerland, by the Baptist Foreign Mission Board, Richmond, Virginia, was transferred to European Baptists. Providing theological training at graduate level for young preachers from all over Europe, in the English language, this institution ignores national boundaries and discourages national animosities and hatreds by promoting pan-Europe loyalty on the basis of spiritual motivation. Southern Baptists have contributed substantially to the annual budget.

The choice of Ruschlikon may have been a matter of expediency; a handsome lake-front mansion was available for reasonable cost to an eleemosynary institution. Yet it is ironical that the seminary exists near the site where, in 1527, the bloodiest persecution of Anabaptists and dissenters took place.

Baptist Colleges

With the westward expansion of the nation, Baptists planted their academies and colleges in many communities. A survey made in 1860 disclosed that 180 church-related colleges had been founded, and that twenty-five of these were credited to Baptists. In the next five decades the number more than doubled, although by 1910 the academies were rapidly giving way to public high schools.

Typical of the development of the modern Baptist college is the story of William Jewell at Liberty, Missouri, established in 1849 and named for its founder, a Virginia-born physician living in Columbia, Missouri. Jewell served in the Missouri legislature, and when he launched his plan for a college he secured a charter from that body. William Jewell's charter forbade the state ever to levy taxes upon the property or funds of the college. Originally an institution for Baptist ministerial students, by the turn of the century it had become an accredited liberal arts college, affiliated with both the Northern and the Southern Baptist Conventions. In 1935 William Jewell opened its doors to women students, and during the 1967 term had an enrollment almost equally divided between men and women, with not more than 10 per cent of the men studying for the ministry.

In the Baptist Jubilee year of 1964 the American Baptist Convention was controlling or affiliating with the largest number of educational institutions per membership of all the Baptist bodies in the United States. In addition to the nine seminaries there were seven universities, nineteen senior and two junior colleges, and five academies or institutes, with approximately 3,000 ministerial students and 25,000 others enrolled. A Department of Theological Education was in charge of recruiting young men and young women with the necessary qualifications to become pastors and directors of Christian education, or workers in other careers of religious service. The National Baptist Convention, Inc., and smaller bodies of Baptists reported about a score more senior and junior colleges.

From the end of World War II, Southern Baptists followed the policy of establishing more colleges, at a time when most denominations the nation over were consolidating educational institutions under their control because of rising costs and inability to compete with the burgeoning state schools. Two new Baptist colleges began classes in 1963 and others were in the planning or building stage in five other communities where Southern Baptists were predominant.

This trend was spurred by offers of funds from the taxpayers, by way of the federal treasury in loans, grants, and other financial assistance. Sharp differences of opinion developed among Baptist leaders over the issue of whether such public assistance violated the principle of separation of church and state, with the advocates of receiving the money in the heavy majority.

Dr. W. W. Adams, New Testament Scholar

Standing exceptionally tall among professors of the Baptist seminaries during the past half century was Dr. W. W. Adams.[2] Born on a farm in Alabama, "Bill" Adams was obliged to work until he was twenty-one before he was able to enter high school. After graduating from Howard College (now Samford University) in Birmingham, Adams enrolled in Southern Baptist Theological Seminary in Louisville, Kentucky, in 1919. He served for a time as student assistant to Dr. Gaines S. Dobbins and was graduated in 1922.

Adams was pastor of several churches for three years, and then this southern-born Bible student went north to help organize the Eastern Baptist Theological Seminary in Philadelphia, in 1925. He was the first man chosen for the faculty and served at Eastern until 1946, gaining national recognition for his teaching, writing, and lecturing in New Testament Greek interpretation.

In 1946 Dr. Adams became president of Central Baptist Theological Seminary at Kansas City, Kansas, an institution which was receiving support from both the Northern and the Southern Baptist churches until in 1954 it became the primary responsibility of the Northern Baptist Convention. While administering the seminary, he continued his teaching of the New Testament. He served eight years at Central, then returned to his Alma Mater, Southern Seminary. After another eight years there he accepted the professorship in his favorite subject at the New Orleans Baptist Theological Seminary, retiring in 1967.

Meanwhile, during his long years of teaching and lecturing, Dr. Adams signed his name to diplomas awarded his students, most of them ministers, missionaries, and teachers, from every state in the nation and to most of the countries where Baptists are engaged in missions.

Among Baptist teachers and leaders who had sat under Adams's instruction were Dr. John W. Raley, an Eastern graduate, who served as president of Oklahoma Baptist University for twenty-seven years; Dr. C. G. Rutenber, professor of philosophy at Eastern Seminary and an authority on church history; and hundreds of men and women in church-related vocations.

Bill Adams related how at his birth his mother, after she had borne four other sons, recognized that God had chosen this fifth son to be a preacher, and how, as he grew up, she often mentioned this vision she had for his life and work.

"But my mother did not call me to preach," Adams insisted. "She let God do that!"

In June 1924 Bill Adams was married to Miss Beulah Reeves, daughter of the Reverend A. N. Reeves, a Baptist minister in rural Alabama. He and Mrs. Adams became parents of two sons, both serving with distinction as college professors.

In addition to his seminary teaching, Dr. Adams participated in an average of three Bible conferences each week for thirty years, all over the United States. He was perhaps in the greatest demand of any Baptist scholar and lecturer in the country for such conferences, in single churches, in groups of churches, on college campuses, and in summer assemblies. Even after his retirement he was "called back" for conferences in seminaries and universities until well after his eightieth birthday.

Dr. Adams was so familiar with the Greek New Testament that he could quote from memory—and interpret—long passages of its original texts. He was considered both a conservative and a liberal: a conservative in theology and a liberal in applying theology to modern living and its complex problems. Some Baptist pastors and leaders accused Adams of being "unorthodox." Questioned about this matter, Dr. Adams replied:

"Yes, efforts were made to get me dismissed from all four seminaries where I taught because of my espousal of applied Christianity in the affairs of men and nations today. But I never quarreled with my accusers. I knew that if what I taught is true, I need not worry about it, for it will prevail."

Dr. Adams passed away on Christmas Eve, 1977. A tape library of his speeches and lectures has been established at Southern Seminary, to be shared by that institution and Central Seminary at Kansas City, Kansas.

Old Camp Meeting Modernized

The annual revival camp meeting, so popular in rural America when churches were few and far apart, did not completely die out. Baptists love family reunions, and the denominational counterpart is the summer assembly.

In the place of a two-horse wagon to reach these centers of spiritual renewal, Baptists of the twentieth century use air-conditioned family cars, buses, trains, and planes. Instead of a brush arbor to shield the speaker from sun or rain, with the congregation exposed to the elements in the clearing filled with split log benches, modern Baptists gather in frame or stone buildings furnished with pews or padded chairs, a spacious platform for speaker and choir, piano or organ, and often a cooling system to make lengthy sessions comfortable. Hotel and motel accommodations at reasonable rates, complete with private bathroom, are reserved far in advance for the specific date of the conference of their choice. Couples, families, or groups of young people sleep in individual rooms. Graded, carefully devised activities fill the day. Even mealtime is modern. At cafeterias or in dining halls where Baptist college students serve hot food in well-balanced, scientifically planned meals, nourishment for the body three times a day accompanies the spiritual fare.

The camp meeting spirit is best seen when the whole conference gathers at the evening session. Under the direction of an experienced leader, the Baptists sing hymns with an enthusiasm that stops traffic on nearby highways. Fervent prayer is followed by equally fervent preaching or lecturing.

Ridgecrest Baptist Assembly in the Blue Ridge mountains of North Carolina, first such facility of the Southern Baptist Convention, was fifty years in the making. First dreamed of as a Bible study campground in 1895 by a Baptist engaged in Sunday school work in North Carolina, this assembly ground became a reality in 1905. By 1909 a five-week program was offered to entice those who cared to rough it a week or more for study and spiritual renewal. The 1,900-acre tract of wooded slopes became studded with buildings from two-room log cabins to conference rooms, dormitories, and a steel-girded auditorium with a capacity of 3,500 persons. Total value of the Ridgecrest property in 1965 was estimated at $5 million. During that summer season alone, 35,000 persons attended the programs.

Another Baptist conference center was opened in 1951 on 1,200 acres in a spacious valley between ridges on a high plateau in the heart of New Mexico, at Glorieta Pass. Whereas Ridgecrest was built as result of experiments with housing and other facilities, Glorieta began from complete plans, its architecture appropriate to the setting. All-season comfort, adequate water supply, permanent roads, and professional landscaping perfected and beautified the building program of auditorium, dining hall, residence halls, dormitories for staffers, conference and classrooms, and guest services.

On a June day in 1940 about 2,000 students attending the Southwide student retreat at Ridgecrest moved from the auditorium toward the dining hall, waiting for the bugle call to sound time for the noon meal. Frank H. Leavell, director of the retreat, accompanied his guest, the Reverend Luther Wesley Smith, executive secretary of the American Baptist Publication Society, Phila-delphia, toward the tempting smell of fried chicken. The two Baptist leaders looked out upon the lively hordes of college youth assembled from twenty states for ten days of study and recreation. Smith turned to his host and observed:

"You know, Frank, I've just discovered the secret of Southern Baptists' tremendous success in working together for great objec-tives. Once a year you get away from the routine. You come up here and get all fired up over the job to be done, and you go back to work in your churches and communities. I've decided that what we Northern Baptists need is a Ridgecrest!"[3]

Scouting from Maine to Oregon for a suitable northern assembly grounds, Smith heard about Lawsonia, on the west bank of beauti-ful Green Lake in Wisconsin. It had been the estate of Victor Lawson, editor of the Chicago *Daily News,* and had absorbed more than $8 million as Lone Tree Farm, with prize Guernsey cattle, two water systems, vast greenhouses, a power system, and miles of paved roads. After the death of Lawson and his wife a Chicago real estate firm created Lawsonia Country Club with an invest-ment of $3 million. An 81-room hotel, a swimming pool and a yacht harbor, tennis courts, and an 18-hole golf course, bridle paths, and lots for private homes were designed to attract weekend visitors from the city.

The whole project went bankrupt, and the property was put up for sale. Dr. Smith took his good friend, Chicago Baptist layman James L. Kraft, president of the Kraft Cheese Company, to look over this white elephant. In less than four months the purchase papers were signed, making an $11 million property available for religious purposes for $300,000, and Baptists converted the resort to their camp meeting grounds.

The hotel was named Roger Williams Inn. The water tower be-came a prayer room with a lighted cross on top. The bar was con-verted to a snackery and the casino became an auditorium for pub-lic worship, renamed Morehouse Hall. A large housing unit was created from the barn and renamed John Clarke Lodge. A dining-room wing was added to the hotel. The Green Lake Rural Church Center was one of the first innovations. An old chapel railroad car was delivered to the Assembly grounds, as a relic of home mis-sions. A lake-front home was donated as a library and writing center for religious journalists. A children's village, beautifully equipped for training workers for preschoolers and primary children, was established.

A replica of Hopedale, the spot in the Philippines where eleven American Baptists were martyred during World War II, was created on a woodsy hill site. A new building was constructed for radio-television training to improve Christian communications in America and abroad. Drama, religious music, family camping, and other emphases are provided each summer.

Green Lake, though a Baptist facility, has been used for inter-denominational conferences constantly since it was opened in 1945. Leaders of every major denomination and many smaller ones in the United States have enjoyed the convenience and comfort of this assembly. In 1965 the property of Green Lake Assembly was valued at approximately $15 million, and the total registration of those attending its conferences and programs was more than 30,000.

Baptists in most state conventions and associations have established at least one summer assembly. The visitor to Windermere on the Lake of the Ozarks, which Baptists in Missouri operate on a twelve-month basis, is impressed with the elaborate auditorium and conference rooms, the four-room, air-conditioned stone cottages, which may be rented by the room or by the house, and the efficient cafeteria. Oklahoma Baptists prefer to rough it; they flock to Falls Creek, live in large shacks, cook out, and hold meetings in open tabernacles a week at a time.

All major Baptist bodies in the United States have summer assemblies, either using their own campgrounds or college campuses during vacation seasons, or state or national parks. Since 1950, Baptist Negro Americans have trekked to Hot Springs, Arkansas, where the National Baptist Convention, Inc. acquired a bathhouse. Many local churches provide some or all of the funds needed to assist their people to attend the assembly conferences. Some youths arrive on motorcycles or in jalopies or travel in chartered buses from as far away as a thousand miles.

The Baptist summer assemblies follow a program patterning that brings in various groups for a week of study and recreation. There are the college students fleeing Baptist and state campuses after final exams before summer jobs pin them down, women studying missions, conferences for Sunday school teachers and leaders, for church musicians, for persons interested in Christian social action; retreats for ministers and for laymen. There are special conferences dealing with such subjects as the problems of alcoholism, pornographic literature, civil rights, and mental health. All the wide range of Baptist church activities is covered in the programs of the national and state Baptist assemblies. And always there are the carefully planned, professionally supervised recreational activities—swimming, hiking, dramatics, and games of all kinds.

Whether at Ridgecrest, Green Lake, Virginia's Eagle Eyrie near Lynchburg, Puu Kahea in Hawaii, or Monument Assembly in Colorado, a visitor would hear the same hymns, see the same exuberance, and feel the same inspiration that Baptists enjoy in these modern camp meetings.

From Meeting House to Edifice

Baptists have never been cathedral builders. Being of the common people, and somewhat proud of it, they have held a strong aversion for the trappings of the liturgical churches. They have found God more often in an outdoor meeting, under a brush arbor, or under the stars; and they have been grateful for any kind of shelter when they worshiped in stormy, rainy, or wintry seasons.

How their meeting houses usually were built from the earliest days in the United States until the close of the nineteenth century in the rural communities and small towns when most Baptists lived on farms is illustrated by the story of Olive's Chapel Baptist Church near Apex, North Carolina, in 1851. The church's biographer related:

"The last week in November the men gathered to build a meetinghouse. All material was given, and they had enough tools to keep the work moving along. They made mortar from clay, ashes, and water, and put stones in place for pillars. Twelve-by-twelve inch heart pine sills were extremely heavy, and the men in good humor vied with one another to prove who could lift the most. Four-inch posts went up in a hurry.

"After three days the house was roughed in. On the spot they dressed boards, and the preacher helped to build crude pews out of his lumber. The house was thirty feet long by twenty feet wide.

Pews, eight feet long, were arranged so that the only aisle was in the center. The house faced north, and the pulpit was in the front end. On the east side two pews were left out to make space for a wood-burning heater in the winter. James Ragan made an attractive pulpit stand from heart pine. Windows had shutters to protect them on the outside. Two front steps faced the road. On Saturday of the same week the house was constructed, the church members met for the first time in their new building. The air was heavy with pine, but they loved the newness of it. The structure was a monument to their own creative planning and handiwork, a thing of beauty, a symbol of a living fellowship."[4]

The early Baptist meeting houses were strictly utilitarian, with little or no attention to the architectural design. Most congregations had to be content to worship in buildings that neglected beauty and grace. Somewhat modified in design were the Fee Fee Baptist Church on the outskirts of St. Louis, oldest Baptist church west of the Mississippi, and Little Bonne Femme, near Columbia, Missouri. These rectangular brick church buildings had a double front door centered as the entrance, a pitched roof, and large windows on the long sides.

Baptists in the cities generally kept pace with their neighbors of other denominations in the size and beauty of their church edifices. The First Baptist Church of Providence, Rhode Island, erected in 1775, was one of the most impressive structures of any meeting house of its day. In 1822 the First Baptist Church of Charleston, South Carolina, organized in 1682, built an imposing church house of Greek design to seat a thousand worshipers. Both these buildings survive in the twentieth century.

A new and imposing edifice for the First Baptist Church of Richmond, Virginia, long considered the mother church of Baptists in the South, was dedicated in an October Sunday in 1841, and the occasion, according to the editor of the Richmond *Compiler*, "attracted one of the largest audiences ever congregated in our city." The editor described the building as of the Doric order, and continued:

"The interior is exceedingly chaste. The colors are white and blue, the white predominating—the pew cushions being blue. The walls are a glassy snow-white, and the mouldings and central ornament of the ceiling are both simple and elegant. The pitch of the ceiling is the very best in accordance with the general symmetry of the interior, and in its adaptation to sound; a whisper from the pulpit can be heard to the extremes of the Church. The galleries are so pitched and graded that the portion of the audience seated in them seems to be brought more effectually within the range of the preacher's address than usual. . . ."[5]

Richmond Baptists included in their new house of worship what the *Compiler* editor called a baptismal font, "where the baptizing will take place in the presence of the congregation. This is an invention that will be productive of great convenience." The invention blew up a storm of criticism and debate. Baptists had traditionally immersed their converts in open waters of streams and lakes. Most would gladly have gone clear to the Jordan River for the ordinance if that had been possible. Until after the turn of the twentieth century, many Baptist ministers and lay leaders vigorously opposed the idea of a closed-in baptistry.

In 1910 Southern Baptists expressed interest in giving the churches some guidance in the construction of their houses of worship, and the Reverend P. E. Burroughs was given the responsibility of consulting with building committees who needed expert advice as to plans. In 1917 Burroughs brought out a book on the subject, and in 1940 this informal consulting service became the Department of Church Architecture, Baptist Sunday School Board.

The period between the world wars was one of erecting utilitarian structures, generally of square design with rooms for Sunday school classes surrounding the auditorium like dressing rooms of an athletic arena. There were no steeples or other indications that here was a house of worship except for occasional stained-glass windows.

With the end of World War II when building materials again became fully available, a new era of Baptist church construction began. Baptists of all bodies and varieties decided that their church buildings should look like houses of worship. Colonial design, red or white, was most favored. Whether in cities, towns, or the rural communities consolidating their churches to form one self-sustaining congregation, a general scheme was followed: a sanctuary in the forefront, its entrance crowned by a steeple, with an educational plant in the rear.

The First Baptist Church of Buffalo, Missouri, a small inland town in the Ozarks, exemplified the trend when in August 1966 the congregation dedicated their new meeting house. For generations, since the coming of the first settlers from the Tennessee and Kentucky mountains, Baptists in the Buffalo community had held their services in a small wooden sanctuary seating about 100 persons. Sunday school classes were held in various corners of the single room. Soon after World War I a brick structure with four small Sunday school rooms in the rear was erected by the ninety members, located on the old lot of the original meeting house near the business district of the town.

The 1966 edifice presented a sanctuary of colonial design, built of red brick, with all its trimmings in gleaming white, including its 120-foot steeple. About 500 can be seated on the main floor while a balcony accommodates one hundred more. On either side are the four stained-glass windows, in front are four massive pillars, and an Early American-type spire crowns the entrance. At the rear is a two-story educational unit for a completely graded Sunday school with classrooms, assembly auditoriums, and rooms for various youth-training activities. The pulpit stand is in the center of the rostrum; back of the rostrum are the choir pews; and behind and above the choir is the baptistry. The pastor's study has every convenience for his comfort; the church office, the kitchen, the social area, all have modern equipment, and the entire 15,000 square feet of space has central heating and air conditioning. There are several acres for parking space.

The building program of this small-town First Baptist Church was financed at a total cost of $190,000 by an accumulation of gifts over the previous decade, the sale of $70,000 interest-free bonds principally to the church membership, and a loan from the local bank, extended by the banker with the remark: "We know you Baptists will pay it off."

The Nearest Thing to a Baptist Cathedral

Baptists take great pride in the fact that Baptist layman, John D. Rockefeller, Jr., donated millions to construct Riverside Church in New York City, and they admire the truly imposing cathedral itself. However, the nearest the members of the denomination have come to a cathedral under their control was erected eight blocks from the White House. It is the First Baptist Church of Washington, affiliated with both the American and the Southern Baptist Conventions. Built of gray stone, the interior is in the form of a cross, in traditional cathedral style. Facilities for religious education, fellowship, and recreation are beyond the sanctuary in the rear. The stained-glass windows are considered the most elaborate of any Baptist church in America. Joseph R. Sizoo, a Presbyterian and president of the New Brunswick Theological Seminary, after preaching in this Baptist meeting house, declared: "This sanctuary will make it easy for men to find God and hard for them to forget him."[6]

Within view of motorists and bus travelers on the Pennsylvania turnpike at the Valley Forge interchange west of Philadelphia, American Baptists erected their national headquarters. It was designed to be as different from the traditional architecture of office buildings as was possible—a handsome circular edifice with a 240-foot open court in the center. This ultramodern structure has been variously called the Baptist doughnut, the Baptist coliseum, the evangelical Taj Mahal, and even "religion in the round," but when architect Vincent G. Kling turned the finished structure over to American Baptists, he called it a "statement in stone."

Four basic colors—antique gold, Mediterranean blue, olive, and copper—were used in varying compositions to give individual identity to the segments of this unusual architectural product. Because of its circular design all the offices face the outside and no worker is more than forty feet from a window. The building centralizes the offices of the American Baptist Convention, its societies and publishing activities.

How Baptists Call a Pastor

With no bishop and no annual conference to shift pastors from one church to another, how does a Baptist church get a pastor? It is not always easy. Baptists follow the do-it-yourself method.

One congregation, thirty years old, with 1,300 resident members, lost its pastor to a major church in another state. It took twelve months to fill the vacancy.

Upon the resignation of the minister, according to the church's bylaws, a pastoral search committee was formed. Each of the four boards of the church selected two of its members for the temporary committee; the church members proposed some names of qualified persons, the top eight were referred to the board of deacons, and the deacons voted for four. With the president of the women's organization of the church and the youth council selecting one of its members, this made a total of fourteen.

The organizational meeting was held February 13, and a young lawyer member was elected by the committee to serve as chairman. A young businessman was chosen as secretary.[7] He attended every meeting, and he kept meticulous records of the secret meetings and the committee's work.

The pastoral search committee met in committee session forty-five times. Their meetings totaled eighty-three hours, forty minutes. The average committee meeting attendance was 83 per cent.

The committee in small groups heard thirty-five different prospects preach in their own churches, several of them more than one time. To reach these prospective ministers, the members traveled 18,913 miles by car and 6,042 miles by plane. One member of the committee had access to his company's executive plane on weekends, and three or four members of this committee visited a city where two or three possible future pastors were located. The prospective pastor and his wife visited the church on January 15. The committee reported February 12, and the congregation voted in business session to call the candidate.

The committee totaled up expenses of $7,652.50, although some members endorsed their expense checks back to the church. The new pastor arrived April 16.

Better Business Administration

Baptist executives responsible for the administration of denominational agencies have suffered for their naïveté, their tendency to trust anybody who claims to be a Baptist, or the practice of false economy.[8]

In the early days of this century, the first major scandal occurred at the Home Mission Board. Clinton S. Carnes was an auditor employed by a reputable business firm of certified public accountants in Atlanta. Then he became bookkeeper for the Home Mission Board and, in 1919, treasurer of that agency. He disappeared in September 1928, absconding with $909,461, which brought the board to the verge of bankruptcy.

Carnes had been in the penitentiary in Atlanta at one time, but the Baptists had not investigated his record. "There was not a breath of suspicion against him until he disappeared," as one Baptist historian related. The defaulting treasurer was apprehended in Canada and on February 5, 1929, was indicted in Atlanta for embezzlement. Carnes agreed to a "consent verdict," was sentenced to a prison term of five to seven years, and served less than five.

The reaction among many Southern Baptists was traumatic. "Abolish the Home Mission Board!" some demanded. Others said, "Merge the two mission boards." President George W. Truett of the Convention urged reporters to tell the people: "Baptists are honest. Tell them that we will pay all." The last note was paid off in May 1943.

The treasurer of the Baptist Foreign Mission Board from 1920 to 1926 brought acute embarrassment to the organization by systematic embezzlement of funds. The board was able to recover only a fraction of the missing money.

The Baptist Sunday School Board did business with a printing firm year after year, requiring no bids for its growing volume of literature published in Nashville. Finally, an accounting of costs disclosed systematic overcharges by the printing firm, to an extent that a mansion on an estate near the city, owned by the head of the firm, was often referred to by employees of the board as "the house the Sunday School Board built."

In 1947, the administration of the New Orleans Theological Seminary purchased for $500,000, seventy-five acres of land on Gentilly Boulevard for a completely new campus. The architects for the buildings of the Seminary used wood and plaster for the construction rather than more durable materials. In 1953 the institution moved into its new home. In ten years' time, the foundations were crumbling, copper plumbing was corroded beyond repair, and colonies of termites were in evidence all over the campus. Extensive repairs and rebuilding were necessary. It was an unnecessary and costly error for the Seminary.

Similar unfortunate incidents have been experienced in the past by most Baptist organizations. But all have learned the lesson that their employees must be held to strict honesty and accountability. They no longer assume that an officer who handles their funds is trustworthy just because his name is on a church roll. All such officers and employees must be bonded, in both the national and the state Baptist bodies, thus protecting their organizations from financial loss.

XXI

TELLING THE BAPTIST STORY

The Printed Page

From the small, poorly printed weekly or monthly papers of the nineteenth century, giving some news and trivia of church doings and sanctified by the inevitable sermon, Baptist journalism grew into big business. For many years Baptist newspapers were a form of personal expression for the editor and his contributors. Some of the best known of the early Baptist preachers became famous in the denomination by writing lengthy discourses on the salient theological issues and disputes of the day, fighting the battles of orthodoxy with their quill pens.

Because some of the editors took liberties with the truth, or failed to keep faith with their constituents, or proved to be miserable businessmen, the state Baptist conventions began about 1912 to buy out the owners of the Baptist papers. The state publications became the major source of information for the man and woman in the pew. They informed the members of denominational programs and progress, of new church buildings going up, of the heathen converted in foreign lands, of Indians and Mexicans served by the boards of home missions, of other Baptist bodies in the Baptist World Alliance. The state papers praised the work of Baptist schools, hospitals, and orphans' homes. They encouraged young people to go to Baptist colleges and seminaries, to become ministers and missionaries. They were house organs in every respect.

In the Baptist Jubilee year 1964, Baptist papers in the United States numbered fifty. The *Baptist Standard* of Texas, with a circulation of 380,988, was not only the largest Baptist weekly in the world, but the largest newspaper of any kind in the state. Twenty-seven other Southern Baptist state papers were being issued, the smallest being the *Hawaii Baptist* with a circulation of 1,162. These Southern Baptist papers had a combined circulation of 1,508,400.

In that Jubilee year there were nine American Baptist state papers. All other Baptist bodies, Negro and white, had one or more newspapers.

Despite the journalistic immaturity of some Baptist newspapers and magazines, the influence of the denominational press has made it a power in American life. Although this influence has varied with the times, with the general interest in the problems presented, and with the competency of the occupant of the editor's chair, the man and woman in the Baptist pew have consistently depended upon the state denominational paper and the special magazine for information and inspiration. Subscriptions for many of these were subsidized by being included in church budgets for the members. In addition, American Baptists were issuing a monthly news magazine, the *Crusader,* edited by Paul C. Allen, a veteran newsman. This attained a circulation of 385,000.

In 1920, American Baptists experimented with a plan to merge many of the weekly Baptist papers into one denominational paper of the quality and significance, they hoped, of the *Christian Science Monitor*. The convention bought several of the papers and began publishing one creditable weekly called *The Baptist*. With qualified editors and wide support the paper reached a respectable circulation figure and seemed to be safely launched. But the post-World War I economic depression caused circulation to decline, while production costs rose, and the paper failed.

Dr. Norman W. Cox, first executive of the Baptist Historical Commission, devised a highly original method of teaching modern Baptists church history. It was a syndicated column under the heading "The 17th Century Baptist Press," which reported a single incident of Baptist history in each release in proper news style. With the help of journalists on his staff, one to research the incidents and one to prepare the news story, Dr. Cox produced sixty-two releases on a weekly basis for state Baptist papers from the seventeenth century, seventy-four releases from the eighteenth century, and fifty-two releases from the nineteenth century. Thus was presented the unfolding drama of Baptist history in its most palatable form.

By far the most prolific writer among Baptist women for the first half of the twentieth century was Margaret Tyson Applegarth of New York. Born and reared in a pastorium, Phi Beta Kappa in college, she developed a love of the written word early in life. Her skill in writing led to invitations to speak until she became the most popular devotional leader in the country.

Miss Applegarth authored thirty-four books, some of which she did not take the trouble to have copyrighted. She wrote six or eight interdenominational Junior textbooks for Friendship Press. Books such as *Twelve Baskets Full* and *Men As Trees Walking* filled with anecdote, sprightly interpretations of Bible verses, and eyewitness accounts of missions at home and abroad enjoy continuing sales among preachers in search of fresh sermon materials, and women who have to give talks. Miss Applegarth contributed her talent to the writing of copy for brochures to raise funds for missions, and to prepare the manual and worship service for the annual World Day of Prayer each year for a decade.

Recognizing the need to improve the public image of Baptists, several of the conventions established public relations departments to cultivate a good press. Chief architects of the plan for better public information were W. C. Fields, director for Public Relations for Southern Baptists, and R. Dean Goodwin of the American Baptist Convention.

The Southern Baptist Press

A professional analysis of Southern Baptist state papers was secured intermittently, inducing each editor to attend the annual meeting of the editorial association and see how his paper stacked up. Roland E. Wolseley, in 1978 professor emeritus of journalism, School of Public Communications, Syracuse University, New York, did his homework well as several issues of each paper reached him. His evaluation was hard-boiled but not unsympathetic:

> The Southern Baptist Press, as are many other church-sponsored newspapers and magazines intended only for the constituency, is a cousin of secular country or community journalism, industrial house organs, and news magazines. Because secular media cannot be expected to concern themselves extensively with details and inner problems of one denomination, these Baptist publications are essential if the constituency is to be informed.
>
> Although these publications, which in 1978 numbered 33, are not unique (other denominations, including Baptist bodies, issue them), a few are among the outstanding examples of religion publications. As a group they are better organized, with their own press association. They are not, however, to be compared to other Southern Baptist periodicals, all of which have a different function.
>
> State publications receive no nationwide support; as a result they must restrict their size, use of color printing, and professional staffs.
>
> Other Baptist news publications are fewer in number for any one body and, in general, less professional than those of the SBC, primarily, possibly because other Baptist bodies are so much smaller. They have the same functions, however.
>
> The casual reader with no connection to the SBC or general knowledge of the press might dismiss these papers as mere house organs. But at their best they are more than that because they serve as a forum; some even dare to question and challenge, and all fight for the independence of the Baptist constituency.

Baptist Public Relations

Baptist leaders, especially during the 1960s and 1970s, have upgraded the scope and coverage of their public relations efforts.

Both the Southern Baptist Convention and the American Baptist Churches employ full-time public-relations directors, with staffs to assist them, as do most national denominations. As of 1979, the director of such services for the American Baptists was Philip Jenks and for the SBC, W. C. Fields. The Baptist World Alliance editor and publicist was C. E. Bryant.

Since the SBC comprises the largest membership of any non-Catholic denomination in the United States, Dr. Fields's services as public relations director are worth noting. Appointed by the executive committee of the convention, he uses methods which are legitimate and effective.

Months before an annual meeting of the Southern Baptist Convention opens, in a city selected by vote of the body five to six years in advance of the date, the director visits the site and selects a press room big enough and accessible enough for his operation. Newsweeklies and dailies, as well as editors of state Baptist papers, are notified of where and when they can cover the session.

When the religious editors and reporters arrive and identify themselves in the press room, each is given a press ribbon and a badge, assigned table space, a typewriter, and a telephone in the press room, and shown the stack of trays with his label on one of them where he may find each news release as soon as it is mimeographed. A bulletin board carries notices of press conferences scheduled with big-name speakers, the president-elect, and other newsmakers at the meeting. He is invited to help himself to fresh substantial sandwiches, sweet rolls, and hot coffee to be found in one corner of the press room. The late Casper Nannes of the Washington *Star* was always present.

When the 22,000 men and women flooded Atlanta for the 1978 session, the newsroom had registered 463—nearly a hundred more than in any previous year of the Convention. Said Dr. Fields:

"There is still a great deal of curiosity about Southern Baptists. Anita Bryant along with Jimmy Carter [the two big names on the program] helped to stimulate that interest in the Atlanta meeting."

The staff provided information, suggested qualified spokespersons, and proposed appropriate story lines when needed. Closed-circuit television in the press room eliminated the need to go into the auditorium, where press tables were ample.

Newsweek, Time, U.S. News & World Report produced worthy

accounts of the meeting. The New York *Times*, Los Angeles *Times*, Houston *Post*, Nashville *Tennessean*, and the Nashville *Banner*, not to mention the Atlanta *Constitution* and the Atlanta *Journal*, carried daily coverage and a "wrap up" story on Saturday after the Convention.

If 1977 was, as Bob Bell, Jr., of the *Banner* named it, "The Year of the Southern Baptists!" certainly 1978 proved to be, by virtue of unforeseen late summer circumstances, "The Year of the Roman Catholics." But Catholic publications in America did competent work in news coverage of the Baptist meeting in June. Some excellent stories about Baptists appeared in foreign journals —in the free world and also in communist countries.

Is the American Press Pro-Catholic?

Baptists, plagued with the memory of savage discrimination against their forebears in America and their brothers in some parts of the modern world, are quick to detect bias in the secular press. Some readers believe local secular editors play favorites among religious groups.

Under freedom of the press, a newspaper is obligated to produce a publication which reflects the true character of its community—social, economic, spiritual, and otherwise. Editors, criticized as being pro-Catholic by some readers and pro-Protestant by others, tend to ignore all complaints from both sides.

One student[1] at Medill School of Journalism, Northwestern University, decided to discover the answer, once and for all, to the perennial question, Is the American press pro-Catholic? For her master's thesis she made a qualitative and quantitative analysis of church news in metropolitan dailies, during the war decade. The shortage of newsprint tested editors' judgment of the significance of news. They found space for what they considered was most important for their constituencies.

The student, with faculty guidance, chose three metropolitan dailies: the New York *Times*, a national newspaper in a predominantly Jewish city; the Chicago *Tribune*, a Midwestern paper serving the largest Catholic archdiocese in the world; and the Atlanta *Constitution*, a daily in the Southeast, predominantly Protestant.

Devising a chart on which to record the facts about each church news item, the student measured every issue of March (usually the month of Easter), August (a dull church month), and December (Christmas with activity in all churches) in four separate years: 1939, 1942, 1945, and 1948. She recorded for each item, long or short:

The number of column inches it occupied.

Identification by Catholic, Protestant denomination, Jewish, interdenominational, other faith, or general religious news.

Location in the paper by page, and position on the page (above the fold or below it).

Size of headline (one column, two, three, or eight).

Accompanied by pictures, size of cut, and type (mug shot, action, "still life," architecture, disaster, scenery, etc.)

Subject matter: announcement of future events, report of event, sermon, social affair, church wedding, church funeral, pronouncement by official, tragedy, scandal, etc.

The great sheaf of pages was tabulated and analyzed for final results.

Is the American press pro-Catholic? No, if the amount of space is the only criterion.

According to the student's findings, the casual reader gets the impression that the average American newspaper is biased in favor of the Roman Catholic Church. This is an optical illusion. When all the column inches were totaled, two thirds of the news was in the Protestant column. Quantatively, the American press still reflects the Protestant majority of the nation.

A qualitative analysis of church news explains why many readers get the impression a paper is pro-Catholic. News of the Catholic Church, a worldwide institution, appears on page one more often than Protestant news. Catholic news is often accompanied by newsphotographs, the pictures are larger, and the Catholic personnel are easy to identify as "religious." For a seasonal picture at Easter or Christmas, the photographer chooses a liturgical church, where he finds candles and glistening "props," while Protestant churches are less "religious" in appearance—simple, no ecclesiastical glamour.

Protestant churches use the newspaper to drum up a crowd. Protestants deal in "futures," primarily local in character—announcements of what is going to happen, such as revivals, celebrations, church suppers, sports events, visiting speakers, concerts, dramas, and the like. One editor interviewed by the student said, "I sometimes wonder if these things ever come off. I never hear a thing afterward." The average reader considers it trivia.

By contrast, Catholic events are reported as "hard news"—what the Pope decreed, the cardinal's blessing, what the Catholic Charities accomplished, who was promoted to status of bishop, how the parochial school made its goals, and such news. The Vatican is news worldwide.

Protestant ministers interviewed for the survey seldom showed an appreciation of their duties under freedom of the press in relation to freedom of religion. They revealed two false attitudes when confronted by a newsman: "Here's a reporter. He's here for no good. Throw him out!" or "Show him in! At last I have a chance to get my name in the paper." So, before he arrived, the reporter was blocked in his effort to get the story.

The news stories showed perception and respect but not always complete understanding of Baptists. William Whalen of the *U. S. Catholic* gave a friendly analysis of the Convention, then wound up to ask without malice why Southern Baptists insist on a literal immersion in baptism, then serve grape juice [or Kool-Aid] instead of wine at communion time!

Dr. Martin E. Marty of the University of Chicago congratulated the Baptists on achieving "visibility" at last, especially in the northeastern sector of the United States! He coined the expression "Southern Baptist chic." Baptist terminology is exacting. One visiting lecturer at Ridgecrest, himself well acquainted with "Southern Methodism," made reference to "Southern Baptism"—to the amusement of his audience.

Newsmen unacquainted with Baptist nomenclature have to be cautioned to avoid referring to the Southern Baptist Convention as the Southern Baptist Church in the manner of other denominations. Under denominational policy, the word "church" is capitalized only for an individual congregation, or in the name of a religious organization or agency.

Bill Lipphard—the Baptist Conscience

Chief keeper of the journalistic Baptist conscience for half a century was William B. Lipphard, editor of the American Baptist magazine, *Missions*. Son of a pastor in the New York City church that Walter Rauschenbusch had served, graduate of the Rochester Theological Seminary and Yale University, in 1913 Lipphard was hired by the American Baptist Foreign Missionary Society as their departmental editor for the magazine. Ten years later he became associate editor and in 1933 editor, serving until he retired in 1953. As editor emeritus of *Missions* he contributed a monthly column and filled special assignments while serving as part-time executive secretary of the Associated Church Press.

Lipphard deliberately chose the written word in preference to preaching and gave his entire life to editorial service. He sensed the need for one Baptist publication that would not be a mere house organ but stand as the spokesman for self-criticism and could look at the denomination and its problems objectively. He made *Missions* that spokesman.

During the twenty years that Bill Lipphard was chief editor he wrote 634 editorial interpretations of contemporary events and their bearing upon Christian missions. He also turned out 969 major editorials and 998 editorial comments. He tackled every issue on the religious horizon, breaking a lance with many a stalwart Baptist leader. In May 1933, the month of the repeal of the prohibition amendment, Lipphard launched a feature headed "The Great Delusion," which eventually totaled 196 editorials against the liquor traffic and in favor of continued temperance education. He gleaned from 2,000 speeches of prominent persons a total of 2,191 brief quotations, epigrams, and timely comments, to appear as fillers in *Missions*.[2]

At the press tables of Baptist conventions, world congresses, and interdenominational events Bill Lipphard's face was familiar for five decades, but he was not content to cover the proceedings of these events and regularly traveled during the summers for new and more vital copy. Pastors and church members, more or less confined to their communities, were able to read Lipphard's incisive reports about such items as American-style concentration camps for Japanese Americans, Baptist World Alliance relief efforts in Europe, the birth of the United Nations in San Francisco, which the editor attended as a member of the Committee of Baptists, the tercentenary of John Bunyan, observed in Toronto, Canada. Lipphard gave his readers an eyewitness account of history as it happened, seen through sharp eyes and deep-seated Baptist convictions.

Bill Lipphard was severe in his judgment of what he called ecclesiastical isolationism among Southern Baptists. He noted the absence of the spokesmen for that body at various gatherings of Christians of the world and expressed his regret. In a series of editorials he argued that this largest group of Baptists was neglecting an opportunity to bear a witness where it could mean the most. One high Southern Baptist executive, a very sensitive man, let American Baptist officials know that the editor's censure was resented. A discussion of co-operation between American and Southern Baptists to provide postgraduate theological education in Europe after World War II almost broke up over the dispute. Lipphard was called before the board of the American Baptist Foreign Mission Society, where a resolution to reprimand the editor was being considered. He was given full opportunity to state his case, after which the proposed resolution was toned down and then adopted. The Southern Baptist executive was pleased to receive the official statement that the editor of *Missions* had been reprimanded. Lipphard returned to his desk with full freedom to continue to write as he pleased, which he did—including fresh criticisms of Southern Baptist isolationism.

A letter to the editor that Lipphard greatly relished was a cancellation of a subscription from a Baptist pastor, in these words:

"Every time *Missions* arrives at our home, it angers my wife. In the latest issue you reviewed a book written by Dr. Harry Emerson Fosdick, and your favorable review was to my wife the magazine's unpardonable sin. So for the sake of having domestic peace in my home, please grant my request and remove my name from your subscription list. If I outlive my wife I shall then hope to have the joy of asking you to restore my name to your subscription list and thus have the pleasure and inspiration of again reading *Missions*. Most sincerely, although regretfully yours."

The Radio and Television Commission

Messengers attending the annual sessions of the Southern Baptist Convention in the 1930s were often buttonholed by an Atlanta pastor, lobbying for denominational use of radio. Dr. Sam F.

Lowe was not easy to ignore, but he refused to accept the answers: "Too expensive," "No Baptist experts," and "Maybe later." He persisted and, in 1938, the Convention voted to let old Sam Lowe have his way. It allowed $200 for a survey and put Lowe in charge. The first radio production was a series of sermons by Dr. M. E. Dodd, pastor of the First Baptist Church, Shreveport, Louisiana, entitled "Christ and Human Crises." When Dr. Lowe died, the Commission found a man in the pastorate of the First Baptist Church of Ada, Oklahoma, the Reverend Paul M. Stevens. He was a graduate of Baylor University and Southwestern Baptist Theological Seminary, broad-shouldered, ruggedly handsome, and strong of voice. In August 1953, Stevens became president of the Commission. Under his leadership, Southern Baptists successfully infiltrated a secular, commercial arena.[3]

In its fortieth year, the Commission won its first customer for a series of television programs on purchased time. It was the Convention's Sunday School Board, which signed a contract with the Radio and Television Commission for thirty-nine films at a cost of $15,000 each, designed "to lead people to study the Bible systematically," to be shown on commercial time. *At Home with the Bible* was first aired in October 1978.

"Normally, we do not buy time from anybody to tell our story," Paul Stevens admits. "We won't ask anybody for money and there is no attempt to make Baptists out of the people to whom we broadcast."

His product is so well packaged that Stevens tallied up $11.2 million worth of free time in the year 1977. The Commission offers thirty-nine different radio programs for broadcast every week. Audiences recognize them by original names: Power Line, Master Control, Country Crossroads, Soulsearchers, Streams in the Desert, Night Song, as well as The Baptist Hour. On television, children know "Jot," athletes know "The Athletes," and the rank and file are acquainted with "Listen" and "The Human Dimension."

No Commission-produced television show resembles a religious program when it opens. "The message is subtle, couched in subtle matter and treatment that could appear on any commercial television program," according to one viewer, but conventional subject matter is interpreted in such a way as to give a spiritual message.

The impressive headquarters at 6350 West Freeway, Fort Worth, Texas, built in 1964, recently added a studio wing, making a total of three buildings for the operation.

"We came here in 1955 with three employees and a budget of $269,000. We now have 130 staff members and a budget of about $4.5 million," Dr. Stevens told a Fort Worth reporter. His first objective when he moved from the local church to a worldwide congregation was to make the Commission "completely secure" in the field of radio. After that he tackled television.

"I felt it was time some major faith group go big commercially in television," Stevens confides. "Southern Baptists can't solicit for money, and we can't build any facilities on credit." He talked to his board of trustees, the Convention in annual session, and private individuals about his ideas. Paul Stevens got $4 million.

In service to the theme adopted by the Convention in 1977, "Bold Mission Thrust"—dedicated to an effort to evangelize the world by the year 2000—the Commission produced a series of thirty-second spots telling what Baptists believe. A series of Southern Baptist leaders, made up for the camera, appears on the screen, stating the Baptist viewpoint on basic Christian concepts: God, the Holy Spirit, the Bible, salvation, sin, baptism, the church, the Lord's Supper, and the Lord's day.

Bold mission thrust was a technique Paul Stevens learned to practice early in his job as president of the Commission. He considers one of his primary functions to be a watchdog on commercial television in America. At the height of the controversy in 1977 over sophisticated television comedy, the Baptist in Fort Worth made face-to-face contacts with the top men in television in New York. In total candor, seated across the desk from the presidents of the networks, he appealed to their sense of responsibility to the world.

"What you're producing now is not my primary concern," he told them. "What I'm concerned about is what's next. If we will go this far now, how much further do we have to go next time to be Number One in the ratings? And in the race to be Number One are we going to sell out our nation morally and spiritually? Or is there going to be some network official who realizes this and says, 'You know we've pushed this thing about as far as we can go. We've got to appeal to some other part of human nature than that, because if we go any further we are going to destroy this nation.' "

Relating his experience with the media heads, Paul Stevens concluded: "I'm not seeking any headlines, or any credit for it, but I think we had a profound influence on them. I begged the industry to live up to its highest ideals. We can't compete with satire, sex, and violence—it's part of this life. The law of tooth and fang runs every aspect of life, except in man—and we'd be like that, too, if it weren't for Christ. There are a hundred million people in America who don't belong to any church. God loves them, too. We are the instrument to those people."

With that philosophy, Paul Stevens was planning to use satellites. "We're on every continent with television except Asia, and Baptist radio is strong in Asia," he asserts. "Interface," an ingenious 4½-minute radio production in a series of thirteen programs, is the latest offering. It is a news program with a new dimension, probing time and space to explore the problems and social issues that face people of all ages, and exploits the unlimited audience for news.

Holiday spots, for a minute or less, are cleverly written for a special event or emphasis for each month. Each one refers to the Bible and closes with a spiritual note keyed to the holiday it celebrates.

In April 1978, when his board was in semiannual session in Fort Worth, he provided a demonstration. A program was beamed from the Commission's new television studio to a mobile NASA earth-sending station on a Commission backyard. From there a signal was bounced to a satellite more than 23,000 miles away, then to an earth receiving station in the parking lot of the First Baptist Church, Nashville, Tennessee.

SBC President Jimmy Allen of San Antonio saw this demonstration and commented: "The bottom line of communication is not the flinging of words into space but is the fashioning of a transformed life touching others in love and power while pointing them to the source—Christ Jesus."

Dr. Stevens described the satellite transmission as a demonstration of a way "to bring the exotic down to the practical." "Powerline" was on the verge of reaching the one-thousandth station, making it the first syndicated program in the history of broadcasting to reach that level.

The Voice of Free Romania

The outreach of Baptist influence can be demonstrated by numerous coincidences which people of faith attribute to Providence.

A man from northern Romania became a prisoner of war during the first great war. In Budapest he accepted the Baptist faith and was baptized in a Hungarian Baptist church. Back in Bucovina, at last, Mr. Hodoroaba became a strong preacher and pastor. With his ten children, all of them musical, he spent holidays and Sundays giving open-air concerts in village squares, and preaching.

One of the younger boys, Jeremie, was sent to Germany for education, and was drafted by the Nazi forces during World War II. Following family tradition, he used every opportunity, even in uniform, to witness to his evangelical faith. Encamped near villages in Alsace-Lorraine, he visited house to house, sharing his belief in God. In one home where he found a welcome, he met the teen-age daughter, Madlen, who had become dissatisfied with church as she knew it, yet felt compelled to attend services where her violin was the only musical accompaniment to congregational singing.

The young Romanian kept in touch with Madlen. He was wounded in battle and hospitalized, but eventually escaped to Paris and was reunited with his girl, then a team worker in a refugee center conducted by CIMADE, a Protestant relief agency. They were married in the First Baptist Church of Paris.

After Jeremie and his bride attended the International Baptist Theological Seminary at Ruschlikon, near Zurich, Switzerland, they made use of all their languages, on the frontiers of Luxemburg and Lorraine, to minister to different groups in the French iron industry. Jeremie's use of Ukrainian helped him reach Polish and Russian families and German services were conducted for Lithuanians, while Madlen could minister to Italians seeking work in France. Their home in Metz was open for a Romanian service one evening each week. Always there was music—violin, guitar, and voice.

In 1955 the Hodoroabas moved to Strasbourg, and their ministry to a small group of Christians who had decided on believer's baptism made possible a Baptist church in the capital city of Alsace. By 1959 they returned to Paris upon a call from the Romanian Baptist Church to become pastor of residents and refugees who continued to escape into Western Europe. The demand for broadcasts in the Romanian language continued until, by 1972, Jeremie was conducting nine religious programs a week, four of them for thirty minutes and five for fifteen minutes. A spoken message delivered with enthusiasm, based upon biblical truth, interspersed with music, both vocal and instrumental, brought grateful response.

The department of the cults made life difficult for Romanians. Church life was stunted by reducing the lists of candidates for baptism, limiting the time of the church services, refusing the authorization for the building of new churches (unless foreign currency was available for them), intimidation, and public mockery.

Rare visits to Romania by the Hodoroabas revealed an acute need for Bibles and songbooks with notes and words. It took almost seven years to produce *Cintarile Envagheliei,* but the handsome, maroon-leather-bound book was finally published in Stuttgart with 780 pages. The Baptist Foreign Mission Board, Richmond, Virginia, helped finance the volume; the Hodoroabas' older daughter, Sida (now Mrs. Wesley Roberts), shared the editorial task with her father.

The music-loving Romanian Baptists no longer depend upon handwritten scores for their symphony concerts and orchestral accompaniment for congregational singing. Christian bands on parade or in concert in town squares now play in harmony. Children can be taught traditional hymns as they are sung the world over.

In January 1978 Jeremie Hodoroaba appeared at the National Evangelical Broadcasters conference in Washington, D.C., his first trip to the United States. He visited his daughter, a student of Sacred Music at Southern Baptist Theological Seminary, Louisville, Kentucky, and Baptist institutions; then preached for one or more Romanian Baptist congregations in the States.

He returned to Paris and resumed his broadcasts from Monte Carlo over Trans World Radio—the only member of a large Baptist family who is free to witness to his faith to fellow Romanians.

XXII

THE CHALLENGE OF SOCIAL CONCERNS

In Fields of Social Betterment

In the spirit of Walter Rauschenbusch, Baptists of the United States, white and Negro, have developed programs for social betterment in communities and throughout the nation. In the American Baptist Convention this responsibility has been assumed by its Commission on Christian Social Concerns and in the Southern Baptist Convention by the Christian Life Commission. All other Baptist bodies have assigned to one or more comparable agencies such activities as deal with problems of marriage and the family, crime and juvenile delinquency, industrial and race relations, control of beverage alcohol, narcotics, and pornographic literature, and the duties implied by Christian citizenship.

In 1913 the largest Baptist body, the Southern Baptist Convention, established the Social Service Commission, which for many years under leadership of the Reverend A. J. Barton dealt mainly with temperance. In 1947 the Christian Life Commission began its activities, co-ordinating all Southern Baptist Convention work in areas of Christian morality and social responsibilities.

In 1958, a young admirer of the work and ideals of Rauschenbusch, the Reverend Foy Valentine of Texas, took charge of this work among Southern Baptists. He challenged his fellow Baptists to get into the mainstream of social betterment with these words:

"The social responsibility of the child of God is taught in the creative acts of God; included in the first commission he gave to man, recorded in the Ten Commandments, throbs in the impassioned message of the prophets, taught by Jesus in precept and parable, written by Paul into whole sections of his letters; and Jesus says that in the last judgment the social fruits of redeemed people will be the evidences of their true faith in him."[1]

Finding most of the old opposition to the so-called social gospel fast fading from Baptist thinking, Valentine mapped programs to emphasize the nature and extent of Christian responsibility for social conditions in their communities, and for positive action in assuming them. His plan led to numerous summer Christian Life conferences at national and state Baptist assemblies and in local churches.

Similar activities in fields of social betterment have been sponsored by all Baptist bodies, although not always as completely as that offered the American Baptist Convention by its commission. At the 1966 sessions of the convention the commission's director, Elizabeth Miller, an ordained Baptist minister, offered a program of action involving the churches in studies and projects in behalf of civil rights, integrated housing, reform of penal laws, the fight on narcotics and beverage alcohol, a new spirit between management and labor, increased highway safety, conservation of natural resources, assistance to migrant laborers, and support of laws to extend unemployment insurance. Not all these suggested programs were followed by American Baptists with equal enthusiasm, and some were opposed as leading the church far afield from its true purpose, but Miss Miller replied: "I present them as a challenge to Baptists concerned with social betterment."[2]

The Negro Baptists tend to be more practical than theoretical in their social concern. The National Baptist Convention, Inc., sponsors Freedom Farm in Fayette County, near Somerville, Tennessee, 404 acres being cultivated by six Baptist farmers. They are sharecroppers with the Baptist convention. The National Baptist Convention of America sponsors the United Friends Hospital and Burial Society; the convention's former president, the Reverend C. D. Pettaway, carried the title of Supreme Commander of the benevolent agency, and his office on West 10th Street in Little Rock, Arkansas, is headquarters for both convention and society.

For the Sick and Needy

Baptists early recognized the value of a Christian witness through a ministry of healing. Elementary knowledge of hygiene common to all educated Americans often saved lives of persons overseas associated with the missionaries. Hospitals on foreign soil grew out of clinics established in mission homes, below a church auditorium, or under the spreading banyan tree.

Baptist hospitals in American cities began with the concern of a single individual who enlisted the help of fellow Baptists to meet human need. He was W. G. Mayfield, a physician and layman of St. Louis, who in 1884 took a patient into his home to provide treatment and care. By 1890 Dr. Mayfield had opened a residence with space for a dozen beds as the Missouri Baptist Sanitarium. The need soon required more beds, resulting in the establishment of the Missouri Baptist Hospital, now operated entirely under local auspices in St. Louis. Baptists in many other cities followed this example, founding hospitals under control of local and state associations.

The Georgia Baptist Hospital in Atlanta was born when the pastor of the Tabernacle Baptist Church, Len G. Broughton, a practicing physician before he entered the ministry, led his congregation to open an infirmary in a residence near the church to provide for members who could not afford the cost of hospitalization or had trouble getting admitted. Ownership and control of the Atlanta institution was taken over by the Georgia Baptist Convention.

A woman of New Orleans, Mrs. C. M. Kelly, known to her friends as Mother Kelly, recently converted from the Catholic faith and eagerly participating in activities of her church in that city, expressed the hope that Baptists would create a hospital where Protestants would be admitted without prejudice. The idea went into a resolution in a meeting of the New Orleans Baptist Association, and eventually the executive committee of the Southern Baptist Convention directed the Home Mission Board to establish a general hospital in New Orleans.

By 1965 Southern Baptists were operating, in various patterns of ownership, location, and size, a total of forty-seven medical institutions in continental United States, and twenty overseas with fifty-two clinics. Nineteen of the American hospitals have been opened since 1950. American Baptists were operating eight hospitals. Their Association of Baptist Homes and Hospitals, created in 1933, maintained a professional and denominational relationship for sixty-eight homes for the aging and fourteen children's homes as well as the hospitals. By 1965 all Baptist bodies in the United States had established and were maintaining one or more of these institutional ministries.

Baptists leave no doubt that their hospitals and homes are vitally connected with the propagation of their faith, as expressed in a statement of the Baptist Hospital Association:

"A Baptist hospital exists to bring men into a saving relationship with God through faith in Jesus Christ by means of direct personal witness as occasion presents, and by a positive Christian interpretation of the experiences of disease, disability, and death; functions as an instrument of God's grace in enriching and prolonging human life within the scope of divine providence; enlists and teaches those called to the healing arts . . . and makes available the full facilities of the hospitals to those people least able to pay in such ways as to preserve human dignity and worth."[3]

The most renowned medical institution founded and maintained by Baptists is unquestionably the one in Boston. The New England Baptist Hospital began as a medical dispensary of the Ruggles Street Baptist Church, whose pastor from 1870 to 1888 saw the need for medical care and began to meet it.

Established in 1893, this specialty referral hospital is nonsectarian but is known to the profession and the community as "The Baptist" and accepts patients of any faith or no faith. One of every three who receive treatment comes from out of state; a substantial number from other countries. Such a global constituency is attracted by physicians who are specialists of distinction in their fields.

Doctors from other countries come to Boston to observe the techniques used at the Baptist, and improve their skills. The school of nursing turns out from fifty-five to seventy-five young women each year "equipped to serve."

In the 1970s, the hospital board began to plan to replace the aging, clumsy plant at 91 Parker Hill Avenue with a 266-bed facility. A bill to grant the hospital a certificate of need, which would authorize construction, was introduced and passed both houses of the legislature of Massachusetts, but it was vetoed by the governor.

The hospital feels the pinch of inflation but still plans to find ways to create a more efficient plant to replace the sprawling six-acre complex that has developed over the period of eighty-four years.

Dr. Richard H. Overholt, specialist in lung surgery, has a sunny office with books and plants, comfortable chairs, and on his desk he keeps a beautiful vermeil ashtray. The personal enemy of cigaret smoking for half a century, he finds daily use for that relic. From a desk drawer he produces a half pack of cigarets for a visitor. Dr. Overholt strikes a match and lights up—holding the tip of the cigaret to the flame until it gets black and begins to reek, and he quietly lectures.

"The brain is a computer," he says as he deftly twirls the smoking stub. "It processes and stores images of touch and taste and seeing and hearing, and also serves as a mechanism for protecting us. We draw back from a pinprick, or from a scalding liquid because it sends a warning message to the computer. We can't feel, taste, or see a poison gas. But we do have a warning center for them. The two poisons in cigaret smoke—nicotine and the chemicals in the tars—trigger this warning center, which is in the nose."

At this point the doctor leans forward to give a volunteer a whiff of the cigaret, and she chokes and sputters. This demonstration for a patient is convincing: "If you are going to smoke a cigaret, the only sensible way for you to do it is to hold the weed in your nostrils. And you cannot smoke that way. The warning center just won't let you."

The patient may soon be on the operating table; diseased lungs or parts of lungs may be removed. Dr. Overholt spends his spare time in an avocation: an effort to prevent lung and heart disease. He was among the first to open a human chest for the purpose of repairing living tissue. The practice of preventive medicine is as important to him as superb surgery. He constantly preaches: "It's never too late to stop smoking!"

Neurosurgery, hip-replacement surgery, and gastrointestinal surgery are other specialties at the Baptist (Hospital).

Dr. James L. Poppen, neurosurgeon, was on a field trip in a jungle of Mexico when he received a message, which was stuffed into a bottle dropped by a helicopter: "President Kennedy has been shot. Can you come?"

Another night an insistent ring of the bedside phone forced Dr. Poppen awake. A Texas drawl reported another Kennedy had been shot. It was President Lyndon B. Johnson, and he asked: "Do you mind flying in a small fast jet?" The President ordered the plane to Boston and half an hour later Dr. Poppen was on his way to Los Angeles. It was he who broke the news of Bobby's death to the Kennedy family.

A few years later, in another small jet, Dr. Poppen was the passenger with Mr. and Mrs. Aristotle Onassis, headed for Greece and the hospital where Alexander Onassis, injured in an airplane crash, was a patient. Dr. Poppen reported that the brain damage from the crash was irreversible. The burly, six-foot doctor is one of a score of top-flight specialists at the Baptist who have an international reputation for medical care with a capital C.

Baptists and Civil Rights

All Baptist fellowships in America have repeatedly expressed support of civil rights for Negroes and other minority groups. At its May 1946 sessions, the Southern Baptist Convention appointed a special committee on race relations, assigning it the task to review the services being rendered by the convention agencies to Negroes, to study the moral and religious aspects of Baptists in their efforts for better race relations, and "to recommend to the convention a plan looking toward a better fulfillment of that responsibility." The Reverend J. B. Weatherspoon, professor at the Southern Baptist Theological Seminary, served as chairman.

Four years later the committee made a report, in which Dr. Weatherspoon called attention to one reason for the attitude of Southern people generally: "The problem of race relations is rooted deeply in history and is the product of a series of tragic social experiences that have left their marks on both groups. Slavery, war, sudden emancipation of a people unprepared for full responsibility as citizens, the tragic period of reconstruction that planted deep in both races prejudice and resentment and produced a pattern of discrimination and retaliation that has become traditional—all these elements lie in the background of the present situation."

The committee recommended that the Southern Baptist Convention recognize the responsibility to promote interracial good will, and spelled out specific programs to accomplish the task, including discussions of race relations among Negro and white Baptist pastors and leaders, encouraging definite work by churches in behalf of the Negro Baptist people of their communities, and keeping informed about legislation and other public actions affecting race relations. The committee urged that the convention "recognize its responsibility for the promotion of interracial good will, and urge upon our Baptist people and all Christians the duty of ordering our racial attitudes and actions in accordance with Christian truth and Christian love." At its 1950 sessions the Southern Baptist Convention adopted this report as a program of action.

Northern Baptists had carried on a definite program for the defense of the civil rights of Negroes since the end of the War Between the States, starting with the founding of Morehouse College and other schools for the education of the freedmen. More recently its Commission on Christian Social Concerns encouraged Baptist pastors and church members in community programs to produce better educational opportunities and housing, more jobs and fair employment practices for Negro families.

After the decision of the United States Supreme Court of May 1954, requiring racial integration of educational facilities, American Baptist agencies vigorously supported the ruling in publications and programs of action. Typical of numerous official statements on the subject by this convention was that passed at its 1965 sessions, which read:

"We recognize that any form of segregation based on race is contrary to the gospel of Jesus Christ and is incompatible with the Christian doctrine of man and with the nature of the Church of Christ. Whenever and wherever Christians, individually or collectively, practice segregation by action or inaction, we betray Christ and the fellowship which bears His name. We urge that the membership, leadership, ministry, and staff of every church in the American Baptist Convention be open to all followers of Jesus Christ regardless of their race, and that every congregation should offer its ministries to all persons in the community. We urge that all institutions owned or operated by or affiliated with congregations or denominational agencies of the American Baptist Convention should open their board memberships, staffs, and clientele to persons of all racial backgrounds."

A note of conciliation—and caution—was sounded on the attitude of Northern Baptists by the American Baptist Convention in these words: "While pledging to continue the fight for the civil rights of all American citizens, we express our concern at the implications of guilt by association against countless citizens of both races in southern states who for many years have been working, quietly and effectively, often at the risk of their incomes and lives, to overcome long-established mores and deep-seated prejudices in their states and communities in behalf of civil rights. We recognize that we need to continue to strengthen these citizens of good will in the southern states, who are working quietly and prayerfully to advance the cause of civil rights and its peaceful acceptance in their communities."

One citizen of the South to whom the American Baptist resolution of conciliation aptly applied was Brooks Hays, former member of Congress from Arkansas, later assistant secretary of state and special assistant to Presidents Kennedy and Johnson. In 1959, when president of the Southern Baptist Convention, Hays invited Negro Baptist leaders to confer with white Baptist spokesmen on the broad subject of race relations. As result, the Reverend J. H. Jackson, president of the National Baptist Convention, Inc., and the Reverend C. D. Pettaway, president of the unincorporated Negro Baptist body, with several of their associates, met with Hays and other Southern Baptist leaders in Chicago in early 1960. From this small conference came an expression of co-operation that resulted in a program of exchange of information among Negro and white Baptist pastors, intended to foster greater understanding of mutual problems growing out of differences in race.

Dr. H. Franklin Paschall, pastor of the First Baptist Church of Nashville, Tennessee, discussed the question of civil rights with newsmen shortly after his election as president of the Southern Baptist Convention in May 1966, and declared: "The federal government has provided laws governing integration and equality of all people before law. Southern Baptists respect those laws. If

Christian leaders can strengthen proper attitudes, we shall continue to make significant progress in race relations."

Martin Luther King, Jr.

A Georgia-born Baptist minister who dedicated his life to the cause of civil rights among his fellow Negroes was the Reverend Martin Luther King, Jr., a pastor first in Montgomery, Alabama, and later in Atlanta, in churches affiliated with the National Baptist Convention, Inc. For his leadership in this field he was honored with a plaque of distinction by the American Baptist Convention in 1964, and in the same year was awarded the Nobel Peace Prize, the first Baptist and the second Negro American to be so honored.

Son and grandson of Baptist preachers, Martin grew up with better-than-average opportunities for a southern Negro American. He was born in 1929 when his father was pastor of a small Negro church and a student at Atlanta's Morehouse College. He shared in family worship daily and was expected every day to memorize a Bible verse to repeat at the supper table. Young King followed his father to Morehouse, and under the teaching of Dr. Benjamin E. Mays as president, he became deeply interested in philosophy. An article he wrote on "The Purpose of Education" for the campus paper revealed what he wanted in life, which he described as "Intelligence plus character, with a concern for people." He studied the life and work of Rauschenbusch.

At Morehouse College this Southern student met the best of the Negro ministers of America. He enrolled at Crozer Theological Seminary in Pennsylvania. There he won the award for most outstanding student and was given the Crozer fellowship for study in the graduate school of his choice. At Crozer, Martin Luther King was greatly influenced by Dr. Mordecai Johnson, then president of Howard University, who lectured at the seminary soon after a visit to India. Dr. Johnson was convinced that the tactics of Mahatma Gandhi could be useful in the struggle of American Negroes for civil rights. Young King thought so, too, and planned then to make a career of leadership among the people of his race. He won his doctorate from Boston University and married an Alabama Baptist music student there.

King turned down many attractive offers of teaching and school administration to become pastor of the Dexter Avenue Baptist Church, Montgomery, and while there led the first movements among Negroes of civil disobedience to dramatize their determination to secure integration of schools, transportation, and public services.

In April 1961 Dr. King addressed the student body of the Southern Baptist Theological Seminary at Louisville on the subject "The Church on the Frontier of Racial Tension." In this landmark speech he said:

"I am absolutely convinced that men hate each other because they fear each other. They fear each other because they don't know each other. They don't know each other because they are separated from each other . . . The church has the responsibility to open the channels of communication . . . So often in the church we've had a high blood pressure of creeds and an anemia of deeds . . . God is interested in the freedom of the whole human race, the creation of a society where every man will respect the dignity and worth of human personality."[4]

Dr. King lost some of his appeal among Baptist leaders when in 1965 he announced that he was relating his campaign for civil rights among Negroes with the "peace" movement, particularly with regard to the United States involvement in the war in Vietnam. Many Baptist publications and spokesmen declared that his criticism of American foreign policy threw him into the political arena under a questionable spotlight. Dr. King retreated from this position somewhat, resuming his program of resistance as expressed by marches and demonstrations. Although Martin Luther King was inevitably controversial in a time of tension and change, few Baptists disputed the claim he made to a mass meeting of Negroes in Montgomery soon after the demonstrations for civil rights began:

"If you will protest courageously, and yet with dignity and Christian love, the historians will have to pause and say, 'There lived a great people, a black people, who injected new meaning and dignity into the veins of civilization.' "

Death from a sharpshooter's bullet in Memphis, Tennessee, took his life in April 1968. His brother, associate pastor of the church in Atlanta where the Reverend Martin Luther King (Sr.)

was pastor, drowned in his backyard swimming pool on a hot summer night. Their mother, Mrs. Alberta King, organist in that church, was killed by a gunshot on a Sunday morning while she played for the worship service in 1974.

Pastor King continues to serve the Ebenezer Baptist Church, Atlanta, and his daughter-in-law Coretta Scott King, widowed mother of the four children of the late Martin Luther King, Jr., continues to represent the cause of civil rights. When the elder King canceled his commitment to address the Southern Baptist Convention during its 1978 meeting in Atlanta, because he had an invitation to preach in Eastern Europe, Mrs. King filled the appointment and addressed the session. She cherishes the Nobel Peace Prize awarded her husband in 1964.

Clarence Jordan and Koinonia

Sixty men and women and children in one big happy family break bread together daily at noon in the dining hall at Koinonia Farm, seven miles southwest of Americus, Georgia. Thirty-two of them are Koinonia (meaning "fellowship") Partners, sharing all things in common in the pattern of the first Christians (Acts 4:32), and the others are volunteers for short or long terms. They work together, they study and pray together, and they live out the principles of Jesus Christ as they understand them.

A coauthor of this book remembers how it began: Clarence L. Jordan, graduate student at Southern Baptist Theological Seminary, Louisville, Kentucky, and his wife, former librarian of the seminary, discovered the New Testament in Greek as a handbook in human relations; realized the problems of war, poverty, and race could not be solved in the big cities; moved to his native Georgia and launched "an agricultural, missionary venture" November 1, 1942, on 400 acres of "fairly good" land.

An American Baptist missionary couple, the Reverend and Mrs. Martin England, stranded at home by World War II, first shared the farmhouse and the chores. The Jordans and the Englands went to work. They made a hard living but demonstrated scientific farming as Clarence had learned it at the University of Georgia and Martin had practiced it in Burma. Peanuts, poultry, pigs, and pecans thrived in the sandy soil of Sumter County. Neighbors, black and white, welcomed the man with the slow southern drawl, the kind heart, and the know-how of the educated farmer.

Dr. Jordan (pronounced "jerdan" the same as Hamilton Jordan, his second cousin, presidential assistant in the late 1970s) and his associates practiced brotherhood as they preached, lectured, and taught it in churches, colleges, summer assemblies, and youth camps in the North and West as well as South. That policy met with hostility which developed into violence, even to dynamiting and shootings to drive the "nigger lovers" and "communists" out of the county. But the Jordan family with four children was not easily intimidated.

To amplify his voice and make his message more clear, Jordan began to translate Paul's epistles into the vernacular of the South, mimeographing and later publishing each book under the title *The Cotton Patch Version of the New Testament*.

Slowly the fellowship grew, but black prospects never quite dared to make full commitment to the group. Millard Fuller, an affluent Alabama lawyer, caught the gleam and he and his family joined the community. When the founder died at the age of fifty-seven on October 29, 1969—of heart failure and pneumonia, according to Dallas Lee in his book *The Cotton Patch Evidence* (Harper & Row, 1971)—new leadership was in the harness. Koinonia Farm had been reorganized and renamed Koinonia Partners, Inc. The Fund for Humanity had financed the project and the partners were building sturdy homes for native families, white and black, who had never been able to own a house and had always paid high rent for shacks. The number of houses totaled seventy in 1978.

A memorial service was held in the chapel of the Seminary in Louisville in honor of the former student whose body, dressed in overalls and plaid work shirt, had been buried in a cedarbox at the Koinonia picnic grounds. Their response to that man's witness was the Clarence Jordan Institute, to provide a forum for the discussion of issues which pastors and laymen face. The goal of a $50,000 endowment was voted and approved by the Seminary board of trustees. Paul D. Simmons of the Department of Christian Ethics was named chairman, and Glen Stassen vice-chairman.

During 1977 Koinonia Partners harvested 150 tons of peanuts, shipped 20 tons by mail order, processed 350,000 pounds of pecans, baked 50 tons of fruitcake (made by a recipe Clarence created by trial and error), and grossed $75,000 off the 1,400 acres. "We netted around $20,000," reports cofounder Florence Jordan, "but our profits are small because we do not try to make them great."

The Fullers answered a call to practice in Zaïre the Christian principles they had mastered in Georgia. They served their term and came back to Americus to establish "Habitat for Humanity," incorporated as a separate organization but sharing worship services with Koinonia Partners.

Like many another Baptist, Jordan was not without honor save perhaps in his own country. In an obituary the New York *Times* quoted Clarence as saying, "We are not concerned with integration or segregation, only the fatherhood of God and the brotherhood of man." Being an ordained minister, he was never allowed to register as a conscientious objector, but he was opposed to war.

Today the letterhead for the mail-order correspondence and the quarterly newsletter carry the slogan "We seek a new spirit . . . a spirit of partnership with God and people everywhere." Koinonians are idealists with a realism rooted in the Christian faith.

The United Nations

Among the statesmen responsible for the formation of the United Nations at its organization meeting in San Francisco in the spring of 1945, as World War II drew to its inevitable victory of the Allies over the dictatorial regimes of Germany and Japan, were several prominent Baptists. The names of three are written into the history of the agency devoted to world peace: Harry S. Truman, President of the United States, who inherited the so-called Dumbarton Oaks proposals of the State Department and other foreign offices among the major powers; the other two were official delegates to the founding convention: Harold E. Stassen, former governor of Minnesota and naval aide to General Douglas MacArthur during the closing months of the war in the Pacific, a Baptist deacon, later to become president of the American Baptist Convention; and the Reverend Charles A. Eaton, of New Jersey, member of the Foreign Affairs Committee of the House of Representatives, a former Baptist pastor.

A committee of Baptists, selected by the Baptist Joint Committee on Public Affairs at the invitation of the State Department, served with similar representatives from many other major denominations in the United States during the deliberations of the delegates from forty-two nations to the United Nations organization meeting. The committee was headed by the Reverend Walter O. Lewis, director of Baptist relief activities in Europe during and after the war.[5] While the committee accomplished little by way of changes in the proposals already agreed upon for the new organization, its members did help to originate two recommendations to be incorporated in the Charter of the United Nations: first, that Almighty God be recognized as the father of all mankind; second, a statement of the inalienable liberties of all men, a Bill of Rights, which would in general terms outline the rights which citizens of every member nation should be guaranteed by their governments.

These proposals were passed on to other committees representing religious denominations in the United States. At numerous meetings they were fully discussed, and were generally approved. Spokesmen for the Roman Catholic Church agreed heartily with the Protestant groups that a recognition of God would add spiritual strength to the proposed charter, and that a Bill of Rights would point the way to greater human liberties. Spokesmen for the Jewish faith also agreed, in a remarkable demonstration of interfaith unity.

The church groups, invited as advisers to the official United States delegation, were instructed to clear all recommendations with the secretary-general of the conference. The man who held this powerful position, the one who wielded the gavel to call the organization meeting to order on its first day, was Alger Hiss, trusted adviser to President Truman and spokesman for Secretary of State John Stettinius. He let it be known that he opposed both suggestions. The first proposal, Hiss declared, was objectionable for the reason that there were delegates present who did not believe in God and that sectarian sentiments should not be incorporated in the United Nations charter. Hiss rejected the second idea because the representatives of the Soviet Union, he insisted, did not interpret human rights as did the government and people of the United States.

Baptists and others, unable to influence Alger Hiss, saw their proposals abandoned. The United Nations charter was adopted practically as it had been approved by the Stalinist government of the Soviet Union. However, through resolutions and programs of all the major Baptist bodies, the denomination's efforts to build a just and lasting peace have gone forward. Typical of the pronouncements on the subject was the one adopted at the 1964 session of the American Baptist Convention, presided over by Harold E. Stassen:

"We live in a time of great tension and fear. The stockpiling of nuclear and biological weapons by an increasing number of nations poses a constant threat to the future of the human race. Further tension is created by new nations emerging from colonialism and facing the almost insuperable task of moving from an underdeveloped economy and limited government experiences to take their places in an industrialized and highly complex world.

"It is in this world that the Christian church is called to witness today. As the Prince of Peace came to reconcile the world to himself, so must his followers be agents of reconciliation in a tense and fearful world. As Christ was concerned for mankind in his hunger, sorrow and nakedness, so must we be concerned for men caught in a world of conflict and need and must work for a world of peace with justice and freedom.

"We believe that God, still sovereign amid the unleashing of the atom and the probing of space, seeks for all his twentieth century children a world of nations in a community where peace is enduring precisely because it offers and contains equal justice and equal opportunity for the fullest development of his human family. Therefore, we reaffirm our faith and hope, we state our continuing concern, and we request our people and our churches to study and take appropriate action on issues of international affairs."[6]

Other resolutions of Baptist bodies have called not only for support of the United Nations, but also for the strengthening of the world organization by revising its charter to give it more power to prevent subversion and aggression, and to take more positive action to preserve international peace. Still another move developed in both the Southern and the American Baptist Conventions, announcing support for what may prove to be the final answer to the building of peace, the establishment of world order under enforceable law. Meanwhile, both conventions in varying degrees help maintain the Church Center at the United Nations.

The world Baptist organization and some of its affiliates in the United States were represented at a 1977 meeting of nongovernmental organizations accredited to the United Nations. In this group were Eleanore Schnurr, Baptist World Alliance; Eldon L. Janzen, North American Baptist Conference; Robert Hardmond and Daniel Nickerson, National Baptist Convention, U.S.A., Inc.; Nathaniel Billings, Baptist General Conference; and Vernice Lee, American Baptist Churches in the U.S.A.

Operation Brother's Keeper

Christian social concerns have taken Baptists from the United States to the ends of the earth. There was Robert A. Hingson, for example, the state Baptist Student Union president of Alabama in the 1940s, who as a physician became professor and director of anesthesiology at Western Reserve University, Cleveland, Ohio. In contact with his friend of student days, Robert S. Denny, associate secretary of the Baptist World Alliance, Hingson hit upon a plan to implement his ideas of Christian service.

The result was a medical mission of three months, surveying medical facilities and needs in Asia and Africa. Five other doctors joined Hingson, and the party of fifteen included the wives of several, an interpreter, and one or two medical assistants. Travel expenses of the mission were financed by the Jarman Foundation of Nashville, Tennessee, but travel expenses only. The men gave their time and skills for what they called Operation Brother's Keeper.

The trip was launched with a five-hour briefing session in which Hingson told his fellow doctors: "We will go into slums and jungles. We will get our hands dirty. Some of us may not get back. Some of us may get sick and have to be left behind. Our job is to go on, once we have put our hand to the plow. If any of you think your decision was unwise, now is the time to withdraw."[7]

The team covered 45,000 miles. The traveling doctors rolled up their sleeves, put on their gowns and masks and performed 120 operations, administered more than 90,000 vaccinations for polio, typhoid, cholera, and tetanus, delivered 128 medical lectures to audiences of more than 5,000 persons in missionary and national university centers. They conducted or gave devotions, sermons, and religious talks to ninety-six audiences in twenty-seven countries.

Dr. Hingson and his associates used a new injection device that he had invented, which he called a peace gun, to give antityphoid and other shots painlessly, and with this the team inoculated 486 schoolchildren in a half hour. The doctors demonstrated a plastic air-way for a safer use of mouth-to-mouth resuscitation.

Arriving in Cairo, Egypt, the doctors found government red tape cut to permit them a quick trip to Gaza to visit the Baptist hospital there. In Lamberéné, French Equatorial Africa, they met and visited Dr. Albert Schweitzer. In Europe they visited Zurich and met with members of the Baptist World Alliance commission on world missions, then stopped at Brussels to appear at the Protestant Pavilion of the World's Fair. Summarizing the impressions of his team when they reached New York, Hingson declared that man's worldwide health needs may be stated in words that begin with S: "Sewers, sanitation, soap, shots, soup, schools, screens, sprays, self-respect, and salvation."

By 1977 Brother's Brother Foundation had been established. Bob Hingson found an ally in the Jonas Salk Institute. Dr. Salk (who had discovered an antipoliomyelitis vaccine in 1953) joined in a program, endorsed and partially underwritten by the Baptist World Alliance through its division on Relief and Development, to help rid the world of polio.

Having retired from the medical staffs of Case-Western Reserve University at Cleveland and the University of Pittsburgh, Dr. Hingson could give his full time to the Foundation. His friend at the Alliance, now general secretary of the worldwide organization, Bob Denny, led its 109 member bodies to assume one third of the cost of $3 million as a goal for the crusade to immunize the world's population with the "peace gun."

From Pittsburgh, Pennsylvania, the Hingson team went to Grenada, West Indies, in the mid-seventies for a mass immunization effort against the plagues of young life. In July 1978, Bob and his six associates made an attack on disease in Liberia and booked themselves for a campaign in Haiti for October.

Dr. Hingson acquired his obsession for preventive medicine

when he attended a Baptist Sunday school as a boy in Oxford, Alabama, and made up his mind to follow the biblical commandment, "Love thy neighbor as thyself."

David Carver's Chinese Imports

Another Baptist, a layman, David J. Carver of Baltimore, carried his Christian concerns with him into the importing business. He was the youngest brother of Dr. William Owen Carver, professor of missions at Southern Baptist Theological Seminary. David finished college and went to China, where he taught at the University of Nanking, a Presbyterian-Methodist institution, then in a government high school established to prepare students to study abroad—part of a plan to use the Boxer Indemnity Fund which the United States had remitted to China on condition that it be used for the education of Chinese.

Carver's four years with Chinese students and scholars gave him great respect for the Chinese mind and culture. While getting his graduate degrees he disposed of some old Chinese embroideries and curios to pay expenses, and this led him into importing Chinese goods. He set up his business headquarters in New York and made numerous trips to China and other Far Eastern countries. During World War II when it was impossible to secure Oriental materials Carver copied an Oriental coffee table with ceramic inlay and mass produced it as a reproduction of a genuine import. After the Communist take-over of China he shifted to Japanese and Italian imported merchandise. In his Baltimore church, he was superintendent of a large Chinese Sunday school.

On a visit to his home area in Tennessee David Carver encountered a Chinese student whose parents were originally from the city where Carver had taught, Kaifeng. The student was struggling to get through medical college. About that time some of Carver's friends had appealed to him to help Chinese students in Taipei and Hong Kong who wanted to attend American colleges. He decided to lay aside a large share of the profits he had made from business and devote his money to aiding Chinese students. He induced a Chinese American official of the State Department to resign his position and represent Hong Kong College in the United States.

David Carver's gifts included $100,000 to the University of Richmond for a Chinese scholarship fund, $35,000 to Johns Hopkins University for a similar fund, $150,000 to Hong Kong Baptist College, and numerous other grants to help needy Chinese and other students. When asked to allow the college to name a new campus building in his honor Carver refused, informing the trustees: "If a few educated and dedicated leaders among the Chinese result, that is my reward."[8]

Kyin Oo and James Tanimola Ayorinde

When the Voice of America needed a good man to broadcast news and commentary to Burma, a member of the staff of the United States Information Service in Rangoon was recommended. He was Kyin Oo, and he came to Washington. Son of two Christian teachers in the capital city of the Buddhist nation, Kyin had come through grade school and high school under Baptist mission teachers, and got his degree from Judson College of Rangoon. His young wife and two children joined him in the States after his first year with the Voice of America, and two other children were born to the family.

At nine o'clock every morning Kyin Oo turns the switch to begin speaking to his fellow countrymen in cultured Burmese from a script he has prepared himself. Recorded music, newscasts, and comments on happenings in the free world are supplied to listeners on the opposite side of the earth at a popular hour of their day. Without a foreign accent he gives his own people a nonsectarian message of music and current events, interpreted by one friendly to the United States and one who adopted the faith dominant in America.

This Burmese third-generation Christian layman fought hard to keep his faith in his country. He was familiar with the development of Christianity in Burma, from the day in July 1813 when the Judsons first arrived to 1955 when the number of Baptist church members, not including children, reached 197,000, and the Burma Christian Council reported a grand total of Protestants as 215,415. Kyin Oo had identified himself with a Washington Baptist church on arrival in the States. His day-by-day message from America gives to his own people a fair picture of the nation whose Christians sent an American couple to live and die with them a century and a half ago.

Kyin and his wife own a home in the heart of Springfield, Virginia, due south of the nation's capital. All four children are now on their own, Burmese in appearance but Americans at heart.

At the age of thirty-one, the Reverend James Tanimola Ayorinde from the British Crown Colony of Nigeria, West Africa, came to the United States and enrolled at Virginia Union University. He earned a degree at this Baptist school in two years, then continued his education at Oberlin College in Ohio. His wife, Mabola, accompanied him to the United States and attended the National Trade School for Women and Girls in Washington—Nannie Burroughs' School.

When in 1960 Nigeria became an independent nation, Ayorinde was named by the new government to be chairman of the national broadcasting corporation. It was a tribute not only to his ability as a minister and educator, to the church of which he was pastor and the Nigerian Baptist Convention of which he was president, but also to the Christian minority in a country with a large Muslim constituency. Ayorinde was the first African to become executive secretary of Nigerian Baptists. Dr. Ayorinde lived to be seventy. He was succeeded by another Nigerian, Dr. Emanuel A. Dahunsi, a brilliant student who earned a doctorate at Southern Baptist Theological Seminary.

W. Maxey Jarman—Church Builder

At a major intersection in Barranquilla, Colombia, there was erected in 1946 an attractive modern church edifice for the Baptist congregation of that seaport city. The purchase of that important property and the erection of that house of worship were made possible by the gift of a Baptist layman, W. Maxey Jarman, manufacturer and business executive of Nashville, Tennessee.

Since that time many other such houses of worship have been built largely through the generosity of this Christian philanthropist to accommodate congregations in countries around the world. On tour of South America soon after the close of World War II, Jarman noticed that the missionaries in new centers of activity usually preached in cheap store-front buildings on unpaved side streets until they could win enough converts to start a church. He learned that it was often a missionary lifetime before the congregation was strong enough to build a house of worship that could attract the more affluent people of a city.

In consultation with the secretary for Latin America of the Baptist Foreign Mission Board, Jarman explored the possibilities for modest but attractive church buildings in key cities of South America. "Missionaries deserve a chance to begin their work in a simple, clean church building on a residential street where the whole town can see that the Baptists are in business there," Mr. Jarman reasoned. "We can make greater progress on every new mission field if we can reduce the time it takes to get started."

Jarman reasoned also that an attractive church edifice in a good location would be itself an advertisement of evangelical Christianity and would attract worshipers and members.

Maxey Jarman's father, James Franklin Jarman, when chairman of the board of the General Shoe Corporation, had established the Jarman Foundation to assist worthy causes. As principal director of the Foundation, the younger Jarman drew upon its funds for his project of building Baptist churches. He never permitted the Jarman name to be associated publicly with these churches overseas, insisting that this project represents a part of his Christian stewardship.

Maxey retired from Genesco and later resigned from the board of directors over a disagreement about principles. He helped to create an organization, the Christian Bible Society, whose purpose is to get people to read the Bible. The Bible Society, with the help of the Jarman Foundation, uses radio, syndicated-type columns in rural newspapers, and other devices to promote Bible reading. The non-profit corporation is based in Nashville, Tennessee.

Geren and Nziramasanga

The last American consul-general to the Federation of Rhodesia and Nyasaland before independence was granted that new African country, Paul Geren, joined in a 110-mile annual march from Battlefields to Salisbury on May 24, 1963, and he made front-page news in the *Rhodesia Herald*. With the aid of his wife and three teen-age daughters, who supplied refreshments and a change of shoes and socks while he was en route, this representative of the United States government in Southern Africa walked fifty-five miles of the trek in sixteen hours and fifteen minutes. Of the 175 persons who entered the march, only thirty were still going when the athletic American diplomat dropped out.

Thus Paul Geren identified himself with the Africans in general and the Rhodesians in particular. A native of Arkansas, son of a Baptist pastor, educated at Baylor University, at Louisiana State University, and finally at Harvard, the young economist taught at the University of Rangoon under the American Baptist Foreign Mission Society, then joined the Friends Ambulance Unit when the Japanese forces invaded Burma. In 1942 he trekked 220 miles through Burma's back door into India with General "Vinegar Joe" Stilwell and Dr. Gordon Seagrave.

Once defeated in his home district in Arkansas for Congress, Geren entered the diplomatic service. The State Department sent him back to India as economics adviser to the embassy, then to Damascus, and to Amman as American representative. Home again, he was named deputy director of the Peace Corps. Then he was assigned to Africa, at a time when news of racial troubles in the United States brought out big headlines in papers on that continent—and over the world. In an official speech in Salisbury, Paul Geren told his African hosts: "In the United States we have come tragically short of the glory of God in race relations. We have, however, set our faces toward a nonracial ideal . . . We have never supposed that the problems you face are the same as those we face, but we are quite sure that both Rhodesians and Americans need resolution, imagination, and good will. Above all, each needs not stones but the moral encouragement of the other."[9]

A business school at Nyatsime College in Salisbury was named for Dr. Geren. He established the J. M. Dawson Studies in Church and State at Baylor University, Waco, Texas, during a term as vice-president of the largest Baptist college in the world. An automobile accident on June 22, 1969, when he was president of Stetson University, DeLand, Florida, brought Dr. Geren's life to a tragic end.

Caiphas T. Nziramasanga follows in his steps, although the two men probably never met. Born in Zvimba, Sinoia, Southern Rhodesia, in April 1938, Caiphas was the last son born to a polygamist. By Shona custom, a man is expected to assume full responsibility for the widow of a deceased brother and his children. When two of his brothers died, the elder Nziramasanga had to support three wives and a total of fifteen children.

At the age of six, Caiphas was sent to herd cattle all day. With some ninety-six bulls and cows, he kept busy, for they were prone to stray into cornfields which belonged to strangers. By the time he was ten, Caiphas began to talk of school. His father had allowed the older sons to enter, but he needed the youngest boy at home. Eventually, with his brothers' help, Caiphas learned how to write with his finger in the sand. He ran away from the herd and found a school that recognized his intelligence, and he was granted admission.[10]

Young Nziramasanga graduated from Matopo Secondary School in Bulawayo, got a teacher's certificate at Umtali Teachers College in late 1961, and started teaching. He married Lilian, a fellow graduate at Umtali. With the encouragement of Baptist missionaries, and by careful saving of his income, he was able to win a scholarship at Oklahoma Baptist University, Shawnee. After he had earned his bachelor's degree, his wife joined Caiphas, and the two entered Oklahoma State University at Stillwater, where he took a master's degree in history. Residence work completed, the couple returned home, reclaimed their three children, and joined the faculty of Gwelo Teachers' College. During the first half of 1978, in his final stint for his doctorate, Caiphas was a teaching associate at OSU and completed his dissertation, "African Immigration to Rhodesia, 1890–1945." The Rhodesian student represented the Baptists of his country at the Second World Baptist Men's Conference in Indianapolis in April 1978.

This man considers himself a product of the mission opened by Southern Baptists in 1950. In time, a seminary, a bookstore, a medical center, a publishing house, and a radio and audiovisual center were established in various cities of Rhodesia. The shock of the assassination of an American administrator at the Sanyati Baptist Hospital was felt more strongly by Rhodesian Baptists than by missionaries, because it signified the launching of guerrilla warfare against Christian mission outposts and Christian nationals.

The future of the country as a free nation was threatened by the struggle for power among black leaders in 1979, yet herdboys who have become "intellectuals" are the hope of Rhodesia in its search for leaders of integrity for Zimbabwe.

XXIII

THE SINGING BAPTISTS

Church Music Has Come a Long Way

Climaxing the Jubilee observance of the birth of denominational life in the United States was an oratorio entitled *What Is Man?* presented, in May 1964, at Atlantic City where most of the cooperating bodies of Baptists were holding a joint session. It was a star-studded performance.

The modern oratorio was the product of American Baptist artists: Ron Nelson, chairman of the Music Department of Brown University, was composer, and Samuel Miller, dean of Harvard Divinity School, wrote the libretto. The American Baptist Foreign Mission Societies proposed it, and the organizers of the North American Baptist Jubilee commissioned it.

Thor Johnson of Chicago, director of orchestral activities in the Music Department of Northwestern University, was secured to conduct the 60-piece orchestra from the Baltimore Symphony, while Philadelphia's Singing City Choir rendered the choruses. Robert Elmore, born in South India of American Baptist missionaries, was the organist and musical conductor. Irene Jordan of the Metropolitan Opera was one soloist, Sherrill Milnes, winner of the 1962 Ford Foundation Grant Award, the other. Carl R. Greyson of Chicago, radio-TV announcer, served as narrator.

The statement about the oratorio in the printed program concluded with this paragraph: "Today man, excited with the cosmic effects of his human possibilities, yearns to touch new horizons. To us, living in such a mood, this oratorio presents the biblical message of the original majesty of man, marred by rebellion and sin, but restored by redemption in Christ to become an instrument of grace and power. This message, illustrated in Judson's life, calls us to look into our own hearts and outward to the frontiers of mankind where God is at work today."

The music for *What Is Man?* was far different from the traditional church music to which most of the hearers were accustomed, and met a mixed reception. Baptist musicians—organists and pianists, choir directors, and professional singers—hailed the oratorio with high praise as an impressive work of modern religious music. Many rank-and-file Baptists, however, were left confused and baffled by its type of harmony and melody they could not understand. Most of these Baptists would have been happier with the Hallelujah Chorus from Handel's *Messiah,* or perhaps would have preferred to join in singing "How Great Thou Art" as a fitting climax to the Baptist Jubilee.

One thing all Baptists at the 1964 meeting could agree upon: Church music had come a long way from the simple tunes sung in Baptist meeting houses in the early nineteenth century.

Early Baptist Songs

Baptists in the American colonies began singing at public worship as early as the middle of the seventeenth century. Some of the English Baptists frowned upon what they called promiscuous singing, with believers and unbelievers together; but one Benjamin Keach, a Particular Baptist, encouraged congregational singing, and when his son Elias emigrated to America in 1686, he brought along his father's enthusiasm for public singing. As pastor of the Pennepek Church in Pennsylvania, he led his church with its twelve faithful members to make a joyful noise unto the Lord.

"Disturbing the peace" is what the officials called it in July 1651 when they arrested John Clarke of Newport and his friends who came to Lynn, Massachusetts, to visit the invalid William Witter and hold a worship service along Baptist lines for him. The visitors got a whipping for singing.

The Welsh Baptists, arriving in New York in 1701, settled at New Castle, Delaware, two years later. Their Welsh Tract church introduced singing among Baptists in the middle colonies, and other Welsh Baptists made singing a vital part of the Great Valley church near Philadelphia, founded in 1711, and Montgomery church, founded in 1719.

The Keaches, father and son, believed so strongly in this phase of public worship that they added articles on singing psalms, as well as of the laying on of hands, to the Assembly Confession of Faith. A new edition of it was ordered, and Benjamin Franklin did the printing in 1743.

Calvinistic though it was, this confession of faith with the provision for public singing became widely accepted among the Baptist associations and had considerable influence on churches in the South.

Benjamin Keach discovered that, by reminding his opponents that a hymn was sung by Jesus and his disciples after the Lord's Supper in the Upper Room, he could win their consent. He also cited them to hymns written for use during the ordinance of baptism. *The Newport Collection,* the first Baptist compilation of hymns in the colonies, published in 1766, opened with sixteen on the subject of baptism, and this section was followed by seventy-four hymns for the Lord's Supper.

It took the Great Awakening to popularize hymn singing. The favorite hymnal of the period 1734–70 was *Watts' Hymns and Spiritual Songs,* published first in England in 1707. It was reprinted in Boston in 1739, in Philadelphia by Benjamin Franklin in 1742, and ten years later in New York. This was by all odds the most popular book among Baptists, although a hymnbook of 588 hymns, published by John Rippon, famous pastor of the Baptist Church in Carter Lane, London, in 1787, was reprinted in America in 1792, and was promptly accepted by the Baptists.

Some Baptist associations collected hymns and published their own books. The Philadelphia Association got one out in 1790; the Dover (Virginia) Association, the largest Baptist Association in America by 1830, produced the *Dover Selection.*

The camp meeting boosted the custom of congregational singing even more. Baptists in all the states liked the camp meeting, but especially those on the Western frontier and in the South. In 1825 a Baptist collection of camp-meeting songs was published in Baltimore.

Hymn collections began to appear in the South, and before the

War Between the States these collections were always published by individuals. Jesse Mercer of Georgia brought out in 1813 his volume: *The Cluster of Spiritual Songs, Divine Hymns and Sacred Poems*. William Walker of Spartanburg, South Carolina, published his book of hymns with the tunes written in oblong shape notes, in 1835, entitled *Southern Harmony*. *Sacred Harp* appeared in 1844, published by B. F. White of Georgia. *Baptist Psalmody,* the work of Basil Manly and Basil Manly, Jr., contained 1,295 hymns. It won the approval of the Southern Baptist Convention in 1851.

After the war, hymnbooks were published only by the various publication societies. The American Baptist Publication Society brought out *The Baptist Hymn and Tune Book* in 1871, *The Baptist Hymnal* in 1883, and *Sursum Corda* in 1898. The Baptist Sunday School Board published *The Baptist Hymn and Praise Book* early in the present century.

Baptist Hymn Writers

Numerous Baptist poets and composers of hymnal music have enriched public worship throughout America and the world. Samuel Francis Smith, who was a student in Newton Theological Institute near Boston, received several songbooks from a friend who had mastered German and wanted Smith's opinion as to whether some of the tunes could be set to American words. Smith noticed a tune that had already been borrowed by the British for the words of "God Save the King." He reached for a sheet of paper and within half an hour had written the words of "My Country! 'Tis of Thee." The hymn was first sung at Park Street Baptist Church near Boston Common on July 4, 1831. It later barely missed being recognized by law as the national anthem of the United States.

"He Leadeth Me, O Blessed Thought!" has probably been sung in every Baptist meeting house in America since its words were written in 1862 by the Reverend John Henry Gilmore. The preacher-poet, son of the governor of New Hampshire, wrote the hymn after leading a prayer meeting in the First Baptist Church of Philadelphia. His subject at the prayer service had been the Twenty-third Psalm. Discussing the meeting with his host, Deacon

Wattson, who lived next door to the church, Dr. Gilmore felt inspired to put the words of the hymn on paper.

The Reverend William H. Doane, member of the Baptist Church at Norwich, Connecticut, later Mount Auburn Baptist Church, Cincinnati, Ohio, was one of the most prolific song composers of the nineteenth century. He composed the music for several productions of the blind poet, Fanny J. Crosby. Among the gospel songs for which Doane wrote the music are the familiar "Rescue the Perishing," "Pass Me Not, O Gentle Savior," "Take the Name of Jesus with You," and "Safe in the Arms of Jesus."

Two Baptist ministers teamed up to produce "Savior, Thy Dying Love," the words by Sylvanus D. Phelps and the music by Robert Lowry. Pastor of Hanson Place Baptist Church in Brooklyn, Dr. Lowry encouraged one of his members, Annie Sherwood Hanks, to write poems suitable as hymns. One of Mrs. Hanks's best-known productions was "I Need Thee Every Hour," for which Lowry wrote the music.

Dr. Adoniram Judson Gordon, pastor of the Clarendon Street Baptist Church, Boston, was composer of "My Jesus, I Love Thee."

Dr. Harry Emerson Fosdick, pastor of Riverside Church in New York for years, reared in a devout Baptist home, added inspiration to every worship service that has used his stately hymn, "God of Grace and God of Glory." For the occasion of church anniversaries, the Reverend Edward Hughes Pruden wrote "Anniversary Hymn" when he was pastor of the First Baptist Church, Washington, D.C.

Best known among all twentieth-century Baptist songwriters and composers was B. B. McKinney, who served the Baptist Sunday School Board as its first music editor and later as secretary of the Board's department of church music. He wrote both the words and music for 150 gospel songs, and composed tunes for 115 texts by other authors. This music master edited the *Broadman Hymnal,* published in 1940 in both round and shaped notes, and more than eight million copies were in use by 1965. *The Baptist Hymnal,* which W. Hines Sims edited and issued in 1956, sold four million copies during its first eight years.

A Baptist layman of Dallas, Texas, Robert H. Coleman, encouraged by his pastor, George W. Truett, and assisted for several years by McKinney, became the greatest single hymnic influence among the Southern Baptists between the two world wars. From 1909 to 1935, Colman published thirty-three collections of hymns, including the highly popular book *The Modern Hymnal* and the equally successful volume *The American Hymnal.*

Rauschenbusch's Record in Translating

All Baptists have engaged in worship by song, but probably none more unanimously than the German Baptists, who have a long heritage of singing. Paul Wengel says in the centenary history of his group in North America, "If they could do nothing else, they sang. They sang in their homes around the family altar or at family social gatherings. They would sing when they had their picnics (*Ausfluege*). In fact, these excursions to some natural beauty spot were nothing if not an opportunity to sing. Many churches had a band, which would lead the parade into the open. There would always be time for singing, if not directed, surely spontaneous."[1]

At no time of the year was singing more popular with the Baptists of German descent than at Christmas. All the world became richer for sharing two festal songs from Germany: "Silent Night" by Franz Gruber, and "Away in a Manger," Martin Luther's cradle song. The children of German Baptists were taught to sing hymns from memory, and adults half a century later could sing four stanzas of children's hymns which still had significance for them.

Among German Baptists in America, hymn translators had an important role to play. They put into English the best they could find from their native language. One of the most effective hymn translators was Walter Rauschenbusch. Of 272 translations in one German hymnal, 137 carried his signature—probably a record for translations without parallel. Rauschenbusch used simple but picturesque words. He was a master of German idioms and used them with telling effect in his many translations.

The last German hymnal of North American Baptists, *Neue Glaubensharfe,* was chiefly the product of Professor Herman von Berge, whose entire musical education consisted of ten lessons from a fifteen-year-old boy when Herman was sixteen. His instrument was an old melodeon. His only practice time was evenings because he had to work all day. He used a silent keyboard, since his family's home was small and he could not disturb their rest in upstairs bedrooms. He published more than 200 anthems for church choirs.

Marian Anderson

Negro Baptist churches have used music most effectively to win and hold their young people for a spiritual emphasis. Their choirs have also discovered countless talented voices and their singing leaders have encouraged those with special musical ability to enter professional careers.

On his annual visit to Philadelphia for a concert at the Union Baptist Church, Roland Hayes once found himself sharing honors with a little contralto by the name of Marian Anderson. So impressed was Mr. Hayes with the quality of the voice and the sincerity of the message in song that he urged Mrs. Anderson, the widowed mother, to give her daughter voice training. He began to mention Marian to those who asked him for suggestions for soloists.

The eldest of three daughters in her family, Marian lost her father, as Hayes did, in childhood and, like him, she was reared by a devout, self-reliant mother. She was taken to church every Sunday and when six years old she was enrolled in the junior choir of the church. The choir director asked Marian and a playmate in the choir to learn "Dear to the Heart of the Shepherd," a hymn, to sing as a duet. He played the melody through for the girls, and they rehearsed it carefully. The next Sunday they performed it for the main service at church. This was Marian Anderson's debut.

Marian grew up with a conscious love of singing. When she was eight, the family acquired a piano from relatives who weren't using it, and she began to pick out melodies with one finger. Marian's aunt, who sang in the senior choir, arranged to sing duets with the child. A struggling store-front church in Philadelphia announced a benefit concert for its building fund, with the aid of the Union Church choir member. Marian knew nothing about it until on her way to the grocery store she picked up a handbill carrying her picture with the invitation, "Come and hear the baby contralto."

Living for a time in her grandmother's home, Marian had the use of an old-fashioned organ. She continued to sing, and in the school choruses she was given occasional solo parts. When the family could afford it, she received piano lessons. She was active in B.Y.P.U. and enjoyed making speeches, but music was her chief interest in both church and school. At thirteen she joined the adult choir, staying with the junior choir as director until she was past twenty.

Marian Anderson was the first Negro to win top prize in the Philadelphia Philharmonic Society's annual auditioning. With more training she began to be in demand for concerts outside Philadelphia, but like Hayes she toured the capitals of Europe before she won recognition at home. She also toured Latin America, the first Negro woman to appear in concerts in many of the cities of that area. In New York Miss Anderson presented a sacred concert on Easter Sunday in the Metropolitan Opera House and sang with the New York Philharmonic orchestra at Lewisohn Stadium.

Coming into national prominence, Marian Anderson was booked for a concert in March 1939 in Constitution Hall in Washington, D.C., an auditorium owned by the Daughters of the American Revolution. Shortly before the day of the concert she was informed by her business manager that her use of Constitution Hall had been canceled. Soon afterward Miss Anderson was surprised to receive an invitation from Secretary of the Interior Harold L. Ickes, to give a concert on April 9, Easter Sunday, on the steps of the Lincoln Memorial in Washington. She was even more surprised to be given home hospitality by the former governor of Pennsylvania, Gifford Pinchot, in a city whose major hotels were not yet open to Negroes.

When Marian Anderson reached the Lincoln Memorial on that Easter Sunday she was overwhelmed with emotion at the sight of the crowd. After singing the national anthem Miss Anderson sang "Ave Maria," "Gospel Train," "Trampin'," and "My Soul Is Anchored in the Lord." She sang in Constitution Hall many times afterward, including a concert to benefit China relief. She was the first Negro to sing as a regular member of the Metropolitan Opera Company. She and her husband retired to a home in Connecticut.

By popular demand, Miss Anderson sang one spiritual more frequently than any other number, "He's Got the Whole World in

His Hands." It was brought to her attention by Marian Kirby, collector of folk songs of American Negroes and mountain people. In many concerts, even where her audiences did not understand English, she was called back to repeat this spiritual. Marian Anderson explained: "I chose it not alone because I thought the audience would like it, but because it has a cry, an appeal, a meaning to me. It is more, much more, than a number on a concert program."[2]

Mahalia Jackson

Generally billed as the world's greatest gospel singer, Mahalia Jackson owed her inspiration to Marian Anderson. Born in 1911 in New Orleans, Mahalia was the daughter of a man who was a stevedore by day, a barber by night, and a Baptist preacher on Sunday. She was singing by the time she was five. Losing her mother when she was six, Mahalia was raised, as she expressed it, in a Baptist church. Singing with the congregation, she felt at home. All around she could hear the feet tapping and the hands clapping, and that gave her what she called bounce.

Mahalia went to school through the eighth grade. After that she used the Bible as a teacher. At seventeen she moved to Chicago to live with an uncle and aunt, and worked at various jobs. She joined the Greater Salem Baptist Church where she remained a member through her active career. At Greater Salem Mahalia Jackson began her gospel-singing concerts. She conducted songfests in many Baptist churches, and made several cross-country tours in the early 1930s. In every audience there were those who urged her to take up blues singing, but she declared she would not. "I knew that wasn't the life for me. Blues are the songs of despair. Gospel songs are the songs of hope. When you sing gospel, you have a feeling there is a cure for what's wrong; when you're through with the blues, you've got nothing to rest on," Mahalia explained. She also avoided jazz as not worthy of a gospel singer.

In 1946 a recording of "Move On Up a Little Higher" called wide attention to Mahalia Jackson's gospel songs. By 1963 this record had sold two million copies, and many other successful ones were on the market. In 1950 Miss Jackson made her first appearance at Carnegie Hall, New York, and she appeared there many times afterward. In 1952 she won a prize from the French Academy of Music for her recording of "I Can Put My Trust in Jesus." When she went to Paris to receive the award, she gave a concert and received twenty-one curtain calls. She later toured Europe and the Holy Land.

Recalling the reception given her concert in Tel Aviv, Israel, Miss Jackson reported: "They may not accept my Lord Jesus, but they certainly accepted my songs and his gospel when I sang about it." In the Berlin Sportspalast, Miss Jackson received an ovation that was second only to the one given Hitler when he spoke there in 1938. When she was informed of that, she shuddered. "Hitler stood in that spot and talked to the people and made war. I stood there twenty-three years later, and I hope that I was able to talk peace and the love of God."[3]

When she was not on tour or engaged in community relations projects, Miss Jackson found her way to small, obscure meeting houses of her people, declaring that the humble churches were her spiritual filling stations. Her reason was simple, and she expressed it in these words: "The Lord took me when I was nothing and he put me up. If the Lord can bring me this far, he can do as much for others." Like Marian Anderson, Mahalia Jackson sang in front of the Lincoln Memorial, to 200,000 people who had taken part in a civil rights march.

Miss Jackson had her critics, the most severe of which were among Negro Baptist leaders, who said she commercialized her religion for profit. She admitted the profit, but added: "I believe I have a mission to sing for people." And this she did, until she drew her last breath on January 27, 1972.

XXIV

BILLY GRAHAM

Bright Star in the Evangelical Sky

Until long after the turn into the twentieth century most Baptists considered that an annual revival, often called the protracted meeting, was necessary for the spiritual health of the church. In rural areas the revival meetings occupied a week or two in the summer, after the crops had been laid by; in the cities the revival usually came in the winter season, when there were fewer distractions to fill the evenings of church goers than in summer. Whatever the season, the protracted meeting was a time for the saints to gain spiritual refreshment from praise, prayer, and preaching, and for the sinners to quit wicked ways and join the ranks of the believers.

Just as in pioneer days any man could become a Baptist preacher by announcing himself one, starting to preach, and inducing a church to ordain him, so self-appointed evangelists roamed the Baptist preserves hunting churches in which to hold their revivals. They accepted the hospitality of the local pastor and his members, happy if they could count a substantial number of converts and additions to the congregation, along with reviving the spirits of any laggard church members. They left with a "love offering" raised by the congregation at the last service. If high enough in the ranks of recognized evangelists, the preacher would bring his own song leader, or a local singer might have charge of the music.

Like a meteor in the religious sky of the early twentieth century came Billy Sunday, former baseball player from Chicago. He had with him his helpmate "Ma" Sunday and his handsome bachelor song leader and trombone player, Homer Rodeheaver. He built big wooden tabernacles with aisles covered with sawdust, and after his stirring sermons unnumbered thousands of converts "hit the sawdust trail" (as Sunday himself expressed it). Billy Sunday was not a Baptist, but in two ways he definitely influenced Baptist history: He prompted many young Baptist ministers to seek the roadways as traveling evangelists, and he opened the eyes of Baptist leaders of all varieties to the importance of giving some guidance to their churches in the selection of evangelists and planning their meetings for the greatest benefit to the congregations.

From the first decade of the present century, departments of evangelism were organized in most major Baptist bodies, to co-ordinate plans for revival meetings and for continuous evangelism under leadership of the pastors. In the Southern Baptist Convention, the Reverend W. W. Hamilton developed a systematic plan. It called for simultaneous revival services in the churches of larger cities, whereby every Baptist church in the area that would co-operate scheduled special preaching services with a local or out-of-town evangelist. The plan was adopted by many state and national conventions of Baptists, and departments of evangelism became a definite division of denominational work.

Many churches, however, while honoring the ritual of revival, came to place greater dependence upon a continuous enlistment of children and youths of church families. The young people attended instruction classes led by the pastor and were thus led into believer's baptism and church membership.

During World War II, when the energies, incomes, and manpower of the American people were being thrown into winning the global conflict, many Baptist leaders, and Protestant officials generally, assumed that the day of mass evangelism was past. The idea was strengthened during the immediate postwar period when indifference toward spiritual matters became the mood. A dynamic young ministerial student of fundamentalist leanings thought differently. He was Billy Graham.

Baptist morale in the twentieth century got a tremendous boost when Billy, still young and dynamic but nationally known as an evangelist, chose to identify himself with Southern Baptist people.

It was the largest body of evangelical Christians in the world, he said, who had consistently supported mass evangelism and he felt he belonged with them.

Conversion in a Tent

Native of the piedmont area of North Carolina, son of a dairy farmer, reared in the Associate Reformed Presbyterian church, young Graham and his pal Grady Wilson sauntered into a tent revival meeting conducted by the Reverend Mordecai Ham one summer evening. It was not religion they sought, but rather relief from boredom. On the second night they attended with seriousness of purpose, and Billy walked down the aisle as a convert with Grady close behind him.[1]

Billy, whose full name is William Franklin Graham, Jr., knew right away that he could not be content to be a pew warmer. If God wanted him at all, it was for something all-consuming, and that probably meant preaching. At any rate, the thing to do immediately was to go to school. Billy went through public high school at Charlotte, then on to Bob Jones College in Tennessee, an institution now located in Greenville, South Carolina. Later he enrolled at Florida Bible Institute, Tampa. In both schools, and during summer vacations, Billy heard the evangelists of his day. He studied their sermons, their appeals, their results, like a man who was looking for the ideal pattern to follow. He encountered such successful professional evangelists as the Reverend J. Harold Smith of Spartanburg, South Carolina. More and more Billy Graham felt called to the field of preaching for decisions. His first few attempts in the pulpit were agony. The right words did not seem to come. At street preaching somehow he felt more at home. He kept trying, and he kept studying.

Off to Illinois to enroll at Wheaton College, the young preacher had to work his way through school and invested in a truck for an extracurricular hauling business. After a year at Wheaton he had so many engagements to preach that Billy no longer needed to engage in trucking to pay his fees. But something in the way the lithe, six-four-three-inch sophomore with a soft southern accent moved furniture, and the way he could hold a congregation caught the attention of dark-eyed Ruth Bell, daughter of missionaries to

China. Billy Graham soon began dating the coed, one of three girls born to Dr. and Mrs. Nelson Bell.

After a banquet for Wheaton alumni fifteen years later, the evangelist said of his wife:

"What a wonderful girl. She looks twenty-five instead of thirty-five. I remember the autumn day when I was introduced to her. The light in her face! I had been told she was a woman who got up at five every morning to pray. She still gets up ahead of any of the rest of us to spend time alone with God."

After graduation Billy was in much demand to speak for meetings of Youth for Christ, and he traveled for the organization, backed by funds from the inventor and manufacturer of earth-moving machinery, the Christian lay speaker Robert G. LeTourneau. After a rally in a suburban New York church in 1946, Billy accepted a ride on the LeTourneau business plane to another rally in Lincoln, Nebraska. A writer for a national magazine (the coauthor of this work) was aboard the same flight. The writer and the youthful preacher soon got acquainted as they flew west.

"And what do you expect to do in life?" the writer asked Billy.

"I plan to be an evangelist," he said with enthusiasm. "I believe that this nation is ripe for a great religious revival. In fact, I believe that the whole world is ready for a great spiritual awakening. I'd like to be the one to help start it."

Billy Graham's associates date the story of his crusades back to 1947, when he held a series of meetings in Grand Rapids, Michigan, with a total of 6,000 persons in attendance and 500 coming forward as "inquirers." In November of that year, he held a two-week revival in his home town, Charlotte, North Carolina, and found his attendance climbing to 42,000 with 1,200 inquirers.

Billy Graham's faith in himself and in God's will for his mission carried him into revival meetings that grew with each engagement in cities all over the country. During the next four years, Billy held two crusades in 1948, four in 1949, six in 1950, and eight in 1951. He added Cliff Barrows to his evangelistic team as song leader, George Beverly Shea as soloist, and other personnel as advance agents and field representatives. The cities visited during that four years of crusades and rallies included Miami; Los Angeles; Boston; Columbia, South Carolina; Portland, Oregon; Atlanta; Memphis; and Hollywood, California. He preached in scores of cities and towns on tours of New England and the southern states. More than four million persons had attended his meetings by the end of 1951, and almost 90,000 men, women, and young people had come forward at his invitation to seek Christ.

In early 1951 *Time* magazine recognized the unusual quality of Graham's preaching, and his effective approach to big, worldly, blasé Los Angeles and Hollywood. There was something more than showmanship, the reporter declared, about this young man's preaching from the Bible and the ready response of hundreds of persons, of all ages and of all social and economic backgrounds, who came forward at his invitation to make a decision for Christ.

At the Columbia, South Carolina crusade, the evangelist met a crisis. After the final service, when the team member who usually took care of the offering asked Billy to get it to the hotel for safekeeping until the banks opened, he agreed. An alert newsphotographer back stage caught Graham in the act of carrying a heavy bag of cash from the stadium.

The picture was run on page one. It seemed to spell out the damaging falsehood that Billy Graham was getting rich off his preaching. In desperation the young preacher put in a long distance call to a new friend, the Reverend Jesse R. Bader, in the stewardship department of the National Council of Churches.

"What can I do to save my ministry?" he pleaded.

Dr. Bader lost no time telling him. "Put yourself on a salary, Billy, and let the world know you are not in evangelism for the money."

From that time, the offerings at Billy Graham crusade services were handled with scrupulous care, full audit made locally, and publicized through the press. All funds were turned over to the evangelistic association with headquarters at Minneapolis, and Billy and all his team members drew salaries and necessary expenses from that source. On a sound financial footing, Billy also developed methods for the orderly conduct of his meetings—recruitment of choir members, training for counselors of those who responded to his invitations, organization of ushers, a press-relations specialist experienced enough to handle any news angle, skill in dealing with fire and police regulations. Perpetuating the impact of the crusade for each one who made a profession of faith is a subscription to *Decision,* a slick tabloid published monthly by the Billy Graham Evangelistic Crusade in the Minneapolis office. With news photographs in color, devotional messages, and a Billy Graham sermon, this handsome periodical had reached Volume 20 in 1979.

Invading the Capital

In the autumn of 1951, Billy Graham's advance workers arrived in Washington to see if it was possible to arrange a crusade in the nation's capital. While some of the leaders of the city had heard of him, Graham was not universally accepted as a God-called evangelist. In a cosmopolitan city like Washington, to many church leaders mass evangelism seemed highly improper. Graham's emissaries had difficulty selling the idea and enlisting local personnel.

They found one Baptist pastor, the Reverend J. W. Carpenter, pastor of the Metropolitan Baptist Church, who was willing to lead the crusade. Carpenter recommended as cochairmen two Baptist members of the House of Representatives, one a Democrat from Tennessee, the other a Republican from Missouri. Both accepted the responsibility. The three men set out to enlist the support of Washington's Protestant pastors.[2]

"Sorry, our church calendar is already full!" was a stock reply. "Billy Graham—who's he?" was a frequent query.

One minister gladly joined the committee: the Reverend W. H. Jernigan, veteran leader of the National Baptist Convention in the nation's capital. He promised the support of the Negro Baptists for Billy. "I know our people in Washington need a revival," he said. "And I think some white churches need it, too!"

When about a dozen pastors and laymen had been enlisted, Billy Graham himself met with them. He exuded confidence in the success of his forthcoming assault upon the forces of evil in Washington, and asked for the advice and the questions of his local committee.

"What'll you do with colored people who attend these meetings?" asked one of the members, a white minister. Billy was thoughtful a moment.

"I will do what Jesus would do if he were holding the crusade. I will welcome everyone, regardless of color."

Never before that crusade in January 1952 had America's capital city seen a major revival campaign opened to everybody without regard to racial origin. For the first time in their lives, some ministers and many church members of the District of Columbia participated in a racially inclusive worship service, where Negroes sang in the choir, served as ushers, took up the offering, and helped as counselors on a par with white Christians. No one publicly complained or objected.

Also, for the first time in their lives, many persons in the audiences, which averaged about 14,000 during this first Billy Graham crusade in Washington, clasped hands with leaders of churches of other faiths in the common evangelistic effort. Pastors who had been wary of this venture saw the armory filling an hour before the time of the service, and heard the wholehearted song services of the choir led by Cliff Barrows. George Beverly Shea stirred their souls with solos in his rich baritone, preparing the way for the simple, hopeful messages of the man who believed completely in what he said, because, as he kept repeating, "The *Bible* says—"

Still some criticisms of Billy and his methods were heard. One Washington minister who had co-operated with the crusade, the Reverend Clarence W. Cranford, pastor of Calvary Baptist Church and later president of the American Baptist Convention, answered the critics with this statement from the pulpit:

"Some question whether the converts of Billy Graham's revivals will stick with their Christian profession and the church. The same question was raised about Billy Sunday's converts. The answer is that some may not but many will. I know one man converted under Billy Sunday's preaching who was true to his profession of faith. He was my father."

Before the crusade was over, numerous members of the Senate and the House of Representatives were being seated on the platform at the armory, and were gladly taking part in Billy's ministry to the nation's most influential city.

By now Billy was sure that his special mission under God's leadership needed the full backing of a group who had never doubted the validity and the significance of mass evangelism. Of 30,000 Southern Baptist churches, which one should he affiliate with? Many pastors and some laymen have questioned Dr. Graham's motive in going all the way to Dallas to put his name on the church roll of the largest white Baptist congregation in the world, the First Baptist Church, made famous by George W. Truett, its pastor for half a century. It is far from his North Carolina home. Billy pledged his tithe as an offering through that church. He made it a point to be on hand to preach at least one Sunday a year.

A Busy Schedule

But a man who travels the world cannot be expected to punch the denominational clock in Sunday school and Church Training Union. On his first revival campaign overseas, with London as the center, Graham became an international figure. Within a year he was so swamped with invitations to hold revivals at home and abroad that he began scheduling them two and three years in advance. Baptists, proud of their priority with him, sought to build every national conference and convention with Billy Graham as the great drawing and holding card. At the Baptist world congresses in Rio de Janeiro in 1960 and in Miami Beach in 1965, he packed athletic stadiums with from 150,000 to 200,000 people.

It was understandable that Billy Graham's popularity with the masses would attract the interested attention of politicians, great and small. Anyone who can draw 200,000 people to hear him speak is considered worth studying and cultivating. The noted evangelist met the public figures half way, without seeking them out or fawning upon them. He was the principal speaker at the first Presidential prayer breakfast, in February 1953, sponsored by the Christian Leadership Conference in Washington, at which President Dwight D. Eisenhower was honor guest, and he spoke at every subsequent annual prayer breakfast honoring Presidents Kennedy and Johnson. He was a frequent guest and golfing partner of both Kennedy and Johnson, and of Richard M. Nixon when he was the nation's Vice-President. On state occasions, Ruth Graham graciously shared the event.

Graham was besieged by leaders of both major political parties to endorse their candidates in 1960 and 1964, with the accurate appraisal that such an endorsement would sway countless votes. Graham refused, politely but firmly, pointing out that whoever was elected chief executive of the United States would need his help in maintaining the nation's moral and spiritual strength. President Lyndon B. Johnson evidently agreed, for he had Billy Graham come for a special religious service at National City Christian Church on the morning of his inauguration, January 20, 1965, an event covered fully by all news media. In his sermon at this service the modern prophet reminded the President, Vice-President Hubert H. Humphrey, other dignitaries of the administration and their wives:

"In foreign affairs we are faced with overwhelming problems, from Southeast Asia to the Congo. In domestic affairs we are faced with an alarming crime rate, a moral crisis, and many individual psychological problems. These problems may become more intense and demanding during the next four years . . . I know the leaders of this administration well enough to know that they believe that our problems are basically spiritual and that they require a spiritual solution. That spiritual solution was outlined by God to King Solomon long ago in the words, 'If my people, which are called by my name, shall humble themselves, and pray, and seek my face, and turn from their wicked ways; then will I hear from heaven, and will forgive their sin, and will heal their land.' To approach the problems of the next four years in a spirit of prayer and humble dependence on God would bring a freshness of vision and purpose that could capture the imagination of the world."[3]

The procedures for a Billy Graham campaign in any city have been standardized for efficiency and for maximum public appeal: ample announcements in all media, local and national, of the forthcoming crusade; selection of a Billy Graham campaign committee, composed of outstanding ministers and lay leaders of the community; a series of prayer and dedication services in spiritual preparation for the event; enlistment of singers for the choir, counselors for those who come forward, and ushers for the meetings; and continued publicity leading up to the arrival of the evangelistic team.

For Billy Graham's crusade in Kansas City, Missouri, in September 1978, for the first time a black minister served as general chairman. He was the Reverend John W. Williams, pastor of St. Stephen Baptist Church. Many black ministers and laymen have served as members of local evangelistic teams for the Graham meetings.

Much of 1955 was spent in crusades and shorter rallies in foreign countries, including Scotland, England, France, Switzerland, Germany (where Dr. Graham toured U.S. military bases), the Netherlands, Norway, Sweden, Denmark, and Canada. An estimated total of more than four million people attended these crusades with more than 115,000 coming forward as inquirers.

In sixteen weeks of crusades in New York City, May to September 1957, 2,397,400 persons heard Billy Graham's evangelistic message. In 1958 Dr. Graham's Caribbean tour reached a million persons in attendance. The next year Billy was in Australia and New Zealand, preaching to a total of 3,362,240 hearers. In 1960 he toured many countries of Africa, from Liberia to Ethiopia and Egypt, then to the Holy Land. The evangelistic team came back for another crusade in Washington, then went to Rio de Janeiro and to several European countries. Since that year, Dr. Graham has held crusades in at least fifty important cities in the United States and again in scores of foreign cities. In Seoul, Korea, in one week's crusade, he spoke to more than three million people, with 72,000 coming forward at his invitation.

One of the outstanding accomplishments of Billy Graham's career as a world religious leader was his sponsorship of the World Congress on Evangelism in the Congresshalle at West Berlin, Germany, October 24–November 4, 1966. With him as cosponsor was Carl F. H. Henry, editor of Christianity Today, who originated the idea and passed it on to Graham to activate. A total of about 1,250 delegates and observers from more than a hundred countries assembled for the first ten days of discussion of plans and programs to extend the influence of the Evangelical faith throughout the world. Graham reminded his fellow leaders of evangelism, in this the greatest meeting of its kind in the twentieth century, that modern evangelism must concern itself with two major fields: the great cities and the student world.

He said: "Church historians of the future may indeed write that true evangelical ecumenism was born here in Berlin."

To the Ends of the Earth

In 1977 Billy Graham penetrated the iron curtain of Communist control with his preaching. The first such country was Hungary, in September. He reported that his campaign in Budapest and its environs was a success, with the people eager to hear the message of the gospel.

Dr. Graham encountered some criticism, however, from Hungarian-American Christian leaders because of certain circumstances in connection with his being invited to hold a crusade in that country and the restrictions placed upon the crusade itself. A leading official of the Hungarian Baptist Union of America and writer for the *Gospel Messenger,* a publication of that organization, declared:

"When the government of Hungary invited Dr. Graham to hold a crusade in that country, it had political and economic aims. The government leaders knew that Dr. Graham's fame could be used to improve the image of the Communist regime.

"Since Hungary officially is a Communist country, and therefore an atheistic country, and since such religious practices like open evangelistic meetings with invitations to accept Christ are forbidden, the problem was how to counteract the expected impact of Graham on the Hungarian people. It was decided that the economic-political advantages would outweigh the ideological disadvantage. Still they had to minimize the effect of Dr. Graham's personality and message as much as they could."

In October 1978, Dr. Graham went again to an Eastern European nation, Poland, with an evangelistic crusade. In that country, predominantly Roman Catholic in religion and under the Soviet Union's political control, Billy Graham preached to about 25,000 people at nine churches in six cities. The meetings brought Roman Catholics and Protestants together, worshiping under the same roof. As one of his principal themes, Graham stressed the responsibility of Christian people for world peace, a subject that drew an emotional reaction from many listeners. The Polish people were the victims of the joint decision of Hitler of Nazi Germany and Stalin of the Communist Soviet Union to divide and conquer their country.

Dr. Graham preached to about a total of 6,500 in meetings in a Catholic church in Katowice. He preached in Krakow, the home city of a Catholic cardinal, whose selection as the new Pope John Paul II was announced soon after the Graham meetings had ended. Instead of asking inquirers to come forward at the close of his message, the evangelist asked them to raise their hands. Graham's associates estimate that at least 1,000 persons responded.

"I would like to preach the gospel to as many people as possible all over the world. I want to see how the Christian church exists in socialist [Communist dominated] societies and to help build bridges between the peoples of the world."

On an eight-week tour of India and the Far East, Billy Graham preached to a total of 800,000 people. During September 1978 Dr. Graham held crusades in Oslo, Norway, and in Stockholm, Sweden.

On through one crusade after another Billy Graham's meetings have drawn millions of people to hear his message of "good news." They have made Dr. Graham recognized as the foremost Christian evangelist of this age, eclipsing the accomplishments of the late, great Billy Sunday in winning masses of people to accept Christ and affiliate with the church of each convert's preference.

Billy Graham's association officials estimate that, as of September 1978, this evangelist has addressed in person a total of 87,197,764, and that between two and three million have received counseling from members of his team during the crusades. At the beginning of 1979, Dr. Graham could humbly say that he had had the opportunity to preach personally to more people, in more countries of the world, than any other person in history.[4]

On Tuesday, November 6, 1978, Dr. Billy Graham turned sixty years of age. At a dinner honoring his four decades of preaching, Billy said:

"I expect to continue my efforts to save human souls. I have no plans whatsoever to retire."

How can modern Christians, of all kinds and denominations, explain Billy Graham's success?

"He reminds me of Billy Sunday!" said an elderly man in a crusade congregation.

"He's so sincere!" remarked a young homemaker, who doubtless saw and heard in him the personification of all she wished her husband might be.

"He speaks with authority, and not as the theologians," said a counselor for those who were sure to respond to the message of the day.

Billy Graham has faced some cynical comments of some of his fellow ministers in America. Said one of the nation's most noted pulpiteers: "In my opinion, Billy Graham has set Christianity back a hundred years."

Asked in his news conference the next day to comment on this assertion, Billy Graham showed no signs of anger. "I suppose I've failed," he said. "It was my purpose to set it back nearly 2,000 years!"[5]

XXV

ECUMENISM—BAPTIST STYLE

*

The Baptist Meaning of Unity

There is an old Baptist saying that expresses the sentiments of many members of that denomination on the question of ecumenism—a movement seeking greater unity among the Christian bodies and their churches throughout the United States and the world. The saying runs: "We Baptists will walk along the spiritual road with the people of all other faiths—if they are going in our direction!"

For Baptists, ecumenism has grown to mean two things: first, unity within their own denomination, among the great variety of Baptists; second, unity with other denominations.

Unity likewise has two sides in Baptist thinking: first, movements toward organic union, or merger, with other Christian churches—which most Baptists have steadfastly avoided; second, co-operation in common tasks which have become the responsibility of churches of all names and kinds, both within the world-wide Baptist family and with non-Baptists as well—which most Baptists have supported heartily.

From the earliest colonial days, Baptists in the United States practiced unity with other faiths in the matter of standing for religious liberty. In the early days of the town of Philadelphia, Roman Catholics set up their first meeting house there. Some religious leaders protested to the town council that this was "contrary to the laws of England." Baptists, joined by Quakers, came to the defense of the right of Catholics to worship as they pleased, and the council took no action against them. When Jewish immigrants met persecution from the Dutch authorities on Long Island they moved into Rhode Island and found the haven of freedom that Baptists had established there. Baptists of New England contributed substantially to the interdenominational American Board of Commissioners for Foreign Missions before the Triennial Convention was formed in 1814. Throughout the nineteenth century, whenever a trumpet sounded the call to defend religious liberty, Baptists fell into battle line.

As the twentieth century progressed, in almost countless ways the leaders and worshipers in all Christian faiths began going in the same direction. They began closer co-operation in missionary activities on foreign fields to avoid overlapping and conflicting programs. They joined in fighting for better wages and working conditions for labor, and against the exploitation of women and children. They pooled their personnel and resources in numerous projects for social betterment, such as assistance for migrant workers, and in the 1950s, 1960s and 1970s for the protection of civil rights. They united to study and publicize policies intended to advance the building of a just and lasting peace. Many Baptists assumed leading roles in these expressions of unity.

The Northern Baptist Way

Especially was ecumenism, by way of co-operation, a goal of the Northern Baptists. In 1908, one year after the Northern Baptist Convention was formed, it became a founding member of the Federal Council of Churches in America, an organization that brought together in numerous activities several major denominations. Two years later the Baptist Foreign Mission Society sent representatives to the International Missionary Conference, held at Edinburgh, Scotland, with full backing of the convention.

In 1938 the World Council of Churches was formed, at Utrecht, Holland, and ten years later its first assembly brought together at Amsterdam representatives of 150 Christian denominations from forty-four nations. In 1950 the Federal Council of Churches joined several other ecumenical groups to form the National Council of Churches of Christ in the United States of America.

Support of the Federal Council and its successor was never unanimous among Baptists. Vigorous criticisms of the organization have erupted time and again in the annual sessions of the Northern Baptist Convention, as leaders of fundamentalist churches and groups tried to vote the body out of affiliation with it. This conflict was a principal factor in the withdrawal of many churches from the Northern Baptist Convention to form the General Association of Regular Baptists.

In 1948 a special committee of the convention, headed by the Reverend Edward H. Pruden, outstanding Baptist pastor and leader of Washington, D.C., reported recommendations designed to assure the autonomy of each local Baptist church supporting the councils of churches, "while maintaining our denomination's rightful place in co-operative Christianity." The report definitely committed Northern Baptists to continue affiliation and support of the National and the World Councils of Churches.

While remaining steadfastly affiliated with the Councils of Churches, the American Baptist Convention has sometimes used its Baptist prerogative to disagree with council policies. Usually, disagreement has involved foreign affairs. At the annual convention meeting in 1959 a resolution was presented calling for careful consideration of a report of a study conference sponsored by the National Council of Churches during the previous year. The report favored establishing official recognition of the People's Republic of China and its admission to membership in the United Nations. A substitute for the resolution was offered from the floor, calling upon American Baptists instead to support the United States policy of refusing recognition of and diplomatic relations with the Communist regime, and to support also the policy of the United States government and the United Nations of refusing a seat in the UN to the regime "so long as it remains an unrepentant aggressor." The substitute was adopted.

Scores of Baptist men and women, white and black, have occupied positions of leadership in the National and the World Councils of Churches, and hundreds more have served as officers and committee members of local councils in communities all over the United States. Dr. Edwin T. Dahlberg, Baptist pastor in St. Louis and former president of the American Baptist Convention, headed the National Council of Churches from 1955 to 1959. At the time of the 1964 Baptist Jubilee anniversary, R. H. Edwin Espy, Baptist layman, was serving as general secretary of the National Council; R. Dean Goodwin, general director of the Division of Communication of the General Council, American Baptist Convention, was a member of the National Council's Broadcasting and Film Commission; Mrs. John W. Bradbury, leader among American Baptist women, was national president of the Protestant Motion Picture Council.

In addition to the American Baptist Churches, the National Council of Churches in 1979 listed as members of its organization the National Baptist Convention, Inc., the National Baptist Convention of America, and the Seventh Day Baptist General Conference.

In 1978 the National Council of Churches elected a black Baptist from Americus, Georgia, as president. He was the Reverend M. William Howard, born in 1946, educated in the public schools of Georgia, and, after graduation from Princeton University, he was made executive director of the Reformed Church in America.

Mr. Howard's hometown, Americus, is only a few miles from the late Clarence Jordan's Koinonia Farm (now Koinonia Partners). Asked about his contact with the Farm during the violence caused by opposition to Jordan's interracial policies, Mr. Howard replied:

"It cannot be said that Dr. Jordan had any particular influence on my upbringing. For that, I must credit the Black community of Americus, Georgia. Of course, I knew of the existence of Koinonia and have met members of the Jordan family."

Where Were the Southern Baptists?

Conspicuous by its absence from this area of ecumenical activity has been the Southern Baptist Convention. Many of the churches affiliated with this largest body of Baptists have supported the work of the councils of churches, from the local to world level. What reasons prompted this convention officially to decline to join the councils-of-churches movement?

The reasons are both negative and positive. On the negative side is the resentment against the attitude of many who agitate for the movement. Some Southern Baptists smart under the epithet coined by the *Christian Century,* which won no subscribers by referring to the convention as "the problem child of the denominations." Many leaders of Christian interdenominational groups have made Baptists—and especially Southern Baptists—a favorite "whipping boy." While many Baptists are blissfully unaware of such treatment in modern times, still Baptists have long memories. They can remember the ecclesiastical bigots and the persecution suffered at the hands of Lutherans in Germany and Scandinavia, Anglicans in England, and Episcopalians in America, not to mention Roman Catholics in Latin America, France, and Italy.

In 1940 leaders of the World Council of Churches, representing most of the major denominations in the United States, sent an invitation to the Southern Baptist Convention to join the organization. The convention replied with thanks and this reminder: "Our convention has no ecclesiological authority. It is in no sense the Southern Baptist Church."

The reply pointed out that all the churches affiliated with the Southern Baptist Convention would disapprove of any attempted exercise of authority over them and added these words:

"In a world which more and more seeks centralization of power in industry, in civic government, and in religion, we are sensible of the danger of totalitarian trends that threaten the autonomy of all free churches. . . . Permit us to express the sincere desire of our hearts that the followers of Christ may all be one, not necessarily in name and in a world organization, but in spiritual fellowship."[1]

Another reason for refusal of Southern Baptists, in whatever area of the country they lived, to join the ecumenical movement by membership in the National and the World Councils of Churches has been their stern opposition to the political philosophies frequently expressed at meetings and conferences sponsored by these organizations to discuss subjects such as the United States' relation to Red China or, in 1966, the war in Vietnam. Apart from disagreeing with statements that many Southern Baptists consider leftist, radical, or even Communist-inspired, there are those, like the late Dr. H. H. McGinty, editor of the Missouri Baptist paper, *The Word and Way,* who questioned the general propriety of church gatherings venturing into discussion of politics. Doubtlessly expressing the overwhelming sentiment of Southern Baptists, McGinty asked this question:

"How can a group of religionists arrive at the conclusion that they are authorities in so many fields? In other areas, men who have given a lifetime to specialized study frequently are modest about the possession of superior knowledge. . . . In this country it would be resented if the state revealed any disposition to take over the control of the church. Is it any less reprehensible if the church undertakes to assume direction of the affairs of state?"[2]

Further emotional and psychological reasons for Southern Baptist refusal to join the councils of churches have often raised their heads. Many in the states of Old Dixie have considered these organizations as Yankee inventions. They have long been influenced by stories of the bitter humiliation of Reconstruction days, when Northerners exacted the penalty among southern people for slavery and the Civil War. In addition, the knowledge that they were once a despised minority, without rights and with little or no chance to secure justice, has colored the attitudes of many Southern Baptists.

If this appears to be slightly absurd, considering the time that has elapsed since the atrocities in Zurich and the oppression in Virginia, there was a more recent recollection. Baptists were denied the use of the only church sanctuary in Copenhagen, Denmark, large enough to hold the Baptist World Alliance at its 1947 congress in that city. The reason given by the state-supported church was that Baptist ministers were not truly ordained. Southern Baptists—and some others—asked: "If there is no equality, can there be spiritual unity?"

Dr. T. B. Maston, long-time professor of Christian ethics at Southwestern Baptist Theological Seminary, expressed the prevailing sentiment of the predominant body of Baptists in America at mid-century when he wrote:

"There is a danger in the ecumenical movement and in Christian groups in general, including local churches, that organizational strength will be considered a substitute for spiritual power. The church may need great unification but what she needs far more is a deepened sense of a divine mission, a clearer insight into the distinction between the church and the world, and a more deeply spiritual approach to the problems of the world."[3]

When Dr. J. B. Gambrell was president of the Southern Baptist Convention in 1919, this Texas Baptist and Confederate veteran had gladly endorsed the idea of admitting women as messengers to the Convention and had inaugurated other progressive reforms. But when the issue of joining the Interchurch World Movement came to a vote, he killed it with a double-edged comment:

"Southern Baptists do not ride a horse without a bridle! Furthermore, you cannot unite two bushes by tying their tops together!"

Baptist Co-operation

Despite this historic attitude on the part of the Southern Baptist Convention, this largest body of Baptists has a long and solid record of co-operation both within the denomination and with other Christian churches. As far back as 1889 Dr. John A. Broadus, who helped establish the Southern Baptist Theological Seminary in 1859 and taught at the institution for thirty-six years, gave the Yale Lectures on Preaching. Since that time countless other distinguished Southern Baptist ministers, educators, and journalists have given lectures and participated in conferences under religious auspices other than Baptist.

A striking example of Baptist leadership in interdenominational co-operation was given in the production of uniform Sunday school lessons, starting in 1921 when Dr. John R. Sampey became chairman of the International Sunday School Lesson Committee. This was a plan on the part of most of the major Protestant denominations to furnish an outline of study with the same subjects and Scripture passages for Bible classes. For fifty-seven years Sampey was a member of the faculty and for thirteen years chairman of the faculty of the Southern Baptist Theological Seminary; for forty-six of those years he served continuously as a member of the lesson committee. In 1937 Sampey was appointed the Southern Baptist representative to the Conference on Life and Work in Oxford, and also to the Conference on Faith and Order in Edinburgh, thus helping to lay the foundations for the development of the ecumenical movement.

Archibald T. Robertson, one of Sampey's students and later a colleague at the seminary, as a world-renowned Greek scholar and author made many contributions. As professor of New Testament Interpretation, he delivered the Stone Lectures at Princeton University two different years, and was Bible interpreter repeatedly at Northfield and at Winona Lake assemblies. Still recognized as a major contribution to the training of Christian ministers are Dr. Bob's *Big Grammar* and forty-four other books that included grammars, commentaries, and word pictures of New Testament characters. Dr. John Claypool, Southern Seminary graduate of 1957, pastor of Northminster Baptist Church, Jackson, Mississippi, was the preacher chosen by Yale Divinity School in 1979 for the Beecher Lectures at the annual convocation.

Among Southern Baptist leaders of the early twentieth century, Dr. I. J. Van Ness was an outstanding example of personal ecumenism. While giving nearly half a century of service to the Sunday School Board, he was an officer of the International Lesson Committee, the editors' section of the International Council of Religious Education (later the Division of Religious Education of the National Council of Churches), the Sunday School Editorial Association of the United States and Canada, the Sunday School Council of Evangelical Denominations, and the Executive Committee of the World Sunday School Association. Van Ness was easily recognized as the principal authority on Sunday school publications by all Protestant bodies in the United States.

Frank Hartwell Leavell, native of Mississippi who launched a denominational student movement in 1922, made a worthwhile contribution to the United Student Christian Council and was a popular member of the National Executives of Student Work.

Southern Baptists have contributed substantially every year to the American Bible Society since its founding, and the Baptist Foreign Mission Board sent representatives to the annual meetings of the Foreign Missions Conference of North America from 1893 to 1919, and from 1938 to 1950, for mutual benefit. The Baptists received valuable help on overseas problems of their missionaries, in the areas of health, transfer of funds, language instruction, transportation, diplomacy, taxes, and literature for adult converts.

The big business of publishing religious literature and books has brought about an indirect ecumenism for Baptists. Friendship Press of New York, the publishing arm of the Missionary Education Division of the National Council of Churches, has obtained its largest annual order for the books it publishes from the Baptist Sunday School Board for the fifty-eight bookstores under the board's control. The books have been used as auxiliary references for study courses mapped by the Missionary Education Council of the Southern Baptist Convention for all churches in that body.

Broadman books and supplies found a greater market when the term "Southern Baptist" was eliminated except for precise identification in legal and commercial labels. Vacation Bible school texts and craft materials, music for choirs of all grades, and church record equipment are non-sectarian, and the popularity of the products from the Nashville Baptist headquarters has encouraged the editors and designers to omit the propaganda. This policy expanded the usefulness of church materials among churches that had no publishing house of their own, and added to the profits of the Baptist publishing center.

The Consultation on Church Union

In the 1960s an inviting door was opened to Baptists that gave promise of leading them into what seemed like the peaceful shelter of union with several other denominations. The movement was called the Consultation on Church Union. It began with a notable sermon preached by Dr. Eugene Carson Blake, stated clerk of the United Presbyterian Church of the United States of America, in Grace Cathedral, San Francisco, a Protestant Episcopal church in which James A. Pike was consecrated a bishop. In his carefully worded sermon Dr. Blake declared that the time had come for Protestant Christians "to look toward the reunion of Christ's church."

Bishop Pike publicly endorsed the proposal. The result was an agreement to invite selected Protestant leaders to consult officially on the matter. The consultation was set up, in which the denominations of these two religious leaders, the United Presbyterians and the Protestant Episcopal Church, were joined by representatives of six other bodies by mid-1966. Already the trail of Christian organic union had been blazed by several outstanding mergers, particularly that of the major Methodist bodies of the United States, and by a more recent union of the Congregationalists and the

Evangelical and Reformed Church to form the United Church of Christ.

The only Baptists to give the invitation more than a polite "No, thank you!" were the leaders of the American Baptist Convention. It was a foregone conclusion that the traditional stand of Southern Baptists against such an involvement would remain unchanged. Understandable also was the attitude of the great majority of Negro Baptists in the United States, who have been happy to have and to hold their own well-earned identity as important members of the Baptist family. They had made their voice more than an echo of white Baptist programs, and they displayed no desire to lose, by amalgamating with other denominations, an identity that has given them status and responsibilities.

Although American Baptist leaders knew that the question of organic union was highly controversial they placed it before their church membership and on the agenda of their general council for consideration. Eighty professors on the faculties of American Baptist seminaries signed a petition addressed to the general council, urging that the convention's Division on Co-operative Christianity join the consultations.

Hundreds of letters poured into the American Baptist Convention headquarters at Valley Forge, Pennsylvania, some writers rejoicing that Baptists could now demonstrate their willingness to help reach the goal of a united Christendom, others heartily opposing the plan. Evaluating the replies, Dr. Edwin H. Tuller, general secretary of the convention, discovered that only about 17 per cent wished full participation in the consultation, while 70 per cent desired their convention to be represented only by observer-consultants. The Baptists were heavily influenced in their stand by an announcement in late 1965 from leaders of the consultation that "anyone who would come into the consultation as full participants at this point would have to be rather strongly committed to the agreements which we have reached so far."

The agreements already reached for the proposed united church were defined as including: some form of the episcopacy, with recognition of apostolic succession; acceptance of baptism of both infants and adults by various methods; a minimum common liturgy; and some form of creedal statement.

Most American Baptists interpreted these agreements as involving some sacrifice of principles highly cherished by all Baptists throughout their history. Since some form of episcopacy would be required in the new union of Christian churches, many a Baptist pointedly asked: "And what would Baptists do with a bishop? And what on earth could any bishop do with Baptists?"

Furthermore, there was almost unanimous opinion among the rank and file of Baptist members that the agreement on baptism of both infants and adults by various methods would pull the plug on every Baptist pool in the country, leaving high and dry a most fundamental Baptist tenet of all, believer's baptism by immersion.

Dr. Robert G. Middleton, pastor of Hyde Park Baptist Church, Chicago, led the forces within the denomination favoring participation in the consultation and ultimate organic union. He declared that the failure of American Baptists to join this movement was a serious defeat for those working for the union of Christian churches. He added: "American Baptists have turned down an opportunity to stay in the mainstream of American Protestantism. By the action of the General Council we are now relegated to a place among small sectarian groups. We could have been responsibly involved in an exciting venture of church union."[4]

Dr. Middleton's opinion was not shared by a majority of those attending the annual session of the American Baptist Convention in May 1966. A resolution presented to the meeting approved the action of the convention's general council in establishing a Commission on Christian Unity. An amendment to the resolution, which the convention adopted, stated that "for the further guidance of the commission" the convention reaffirmed its adherence to certain historic Baptist principles, which were spelled out, and then gave the commission these two added duties:

"We urge our Commission on Christian Unity to continue and if possible to increase every appropriate effort for greater unity with other Baptist bodies in the United States; and for greater unity with other free churches, in a federation or other co-operative organization that would involve no sacrifice of the New Testament principles which have been, and will ever be, the source and reason for our Baptist witness in the world."

Thus, Baptists demonstrated, as they have many times in their history, that while enjoying the unity resulting from countless programs of fellowship and co-operation with Christians of other names, they have never given up the privilege of deciding which road leads the ecumenical procession in the right direction.

The Great Southern Baptist Invasion

While closer unity became the goal among Baptist churches, one movement definitely drove a wedge between Southern and Northern (American) Baptists. It was the effort of Southern Baptists to establish churches, associations, and state conventions affiliated with their body, in every state of the nation. The movement gathered swift momentum during World War II. By 1964, the year that brought American and Southern Baptists together to celebrate the 150th anniversary of the Triennial Convention, Southern Baptist churches could be reported in all fifty states.

Beginning in 1894 there were comity agreements, some explicit and others implied, between Northern and Southern Baptists that in effect divided the United States into two areas. One was made up of the Old South and the border states, in which Southern Baptist churches were predominant, from Maryland to Texas and northward to Missouri and the Ohio River. All north and west of Dixie and its frontiers was considered a region open to the organization of churches and home mission work by Northern Baptists. In 1912 this comity agreement was restated, although an increasing number of Southern Baptist leaders expressed dissatisfaction.

Meanwhile, the agencies of the Southern Baptist Convention were going forward vigorously with their educational and organizational programs. Under the Baptist Sunday School Board in Nashville, "manuals" for Sunday schools and for Baptist Young People's Unions were being taught, and the best methods of church organization were studied and adopted. "Standards of Excellence" spurred attendance, contributions, and enlistments throughout all the churches of the Southern Baptist Convention.

The Foreign Mission Board, located in Richmond, Virginia, was sponsoring a most successful program of support of missions and recruitment of missionary personnel for service overseas. The Home Mission Board in Atlanta was expanding its financial services to assist in building new churches and church facilities in Southern Baptist areas.

State Baptist "assembly grounds," featuring training for young people in church membership, became annual outings for thousands of Baptists who combined vacations with church-sponsored study and activities. The steady tide of recruits for the ministry and the mission fields grew to require more seminaries for their training and higher academic standards for their degrees.

This Southern Baptist fervor expressed itself not only in expansion, but also in what many Northern Baptists considered attempts to dominate. In Missouri, for example, in 1919 state Baptist officials sponsored a movement to induce all Baptist churches to "align" with the Southern Baptist Convention, and the state convention led the way by such an alignment.

Came the Second World War and an unprecedented movement of southern workmen and their families into war industries of northern states. Men in military uniform were sent to all parts of the nation. They went from Atlanta to Chicago, from Charleston to Denver. They migrated from the rural South to duty posts from New England to California. Statistics of the Home Mission Board estimate that from the late 1930s at least 800,000 Southern Baptists had moved to the North. They carried their Southern Baptist customs and practices with them. Many found themselves at home in American Baptist congregations in their new communities. Many others did not; they found the hymns, the sermons, the Sunday school methods, and even the prayers different from the Southern Baptist worship to which they were accustomed. As expressed by the Reverend Blake Smith, pastor of the University Baptist Church of Austin, Texas, in an address to the American Baptist Ministers Council in May 1959:

"With us (Southern Baptists) the church is a primary center of social life. The ground is still mighty level in a Southern Baptist church. This feeling of belonging to one another is achieved through the forms and structures with which all of us are familiar and in which we all participate. The songs we sing and the manner in which we sing them; the loose and sometimes crude orders of service which we follow, or method of evangelism, with the long, drawn-out, and highly emotionalized invitation; the friendly atmosphere, the way we are organized up and down and sideways— all of these things constitute the external structures within which our people experience their oneness with Christ."[5]

Missing those familiar external structures, many Southern

Baptists preferred to meet in homes with fellow exiles from the South and have private worship than brave the uncertainty of Yankee churches. Some Southern Baptist congregations in the North started in just that way.

Officially, Southern Baptist leaders have contended that there was no invasion of Northern territory. They have explained that great areas of the North and West lay neglected by Baptists, and constituted a challenge to Southern Baptists to go in, establish churches, and possess the land. Two other reasons, shrouded in emotion and prejudice, have stood always in the background of the discussion: First, Northern Baptists have traditionally had ecumenical connections with councils of churches that advance policies with which Southern Baptists do not always agree. Second, most American Baptists have accepted as members of their churches persons who have been immersed by ministers who were not Baptists and have practiced "open communion" with church members of other faiths. Many Southern Baptists thought of these as heresies that could be corrected only by forming congregations that hold to what they considered the true faith.

Whatever the explanation, sponsoring new churches in every state of the nation became the official policy of the Southern Baptist Convention, through its Home Mission Board. The board furnished loans and grants to assist churches on Southern Baptist frontiers. The Reverend Courts Redford, executive secretary of the board, triumphantly reported the progress of the campaign for new churches at every annual session of the convention. His report to the 1964 session announced that a Southern Baptist church had been organized in Vermont—last of the fifty states to be entered by Southern Baptists—and that two thirds of the $4,065,000 spent by the board's missions division and most of $6,500,000 sent in loans to Southern Baptist churches, went to what Redford called the "newer areas"—meaning those outside the original territory of the South.

In 1979 Southern Baptists could count one hundred eighteen churches and chapels in New York State, all established within the preceding twenty-one years. Some of the congregations were worshiping in new meeting houses, some in refurnished structures, and others in rented quarters of apartment and office buildings. In answer to the question "Why are Southern Baptists in New York?"

the Reverend Paul S. James, director of the Metropolitan New York Baptist Association, declared: "We are here, primarily, because of the multitude of people who need Christ as their Savior from sin and the Lord of their lives. A burgeoning population, whole communities being built without churches, young people by the tens of thousands who have never heard an evangelical witness —these are the compelling needs."[6]

In some areas Southern Baptist churches were organized by ministers from distant states who made no effort even to meet the local American Baptist pastor, much less discuss with him the needs and problems of Baptists in that community. Resentment and friction inevitably resulted. On the other hand, many Southern Baptist churches were started in communities that Northern Baptists had indeed neglected. The Reverend James S. Eckles, pastor of the Baptist Community Church of Afton, Wyoming, affiliated with the American Baptist Convention, reported:

"I am happy to say that a Southern Baptist church is starting in Kemmerer, Wyoming, where there is no Baptist church. There is evident in this situation a real sense of Christian mission and teamwork. We hope it continues. American Baptists will not try to establish work there, since this Southern Baptist work is going well."[7]

Counterinvasion from the North

Something of a counterinvasion was launched by the Northern Baptist Convention when at its 1950 session it changed the name to American Baptist Convention, with a resolution that included these words: "Affirming, as we adopt the name American Baptist Convention, that we hold the name in trust for all Christians of like faith and mind who desire to bear witness to the historic Baptist convictions in a framework of co-operative Protestantism."

Eight years later the general council of the convention opened wide the door for Baptists in the South who were dissatisfied with the Southern Baptist Convention to affiliate with the American Baptist Convention, in a statement which declared that the body was ready "to proceed at the earliest possible moment to confer with any group of Christians of like faith and mind in the United

States of America without regard to geographical location, cultural, social, and racial background."

By May 1964 there were churches affiliated with the American Baptist Convention in Baltimore, Maryland; Richmond, Lynchburg, and Norfolk, Virginia; Dallas, Texas; Tulsa, Oklahoma; and St. Petersburg, Florida. Some of these churches were of predominantly Negro membership, affiliated also with one of the Negro Baptist conventions. American Baptist leaders recoiled from any suggestion that the challenge of the Southern Baptist invasion was being accepted by a counterdrive from the North. Rather, they explained, Baptist churches in the South that desired to express ecumenism and co-operation with other Protestant bodies should have some place to go.

Other Places to Go

Despite the rivalry between the two major predominantly white Baptist conventions, countless leaders among them, dedicated to greater unity among all Baptists and all Christians, have been working at the task since the turn of the century. In 1905 the Southern Baptist Foreign Mission Board reported to its convention that missionaries in China and Japan, sent by both Northern and Southern Baptists, hoped for a plan whereby these agencies would unite to supervise Baptist schools in those oriental lands. As a result, the two groups of Baptists agreed to operate the schools jointly, each with a half interest in the school property.

In 1911, committees representing the two conventions formulated a plan to quiet friction in the Territory of New Mexico stemming from a dispute as to which convention should organize churches in that area, and the following year they assigned New Mexico, with the consent of the Baptist churches of that territory, to the work of the Southern Baptist Convention.

Soon after the end of World War I, the Baptists of the District of Columbia exemplified the determination of many Baptists in the United States to create greater unity among the churches of the two largest white Baptist conventions. Traditionally supporting by dual alignment the work of both Northern and Southern Baptists, they joined in erecting the National Baptist Memorial Church, at a cost of about half a million dollars. This congregation's constitution states that the church must forever be affiliated with both conventions. Numerous other churches, particularly in the border states, have been aligned with both the Southern and the American Baptist conventions, while many of the Negro Baptist churches have affiliated with both the Southern Baptist Convention and one of the National Baptist conventions, or with American Baptist Churches and the Progressive National Baptist Convention.

In the 1950s Baptist women of most of the major bodies in the United States and Canada formed the North American Baptist Women's Union, for co-operative efforts in missionary work at home and abroad. Following the lead of the women, in the early 1960s officials of six Baptist groups on the North American continent founded the North American Baptist Fellowship. They included the American, Southern, Canadian, Mexican, and the incorporated National Baptist convention, and the Seventh Day Baptist General Conference. At the 150th anniversary celebration of the Triennial Convention in 1964, the fellowship proposed that an evangelistic campaign be launched in 1969 in both North and South America, to be called the Crusade of the Americas. In gaining acceptance of Southern Baptist participation the Reverend C. C. Warren, then a pastor of the First Baptist Church of Charlotte, North Carolina, and a former president of the Southern Baptist Convention, told the convention that the Crusade of the Americas did not contemplate an organization to control, or even to duplicate, programs already being supported by that body. He added: "This is not an attempt to drag Southern Baptists into an ecumenical movement or the World Council of Churches." Thus assured, Southern Baptists joined plans for the big campaign.

Robert G. Bratcher, "Good News for Modern Man"

"How would you like to do a translation for Southern Baptists?" an American Bible Society executive, Eugene A. Nida, asked Bob Bratcher, a research associate in the Translations Department at the New York office.

Dr. Nida showed Bob a letter from Wendell Belew of Atlanta, an official of the Home Mission Board of the Southern Baptist Convention, responsible for language missions. Home missionaries, it seems, were struggling to teach English to first- and second-generation Americans so they could learn to read the Bible for themselves. No Bible was simple enough for these new Americans.

Robert Galveston Bratcher went right to work on this project. His first draft of the Gospel of Mark so pleased the Society's board that the members urged Dr. Bratcher to follow the same style through all twenty-seven books of the New Testament. Bob ordered a copy of the 3,000-word list developed by the United States Information Service; he found it adequate except for a very few specialized terms.

When the whole manuscript was approved and ready for the press, an artist was enlisted. Annie Vallotton of Switzerland was the inspired choice. Her line drawings could illumine the text as could no other illustrations. Dr. Nida expected only a modest demand for the new translation, but the first 150,000 copies, priced 25¢ each, were gone in three months. The Bible Society, devoted to the distribution of Scripture, was now in the publication business. To cover printing costs only, the price was increased and another batch was ordered.

Immediately the Society began to receive requests for the Old Testament in the same style. Bob Bratcher and his team of specialists got down to work. It took nine years, but at last the Good News Bible was published, complete with its vivid line drawings by the Swiss artist. More than 55 million copies of the paperback have been sold, breaking all records for paperback sales worldwide.

Born in 1920 at Campos, Brazil, where his parents were Baptist missionaries, the Bible translator was educated in Rio de Janeiro and in his family's home state of Kentucky. He earned a bachelor's degree at Georgetown College in 1941, summa cum laude, and both master's and doctor's degrees in theology from Southern Baptist Theological Seminary, in Louisville. In 1944 he married June Heaton, a girl he met while he was on the staff at the Baptist summer assembly, at Ridgecrest, North Carolina.

Following a year in a pastorate in Indiana, young Bratcher served as a U. S. Navy chaplain for two years. Then in 1949, the Baptist Foreign Mission Board appointed the young Bratchers for Brazil where the elder Bratchers had served since 1918.

The South Brazil Baptist Seminary needed a professor of New Testament Interpretation; Bob accepted that assignment and was soon made dean of the institution. His first furlough was spent in Louisville as a visiting professor of New Testament at his Seminary alma mater. He chose to spend a year in graduate research in theology at Victoria University in Manchester, England, an experience which led directly to his career in the Translations Department of the Bible Society, beginning in 1957.

The Bible Society presented Dr. Bratcher a "Citation of Special Merit for his widely acclaimed translation of the New Testament in Today's English Version," in June 1967. The speech the honoree made on that occasion reveals the measure of the Christian scholar. In the midst of his colleagues at the Bible House on Broadway, he chose to express his gratitude for those who made it possible for him to achieve the honor.

Young Bratcher mentioned the grandfather whose first name was Bob's middle name: Galveston Bratcher—a farmer in Black Rock, Grayson County, Kentucky. There was Grandmother Bratcher who had given him ten sons and three daughters and "kept that farmhouse a home until she died at the age of eighty-four," still illiterate. Her ninth child became the missionary to Brazil, and Bob's father.

"The foundation upon which that home was built," Dr. Bratcher continued, "was faith in Jesus Christ and a deep love for the Bible." Then he quoted the late Lewis M. Bratcher's description of the daily experience in that farmer's Kentucky home:

> The sitting room was the place of meeting. There the old family Bible was brought out. Thank God it was never treated like another book. Thank God there was a reverence in its reading and in the treatment of it that left their impression on plastic minds and hearts. It was treated as the Word of God, as the message which the Father had sent to his children. Reverently it was opened and reverently the voice of the father, or of the one who had been chosen to read the message, told of the love of God and of his desire to make that love known.

In gratitude Dr. Bratcher then mentioned others: the professor of Greek and Latin at Georgetown (Baptist) College in Kentucky; Dr. William Owen Carver, professor of Missions, and Dr. William Hersey Davis, professor of New Testament, both of whom guided Bob's studies at the Louisville seminary.

Dr. Bratcher concluded his address with: "One finishes the translation and says to God, 'It's the best I can do. Forgive me!' "

The translations were done in the Bratcher home in Setauket, Long Island. After each day's work Bob brought to the dinner table the sheaf of pages written in longhand for the family's criticism. June Bratcher, teacher of sixth-graders, joined the three children in an honest, intelligent appraisal of the passages Bob had dealt with all day.

Says Dr. Nida of Bob Bratcher and his skills: "His rare combination of scholarship, wit, and personal devotion to the cause of Christ was the directive catalyst in our committee's work."

The children are now grown, and Bob and June Bratcher have moved south, making their home in Chapel Hill, North Carolina, the seat of the state University. In Nashville, Tennessee, on display in the archives of the Southern Baptist Convention is the symbolic 25 millionth copy of Today's English Version of the New Testament, the answer to a need first reported by Baptist home missionaries.

Nearly 60 million copies of the revised New Testament captioned "Good News for Modern Man," first published in 1966, were in circulation in 1979, according to *Christianity Today*. More than seven million copies of the Good News Bible, published in 1976, were sold in two years.

How Great Is the Difference?

One Baptist pastor, the Reverend Howard R. Stewart of Dover, Delaware, faced up to the question: How much actual difference in doctrinal opinions is there between American Baptists and Southern Baptists, as represented by pastors of local churches? To test the matter, Stewart sent a detailed questionnaire to Baptist pastors in Pennsylvania, a typical American Baptist state, and in Virginia, a stronghold of Southern Baptists. He asked such questions as "Do you believe in the Trinity?" "Do you believe in the deity of Jesus Christ?" "Do you believe the Bible is the inspired word of God?"

Replies from the two groups were remarkably similar. After computing an average on all his questions dealing with what Baptists consider orthodoxy in basic principles, Pennsylvania pastors made a score of 93.8 per cent, and Virginia pastors 96.3 per cent. Reporting the findings to Baptist publications, Stewart declared that the differences in theology between ministers in the two conventions were too negligible to hold them apart.

Outstanding example of Baptist unity in action came with the five-year program called the Baptist Jubilee Advance, which began in 1959 and culminated with the 150th anniversary celebration of the founding of the denomination, at Atlantic City, New Jersey, in May 1964. The movement started with a meeting of representatives of seven major Baptist bodies in North America, in which they frankly admitted some conscientious differences among themselves, but asserted their intent to band together in the five-year program.

"It cannot be denied," they agreed, "that unhappy tensions have at times barred relationships among Baptist bodies in North America, even when these bodies have affirmed their oneness in things essential and their membership in one great world family of Baptists. Neither can it be denied that at times one or another body has appeared to ignore the rights, feelings, and best interests of fellow Baptists. Not as competitors, but as compatriots; not in fear of one another, but with deeper faith in one another; not with jealousy, but with shared joy, Baptists of North America should march forward toward a nobler destiny."

During the Baptist Jubilee Advance, pastors and members of their churches met in study courses and discussions on such subjects as Baptist history and witness, stewardship and enlistment, church extension and leadership training, and world missions.

The Reverend James E. Mugg, pastor of University Heights Baptist Church, Springfield, Missouri, has a healthy point of view. Native of Oklahoma City, graduate of Wheaton College in Illinois and Northern Baptist Theological Seminary, with a doctor of ministries degree from McCormick Seminary in Chicago, he served the First Baptist Church of Wyandotte, near Detroit, Michigan, for nine years.

As senior minister of the Missouri congregation from April 1978, a church that affiliates with both the Southern Baptist Convention and the American Baptist Churches, supporting home and foreign missions through both channels, Dr. Mugg expressed optimism in these words:

"While it is clear that the old 'comity agreements' between the Southern Baptist Convention and the American Baptist Churches is at an end, I have faith to believe that a new spirit of brotherhood and co-operation between our two great bodies of Baptists is being revived. As we get to know one another better, and as we work and pray together in our agencies for mutual accomplishment of the task of spreading the Good News through all the world, the new spirit of unity among all Baptists will continue to grow."

XXVI

BAPTIST ALLIANCES

The Baptist World Alliance

They came into the big convention hall at Miami Beach, Florida, in late June 1965, 19,598 registered delegates from seventy-nine countries, from every continent of the world. Many were dressed in the colorful apparel of their homelands: Japanese, Chinese from Hong Kong, Africans from the Congo and other newly independent regions of that continent; delegates from Taiwan, Australia, New Zealand, the Philippines; from every country of Europe except where Communist control had shut the exits; from every republic of Latin America.

They came as representatives of the Baptists of their nations and communities to this the eleventh congress of the Baptist World Alliance. They gathered for five days of fellowship, inspiration, and information on the progress of their worldwide religious denomination. They heard the great and the near-great men and women of their fellowship discuss their mutual accomplishments and their common problems.

These Baptists from all over the world heard Evangelist Billy Graham address 120,000 people jammed into the Orange Bowl stadium, denouncing the so-called new morality and calling for a revival of religion. They heard a former president of the Alliance, Dr. C. Oscar Johnson, call for a new unity of Christian people. They heard the Reverend J. H. Jackson, president of the National Baptist Convention of the U.S.A., Inc., plead for a Christian approach to civil rights as he preached the Sunday morning sermon to the shouts of "Amen! Preach on, Brother!" from his fellow Negro Baptists who made up about 15 per cent of the registered delegates.

The Baptists who gathered there represented twenty-three United States bodies, including the Southern Baptist Convention, the American Baptist Convention since changed to the American Baptist Churches of the U.S.A., the National Baptist Convention, U.S.A., Inc., the National Baptist Convention of America, the North American Baptist General Conference, the Seventh Day Baptist General Conference, with the foreign mission agencies of each of these major bodies; the Lott Cary Baptist Foreign Mission Convention, and eight bilingual conferences affiliated with the American Baptist Convention.

The delegates listened intently as Mrs. J. T. Ayorinde, an African, chairman of the All-Africa Baptist Women's Union, spoke for the Baptists of her continent. They listened with great concern as former Governor of Minnesota, Harold E. Stassen, president of the American Baptist Convention, challenged Baptists to seek ways to insure world peace, and as former Congressman from Arkansas, Brooks Hays, a past president of the Southern Baptist Convention, spoke for Christian statesmanship.

For the first time in the sixty-year history of the Baptist World Alliance the delegates elected a Negro, the Reverend William R. Tolbert, Vice-President of Liberia, as president. For one of the vice-presidents they elected a Japanese pastor, the Reverend Shuichi Matsumura of Tokyo. They voted to hold the 1970 convention in Asia for the first time. A single collection, announced for B.W.A. relief, amounted to $10,400.

The Baptist World Congress began in 1905 with the organizational meeting in London, the result of years of discussions among Baptists of the United States and Europe. The American leader in the movement for the worldwide organization was Dr. Edgar Y. Mullins, president of the Southern Baptist Theological Seminary at Louisville. Meeting alternately in North America and Europe, the B.W.A. met in Philadelphia in 1911; Stockholm, Sweden, in 1923; Toronto, Canada, in 1928; Berlin, Germany, in 1934; Atlanta, Georgia, in 1939; Copenhagen, Denmark, in 1947; Cleveland, Ohio, in 1950; and back to London, in 1955.

In 1960 the international convention was held at Rio de Janeiro. Emblazoned upon the banner over the stage of the great hall was the theme of the Congress, JESUS CRISTO É O SENHOR (Jesus Christ Is Lord). A choir of 3,000 Brazilians, ranging in age from eight to the elderly, all dressed in white, led in the song that has become the Baptists' international anthem: "All Hail the Power of Jesus' Name!"

"Just sing it in your own language!" said Dr. Theodore F. Adams, pastor of the First Baptist Church of Richmond, Virginia, the Congress president. The Reverend Joao F. Soren, pastor of Rio's First Baptist Church and outstanding leader of Baptists of Latin America, was elected to succeed Adams.

In 1970 the Congress was held in Tokyo, Japan, and Dr. V. Carney Hargroves of Philadelphia was elected president. Five years later, at the Baptist World Congress in Stockholm, Sweden, Dr. David Y. K. Wong, of Hong Kong, was given the reins of world Baptist leadership—the first Asian to hold the office.

As of 1979, plans were underway for the fourteenth congress, to be held in Toronto, Canada, July 6 to 13, 1980. Robert S. Denny, a Baptist attorney, former chairman of the B.W.A. Youth Committee, became general secretary of the organization on the death of the Reverend Arnold T. Ohrn of Norway in 1958.

In the United States, the fifty-two groups affiliated with the Baptist World Alliance in 1979 reported 99,052 churches, with a membership of 28,773,731. Adding Canada, Mexico, and Bermuda, the reports for North America totaled 101,245 churches and 29,016,036 members.

The international fellowship of all Baptist conventions and unions that comprise the Baptist World Alliance claimed approximately 33,300,000 baptized believers in 138 countries of the world. This represented a gain in North America alone, in one year, of 283,347 members, and over the decade, of nearly five million. The Baptist "community"—children and other persons receiving pastoral care in homes and elsewhere—is reasonably estimated at 46,227,319.

The Alliance, as declared in its constitution, "exists as an expression of the essential oneness of the Baptist people in the Lord Jesus Christ, to impart inspiration to the brotherhood, and to promote the spirit of fellowship, service, and co-operation among its members." *The Baptist World* is the official publication of the

Baptist World Alliance. Its purpose is to report on progress and problems of Baptists in every country of the world.

According to General Secretary "Bob" Denny, the Baptist World Alliance serves as an agency of communication and discussion among Baptists through personal visits, correspondence, publications, films, and electronic media. It promotes fellowship and understanding, sponsors evangelism, and extends aid to those in need in any part of the world.

The Baptist World Alliance has organized a plan whereby individuals may join a group known as "Friends of the Alliance." Secretary Denny describes it as "an inner circle of men, women, and youth who make personal contributions to the work of the Alliance and in turn receive special newsletters on various aspects of its activities."

Dr. W. A. Criswell, in 1979 still the pastor of the First Baptist Church, Dallas, Texas, serves as chairman of Friends.

Protests in Moscow and Havana

While worldwide Baptists appreciate the opportunity their Alliance Congress presents for inspiration, information, and fellowship, they realize that the foremost value of the Baptist World Alliance is this: It gives to the peoples and governments of the world a solid phalanx of influence, ready to do battle, under the leadership of Baptists of the United States, for religious liberty.

The constitution of the Alliance states: "The Baptist World Alliance shall have as one of its primary purposes the safeguarding and maintenance of full religious liberty everywhere not only for our own constituent churches but also for all other religious faiths."[1] To fulfill this responsibility the Alliance leaders gather facts relating to religious liberty and human rights and make them known to the Baptist constituency around the world. Working through American embassies and other governmental channels they intercede in cases of violations of religious liberty, protest against discriminations and persecutions, and plead for the lifting of restrictions. In this task Baptists rally staunch allies among other denominations.

In January 1963 a group of thirty-two Siberian peasants—men, women, and children—sought asylum in the United States embassy at Moscow. The Siberians were Evangelical Christians and claimed they were being severely persecuted by Soviet authorities in their home region of Chernogorsk. They were persecuted, they declared, because of their religious faith and their insistence that they be allowed to teach religion to their children. The American authorities refused asylum to these devout refugees, on the ground that it would be embarrassing to U.S. relations with the Soviet Union. They were turned over to the Moscow police, who sent them back to their home community.

Newsmen were not permitted to interview these Siberian refugees, but members of the Baptist World Alliance staff, under direction of Dr. Josef Nordenhaug, executive secretary, sprang into action. Through contacts in Siberia they learned that these Evangelicals were given various severe punishments—some being deprived permanently of their children. Dr. Nordenhaug and other Alliance officials in Washington made direct contacts with Soviet Ambassador Anatoly Dobrynin, informing him of their feelings in these terse words:

"Regardless of the precise religious convictions of these Siberians, the Baptist World Alliance desires to express its deep sympathy with them in their feelings of religious oppression and to express the concern that religious liberties should be accorded to all peoples of all religious convictions in every nation."[2]

Pointedly reminding the government of the Soviet Union that the constitution of the U.S.S.R. guarantees all citizens the right to religious worship, Dr. Nordenhaug asked for detailed information regarding the beliefs, and the fate, of the Evangelical Christians. As expected, the government of the Soviet Union refused the information. But the Baptists' protests and statements in behalf of religious liberty were published in every language of every country not under Communist control. The words were read and pondered by countless statesmen and diplomats. Cyril E. Bryant, editor of *The Baptist World,* summarized the reaction in a statement that included these words:

"Only one conclusion was possible for governments and peoples everywhere, and it was this: Baptists believe in religious liberty, and stand ready to fight for it anywhere in the world!"

In May 1965 news from Cuba confirmed that two Southern Baptist missionaries had been sentenced to prison on charges of counterrevolutionary activities—meaning simply that they were religious leaders. One was Dr. Herbert Caudill, veteran missionary, sentenced to ten years in prison; the other his son-in-law, the Reverend David Fite, sentenced to six years. Both had chosen to remain in Cuba after Castro's seizure and betrayal of the Cuban people to Communist control.

The Baptist World Alliance, joined by Southern Baptist Convention officials, issued stinging protests. The matter was taken up through the Swiss embassy in Havana. After feeling the lash of adverse world opinion, Fidel Castro issued a promise that the sentences of these two Baptists *might* be materially reduced—which they were.

During years of restrictions upon and persecutions of Protestant church people in Spain, the Baptist World Alliance pressure for religious liberty was brought to bear upon the Spanish Government. In recent years, many of the restrictions upon Protestant worship have been lifted and greater religious liberty granted.

The Other Concerns

There are four other major concerns of the Baptist World Alliance. One important function lies in establishing, widening, and maintaining communications among Baptists of the world. This is done through personal visits by officers and leaders of the organization, through correspondence, and through publications. *The Baptist World* carries news and inspiration to and from Baptists in all countries. This publication established a high reputation for accurate reporting and for articles of interest to Baptists of all races and kinds. The news service of the Alliance is circulated to editors in ninety nations and is widely used.

The Alliance offers a channel to member conventions, mission boards, churches, and individuals to render relief to hungry, sick, ill-clad, and homeless people. Under the direction of the relief coordinator, food, medical supplies, and clothing to fit persons of all ages goes to Eastern European countries, to the Far East, and to central Africa. In the five years from 1960 to 1965 the Baptist World Alliance provided relief supplies with a total value of $490,327.

Four study and research commissions of the Alliance encourage continuous discussions among Baptists of the world on church doctrine, religious liberty, human rights, evangelism, missions, Bible study, and membership training. Scores of especially qualified Baptist leaders, clergy, and laity, are engaged in these activities.

The Alliance sponsors and arranges international meetings of Baptist leaders, from regional to worldwide. Many of the regional meetings are held in the United States, at centers of Baptist education. Unrecorded and unpublicized is the unofficial but constant liaison between American embassy officials in capitals all over the world and leaders of the Baptist World Alliance, with respect to problems arising from denial of religious liberty and violations of human rights. The impact of this worldwide organization on the domestic and foreign policies of the United States government is immeasurable.

President of the Worldly Baptists and Mr. Baptist

Since the Baptist World Alliance is strictly a voluntary co-operative organization among Baptists and has no authority whatever over the churches, non-Baptists sometimes misunderstand the functions of its leaders. This was illustrated by a misplaced comma in a broadcast by a well-meaning radio newscaster in a large Australian city who told his listeners: "Dr. F. Townley, Lord President of the Baptist World Alliance, will arrive today for conferences with Baptist pastors." Dr. Lord forgave his fellow Britisher.

Dr. Soren was presented to a large audience in a South American city by a chairman unfamiliar with B.W.A. titles, startling many of Soren's friends by saying: "And now I take pleasure in presenting His Holiness, Dr. Joao Soren, president of the Worldly Baptists!"

"I am so grateful for this introduction," Soren responded, "and I hope that on my next visit I may have Mrs. Holiness Soren with me!"

Typical of the B.W.A. leaders, these men and women who have made up the working force of the Alliance from its founding, is Dr. Adams. While he was at the helm of the organization from 1955 to 1960, Adams became known by millions of Baptists all over the world as "Mr. Baptist." With ease and grace he presided over the Rio convention. With a firm hand he led in making Baptist principles felt among the peoples and governments of the world.

Born in Palmyra, New York, in 1898, into the home of a Baptist pastor who had studied under Rauschenbusch at Colgate-Rochester Seminary, Ted Adams moved with his family to his father's pastorates in Oregon and Indiana. He was baptized by his father and while a student in high school Ted decided to become a preacher. With a degree from Colgate-Rochester he served as pastor at Cleveland Heights (Ohio) Baptist Church, then at the First Baptist Church of Toledo.

In 1935 the First Baptist Church of Richmond, Virginia, loaded with history and debt, was looking for a pastor. For fourteen months the church leaders at Old First had embraced the Baptist privilege of failing to agree on various prospective candidates from over the Southern Baptist Convention. The pulpit committee went north to Toledo and brought back Ted Adams and his wife, Esther.

Dr. Adams' story at Richmond is a summary of the reasons for Baptist growth throughout the United States and the impact of the Baptists during the three decades following 1935: forceful, effective preaching; wise administration of church programs; excellent relations with the public; and outstanding leadership in the denomination.

At the time of the Baptist World Alliance meeting in June 1965, Adams' congregation had grown from its 1935 membership of 1,600 to 4,500. An average of 3,500 children and adults were enrolled in Sunday school. Constantly emphasizing the importance of tithing, Adams had enlisted more than a thousand members who regularly gave at least one tenth of their incomes to the church and its many programs. From total contributions of about $71,000 during Adams' first year as pastor, the budget grew to more than $300,000 for 1965—all of it pledged on one Sunday morning by the congregation. The church staff had grown to two associate ministers and twelve other full-time employees. The physical plant of the Old First grew with the membership and budget to include a Georgian sanctuary on Richmond's famed Monument Avenue that with accessory buildings cost more than

$2,000,000. In its baptistry Pastor Adams has immersed an average of ninety new members a year since 1936.

During the five years Adams served as president of the Baptist World Alliance, he spent six weeks in Africa, addressing Baptist meetings in the cities and visiting Baptist chapels far back in the jungle. Presiding at the Rio Congress, Adams led the Baptists of the world to issue a "Manifesto on Religious Liberty" that breathes the denomination's historic stand on freedom of conscience and worship. It states:

"We believe that God created man in his own image and endowed him with freedom to respond to his redemptive love; that man is responsible to God for his religious belief and practice; that religious faith and participation must be voluntary in order to be real.

"We rejoice that God gives grace to endure oppression and to use freedom; that friends of religious liberty are found in all Christian communions; that recent legislation in several countries is favorable to religious liberty.

"We earnestly desire that all forms of discrimination against religious minorities shall cease; that all religious bodies shall make an unequivocal commitment to full religious liberty for all people; that all nations shall guarantee the right of all citizens to believe, to worship, to teach, to evangelize, to change their religious affiliation, and to serve their God as their consciences dictate.

"We solemnly covenant to study and to proclaim the freedom men have in Jesus Christ, the Lord; to show Christian understanding and love towards those whose beliefs and practices are different from our own; to pray and use our influence for the preservation and extension of religious liberty for all men."[3]

Retirement from the pastorate freed Ted Adams to a new ministry: professor of preaching at Southeastern Baptist Theological Seminary, at Wake Forest, North Carolina. He and Esther retained their home in Richmond, near their children and grandchildren, and drove to the seminary each Monday for a week of classes. They also continued to attend Baptist World congresses and build international friendships.

The Joint Committee on Public Affairs

Most of the major Baptist bodies in the United States, working together in the Alliance, take advantage of other opportunities to
co-operate in projects that advance the interests of their respective
fellowships and the entire denomination. Such an opportunity
came in the five-year celebration of the "Baptist Jubilee Advance," which began in 1959. Christian social concerns, church
extension, world evangelism were among major subjects offered by
Jubilee officials to Baptist pastors and church members for study
and discussion during the period. "For Liberty and Light" expressed the overall theme of the Jubilee, with special emphasis
upon the importance of these two words in past Baptist history
and current Baptist programs.

While the 150-year Jubilee observance was temporary, another
Baptist co-operative effort is permanent, so far as religious activities go. It is the *Baptist Joint Committee on Public Affairs*. Its
work began in 1936 when the Northern and the Southern Baptist
Conventions took a long step forward in a move their leaders at
the time called fraternal co-operation.

Previous to the founding of the Joint Committee, efforts to
maintain Baptist principles in public matters were conducted by
separate conventions or associations, with their leaders as spokesmen. For example, when in 1925 the General Assembly of Virginia was considering making Bible reading compulsory in public
schools of that state, the Reverend George White McDaniel of
Richmond represented the Baptist state and local associations in
vigorous opposition to the bill. He contended for the principle that
compulsory Bible reading, prescribed for the purpose of religious
worship, would be unconstitutional as a violation of the First
Amendment. Due to Baptist opposition, the proposal failed to
pass. The United States Supreme Court later affirmed the principle.

At the insistent urging of a vigorous modern exponent of separation of church and state, Dr. Rufus W. Weaver, pastor of the
First Baptist Church of Washington, the conventions organized
what they called the "Joint Conference Committee on Public
Relations for the Baptists of the United States." This lengthy title
expressed the hope of Dr. Weaver, who headed the Committee for

several years, that all Baptist conventions would some day join in common efforts to maintain Baptist principles in public affairs and also build a measure of ecumenism among themselves.

In July 1946 the Joint Committee selected the Reverend Joseph Martin Dawson, then pastor of the First Baptist Church of Waco, Texas, as its first executive director. Six Baptist conventions were then affiliated with the Committee. To the two founding groups had been added two conventions of Negro Americans, the National Baptist Convention of the U.S.A., Inc., and the National Baptist Convention of America; the Baptist General Conference, and the Seventh Day Baptist General Conference. In 1956 two other national Baptist bodies joined the group, the North American (German) Baptist General Conference, and the Baptist Federation of Canada. On the retirement of Dr. Dawson in 1953, Dr. C. Emanuel Carlson of the Baptist General Conference, founded by and for Swedish Americans, became executive director. The Reverend Frank H. Woyke, executive secretary of the North American Baptist General Conference, took his turn as chairman of the B.J.C. in 1966.

Through the years since its organization the Baptist Joint Committee on Public Affairs has been the eyes, ears, and voice of the millions of Baptists it represents on matters affecting the American and the worldwide fellowship of Baptist churches and members. The Committee is authorized by its supporting conventions to act in the wide field of public affairs, to make pronouncements, and to take positions on church-state problems. However, its executive director in 1961, Dr. Carlson, made clear: "It must always function in harmony with actions and positions taken by its co-operating conventions."

The four principal areas of activity of the Baptist Joint Committee, called "concerns" by Baptist leaders, are these:

First, the concern for the effectiveness of the Baptist witness by means of a consistent declaration and practice of religious liberty.

Second, the concern for the consistent practice of separation of church and state by the United States government.

Third, the defense of Baptist rights to equality before the law and the aversion to privileged ecclesiastical organizations.

Fourth, the expression of moral support for those people suffering injustices because of their religion at home or abroad.

A study of the instructions given the Baptist Joint Committee by Baptist leaders discloses an interesting list of verbs: Some of the more frequently used: *Petition, contact, reject, approve, confer, communicate, influence, endorse, demand, recommend, urge, defend, represent.* Plenty of action is indicated by those words! The B.J.C. has never been reluctant to take a positive stand when historic Baptist principles are at stake.

The Baptist Watchdog

Running comments are issued in a monthly magazine called *Report from the Capital* and in a weekly B.J.C. news release on current subjects, sometimes in support, sometimes in opposition, frequently in critical analysis. Federal aid to the arts and humanities, a congressional bill to designate a "Year of the Bible" to pay tribute to the work of the American Bible Society, nondiscrimination requirements of the Civil Rights Act, the outlook for greater religious freedom in Spain, federal treatment for narcotic addicts, distribution of American surplus food overseas—these are some of the matters discussed as they become of general interest to the public and of special interest to Baptists.

The B.J.C. has served as watchdog for Baptist churches and their associations and conventions on a long list of subjects covering every phase of public affairs, especially church-state relations. Its officials have issued legal briefs in cases affecting what the organization felt to be efforts to breach the wall of separation between religious organizations and all levels of government. The Committee's stand on the Federal Aid to Education Act of 1965, for example, was stated in these words:

"We, the members of the Baptist Joint Committee on Public Affairs, recognize that many of our nation's people face serious economic, educational, and health problems. Congress has enacted bold legislation to cope with these acute social problems. We are concerned, however, that all attempts to deal with these problems, both through the enactment and administration of appropriate programs, be consistent with the following general principles and procedures in church-state relations which we affirm.

"We favor public administration of all such programs. If a public agency is not available to administer such a program in a given community, we would look with favor upon a broadly representative *ad hoc* committee in a local community to administer such programs. We do not favor nation, state or local *ad hoc* committees whose representatives are selected on the basis of religious affiliation to promote or administer such programs. We are opposed to any program supported by government funds being placed under the administration of a church or church-sponsored institution.

"We favor the use of public facilities for all such programs. However, if public facilities are not available, church facilities could be used, provided that (a) the programs are not under church sponsorship or administration, (b) the use of church facilities does not prejudice the program, and (c) no public funds shall be used to build up the resources, the programs, or the equipment of any church or other organization dedicated to religious objectives."[4]

While the Aid to Education bill was under consideration a trusted adviser to President Lyndon B. Johnson, a graduate of Southwestern Baptist Seminary at Fort Worth, Texas, William D. Moyers, came to the meeting of the Southern Baptist Convention in Dallas and addressed the messengers of this the greatest body of Baptists to assure them that there would be no violation of the principle of separation of church and state in the proposal. Some messengers still expressed themselves as skeptical. After passage of the act, it was freely conceded, both by congressional leaders and by spokesmen for the White House, that the forthright stand of Baptists through their Joint Committee on Public Affairs was a major influence in the final wording of the law.

The 1963 U. S. Supreme Court decision outlawing prescribed religious devotions in public schools split Baptists down the middle, precipitating conflicting opinions and debates that resounded from pulpits and church forums all over the nation. The principle of religious freedom was called upon by ministers, writers, speakers, and lay leaders on both sides of the controversy. The Baptist Joint Committee volunteered to be helpful to all the dialogues and discussions with this statement:

"Get the facts about the Court decision on prayer: Much misinterpretation and misinformation has been published about the recent Supreme Court decision on 'official prayer' in public schools.

As a service to the Baptist people and to the general public the Baptist Joint Committee on Public Affairs is making available mimeographed copies of the complete text of the decision, including the one dissenting opinion."

An Age of Exciting Change

An outstanding project of the Baptist Joint Committee on Public Affairs has been its annual "Religious Liberty Conference," held in Washington where its discussions and recommendations can have the greatest possible impact upon the nation's political leaders. One of the most significant of these conferences, that of 1960, dealt with "The Churches and American Tax Policies." From the discussions of this meeting came the formulation of a policy which held, in summary:

In keeping with the principle of separation of church and state, the state, on whatever level of government, has no constitutional or legal right to levy taxes upon property devoted exclusively to religious purposes, such as the church sanctuary and other buildings used in connection with worship or other church affairs. The state also has no constitutional or legal right to levy taxes upon incomes to churches and religious organizations derived from materials produced exclusively for religious purposes, where incomes are not made a part of profits to firms or individuals but are utilized solely for religious causes. Conversely, no church or religious organization should claim tax exemption on property used for profitable business purposes, such as office buildings, parking lots, and cafeterias, nor upon incomes derived from profitable business enterprises not a part of the program of worship and religious activities of such church or religious organization.

This policy, given wide publicity in the Baptist press and in publications of other religious bodies, as well as by nationwide news media, had a definite impact upon public thinking. It was cited before congressional hearings on taxation. It helped to clarify the Baptist attitude on the thorny question: *Should churches pay business taxes?* The old text, "Render unto Caesar the things that are Caesar's, and unto God the things that are God's," was dusted off for many a Baptist sermon on the subject.

The B.J.C. Religious Liberty Conference of 1965 dealt with the church-state financial issues that emerged in the antipoverty program, in higher education, in federal support of elementary and secondary education, and in various fields of public welfare. Executive Director Carlson expressed the concern—and hope—of Baptists in his invitation to the Conference:

"Ours is an age of exciting change. So many new ideas and modes of procedure are descending upon us that at times we are perplexed lest the good things of the past be passing. Yet we can see so much good in the new that we are sure that God is still working. Can we save what is basically good from the past and use it together with what is as basically good in the new?"

After days of deliberation and discussions that brought out sharp differences of opinion among the most prominent of Baptist leaders of that year, the members of the Conference decided they could indeed save what is good from the past and blend it into the needs of citizens of all kinds and classes in the present and in the future.

Despite its constant recognition of exciting change, the B.J.C. never neglects the task of reminding Baptists that the fundamental principles of religious liberty do not change. A summary of the modern Baptist stand on freedom of conscience, issued by the Committee, reads:

"A person who enjoys freedom of conscience must in actual practice be free to: Decide whether to worship or not to worship, join the church of his own choice, change his ecclesiastical allegiance without hindrance, nurture the faith of his children, express his faith and convictions personally and in group activities, travel for the advancement of his faith, associate himself with others for corporate religious interests, use his home and his property for religious purposes, determine the causes and the amounts of his religious stewardship, make his own best judgments on moral and public issues, and have free access to information from various sources."[5]

Roger Williams and John Clarke, Isaac Backus and John Leland, all would have nodded approval of this pronouncement on freedom of conscience, and also on the Joint Committee's statement on the freedom of the church: "The independence of the church can be used as a kind of loadstone for the discernment of the boundaries of religious liberty. If the *churches* are not free, then the *people* are not religiously free."

Numerous special projects have claimed the attention of Baptists through their staff of the Baptist Joint Committee on Public Affairs. One of major importance was to keep an eye on the Catholic Ecumenical Council sessions in Rome, called first in 1963 by Pope John XXIII and continued by Pope Paul VI. Representatives of the B.J.C., certified at the Vatican as observers, attended all the sessions of the Council from its beginning, reporting faithfully the discussions and decisions of this historic gathering of Roman Catholic bishops with their Pontiff.

The reports of the Baptist representatives at the Council were distributed by the organization to Baptist pastors, lay leaders, and publications all over the world. They presented an objective summary of the proceedings of the "Catholic Brethren" in Rome, along with comments indicating areas of both agreement and disagreement on the part of Baptists with the decisions made by the Roman Catholic hierarchy. Always there appeared to be a searching on the part of the Baptist representatives at the Ecumenical Council to find statements issued by Catholic spokesmen that favored a greater approach to unity among the great Christian bodies of the world, however difficult and gradual that approach might seem to be.

XXVII

BAPTISTS IN THE WHITE HOUSE

Three Became Presidents

While Baptists have been well represented among members of Congress, governors of the states, and other high officials of the federal and state governments, only three of thirty-nine have attained the presidency: Warren G. Harding of Ohio, Harry S. Truman of Missouri, and Jimmy Carter of Georgia.

Harding became a member of Trinity Baptist Church in his hometown of Marion, Ohio, on May 6, 1883, when he was seventeen years of age. He was a member of that church until he died on August 2, 1923, spanning a period of nearly forty years. He served as trustee of Trinity Church for a quarter of a century. He frequently performed the ministry of greeter for the congregation, standing at the church door and shaking hands with the worshipers.

When Harding moved to Washington as a senator, he attended Calvary Baptist Church, at the corner of Eighth and H streets, N.W., a church founded during the administration of President Andrew Jackson. During the illness of the long-time pastor, Dr. Samuel H. Greene, Senator Harding wrote him a letter which included these words:

"I want to say to you that while I have often been obliged to be away, it has always been with regret. I enjoy and profit by the services in Calvary Baptist Church."

After President Harding entered the White House, he and his

wife continued to attend Calvary. The President never mentioned his Baptist faith to gain political prestige.

When news of the sudden death of President Harding reached his hometown, the pew he and Mrs. Harding usually occupied in Trinity was draped in black and remained with its symbol of mourning for thirty days. Later a bronze plaque was placed at the end of the pew. The church doors were kept open for many days, and 11,000 persons took advantage of the opportunity to register their presence. Trinity Baptist Church was remembered in the will of the late President.

During the Bicentennial celebration, a Heritage Tour of historical places was conducted by the Marion Historical Society, and again many people passed through the church sanctuary to note the Harding pew.

At a memorial service held for the late President at Calvary Baptist Church on August 10, 1923, Dr. Alvah S. Hobart paid Harding this tribute:[1]

"The sudden death of our beloved and honored President, Warren G. Harding, which shocked and saddened the world, comes very close to the hearts of the people, not only of our denomination at large, but especially of Ohio Baptists, for it has removed a brother Baptist. His family have been Baptists for generations, and the late President himself was vitally and actively interested in all the affairs of the denomination. . . .

"One of the beautiful and touching things connected with the life of President Harding was the fact that, when shortly before his inauguration, his own pastor was stricken with paralysis and unable to perform the duties of his pastorate, so that the church was compelled to secure an associate pastor, President Harding himself assumed the support of the invalid pastor, whose death preceded that of the President by only a few days. Our country may take hope in the fact that, moved by some great common impulse, the people of this country have long been choosing for its highest office, men of God."

President Truman was a casual churchman. He attended the Baptist church in Independence, Missouri, before his election as senator, while his wife and daughter worshiped elsewhere. When the family moved to Washington on his election to the U. S. Senate, and for a while after he occupied the White House, Truman attended the First Baptist Church at Sixteenth and O streets, N.W. The President walked the eight blocks from the official residence, swinging his cane, always accompanied by a secret service man, and sometimes by newsmen who took that chance to interview the President informally.

As in the Harding administration, when a Baptist occupied the White House, casting politics aside Baptists generally were proud to have one of "their own" statesmen at the helm of government. In one area of Baptist faith and practice, however, the vast majority of Baptists disagreed with President Truman. They held firmly and vigorously to the cherished principle of separation of church and state, while many feared that Truman would violate that policy in the country's relations with the Vatican in Rome. His predecessor, Franklin D. Roosevelt, had appointed a "personal representative" to the Pope. He was Myron C. Taylor and was given the specific responsibility to represent the President of the United States at the Vatican.

While most Baptist leaders did not approve of this arrangement, they did not raise serious objections to it during the Roosevelt presidency. But President Truman desired to establish formal diplomatic relations with the Holy See. He named General Mark W. Clark as his personal envoy and announced that he would raise the status of General Clark's office to that of ambassador. Truman sent the nomination to the Senate for confirmation. The matter was referred to the Foreign Relations Committee, of which Senator Tom Connally of Texas was chairman.

Before Senate ratification could be brought to a vote, Senator Connally announced that his committee had received about a hundred letters approving the appointment and more than 50,000 letters and messages opposing it. While the discussion was gathering momentum, the nation's most distinguished Baptist of that day, President Truman, went to church as usual one Sunday morning. The preacher, with full knowledge that the President was in his pew, declared in his sermon that Baptists would never approve action for an official tie with the Vatican or any other church body.[2]

President Truman found it inconvenient ever again to attend services at the First Baptist Church of Washington. But politician that he was, and keenly responsive to popular opinion however controversial, he withdrew the proposed appointment.

In the presidential campaign of 1960, John F. Kennedy, the Democratic candidate, a Roman Catholic, was invited to address a conference of Baptist ministers in Houston, Texas, and to state his position on church-state relations. Somewhat to the surprise of his listeners, Kennedy declared forthrightly that if he was elected President he would adhere strictly to the policy of separation of church and state—a pronouncement which in the opinion of many political observers had much to do with his election in November of that year.

On March 4, 1969, President Nixon said in a press conference that he was looking forward to the appointment of a personal representative to the Vatican. In response to that statement, the Baptist Joint Committee on Public Affairs, in plenary session on March 6, unanimously adopted the following resolution:

"Recognizing that the intricate relationships involved in world peace require the widest range of perception and communication, we believe that the national interests and the cause of peace are served best by flexible and informal means of church-state consultations rather than by formal diplomatic relations. In line with the Staff Report of the Baptist Joint Committee on Public Affairs, *Diplomatic Relations with the Vatican,* published in April 1968, we respectfully request the President to make widest use of the present and emerging informal relationships open to him; and, consistent with the American model of church-state relationships, to avoid naming a permanent representative to the Roman Catholic Church or to any other church."

Ignoring this expression of Baptist policy, in 1970 President Nixon appointed Henry Cabot Lodge, former U. S. senator and former United Nations ambassador, as his personal representative to the Vatican. Mr. Lodge served during the administrations of Nixon and Ford.

A century-old statute, passed by Congress in 1867, prohibits appropriations from public funds for a United States ambassador to the Vatican, so the President's personal envoy draws no salary. He is paid expenses in connection with his travel to and from Rome. In addition, his office in Rome receives from the public treasury his subsistence, pay for the clerical help, and miscellaneous office expenses. In fiscal 1978 these totaled $37,500. The annual average for the years 1970–78 was approximately $42,000.[3]

The First Southern Baptist President

When the "summit talks" on the Middle East took place among Prime Minister Menachem Begin of Israel, President Anwar Sadat of Egypt, and President Jimmy Carter, in late summer 1978 at Camp David, the television newscast from the White House lawn announced the meeting of "a Jew, a Moslem, and a Southern Baptist."

Protocol may have required that the visiting heads of state be announced first, or the newscaster may have chosen to name the religious faiths in alphabetical order. But the Christian, who was host, was designated by his church affiliation, rather than by the broader term.

National and international attention to Southern Baptists began in 1975, when Jimmy Carter came into the headlines as a candidate for President, and newsmen became curious about his religious faith and practices.

President Jimmy Carter is unquestionably a birthright Baptist, "born and bred in the briar patch of Georgia" on a farm now producing many tons of peanuts. He is the first authentic Southerner to be elected President of the United States since the War Between the States. Reared in the Deep South and married to a neighbor Southerner, Carter is the product of Georgia and of Georgia Baptists.

President Carter does not smoke, and he drinks sparingly. He shuns all physical dissipation. He dresses casually but neatly, and conforming to the advice of his public relations personnel, he dresses to suit the occasion. For example, for Jimmy Carter's first "fireside chat" he spoke from his living room, dressed in an open-neck sweater. He gives no evidence of extravagance in taste. He practices the concept of Christian stewardship, and in all likelihood (though not for public record), he tithes his income.

A major test of his integrity as a Christian came during his campaign for the presidency. His home church became involved in a controversy over race when a black man from another state made application for membership in the Plains Baptist Church. The church voted to refuse to accept black members. Jimmy Carter expressed to his friends and relatives at the church's business session his opposition and followed the minority members under the rejected pastor to establish another Baptist church in the small township of Plains.

During a period of violence in the 1950s, at a neighboring communal farm, now known as Koinonia Partners, Inc., established in 1942 by the late Clarence Jordan, a native of Georgia, a roadside refrigerated stand was bombed and burned, shotgun blasts were fired, and black schoolchildren were threatened for their participation in the vacation Bible schools at the farm. The Carter family lived at Plains six miles away.

Jimmy Carter, a fellow Baptist, followed the example of most of the white citizens of Sumter County. He stayed away, but he refused to join the White Citizens' Council. Says Mrs. Jordan, a charter member of the agricultural missionary enterprise: "To my knowledge, he was never on the place."

President Carter frankly bears his witness to his faith in God and his faithfulness to church attendance. Within a month of his arrival in Washington as Chief Executive, he and his family joined the First Baptist Church by "transfer of letter" from the Plains Baptist Church. He joined the Sunday school class for those of his age group; he offered to teach the class when needed. He and his wife Rosalynn and daughter Amy, and occasionally a son and daughter-in-law, attend the worship service.

The news media have let the world know this President's lifestyle. He observes a "quiet time" at his desk daily before his associates enter for the day's work. He has "grace" before meals, whether it is at state dinners or over soup and sandwich on trays with the Vice-President. He attends Sunday worship services whether in a log church in Moose, Wyoming, when he is on vacation, or at Camp David during conferences, or in the First Baptist Church of Lagos, Nigeria, on a state visit to West Africa.

A Very Active Layman

Within six months of his occupying the White House, Jimmy Carter invited the dozen major executives of the Southern Baptist Convention for a "strategy conference" in his office. He asked these leaders to tell him what he could do for Southern Baptists while he is President.

The result was his endorsement of a crusade they had decided upon. Its purpose is to inspire the 33,000 congregations to launch an evangelistic campaign to proclaim Christ to every human being before the year A.D. 2000. At the annual meeting of the convention, in June 1977, a personal message by videotape from their fellow Baptist in the oval office was shown, appealing for a "Bold Mission Thrust." Primary request was for men and women to volunteer two years of their lives to serve in some needy field on American soil or overseas.[4]

At the 1978 annual meeting of the Convention, Jimmy Carter appeared at the Baptist Men's breakfast in Atlanta, following adjournment of the session, and spoke from notes he scrawled on the backs of old envelopes. Again he urged Christian laymen to take the "Great Commission" more seriously and plan their retirement, their vacations, or their leaves of absence to use their experience and skills in the cause of missions.

The First Baptist Church of Washington, D.C., has accepted this mixed blessing of the President's participation, with the constant presence of secret service men and the occasional disruption of the service by those who want to discuss personal problems with the President. Says the Reverend Dr. Charles A. Trentham, the pastor:

"I can say very honestly that President Carter's commitment to Christ has become more and more obvious to those who see him at worship, hear him teach his Sunday school class, and then stand solidly behind his Christian commitment during his administration."[5]

In 1978 President Carter invited some twenty-eight religious leaders of various denominations to the White House for consultation. Dr. Robert C. Campbell, executive secretary of the American Baptist Churches of the U.S.A. (formerly American Baptist Convention) and Dr. Sloane S. Hodges, the executive of the Progressive National Baptist Convention, Inc., were the two Baptists present. As reported in the May 1978 issue of *The American Baptist,* a monthly, President Carter spoke of the National Council of Churches in the United States as a "major and constructive voice in society," although he is a member of a Baptist body which does not affiliate with it. The President expressed to those interdenominational leaders his deep concern over a "growing quiescence in the churches" and pled with them to get their congregations more involved in outreach and social programs.

George W. Cornell, Associated Press Religion writer, reported a later conference with fellow Southern Baptists. Jimmy Carter in more than usual frankness described a continual tension between a person's inner convictions and his external public life. "The individual ideals usually surpass the performance, but they keep pushing one to do better," the columnist reported, quoting the President.

Again—the Separation of Church and State

President Carter has not escaped the controversy over the position of his fellow Baptists, and many other Protestant denominations, on the question of separation of church and state as it relates to the appointment of a personal envoy to the Vatican. In fact, he walked right into it, by agreeing to a plan for the repeal of the old statute which prohibits any appropriation for an ambassador to the Holy See.

During his campaign for the presidency in 1976, in an interview with C. L. Sulzberger of the New York *Times,* Carter declared that he had no objection to an exchange of ambassadors between the United States and the Vatican. On July 6, 1977, he announced the appointment of David M. Walters, a Roman Catholic of Miami, Florida, as his personal envoy to the Vatican.

In reporting the appointment the National Catholic News Service disclosed that the move had been cleared with the president of the National Conference of Catholic Bishops, Archbishop Joseph Beradin of Cincinnati, according to Russell Shaw, secretary for public affairs of the U. S. Catholic Conference. Mr. Shaw further revealed that Mr. Walters was recommended on a personal level for the Vatican post by Terence Cardinal Cooke of New York and by Archbishop Coleman Carroll of Miami.

"These disclosures confirmed the ecclesiastical nature of the appointment and the concern of the President for ecclesiastical approval of the first Roman Catholic to serve as envoy to the Vatican," declared Dr. James E. Wood, executive director of the Baptist Joint Committee on Public Affairs.

Meanwhile, the U. S. Senate voted to repeal the century-old statute which prohibits any funds for an ambassador to the Vatican, by an amendment introduced by Senator Richard Stone of

Florida. The amendment was not in the House version of the bill, and it was eliminated by a conference committee of both houses.

Although Mr. Walters withdrew from the appointment as envoy to the Vatican after the defeat of the move to appropriate funds for an ambassador, President Carter still confronts the old conflict between his fellow Baptists and those who advocate official relations with the Pope of Rome. Separation of church and state is a firm conviction of Baptists in the United States and, for the most part, of Baptists worldwide. In America, the conviction is rooted in their interpretation of the United States Constitution. It is burned into their souls by the inherited memory of persecutions of their forebears in Europe and in America before the Constitution was adopted. As expressed by the Baptist Joint Committee on Public Affairs:

"Whatever the merits of the appointment, including any marginal political gains for the President among Catholics, the losses to both church and state far outweigh the gains."

"Every President Has Rights"

Dr. Wayne E. Oates, professor of psychiatry and behavioral sciences at the School of Medicine, University of Louisville, in Kentucky, formerly a member of the faculty of Southern Baptist Theological Seminary, Louisville, was asked for his opinion about Jimmy Carter as an active Baptist. He replied:

"Every President has rights in addition to power. He has a right to the exercise of his own personal religious faith and to participate in his own religious group. However, he also has a responsibility to preface these public exercises by saying forthrightly that this is what he is doing. He needs to clarify his relationship as *not* speaking or acting as President of the United States to propagandize persons of other persuasion. Every responsible leader—high and low—has the ever-present responsibility to clarify what his or her relationship is before seeking to communicate. Otherwise the message will be garbled."[6]

In simpler words, a fellow member of the First Baptist Church of Washington, widow of a former diplomat who served in strategic foreign posts, expressed her opinion: "It has been a blessing to our church to have the President and Mrs. Carter and family as members and attendants. I had the privilege of hearing the President teach his Sunday school class and was impressed with his knowledge of the Bible."[7]

When the head of state of the most powerful nation in the world pays a visit to Nigeria, the first nation of Africa to win its independence from the mother country, Great Britain, and to the African country founded by freed slaves from the United States, Liberia, that choice of places to visit gives the two nations added prestige. The heads of African states chosen were Baptists. General Olusegun Obasanjo of Nigeria took his guest to church, read the Bible during the service, and asked President Carter to lead in the responsive reading at the First Baptist Church of Lagos. In Monrovia, the President, Dr. William R. Tolbert, a pastor of churches in Liberia, president of the Liberian Baptist Convention, and a former president of the Baptist World Alliance, received the fellow Baptist from the United States. It was during the Easter season, and it was the first time an American President had visited West Africa.

Cynics may charge Jimmy Carter with religious propaganda, but the Baptists call it simply "Christian witness." Most religious leaders, whatever their faith, would agree.

XXVIII

PROBLEMS OF THE FUTURE

Some Common Problems

With all their accomplishments, with all their victories for freedom of conscience and worship, all their progress in organization, and all their growth in numbers, Baptists of the 1970s faced problems as serious as at any time in their history.

They were not alone in this. The same problems beset in some degree leaders and members of all other religious bodies. They stemmed from the political, social, and economic complications of the period variously called the post-World War II era, the atomic age, the age of scientific engineering, the decades of undeclared wars, the time of perplexity, the era of questioning and doubt.

One pressing problem was the decreasing rate of Baptist growth. With all its elaborate organizational structure to win converts and establish new churches, the Home Mission Board of the Southern Baptist Convention reported in 1966 that baptisms in this largest Baptist body had dropped from 416,876 in 1955 to 361,643 in 1965. The latest year to report more than 400,000 baptisms in churches of the Southern Convention was 1961 with 403,315. Almost the same ratio of slump in baptisms and additions to church membership prevailed in most of the various Baptist bodies.

What were the reasons? Baptist leaders listened carefully while C. E. Autrey, director of evangelism for the Home Mission Board, in a gloves-off manner supplied what he considered them to be:[1]

"There are four major factors: lack of concern for the lost on the part of pastors and church leaders; neglect of ways and means to develop and maintain an evangelistic church; the tendency to conduct brief routine revivals, even at times cut to weekends only."

The fourth reason indicated Autrey's belief, shared by many leaders in the various Baptist fellowships, that with all the elaborate organizations in churches, associations, and conventions, more ecclesiastical machinery had been set up than there was spiritual steam to run it. Said Autrey:

"The necessary emphasis conventionwide on program study and agency co-operation has sapped momentum from grass-roots gospel preaching. We've taken the emphasis off reaching the lost. As soon as we're through with these projects we'll get back to baptizing people."

A Middle-Class Denomination?

To Dr. Autrey's explanation many Baptist leaders added another possible one by way of a question: "Are Baptists sloughing off at both the top and the bottom, rapidly becoming predominantly a middle-class fellowship?"

In the opinion of these leaders the loss at the top involved members in the upper economic and social brackets, who joined other churches, such as the Episcopal, which offer more formality in worship than the Baptists prefer. Loss at the bottom was to the Assemblies of God and other strongly Pentecostal churches, where emotional expression in worship prevailed.

At one time, Baptists and Methodists of the older American stock had undisputed claim to converts in the lower income and educational scales. It was often said to the Baptist preacher in the period of the expanding nation that "the common people heard him gladly." With little or no emphasis upon the liturgical in worship, Baptist congregations developed an informality in their services that satisfied the needs of the common people and has remained the hallmark of rural and small-city Baptist churches. It has been expressed in the hubbub on Sunday mornings as the congregation moved from Sunday school classes into the sanctuary for the church service; in the clarion call by the song leader that everybody should get songbooks and prepare to make a joyful noise unto the Lord; the numerous announcements by the pastor concerning meetings of all kinds during the week, from deacons to boys who want to try out for the church baseball team; the presence of numerous babies in the arms of their mothers, ready to test their lungs in competition with the preacher's; and on through the sermon to a lengthy plea for somebody to come forward and join the church.

Illustrating this informality, W. L. Howse, director of the educational division of the Baptist Sunday School Board, related to a summer assembly audience that he returned to Texas where he had taught Christian education for twenty-five years and dropped into a Baptist church in Dallas to worship one Sunday morning. Shown to the men's Bible class for his age group, Howse was introduced to several of the members before the class session was called to order. After a hymn, one of the members was asked to lead in prayer. Unhesitatingly, the layman launched into his petitions, and then remembering the stranger in their midst he prayed: "And now, Oh Heavenly Father, we ask you to bless Mr.—er, uh, we thank you for our visitor from Nashville." Then suddenly the layman broke into his prayer with a parenthetical statement: "Now, isn't that the funniest thing. I met him less than five minutes ago, Lord, but I can't remember his name!"

As American communities became urbanized and the economic, social, and intellectual status of their citizens steadily rose, Baptist churches in those communities gradually changed to answer the demand for more formal worship services. The First Baptist Church generally became the one with a plate-glass curtain, a partition which was obviously there but so spotlessly clean as to be invisible.

In any city in America of 25,000 or more inhabitants in the mid-1970s, Baptist churches ranged from high church to low church, or from First Baptist to poor-neighborhood Baptist churches, and each could be identified by the degree of formality in its worship, the style and quality of its physical plant, the educational qualifications of its minister, and the geographical location of the meeting house. All were filling a place in the spiritual life of the community.

Dr. Wayne E. Oates explained to college students meeting at Green Lake Assembly the debt he owed to a humble Baptist church: "It was they who found me in the fringe of Greenville, South Carolina, in a mill village. They put shoes on my feet, taught me the difference between a knife and a fork, and helped me to know about God."

The holiness and other emotion-packed sects, with their fast growth at mid-century, won away many of the members and potential converts from the mill-village and Mount Pisgah churches. At the same time, those in the First Baptist churches, especially the young couples, the young business-executive type and his wife, who desired even greater formality, quietly left to worship where they could find it.

Here was a problem for the solution of which Baptists in the United States directed their thinking as they looked forward to the twenty-first century: Could they stop the erosion at both ends of the social scale of their denomination? Their leaders seemed determined to try.

The Power Structure

By the mid-twentieth century, Baptists in America also faced a growing criticism of the power structure that had developed within their associations and conventions, creating what many church leaders and members considered a *de facto* hierarchy in a denomination that had fought hierarchies throughout its existence. Some of the power structure clearly came about because of the enjoyment of ecclesiastical authority on the part of some denominational leaders, which, as we have seen, split several of the fellowships and created new and sometimes rival bodies of Baptists. However, most of the structure of control over local churches simply grew from the orderly functioning of the huge organizations dealing with missions, publishing, institutions, and all other denominational programs.

One woman, Rachel Caldwell, and her husband, Baptist pastor and college teacher, reluctantly gave up their membership in a Baptist church. A Presbyterian church asked Caldwell to be its pastor and he accepted. In words that shook many Baptist leaders into thoughtful soul-searching, Mrs. Caldwell gave their reasons for giving up the church in which they were reared. The following was a part of her discussion:

"How independent, really, is the local Baptist church? What can it do that really matters, without the sanction of the 'state office'? Of course, the pressure that is applied for conformity is a great deal less obvious than that of the Roman Catholic hierarchy, but it is just as real, and just as effective. There are still some Baptist churches large enough, and some pastors strong enough, to resist pressure of this type and to maintain a measure of independence—but they are few. By and large, Baptist pastors are expending the greater part of their energies attempting to curry favor with the powers-that-be by fulfilling or even exceeding the expectations of the human beings into whose hands has been given control over Baptist churches. The Holy Spirit has had to take second place to the power structure, with the result that He rarely has a chance to direct at all. God and his wooing spirit must play ball with the System or get out of the stadium."[2]

Another criticism within the Baptist ranks dealt with the hope for greater freedom on the part of ministers and teachers to interpret the Bible without fear of pressure from self-appointed guardians of Baptist orthodoxy. From that discussion these questions arose: "If the Bible is the eternal word of God, why fear man's exploration of it? Why should one professor's interpretation of Genesis, differing from the ancient one, force him out of a Baptist seminary?"

Still another concern of many Baptists was the emphasis placed upon numbers in every area of church life. Generally, these critics faced both ways. They regretted the decrease in converts and baptisms among Baptist churches, granting readily that numbers were important to denominational strength. But they asked whether the goal of size was in danger of overshadowing spiritual commitment. They asked whether a pastor should be judged largely by the total of members he had lured into his congregation, whether the success of a revival should be not how many converts were recruited but rather to what extent had conversion prepared the new members for living spiritually directed lives.

Some terse words were spoken on the subject to the leaders and messengers of the Southern Baptist Convention at its 1964 session by Owen Cooper, Baptist layman of Yazoo City, Mississippi, president of the Mississippi Chemical Corporation. As a member of the executive committee of the convention Cooper could speak as a Baptist concerned with the future of his denomination. He raised this question: "Why the diminution of spiritual momentum in the world, in our country and in our denomination?" His blunt answer included this opinion:

"Southern Baptists have grown to such large numbers that it is difficult to maintain spiritual enthusiasm, missionary fervor, and Christian zeal throughout its entire membership. We may find ourselves somewhat in the position occupied by Gideon when his followers included the curious, those desiring social acceptance, those seeking to create the impression of loyalty, those who wanted to do that which was esteemed popular, those who follow the crowd, as well as the earnest and dedicated."[3]

Another problem faced by Baptists was the insecure position of their pastors. Many leaders and members were asking: "When a congregation has immediate and ultimate control over the tenure of the pastor, has he sufficient freedom of mind and of action to give effective leadership to his church and to the community of which it is a part? Can the minister retain the dignity that requires security, when his very existence as a pastor is always in question?"

Before the modern era of Baptist soul-searching for ways of improving the functioning of their churches the answer would doubtless have been: "This is the price a Baptist minister must pay for the autonomy of the local church and its freedom from both ecclesiastical and state control." Seminaries and associations of ministers were wrestling with this matter so vitally affecting their denominational and local leadership. They wanted a better answer than the traditional one. They sought a plan that would develop within any Baptist church the responsibility to protect the pastor from unwarranted and unfair attacks growing out of misunderstanding, jealousy, or downright stupidity, and at the same time give the local church assistance in dealing with a pastor whose ministry had become too beset with problems to permit his further effective leadership of that congregation.

Baptists have a reputation for dealing forthrightly with devils representing problems whose horns and tails they can see and take hold of. In the mid-1960s they were startled by one that blew up like a sudden whirlwind under a cloudless sky. It was a question that broke upon churches of all faiths and left their ministers and workers gasping: "Is God dead?"

Some Baptist ministers were so busy trying to refute the idea that God is dead that they neglected the ministry of the church that would have answered the question and at the same time might have filled their pews with worshipers. The Reverend Franklin D. Elmer, pastor of Woodside Baptist Church, Flint, Michigan, expressed the forward look of Baptists when he wrote in the American Baptist publication *Missions:*

"We must be ready to admit that the tragedy of religion in our times has resulted because so many of us were brought up in churches and synagogues and mosques and temples where the idea of God we were taught is so limited and inadequate that it was destined only to die. And what we must see in the marvelous, disturbing, revolutionary developments of our time is that, while the inadequate ideas of God are properly dead, a greater idea of God cries out for our acceptance. If the ancient womb of religious faith seems suddenly empty, it is not because the living faith in God that was there has died and been aborted, but rather because a growing, greater concept of creation and man's place in it has come to birth and is crying out for our acceptance."[4]

The Challenge of Urbanization

The movement in the 1960s to merge several major denominations in the United States in organic union to form a greater Church of Christ, and the reaction of Baptists toward it, forced leaders of the denomination to face such questions as these: Are denominations—including our own—obsolete? Is the real sin a separate denominational existence, or is it a lack of co-operation across denominational lines? Must there be one superchurch with hierarchical muscles to oppose the great economic and political power structures of our day? Contemplating such questions as these that confronted Baptists, Paul Allen, editor of the American Baptist *Crusader,* sadly remarked in his magazine: "A thorough exploration of such questions will underscore again the old saw: where there are two Baptists there will be three opinions."

Another challenge to Baptists of all varieties was the changing constituencies to which they have traditionally ministered due to rapid urbanization of the United States. Baptist historian, the late Kenneth Scott Latourette of the faculty of Yale University set this challenge in clear perspective in these words:

"A rapidly declining proportion of the population is on the farms and in the rural towns and villages where we have heretofore had our main strength. That is true in both the South and the North and among both the whites and the Negroes. With urbanization has come rising prosperity and a striking increase in the number of Baptist youth who are going to colleges and universities. There they are being exposed to intellectual currents and the attendant questions which the older generation did not know. Strains have developed in the effort to answer these questions. The issue is particularly acute in the South among the whites, for Southern Baptist youth are flooding Baptist colleges and the state universities, where these questions are clamant.

"Can we enable youth to see that no contradiction exists in God's truth and that the wonder of the gospel is only enhanced by all insights into truth? Can we so utilize the rising prosperity that it will not bring a mounting absorption in the gadgets and luxury brought by wealth but will enhance dedication and be used for the spread of the gospel?"[5]

The Reasons for Being Baptist

Ecclesiastical, economic, social, and political problems of the mid-century brought into clearer relief than at any time in previous decades the fundamental question for all Baptists: Are the reasons for being a Baptist the same as they were from the beginning of our history? The composite answer of an overwhelming majority of the leaders and members of the denomination, white, Negro, and others, Northern and Southern, liberal and conservative, was this: "We have a distinctive message, and our witness to it has helped to shape the destiny of our nation and the world. We have stood for spiritual liberty, for freedom of conscience, for the right of each individual to worship or not to worship as he pleases. We have stood, and will forever stand, guarding the wall of separation of religion and government. We are not about to abandon our distinctive witness at a time when our nation needs it as badly as it ever has."

Baptists have always believed that American democracy is not understandable apart from the background of the free churches, maintaining that the principle of democracy appeared first in the free churches and not in the state. They contend that it was the free church meeting that gave birth to political democracy and not the other way around.

In his book *Fifty Years an Editor,* William B. Lipphard pointed out that he liked pastoral security in the Methodist Church, the Presbyterian form of church government, much of the ritualism of the Episcopal Church, then added:

"In one realm of religious experience the Baptists are admittedly different. This is the realm of freedom. As understood and proclaimed by Baptists throughout their history, religion is a personal relationship between the human soul and God. Into this relationship nothing may intrude . . . Liberty of conscience, freedom from creedal bondage, freedom of doctrinal interpretation, and local church independence—these constitute Baptist ecclesiastical democracy . . . Such freedoms a Baptist not only insists on for himself, but also grants to all others, and in fact demands for them."[6]

The executive secretary of the Baptist Joint Committee on Public Affairs summarized the foremost principle of the Baptists, which is spiritual liberty, in these words: "To Baptists, the purpose of God is that men shall be spiritually free beings, free to live their religious lives and have their ultimate being under the lordship of Christ. This freedom is real only if these same people are free not to be responsive to God, or to respond in such manner as seems right to them."[7]

ACKNOWLEDGMENTS

Thanks to the publishers, Doubleday-Galilee, we authors have the opportunity twelve years after the appearance of our *The Indomitable Baptists* to bring out a revised paperback edition under the title *The Baptists in America*. We acknowledge the valuable assistance of church historians and friends in the production of both the former and the present work; and especially for the helpful and sympathetic criticisms of all who helped to make this new version a better book.

The names of those who have contributed to our efforts would fill too many pages if listed in full, but at least these must be mentioned with the authors' special thanks:

The late Dr. Kenneth Scott Latourette, the late Dr. Gaines S. Dobbins, Dr. Robert A. Baker, Loulie Latimer Owens, and Dr. William J. Reynolds, who gave extensive help.

Also: Porter W. Routh, executive secretary-treasurer, and W. C. Fields, director of communications, Southern Baptist Convention Executive Committee, Nashville, Tennessee.

Philip E. Jenks, executive director, and Helen Sames, associate, Division of Communication, American Baptist Churches, Valley Forge, Pennsylvania.

Arthur C. Borden, secretary for Church Relations, and John A. Duguid, associate, the American Bible Society, New York, New York. Mrs. Faye Pullen, American Baptist Historical Society, Rochester, New York. Rachel Joy Colvin, artist, Radio and Television Commission, Southern Baptist Convention, Fort Worth, Texas. Michael Duduit, director of communications, Southern Baptist Theological Seminary, Louisville, Kentucky.

Dr. James E. Wood, Jr., executive secretary of the Baptist Joint

Committee on Public Affairs, Washington, D.C. C. E. Bryant, associate secretary, Baptist World Alliance, Washington, D.C.

Dr. William E. Dowell, president, Baptist Bible College, Springfield, Missouri. Dr. Charles E. Boddie, president, American Baptist Theological Seminary, Nashville, Tennessee. Professor Timothy Weber, Denver Conservative Baptist Theological Seminary, Denver, Colorado. Donald E. Bailey, director of press relations, Billy Graham Evangelistic Association, Minneapolis, Minnesota. Dr. Martin E. Marty, University of Chicago, Chicago, Illinois. Roland E. Wolseley, professor emeritus of journalism, Syracuse (New York) University. Dr. Wayne E. Oates, faculty, University of Louisville Medical School, Louisville, Kentucky.

Reverend and Mrs. Jeremie Hodoroaba, Gentilly, Paris, France. Dr. and Mrs. Bela Udvarnoki, retired teachers, Richmond, Virginia. Dr. Jitsuo Morikawa, retired director of the American Baptist National Ministries, Valley Forge, Pennsylvania. Dr. Edgar H. Burks, executive secretary, Nigerian Baptist Mission, Ibadan, Nigeria. Richard B. Ogrean, administrator, New England Baptist Hospital, Boston, Massachusetts. Mrs. Clarence L. Jordan, Koinonia Partners, Americus, Georgia.

Juliette Mather, St. Petersburg, Florida. Dr. Charles A. Trentham, pastor, First Baptist Church of the City of Washington, D.C. Reverend Harold Hoffman, pastor, Second Baptist Church, St. Louis, Missouri.

Our special gratitude to Porter Routh of Nashville, Tennessee, who recommended us as a team of writers available for this assignment, and who is retiring after twenty-eight years as executive secretary of the Executive Committee, Southern Baptist Convention.

Finally, our hearty thanks to Alexander Liepa, editor of Galilee Department, Doubleday & Co., Inc., and to Janet V. Waring, his editorial assistant, for their kindness and patience in our struggle to do our best in this rewarding task.

O. K. Armstrong and Marjorie Armstrong

January 31, 1979
The Highlands
Republic, Missouri 65738

SOURCES AND SUGGESTED READINGS

General

Among numerous works on the history and the story of the Baptists in America, the authors found the following of special value:

A History of the Baptists, by Robert G. Torbet, Judson Press, Philadelphia, 1950

The Encyclopedia of Southern Baptists, 2 volumes, Broadman Press, Nashville, Tenn., 1958

Baptist Advance, edited by Davis C. Woolley, copyright Broadman Press, Nashville, Tenn., 1964

A Short History of the Baptists, by Henry C. Vedder, the American Baptist Publication Society, Philadelphia, 1907

A Century of Baptist Achievement, edited by A. H. Newman, American Baptist Publication Society, Philadelphia, 1901

A History of the Baptists, by John T. Christian, Sunday School Board of the Southern Baptist Convention, Nashville, Tenn., 1901

Handbook of the Denominations in the United States, by Frank S. Mead, 4th edition, Abingdon Press, Nashville, Tenn., 1965

A Baptist Treasury, compiled and edited by Sydnor L. Stealey, Thomas Y. Crowell Co., New York, 1958

Specific references and sources

CHAPTER I: JOHN LELAND AND THE BILL OF RIGHTS

1 *Baptists and the American Republic,* by Joseph Martin Dawson, Broadman Press, Nashville, Tenn., 1956

2 Ibid., p. 91

3   *History of the Life and Times of James Madison,* by William Cabell Rives, Little, Brown & Co., Boston
4   *Elder John Leland, Jeffersonian Itinerant,* by L. H. Butterfield, American Antiquarian Society, Worcester, Mass.
5   *The Complete Jefferson,* edited by Saul K. Padover, Duell, Sloan & Pearce, New York
6   *History of the Rise and Progress of the Baptists in Virginia,* by Robert B. Semple, publisher, Richmond, Va., 1810
7   Ibid.
8   Butterfield, op. cit.
9   Dawson, op. cit.
10 *Father of the Constitution,* by Irving Brant, Bobbs-Merrill Co., Indianapolis, Ind.

Besides the general and specific references, we found this work helpful: *In God We Trust,* the Religious Beliefs and Ideas of the American Founding Fathers. Editor, Norman Cousins, Harper & Bros., New York, 1958

CHAPTER II: THE ZEALOUS ANABAPTISTS

1   *A Manual of Church History,* by A. H. Newman, Vol. I, Judson Press, Philadelphia, 1899
2   *The Anabaptist Story,* by William R. Estep, Jr., Broadman Press, Nashville, Tenn., 1963
3   *An Ecclesiastical History,* by John Lawrence Mosheim, Blackie and Son, Glasgow, Scotland, 1737. English edition translated from the German by Archibald Maclaine in 1764
4   *A History of the Anabaptists in Switzerland,* by Henry S. Burrage, American Baptist Publication Society, Philadelphia, 1881
5   Ibid.
6   Mosheim, op. cit.
7   Ibid.

Mosheim's volume, with its excellent translation, is perhaps the most comprehensive account of the Anabaptists in existence.

CHAPTER III: ENGLAND'S FIRST BAPTISTS

1   *A History of Anti-Paedobaptism,* Judson Press, Philadelphia
2   *A Manual of Church History,* Newman, op. cit.
3   Ibid.
4   *The Anabaptist Story,* Estep, op. cit.

CHAPTER IV: ROGER WILLIAMS

1 *Roger Williams,* by Henry Martyn Dexter, American Baptist Publication Society, Philadelphia, 1876
2 *Church History of New England,* by Isaac Backus, American Baptist Publication Society, Philadelphia, 1844
3 Ibid.
4 Ibid.

John Winthrop's journal, telling of his welcoming the Williamses to Boston, is in the library of Thomas Jefferson at Monticello, Va.

A reference work of interest to juveniles on Roger Williams and John Clarke: *They Kept the Faith,* by Ina Smith Lambdin and Loulie Latimer Owens, Broadman Press, Nashville, Tenn., 1954

CHAPTER V: JOHN CLARKE OF RHODE ISLAND

1 *Church History of New England,* Backus, op. cit.
2 Ibid.
3 Ibid.
4 *Baptists and the American Republic,* by Joseph Martin Dawson, op. cit.
5 Ibid.
6 Backus, op. cit.
7 Ibid.

Several works on the Baptists of the colonial period shed additional light on these people from the Roger Williams period to the Revolutionary War.

CHAPTER VI: HOW BAPTISTS GREW

1 *Baptist Foundations in the South,* by William L. Lumpkin, Broadman Press, Nashville, Tenn., 1961
2 Morgan Edwards' manuscript is in the library of Furman University, Greenville, S.C.
3 *A History of South Carolina Baptists,* by Joe M. King, The General Board of the South Carolina Baptist Convention, Columbia, S.C., 1964

Additional material on the Great Awakening is found in several biographies of George Whitefield, Jonathan Edwards, and the Tennents.

CHAPTER VII: ISAAC BACKUS—BAPTIST CHAMPION

1 The account of James Lane of Virginia is from the manuscript by Morgan Edwards, op. cit.

2 Ibid.

3 *Isaac Backus—Pioneer of Religious Liberty,* by T. B. Maston, doctoral thesis, Yale University Press, 1939

4 Ibid.

5 *A History of New England, with Particular Reference to the Denomination of Christians Called Baptists,* by Isaac Backus, Vol. II, privately published, Providence, R.I., 1784

6 Quoted by Backus from copy of original, bearing signature of John Hancock.

CHAPTER VIII: THE FREEDOM TRAIL

1 Maston, op. cit.

2 Backus, op. cit.

3 Quoted in various sources from the original minutes preserved by the American Baptist Convention, Valley Forge, Pa.

4 Backus, op. cit.

5 *Memoir of the Life and Times of the Rev. Isaac Backus,* by Alvah Hovey, American Baptist Publication Society, Philadelphia, 1898

6 *A Century of Baptist Achievement,* edited by A. H. Newman, op. cit.

7 *That Old-Time Religion,* by Archie Robertson, Houghton Mifflin Co., Boston, 1950

We found Dawson's *Baptists and the American Republic* excellent for fast reading on the contribution of Baptists to the nation in this era of American history.

CHAPTER IX: ADONIRAM JUDSON AND THE HEATHEN

1 *The Shoe Leather Globe,* by Saxon Rowe Carver, Broadman Press, Nashville, Tenn., 1965, pp. 109–10 (A brief but vivid story of William Carey.)

2 *Golden Boats from Burma,* by Gordon Langley Hall, Macrae Smith Company, Philadelphia, 1961, p. 30

3 *To the Golden Shore,* by Courtney Anderson, Little, Brown & Co., Boston, Mass., 1956; Dolphin Books, 1961, p. 115

4 Ibid.

CHAPTER X: LUTHER RICE AND COLUMBUS

1 *Ropes to Burma: The Story of Luther Rice,* by Saxon Rowe Carver, Broadman Press, Nashville, Tenn., 1961, p. 134

2 Reproduced from the original manuscript for the cover of *Baptist*

Leader, May 1964, American Baptist Publication Society, Valley Forge, Pa.

3   Carver, op. cit., p. 132
4   "Hitherto-Henceforth," address by J. D. Grey before the Southern Baptist Convention, May 21, Atlantic City, N.J., 1964
5   *A Memoir of the Life and Labors of the Rev. Adoniram Judson,* by Francis Wayland, Phillips, Sampson & Co., Boston, 1853, pp. 121 ff.
6   Ibid.
7   Anderson, op. cit.
8   Wayland, op. cit.

CHAPTER XI: PECK AND THE WESTWARD EXPANSION

1   *Memoirs of John Mason Peck,* by Rufus Babcock, American Baptist Publication Society, Philadelphia, 1864
2   *American Baptist Magazine,* June 15, 1818
3   Babcock, op. cit.
4   *John Mason Peck, the Pioneer Missionary,* by Matthew Lawrence, Fortuny's, New York, 1940
5   *Vanguard of the Caravans,* by Coe Hayne, Judson Press, Philadelphia, 1931
6   *Peck's New Gazetteer of Illinois,* by John Mason Peck, Grigg & Elliott, Philadelphia, 1837

Additional references:

John Mason Peck and One Hundred Years of Home Missions, 1817–1917, by L. C. Barnes and A. K. DeBlois, American Baptist Home Mission Society, Philadelphia, 1917
One Mark of Greatness, by Louise Armstrong Cattan and Helen C. Schmitz, Judson Press, Valley Forge, Pa., 1961

CHAPTER XII: BAPTIST GROWING PAINS

1   *Baptists,* pamphlet by Lynn E. May, Jr., The Historical Commission of the Southern Baptist Convention, Nashville, Tenn., 1964
2   *The Life of Jeremiah Vardeman,* by John Mason Peck
3   Correspondence in the archives of Furman University, Greenville, S.C.
4   Hayne, op. cit.
5   Babcock, op. cit.
6   *A Short History of the Baptists,* by Henry C. Vedder, American Baptist Publication Society, Philadelphia, 1907

CHAPTER XIII: THE RANKS SPLIT

1   *History of the Home Mission Board,* by J. B. Lawrence, Broad-
    man Press, Nashville, Tenn., 1958, p. 9 (quotation from *Our
    Home Field,* Vol. I, No. 1, 1888)
2   *The Southern Baptist Encyclopedia,* p. 1245, monograph by J. W.
    Storer, Broadman Press, Nashville, Tenn., 1958
3   *A History of the Baptists,* by Robert G. Torbet, Judson Press,
    Philadelphia, 1950
4   *These Glorious Years, The Centenary History of German
    Baptists of North America,* 1843–1943, edited by Herman Von
    Berge, Roger Williams Press, Cleveland, Ohio, 1944
5   Quoted from *Standard,* official organ of the Baptist General Con-
    ference (of America), Swedish Baptists' body, Chicago, 1959

CHAPTER XIV: WAR AND PEACE

1   *The Southern Baptist Convention,* by W. W. Barnes, Broadman
    Press, Nashville, Tenn., 1954, p. 46. Quote from *The Western
    Recorder,* Louisville, Ky.
2   Ibid., p. 45
3   Ibid., p. 45
4   Ibid., p. 63
5   Ibid., p. 76
6   *Proceedings of the Southern Baptist Convention,* 1893, Appendix
    B, p. LXX
7   *Fifty Fruitful Years,* by P. E. Burroughs, Broadman Press, Nash-
    ville, Tenn., 1941, p. 47. Quote from the *Religious Herald,* Feb.
    27, 1890, Richmond, Va.
8   *A History of American Magazines,* by Frank Luther Mott, Har-
    vard University Press, Cambridge, Mass., 1938, Vol. I, pp. 63–64
9   Ibid., p. 50

CHAPTER XV: RAUSCHENBUSCH AND THE SOCIAL GOSPEL

1   *A Rauschenbusch Reader,* Benson Y. Landis, editor, Harper &
    Bros., New York, 1957
2   *The Social Gospel of Rauschenbusch,* by D. R. Sharpe, Yale Uni-
    versity Press, New Haven, Conn., 1944, p. 54
3   Ibid., p. 60
4   Ibid., p. 79
5   Landis, op. cit.

6 Sharpe, op. cit., p. 273

7 *Walter Rauschenbusch and His Contribution to Social Christianity,* by Anna M. Singer, Richard G. Badger, Boston, 1920

8 *A Baptist Treasury,* by Sydnor L. Stealey, Thomas Y. Crowell Co., New York, 1958, p. 165

9 Ibid., p. 166

10 Landis, op. cit., p. 22

CHAPTER XVI: THE NEGRO BAPTISTS

1 *The First Century of the First Baptist Church of Richmond, Virginia,* edited by H. A. Tupper, printed by Carlton McCarthy, Richmond, Va., 1880, pp. 247–72

2 *The Story of the National Baptists,* by Owen D. Pelt and Ralph Lee Smith, Vantage Press, New York, 1960

3 *Up From Slavery, An American Autobiography,* by Booker T. Washington, Doubleday & Co., New York, 1901. Paperback, 1956, Booker T. Washington Centennial Commission

4 Ibid., p. 163

5 *American Negro Songs and Spirituals,* by John W. Work, Bonanza Books, p. 2

6 *Angel Mo' and Her Son, Roland Hayes,* by MacKinley Helm, Little, Brown & Co., Boston, 1942

Additional reference:

The Negro and His Songs, by Howard W. Odum and Guy B. Johnson, University of North Carolina Press, Chapel Hill, N.C., 1925

CHAPTER XVII: THE GREAT VARIETY OF BAPTISTS

1 Norman W. Cox, secretary emeritus, The Historical Commission, Southern Baptist Convention, Nashville, Tenn.

2 Quote from *History of the General Baptists,* by Ollie Latch, The General Baptist Press, Poplar Bluff, Mo., 1954

3 *These Glorious Years,* edited by Herman Von Berge

4 Don Hook, in *The Quarterly Review,* second quarter, 1959, p. 23, Sunday School Board of the Southern Baptist Convention, Nashville, Tenn.

5 *A Thousand Months to Remember,* by Joseph Martin Dawson, Baylor University Press, Waco, Texas, 1964, p. 130

6 *Baptist Bible Tribune,* Noel Smith, editor, Springfield, Missouri. June and July issues, 1950

7   *The Birth Pangs of the Baptist Bible Fellowship,* Dr. W. E. Dowell, Temple Press, Springfield, Mo., 1977

CHAPTER XVIII: THE BAPTIST WOMEN

1   *Tales of Baptist Daring,* "Helen Barrett Montgomery," chap. 18, p. 196, by Benjamin P. Browne, Judson Press, 1961
2   *The Southern Baptist Convention,* by W. W. Barnes, chap. 10, p. 149
3   *Nannie Burroughs and the School of the Three B's,* pamphlet by William Pickens, privately published, New York, 1921

CHAPTER XIX: TO THE ENDS OF THE EARTH

1   Material on Luther Wesley Smith from Harriet Vaughn Smith and from files of American Baptist Churches, Valley Forge, Pa.
2   Sister of the coauthor.
3   *George Green of Africa,* by Marjorie Moore Armstrong, Broadman Press, Nashville, Tenn., 1953
4   *Bill Wallace of China,* by Jesse C. Fletcher, Broadman Press, Nashville, Tenn., p. 5
5   Ibid.
6   *Lazy-Man-Rest-Not,* Burma Letters of Brayton Case, Judson Press, 1946

CHAPTER XX: THE BAPTIST ASSEMBLY LINE

1   *Baptists in Nashville,* pamphlet of the Baptist Sunday School Board, Nashville, Tenn., 1964. *Baptist Advance,* Davis C. Woolley, editor, Broadman Press, Nashville, Tenn., 1964, pp. 302–15
2   Personal correspondence with the coauthor, O. K. Armstrong
3   Unpublished anecdote, eyewitness account by coauthor Marjorie Moore Armstrong
4   *Biography of a Country Church,* by Garland A. Hendricks, Broadman Press, Nashville, Tenn., 1950, p. 23
5   *The First Century of the First Baptist Church of Richmond, Virginia,* op. cit., p. 34
6   Pamphlet published by the First Baptist Church, Washington, D.C.
7   Ross H. Terry, Springfield, Mo.
8   Material from Southern Baptist Encyclopedia

CHAPTER XXI: THE BAPTISTS TELL THEIR STORY

1 Thesis of coauthor, Marjorie Moore Armstrong
2 *Fifty Years an Editor*, by William B. Lipphard, op. cit.
3 Documents from the Radio and Television Commission, Southern Baptist Convention, Fort Worth, Tex.

CHAPTER XXII: THE CHALLENGE OF SOCIAL CONCERNS

1 From pamphlet *Principles, Purposes, Procedures* published by the Christian Life Commission, by Foy Valentine, Southern Baptist Convention, Nashville, Tenn., undated
2 Report of the Commission on Christian Social Concerns, Elizabeth Miller, American Baptist Convention, 1966
3 *Baptist Advance*, p. 340
4 From King's speech, recorded on tape and mimeographed, April 19, 1961, Southern Baptist Theological Seminary, Louisville, Ky.
5 Other members of the Baptist Committee: J. M. Dawson, William B. Lipphard, and O. K. Armstrong, coauthor of this book
6 Proceedings of the American Baptist Convention, 1964
7 *Baptist World*, Nov. 1958, Cyril E. Bryant, editor. "Project: Brother's Keeper"
8 Personal correspondence of Marjorie Moore Armstrong with Dr. Carver
9 Mimeographed letter to friends in the United States
10 His life story furnished the plot of a children's book, *School Someday*, by Marjorie Moore Armstrong, Convention Press, 1976

CHAPTER XXIII: THE SINGING BAPTISTS

1 *These Glorious Years*, op. cit.
2 *My Lord, What a Morning!*, autobiography of Marian Anderson, Viking Press, New York, 1956
3 "In God She Trusts," by Don Gold, *Ladies' Home Journal*, Nov. 1963

CHAPTER XXIV: BILLY GRAHAM

1 *Billy Graham*, by Stanley High, McGraw-Hill Book Co., New York, 1956
2 The cochairmen: Representatives Percy Priest of Tennessee and O. K. Armstrong of Missouri

3 *Decision,* March 1965, magazine of the Billy Graham Evangelistic Association, Minneapolis, Minn.

4 Statistics supplied by Donald L. Bailey, Director of Media, Billy Graham Evangelistic Association

5 Associated Press, London, April 1965

CHAPTER XXV: ECUMENISM—BAPTIST STYLE

1 Southern Baptist Convention Annual, 1940, published by Baptist Sunday School Board, Nashville, Tenn.

2 *The Word and Way,* Missouri state Baptist weekly, H. H. McGinty, editor, April 21, 1966

3 *Christianity and World Issues,* by T. B. Maston, The Macmillan Co., New York, 1957

4 *Baptist Freedom,* June—July 1966, publication of Roger Williams Foundation, Downers Grove, Ill. Article by Robert G. Middleton

5 Address reported in full in *Crusader,* October 1959, published by American Baptist Convention, Valley Forge, Pa.

6 Bulletin of Metropolitan New York Baptist Association, New York, March 1966

7 Private correspondence of July 1966

CHAPTER XXVI: BAPTIST ALLIANCES

1 Baptist World Alliance Official Report, 1966, Broadman Press, Nashville, Tenn., p. 545

2 *The Baptist World.* Quoted from *Religion Can Conquer Communism,* by O. K. and Marjorie M. Armstrong, Thos. Nelson & Sons, New York, 1964

3 "Manifesto on Religious Liberty"

4 Report of the Baptist Joint Committee on Public Affairs, 200 Maryland Ave., N.E., Washington, D.C., 1965

5 *The Meaning of Religious Liberty,* by C. Emanuel Carlson, pamphlet issued by the Baptist Joint Committee on Public Affairs, 1961

CHAPTER XXVII: BAPTISTS IN THE WHITE HOUSE

1 Memorial cited from Ohio Baptist Annual, 1924, p. 54

2 The pastor was Dr. Edward Hughes Pruden

3 Report of the Appropriations Committee, U. S. House of Representatives, 1978

4   Minutes of the Executive Committee of the Southern Baptist
    Convention, Nashville, Tenn., 1977
5   Personal correspondence
6   Personal correspondence between coauthors and Dr. Oates
7   Elizabeth Geren's letter

CHAPTER XXVIII: PROBLEMS OF THE FUTURE

1   Report of the Home Mission Board to the 1964 session of the
    Southern Baptist Convention
2   Unpublished manuscript
3   Address before 1964 meeting of the Southern Baptist Convention
4   *Missions,* American Baptist Convention, Valley Forge, Pa., Feb.
    1966, p. 19
5   *Baptist Advance,* p. 492
6   Lipphard, op. cit., p. 255
7   Carlson, op. cit.

4395-#412